The Reparations Controversy

The Reparations Controversy

The Jewish State and German Money
in the Shadow of the Holocaust
1951–1952

Edited by
Yaakov Sharett

De Gruyter

The publishing of this book was initiated by the Moshe Sharett Heritage Society.
It was supported by grants from The Conference on Jewish Material Claims Against Germany,
the Daniel Barenboim Stiftung, and the Federman Family Foundation, as well as by friends of the
Society, too numerous to be named.

The Moshe Sharett Heritage Society
30 Ben Gurion Street, Tel Aviv 64588, Israel; msharett@017.net.il; www.sharett.org.il.

Editor: Yaakov Sharett
Translation from Hebrew: Yoram and Yaakov Sharett
Graphics: Adi Chen

ISBN 978-3-11-025508-9
e-ISBN 978-3-11-025538-6

Library of Congress Cataloging-in-Publication Data

The reparations controversy : the Jewish state and German money in the shadow
of the Holocaust, 1951-1952 / edited by Yaakov Sharett.
  p. cm.
Includes index.
ISBN 978-3-11-025508-9
1. Holocaust, Jewish (1939-1945)--Reparations 2. Holocaust, Jewish
(1939-1945)--Reparations--Sources. 3. Israel--Foreign relations--Germany (West).
4. Germany (West)--Foreign relations--Israel. 5. Israel--Politics and govern-
ment--1948-1967. 6. Germany--Politics and government--1945-1990. I. Title.
  D819.G3S53 2011
  940.53'18144--dc23

    2011030929

Bibliographic information published by the Deutsche Nationalbibliothek
The Deutsche Nationalbibliothek lists this publication in the Deutsche
Nationalbibliografie; detailed bibliographic data are available in the Internet
at http://dnb.d-nb.de.

© 2011 Walter de Gruyter GmbH & Co. KG, Berlin/Boston

Cover: Foreign Minister Moshe Sharett speaking at a public meeting, Tel Aviv 1952

Printing: Hubert & Co. GmbH & Co. KG, Göttingen
∞ Printed on acid-free paper

Printed in Germany

www.degruyter.com

Preface

The present volume of *The Reparations Controversy* is an abridged English edition of the original book, published in Hebrew, of the same name. The Hebrew edition (974 pp.), compiled and edited by Yaakov Sharett, was published by the "Moshe Sharett Heritage Society" (Tel Aviv, Israel, 2007).

While the aim of the anthology is to portray the controversy over the idea of reparations in principle, as well as over the conduct of Israeli-German direct negotiations towards their attainment, it was impossible to fully abstain from touching upon the process of the actual negotiations that eventually culminated in the historic Reparations Agreement concluded in September 1952. I thus saw fit to include in the anthology several protocols of Israeli cabinet meetings as well as several additional documents which throw light on the negotiations per se.

The unavoidable abridging of the original Hebrew volume of *The Reparations Controversy* obliged me to omit some parts of the translated protocols as well as some protocols in their entirety. I believe these deletions do not mar the impact of the anthology's contents.

In translating the protocols from the original Hebrew, we endeavored to preserve the spirit and style of the spoken language of the debates. Thanks are due to Tony Berris for his contribution to the first draft of the translation.

Yaakov Sharett   Tel-Aviv, 2011

Table of Contents

Israeli Coalition Governments 1950-1952 X
Main Political Parties in the 1st, 2nd and 3rd Knessets X
The Reparation Negotiations in Israeli Politics.
An Introduction by Yehiam Weitz 1

Documents

[1] Direct Contact With Germany Is Inevitable
     Cabinet Meeting, 15.2.1950 23
[2] Shall We Boycott Germany Forever?
     Cabinet Meeting, 30.10.1950 27
[3] On Sending an Official Israeli Delegation to Germany
     Cabinet Meeting, 27.12.1950 32
[4] The Cabinet Decides to Send a Delegation to Germany
     Cabinet Meeting, 3.1.1951 41
[5] On Individual Compensation and General Reparations
     Cabinet Meeting, 8.2.1951 44
[6] Compensation Claim From Germany; Release of Nazi War Criminals
     Knesset Foreign Affairs and Defense Committee Meeting, 13.3.1951 49
[7] Demand for Compensation From Germany – Statement by the
     Foreign Minister
     Knesset Session 237, 13.3.1951 61
[8] Mitigation of Nazi War Criminals' Sentences; Compensation Claim
     from Germany
     Knesset Sessions 242, 26.3.1951; 245, 2.4.1951 67
[9] Israel Enlists the Jewish Organizations
     Cabinet Meeting, 25.10.1951 89

[10] Review by the Foreign Minister Followed by a Cabinet Debate
      Cabinet Meeting, 28.10.1951 93
[11] The Cabinet Prepares for the Knesset Debate
      Cabinet Meeting, 4.11.1951 98
[12] Israel's Claim for Reparations from Germany
      Knesset Sessions 14-15, 4-5.11.1951 100
[13] The Reparations Agreement with Germany
      Central Committee of Israel Labor Party (Mapai) Meeting, 13.12.1951 ... 113
[14] The Israeli Claim is Accepted as a Basis for Negotiation
      Cabinet Meeting, 16.12.1951 134
[15] Negotiations Immediately – The Opportunity Must Not Be Missed
      Cabinet Meeting, 31.12.1951 136
[16] Reparations: Permissible or Forbidden? Kosher or Non-Kosher?
      Excerpts from a speech by Moshe Sharett, election meeting, 5.1.1952 ... 140
[17] The Foreign Minister Reports to the Foreign Affairs and Defense
      Committee Before the Knesset General Debate Regarding
      Direct Negotiations
      Knesset Foreign Affairs and Defense Committee Meeting, 7.1.1952 142
[18] The Reparations Agreement with Germany – General Debate
      and Decision
      Knesset Sessions 38-40, 7-9.1.1952 161
[19] The Violent Herut Demonstration
      Telegram from Moshe Sharett to Israeli Legations, 8.1.1952 273
[20] Shall We Live in our State as a Diaspora People?
      Moshe Sharett's Speech, Mapai Activists' Meeting,
      Tel Aviv 10.1.1952 275
[21] We Shall Not Relinquish the Plundered Property
      Moshe Sharett's Speech, Open Public Meeting, Tel Aviv 12.1.1952 281
[22] Freedom of Action for the Government
      Knesset Foreign Affairs and Defense Committee Meeting, 15.1.1952 .. 297
[23] The Government is Ready to Enter Negotiations
      Cabinet Meeting, 27.1.1952 303
[24] Meeting With a Delegation of the Jewish Organizations
      Cabinet Meeting, 17.2.1952 306
[25] Facing the Delay in the Negotiations
      Cabinet Meeting, 6.4.1952 312
[26] The Israeli Delegation Reports
      Knesset Foreign Affairs and Defense Committee Meeting, 15.4.1952 .. 316
[27] Waiting for a German Initiative
      Mapai Political Committee Meeting, 5.5.1952 324
[28] No Compromise on Reparations
      Knesset Session 77, 6.5.1952 330

[29] Towards Renewal of Negotiations
Cabinet Meeting, 18.6.1952 339
[30] Who Will Sign the Reparations Agreement?
Cabinet Meeting, 24.8.1952 341
[31] It is an Honor to Shoulder the State of Israel's Obligations.
An Exchange of Letters between the Legal Adviser of the
Foreign Ministry and the Foreign Minister 343
[32] Israel Labor Party Approves the Reparations Agreement
Mapai Political Committee Meeting, 5.9.1952 346
[33] The Foreign Affairs and Defense Committee Ratifies the Agreement
Knesset Foreign Affairs and Defense Committee Meeting, 5.9.1952 351
[34] Israel Demonstrates its Strength
Telegram from Foreign Minister Moshe Sharett to the
Israeli Ambassador in Washington, 5.9.1952 362
[35] On the Brink of Signing the Agreement
Cabinet Meeting, 7.9.1952 363
[36] The Government of Israel Makes its Final Decision
Cabinet Meeting, 8.9.1952 366
[37] An Historic Achievement for the State of Israel
Foreign Minister Moshe Sharett's Telegram to Israel Legations
Abroad, 8.9.1952 368
[38] Moshe Sharett: A Speech Not Made
Signing Ceremony Speech Draft, 10.9.1952 372
[39] The Political and Moral Value of the Reparations Agreement
by far Outweighs its Economic Significance
The Day After: Foreign Minister Moshe Sharett at a Press
Conference, Paris 10.9.1952 374
[40] Political Wisdom and Moral Pragmatism – Moshe Sharett
and the Beginning of Relations with Germany
A Retrospective by Benyamin Neuberger 376

Appendices

Appendix A   200 Hurt As Police Defend Knesset From Herut Riot
The Jerusalem Post, 8.1.1952 385
Appendix B   Biographical Index 389
Index 399

Israeli Coalition Governments 1950-1952

(1st Government: Feb. 1949 – Oct. 1950; 2nd Government: Nov. 1950 – Oct. 1951; 3rd Government: Oct. 1951 – Dec. 1952)

Minister	Ministry	Party	Government
David Ben Gurion	Prime Minister; Defense	Mapai	1-3
Yosef Burg	Health		3
Ben-Zion Dinur	Education and Culture	Mapai	3
Levi Eshkol	Finance	Mapai	3
Eliezer Kaplan	Finance, Trade and Industry	Mapai	1-3
Pinhas Lavon	Agriculture/Without Portfolio	Mapai	2-3
Yitzhak Meir Levin	Welfare	United Religious Front Later: Agudat Yisrael	1-3
Yehuda Leib Maimon	Religions and War Victims	United Religious Front	1-2
Golda Meir	Labor and Social Security	Mapai	1-3
Peretz Naftali	Economic Coordination	Mapai	3
David Zvi Pinkas	Transportation	Hamizrachi	3
David Remez	Transportation	Mapai	1-2
Pinhas Rosen	Justice	Progressive Party	1-2
Moshe Shapira	Interior, Immigration and Health Later: Interior and Religion	United Religious Front Later: Agudat Yisrael	1-3
Moshe Sharett	Foreign Affairs	Mapai	1-3
Zalman Shazar	Education and Culture	Mapai	1
Bechor Sheetrit	Police	Oriental Communities	1-3
Dov Yosef	Agriculture and Supply Later: Transportation, Justice	Mapai	1-3

Main Political Parties in the 1st, 2nd and 3rd Knessets

(Following General Elections of Jan. 1949; June 1951)

Party	No. of Seats 1949	No. of Seats 1951	Political Ideology
Agudat Yisrael	-	3	Ultra Religious, Non-Zionist
Democratic List For Israeli Arabs	3	3	Pro-Mapai
General Zionists	7	20	Conservative
Hapoel Hamizrachi	-	8	Moderate Religious, Zionist
Herut	14	8	Right-Nationalist
Israeli Communist Party (ICP)	4	5	Communist, Soviet Oriented
Mapai (Israel Labor Party)	46	45	Social Democrat
Mapam (United Labor Party)	19	15	Marxist, Pro-Soviet
Progressive Party	5	4	Liberal
United Religious Front	16	-	Religious
Others	6	9	

The Reparation Negotiations in Israeli Politics

An Introduction
by Yehiam Weitz

The Stage and the Cast

The 1951-1952 debate on the entry of the Israeli government into direct negotiations with Germany on the issue of reparations, and on the very idea of demanding and accepting them after the Nazi atrocities against Jews, agitated the Israeli public for many months. Opposition to these negotiations was vehement, sometimes even violent.

Opposing negotiations on one side of the political spectrum were the Zionist Left (the Marxist, pro-Soviet Union United Workers Party, Mapam) and the non-Zionist Left (the Israel Communist Party, IPC). Both these parties contended that negotiations with the Federal Republic of Germany would constitute a desecration of the memory of Holocaust victims. It would also clearly prove Israel's subservience to the "imperialist-capitalist bloc" and its readiness to serve the policy of the Western bloc to make West Germany "a military tool against the Soviet bloc in a future third world war."

At the other end of the spectrum, the Herut Party argued that any discourse with the Germans – the "modern Amalekites" – would gravely tarnish Israeli national honor. Members of Herut also contended that anyone negotiating with the German Satan was also endowed with satanic qualities. On Herut's part this was a total, "life or death" war in which conventional rules of the political game could be broken. The religious parties, who were all coalition partners, found themselves in the middle of the spectrum. Clearly, without their support, there was no chance of obtaining a majority in the Knesset for the government's motion to open negotiations with the Germans. Within all these factions there were forces pulling in different – sometimes opposite – directions.

In Israel's Labor Party, Mapai – the kingpin of the ruling coalition – there were also groups opposing any contact with Germany; the most vehement opposition came from the Holocaust survivors themselves.

Facing this broad front of opposition stood the leadership of Mapai. They supported direct negotiations with the Germans not only for purely practical reasons. Their ideological rationale played a leading role in the dynamics leading

them to this view. This group propounded a series of arguments justifying
negotiations: the catastrophic state of the Israeli economy; the feeling that if Israel
did not claim reparations from the Germans she would miss the boat since, due to
the Cold War and the West-East conflict, Germany would be welcomed back into
the community of nations without paying its debt to the Jewish people; the belief
that allowing a murderer to inherit the victim's property would be adding insult to
injury; and the contention that payment of reparations to the State of Israel should
in no way be interpreted as atonement for sins that could never be forgiven.

In its drive to obtain Knesset approval for direct negotiations with Germany,
this group of leaders exercised great caution, derived for three reasons: first and
foremost, the fear of breaking the taboo on anything pertaining to Germany since
at the time, only five years after the Holocaust, a total boycott of Germany, Germans
and all things Germanic reigned in Israel. The second factor was the awareness that
a majority favoring negotiations was not assured. The Knesset might possibly fail
to endorse the government's decision to open direct negotiations. The fact that
ultimately 61 Knesset members supported the government's proposal (against 50)
was perceived as a great and unexpected victory for the supporters of negotiations.
The third factor, connected with the second, was the feeling that the struggle was not
only about the specific issue of direct negotiations on the agenda but rather about the
government's very legitimacy. It seemed that both Right and Left were attempting to
undermine this legitimacy, whereas the majority of supporters of negotiations came
from the upper echelons of Mapai, the ruling party. They realized that there was no
escaping direct contact with Germany and were appalled by the chauvinistic and
extremist slogans that the opposition from both Right and Left employed. They were
led by two figures, men who bore this almost impossible task on their shoulders:
Foreign Minister Moshe Sharett and Prime Minister David Ben Gurion.

Prime Minister Ben Gurion viewed the decision to negotiate reparations with
Germany as an integral part of the price of sovereignty – difficult obligations
that could be avoided in the Diaspora had to be fulfilled when Jews are a free,
sovereign people in their own land. His principal role was to provide political
and public backing to those engaged in negotiations and particularly to Foreign
Minister Moshe Sharett.

Sharett was the leading figure in the establishment of relations with Germany.
Up to the time of his removal from his post in June 1956,[1] it was he, and not Ben
Gurion, who led the highly charged and complicated contacts with the Federal
Republic of Germany, bringing all his capabilities to bear in the raging controversy
regarding reparations. Sharett enlisted all his talents as a statesman, diplomat and
politician to overcome the great chasm between distaste of everything pertaining
to Germany and Germans which characterized the vast majority of Israelis at the

---

1   Due to political and defense disagreements with Prime Minister and Minister of
     Defense Ben Gurion before the Sinai Campaign of October 1956 against Egypt, which
     Sharett opposed.

time and the vital necessity of finding financial resources for the impoverished Israeli economy. Two more names should be added to those of Ben Gurion and Sharett: David Horowitz and Nahum Goldmann.

Director General of the Ministry of Finance David Horowitz, who was also the economic advisor to the government between 1948 and 1952, was one of the first to realize that without urgently needed German aid, the Israeli economy would rapidly slide into wrack and ruin. It was he who first thought of appealing to the Federal Republic of Germany for reparations; it was he who convinced first Sharett and then Ben Gurion that negotiations were unavoidable.

Nahum Goldmann, then acting chairman of the World Jewish Congress, succeeded in his talks with Chancellor Adenauer in removing critical obstacles from the tortuous path to a reparations agreement with the Germans. Their first talk took place in London in December 1951. There Adenauer undertook to accept the Israeli demand that the monetary basis for the reparations negotiations would be one and a half billion dollars, thus removing a final obstacle to direct contact between Israel and the Bonn government. At their second meeting, which took place on April 20 1952 at the chancellor's home in Rhöndorf, Goldmann resolved the crisis that erupted about a month after negotiations began. People close to the matter, like banker Hermann Josef Abs, attempted to reduce the financial basis of the negotiations to which the chancellor had agreed some months earlier. At this second meeting, the chancellor decided to study the matter closely and instructed the head of the German negotiating team, Prof. Franz Böhm, to meet with Goldmann. In their talk, held in Paris on May 23, 1952, the financial basis was agreed upon.

Moshe Sharett's Public Standing
In the early 1950s, Sharett's standing in the upper echelons of the government was well-established. Of all the leaders of the Jewish community and Mapai in pre-state Palestine, he was the only one, with the exception of Ben Gurion, who remained at the apex of both the cabinet and the party leadership. During this period Sharett was second in line both in the government and Mapai, his political power derived mainly from his professional talents. His rise to power began in 1933 when he became head of the Political Department of the Jewish Agency, a post he held until he was elected Israel first foreign minister upon the establishment of the State of Israel in May 1948. In 1947 he orchestrated the struggle of the Yishuv and the Zionist Movement at the UN, culminating in the November 29 decision of the UN General Assembly to partition Palestine into two states. Following his enforced resignation in June 1956, he was described as "symbolizing the stability and continuity of Israeli foreign policy."[2] Sharett saw himself not as a leader whose role was to govern but as "the conductor of an orchestra who produces the notes from each instrument and brings them all

---

2   Moshe Zak, "Two Persons – Two Schools of Thought" (Hebrew), *Maariv*, 22.6.1956.

together in harmony."[3] He would consult with his staff at the ministry and air his views to them, and this dialogue enabled him to elucidate new ideas. Ambassador Yaakov Tsur, one of the first members of the Israeli Foreign Service, wrote of him: "He created the Foreign Ministry and left his mark on it."[4]

During the period under discussion – the time of contacts with Germany on reparations – Sharett cooperated closely with Ben Gurion. Although they had their disagreements, such as the one on the decision taken at the end of 1949 to declare Jerusalem the capital of Israel, they were in complete accord on numerous points. They both subscribed to the position that the State of Israel must abandon its policy of non-alignment with either of the two world blocs and join the Western bloc; they both viewed this change as a prerequisite for obtaining the American aid which Israel so badly needed, and for maintaining intimate and effective contact with American Jewry. They were also in agreement in their perception of the State of Israel as the sole representative of the Jewish people, and on the matter of reparations they categorically determined that Israel should be the sole representative of the Jewish people vis-à-vis the German government. Sharett clarified this in a discussion with Goldmann. Sharett's position was clear: "It is evidently desirable that there should be only one representation, that of the State of Israel. ...To appear before the Germans with two financial claims is, first of all, a disgrace, and from a commercial standpoint, too, it is neither desirable nor good. ...The State of Israel speaks for the Jewish people [...] it is the only country the Jewish people has. That is a fact."[5]

Sharett played a dual role in the direct negotiations. He filled a central role at the information level whose main thrust was to prepare both the Israeli political system and public opinion for breaking the total boycott of Germany. He played a no less significant role at the political and diplomatic level of negotiations with the Germans and the allied powers. Thus it was in 1949-1950 and in the early months of 1951 when the matter of German reparations was under discussion in Israel mainly in closed forums and when the central issue was whether direct negotiations with Germany could be bypassed and reparations be obtained through the allied powers. Thus it was too in the last months of 1951 when it became clear that there was no alternative to direct negotiations and the struggle over public opinion began, and also in 1952 after the Knesset endorsed the government's proposal and direct negotiations opened between Israelis and Germans in the town of Wassenaar in Holland.

---

3   Prof. Israel Kolatt in Yaakov Sharett (ed.), *A Statesman Assessed* ("Shoher Shalom") Views and Viewpoints about Moshe Sharett (Hebrew), Moshe Sharett Heritage Society, Tel Aviv, 2008 p.334.
4   Yaakov Zur, *Paris Diary* (Hebrew), Am Oved, Tel Aviv 1968, p. 268.
5   See document no. 9: "Israel Enlists the Jewish Organizations."

Sharett was the leading spokesman on this subject in numerous forums. He presented the cabinet's position in the Knesset plenum and in its highly influential Foreign Affairs and Defense Committee, and played a leading role in discussions devoted to this subject in Mapai Party forums. He also acted as the government spokesman at press conferences on this topic. His public activity on the question of reparations was far more vigorous and continuous than that of Ben Gurion.

1949 and the Early 1950s: The First Discussions on Reparations

The question of reparations from Germany first appeared on the government agenda in the summer of 1949. Minister of Finance Eliezer Kaplan raised the question presented to him by an all-Jewish committee (the Jewish Restitution Successor Organization) dealing with the issue of Jewish property expropriated during the Holocaust: would it be possible to deal with compensation that individuals would receive from the Germans and transfer this to Israel in the form of goods purchased in Germany? Kaplan noted that the decision on this matter could change Israel's position vis-à-vis Germany. "So far there has been opposition to importing goods from Germany and we have permitted only new immigrants to transfer their capital from Germany in the form of goods."[6] At the conclusion of this discussion the cabinet approved Kaplan's suggestion for the shipment of German goods by individuals by an almost outright majority.

Six months later, in early 1950, the government discussed the matter anew against the background of the recommendations of the government committee "for transfer matters with Germany, i.e. the transfer of Jewish assets from Germany," appointed by Ministers Sharett and Kaplan and chaired by Mapai MK Peretz Naftali.

The decisions taken by the Naftali Committee in early January 1951 emerged from the basic premise that direct contact between the Government of Israel and Germany was inevitable: "The committee sees no likelihood of progress regarding adequate transfer without general arrangements that can only be reached by direct contact between the State of Israel and the German authorities." The committee further presented two reasons for this declaration, the first being general – the transfer of Jewish capital through the importation of goods from Germany would be possible "only on a basis of general agreements with West Germany." Such agreements could not be reached "without official talks between representatives of the Government of Israel and the German state." The second reason was different in principle and may be termed "national" – the committee estimated that taking such a decision "is desirable not only from the practical aspect of transferring capital," but also from the standpoint of Jewish honor and the stature of the State of Israel: it would be better to establish direct contact with the Germans rather than have all kinds of alternative, unofficial contacts.[7]

---

6   Minutes of cabinet meeting, 7.6.1949, State of Israel Archives, Jerusalem.
7   Decisions by the Transfer of German Goods Committee, 6.1.1950, State of Israel Archives, Jerusalem.

The Naftali Committee's recommendations were revolutionary in the extreme: the committee was the first forum to deal with the question of how to receive compensation from Germany for Jewish property expropriated during the Holocaust. To a great degree its recommendations were the first step towards breaking the general boycott of Germany.

The cabinet discussed the Naftali Committee's conclusions in early 1950. Minister of Finance Kaplan presented the issue, saying that it had become clear that without direct negotiations with the Germans it would be impossible to resolve the problem of individual reparations and to obtain "very large sums."[8] He proposed that government representatives open negotiations with the Germans. Sharett, who spoke after him, accepted the Treasury's position but was more forthright. For the first time, the argument that the State of Israel must break the total boycott of Germany and establish ties with it was raised in the government plenum. "I think," the foreign minister said, "that we will have no choice but to establish direct and official contact with the German government. This means that we must be prepared to encounter a storm at home and abroad by expediting the arrangement. We will again witness the debate we had during the famous transfer,[9] but even more so." Sharett emphasized that despite the emotional and political difficulties, if twenty years ago it was incumbent on the Jewish Agency to open those negotiations, then today that duty was immeasurably greater: "It is precisely because of what happened during the years of the Holocaust that there is now less reason for foregoing what could be achieved, and also because of the great absorption needs created by the ingathering of exiles."

Sharett went on to give further reasons in favor of negotiations. One was that the government must not claim that reparations were the problems only of individual claimants. It was inconceivable that the government be oblivious to "the interests of a single citizen, all the more so when such citizens are numerous. If Holocaust survivors arrived here with only the clothes on their backs, and if they can now obtain "scores or hundreds of pounds" [in compensation], then we cannot remain indifferent towards these citizens' claims as if their problems are not our concern." Another reason was that the State of Israel was the sole claimant of the heirless property. "The property of the absentees and of Jewish communities

---

8   See document no. 1, "Direct Contact With Germany Is Inevitable."

9   The reference here is to the Jewish Agency's agreement with the Nazi government in 1933 on the transfer of the property of Jewish emigrants. Sharett had a special attitude towards this event, which was particularly traumatic for him. He was secretary to Chaim Arlosoroff, head of the Jewish Agency Political Department, who in my opinion was murdered against the background of the acrimonious debate between the leaders of the Jewish Agency and the Revisionist movement, headed by Ze'ev Jabotinsky, who rejected this agreement outright. As part of this agreement, between 1933 and 1938 goods were shipped to Palestine the value of £8 million, a vast sum at the time. During that period some 60,000 Jews immigrated to Palestine from Germany.

that were destroyed can, in many cases, only be saved by the Jewish people. As we see it, the State of Israel can appear as that inheritor."

Sharett spoke out against the prevailing view held by considerable segments of the population that reparations could be obtained from the Germans without negotiating with them. For his part, the need to negotiate with the Germans was a case of necessity being a cruel task-master. All the actions bound up in these negotiations could not be undertaken "if we do not have contact with them [. . .] we cannot shut our eyes and not see the necessity of contact. On this matter we cannot be of two minds." The State of Israel should not position itself as being "simon-pure from the sidelines;" Sharett believed that there was nothing shameful in attempting to reclaim Jewish property.

In conclusion, Sharett underlined two points: first, that taking plundered property from the thief meant neither recognition of Germany nor the establishment of diplomatic relations with it at present; and second, that these negotiations would not be conducted "by an angel nor by a seraph, and nor by a messenger, but by the State of Israel itself. What moral right has the State of Israel to employ other states to do this?"

The cabinet meeting ended by approving, almost unanimously, the decision "to authorize the ministries of finance and foreign affairs, in coordination with the prime minister and with the Jewish Agency, to attain the payment of compensation and the fulfillment of claims from Germany by means of direct contact with the German government. The public must be provided with appropriate explanation in this regard." This decision widened another crack in the wall of the boycott. While it employed the specific wording of "direct contact" with Germany, the decision was limited: it ratified these contacts with a restricted objective: release of individuals' monies and reparations, but not in order to reach an agreement on an inclusive arrangement with the Germans.

1950: Formulating the Foreign Ministry's Position on Reparations

The issue of reparations re-emerged in the cabinet only at the end of 1950. In the interim, a change had taken place in the position of the Federal Republic of Germany in the international arena, one which necessitated an early decision on the question of making direct contact with it. On June 25, 1950 the Korean War broke out, and consequently the integration of the Federal Republic of Germany into the Western bloc was accelerated.

In July 1950 the three Western occupying powers announced the end of their state of war with Germany. This announcement expressed the readiness of the West for Germany's rehabilitation and reacceptance into the community of nations, a readiness derived from cold war considerations: a war that at the time was at its height. On October 23, 1950 the occupying powers asked Israel to append its signature to the announcement.

At the time the economic situation of the Federal Republic of Germany was improving rapidly, an indication that it would be able to meet the reparations payments. Germany's "economic miracle" was at its peak with an average annual growth rate of 8.2 percent between 1950 and 1954. Israel's Foreign Ministry was following these developments closely.

At a meeting in the summer of 1950, held in the office of Foreign Ministry Legal Advisor Shabtai Rosenne and attended by the ministry's senior staff, the urgent need for a decision on Germany was raised. Kurt Mendelssohn, a senior treasury official who had been sent to Bonn by Sharett and Kaplan to examine the possibility of compensating German Jewry, said that as result of his visit he felt that the only way of dealing with the sensitive issues linked with reparations was through formal state channels. A clear conclusion was drawn: reparations claims from Germany must be left "in the hands of our institutions, i.e., only Israeli ones,"[10] and should not be handed over to international Jewish organizations. The reason for this was that "our country has absorbed 80-90 percent of postwar Jewish refugees in general, and some who have reparations claims in particular." The fact that the State of Israel had absorbed masses of refugees, "poor, crippled and destitute," accorded it the right to be given a full mandate to claim reparations from Germany.

The meeting discussed the phenomenon of the flourishing economic progress of the Federal Republic of Germany. The participants estimated that this was due, inter alia, to the constant decrease in the occupying powers' influence, to "Germany's industrial and mercantile recovery," to its support by the Marshall Plan, and also to the fact that it had been morally rehabilitated in the eyes of the entire world except for Israel and the diaspora. It was further noted that although it had not yet gained full sovereignty, the Federal Republic of Germany had become "one of the most important factors in stabilizing the global political situation."

On the matter of Jewish property in Germany, it was stated that it should be claimed from the Germans. Five principal claims were presented, such as the restoration of "the property of the individual Jew," and "[general] reparations." On this last issue it was decided that there were two alternatives: the first, "to erase this part of the Nazis' deeds from the annals of the Holocaust," and the second, "to influence Germany to make a great and historic gesture towards the Jewish people by the one-time payment of a sum commensurate with the damages caused by it" to the Jewish people. The meeting's participants believed that the Germans would be prepared to make such a gesture.

In conclusion, the participants reached several understandings. The first was that the entire matter was chaotic, the second that the only way of resolving the problem was "through negotiations between the two governments." From this

---

10   Minutes of meeting on 1.8.1950, Yehoshua Freundlich (ed), *Documents On The Policy of Israel* (DPI), Israel State Archives, Jerusalem 1988, pp. 452-455.

second conclusion was derived the third: "An Israeli mission must be established in Germany for the special purpose of winding up the property claims."

This meeting was followed by another headed by Foreign Minister Sharett, Finance Minister Kaplan, and Jewish Agency Treasurer Levi Eshkol, at which it was decided to set up a committee to formulate a clear proposal for organizing the Israeli mission in Germany. At the same time, the senior staff of the foreign service in Jerusalem and its missions abroad came to the clear realization that they must not bury their heads in the sand and ignore the Federal Republic of Germany and its diplomatic corps around the world by continuing the total boycott of that country.

The first to raise this idea was Michael Amir, the Israeli consul in Brussels who at the end of 1950 wrote to the foreign ministry saying that continuation of the boycott policy by Israel meant "continuing with a fine, moral Don Quixote line, which actually means tilting at windmills. While it has beauty and consistency, there is no benefit in it and we shall lose from it."[11] Therefore, the State of Israel must forge ties with the Federal Republic of Germany so that it will admit its responsibility for the crimes of the Third Reich and enter negotiations with Israel in order to pay compensation. If Israel's boycott policy does not change, Amir added, we are likely to miss a one-time opportunity. If we are the only country that votes against them in the UN and other international organizations, "we will be unable to delay or even significantly slow Germany's rehabilitation, and thus the only possibility of obtaining compensation will vanish."

Similar reports by foreign ministry representatives abroad were received in Jerusalem. Israeli consul general in Los Angeles Reuven Dafni wrote that a German consulate had been established in his city, and "soon the German consul will formally announce his arrival and the hope that good relations would evolve between him and his Israeli colleague." Accordingly, "should I have to respond or to leave his message unanswered? In the second case, in view of protocol, it would be regarded as an insult to both the American and the German governments."[12]

Spokesman of Israel's legation in London Eliezer Yappu asked what to do when West German correspondents apply for meetings with him; the problem is not at all simple on several accounts. Some of them, for instance, are Jews or socialists, known for their active opposition to anti-Semitism and reactionary fascism. It is thus quite difficult to "just take a negative position, totally ignoring all aspects involved."[13]

Shmuel Tolkovsky, Israel's Consul General in Switzerland, reported in the summer of 1950 that President Chaim Weizmann and Chancellor Adenauer spent their vacations in the same hotel in the little town of Bürgenstock, and "the

---

11   Letter by Michael Amir to Director General of the Foreign Office, Jerusalem, ibid., pp. 649-650.
12   Israel State Archives, document FO/2413/2, 18.9.1950.
13   Ibid., document 15.8.1951.

picture of the three flags – Israeli, German and Swiss – fluttering over the hotel aroused strong and mixed feelings in my heart." Tolkovsky felt uneasy in view of the possible meeting of the two leaders and did his utmost to evade it. However, he ended his cable to Jerusalem with "Still, I ask myself whether it would not be a pity if such a one-time opportunity of a meeting with the Germans on neutral soil – something we have so far not succeeded in achieving – is missed."[14]

In view of such challenges, in October 1950 Gershon Avner, head of the foreign ministry's Western Europe department, raised the question: "What should be the Israeli government's attitude towards the Federal Republic of Germany in light of its forthcoming entry into the community of nations with Western support: should the diplomatic boycott of Germany be continued or should the line be changed, and is changing this line mandated by the political climate?" Eliashiv Ben-Horin, a senior Western Europe department official, replied that the rapid recovery of the Federal Republic of Germany's leads to "the logical conclusion that if we seek to continue our extreme political boycott of Germany, we shall soon find ourselves totally isolated. Of course, we won't be able even to slow down Germany's giant strides towards the status of a power." For the West, reinforcing Germany is a vital issue and so "on various international issues touching upon Germany that will reach a vote at one of the UN bodies, Germany will go from strength to strength while we will remain in a situation that the world will view as pathetic and, as memories of the past fade, even quixotic." In the upper echelons of the foreign service, a consensus emerged on this difficult and painful issue. The foreign minister and his staff favored direct contact with Germany.

Fall 1950 and Early 1951:
The Government Discussions on the German Question
In the fall of 1950 and in early 1951, the question of Israel's policy vis-à-vis Germany was raised at three cabinet meetings. At the first, at the end of October 1950, the ministers discussed the request of the Western powers to abrogate the state of war with Germany, and this discussion provided Foreign Minister Sharett with the opportunity of presenting his position on this issue. Sharett opened his review with a report on two requests connected with Germany forwarded by the Western powers: the first, to end the state of war with Germany, and the second, a "special request" to support Germany's proposed membership in the International Wheat Council. He admitted that at first he had intended to abstain in the voting on the second issue, but that later he had reached the conclusion that the request should be supported. "For only yesterday, we were knocking on the doors of the nations of the world to support us, and now we must not oppose [such a request]," he explained.[15]

Sharett devoted a large portion of his review to the matter of reparations. He voiced his concern about missing the last chance of claiming compensation

---

14   Ibid., documents 28.7.1959, 23.7.1950, respectively.
15   Document no. 2.

from Germany. The heightening of the cold war, he said, was leading to Germany rejoining "the community of nations" and it was likely to gain complete rehabilitation without repaying its debt to the Jewish people. Later in the meeting Sharett connected this concern with his opposition to the total boycott that Israel imposed on Germany. This position, he stressed, "seems to drive the point home but, in fact, is unlikely to continue, and in any event cannot continue for long." It is not possible to "continue totally negating and ignoring Germany. It exists." Had Germany been eradicated from the face of earth, Sharett stressed, "the problem would have been resolved for us," but that did not happen and so the dilemma we face is "can we see a possibility of some kind of settlement based on compensation, or do we ignore these questions and boycott it [Germany] for ever?"

Sharett expressed this position outside the cabinet as well. On May 14, 1950, the Mapai Central Committee was convened for the purpose of deciding whether the party should participate in the deliberations of the Committee of International Socialist Conference (COMISCO) abroad. A few of the party leaders, such as MK Pinhas Lavon as well as Minister of Labor Golda Meir,[16] who held an unmitigated anti-German position, opposed any participation in this body's conventions because of the German Socialist Party presence there. Sharett's position was somewhat inconsistent. He reasoned first that it is impossible to shun an international arena just because Germany is part of it; and second, the question is rather complicated: "Let us assume that Germany is accepted into the UN tomorrow," said Sharett. "Will we leave the UN because of it? Can we take this path of international policy that will lead us to turn our back on the world, because Germany is part of that world? Insofar as we are talking about principles, then this principle can lead us too far."[17]

In October 1950 the cabinet arrived at a "balanced" decision on two German issues. On the one hand it decided to respond negatively to the Western appeal to abrogate a state of war with Germany; on the other hand it agreed that the Federal Republic of Germany become a member of the International Wheat Treaty. These decisions apparently represented a compromise between the necessity of coming to terms with the new international position of the Federal Republic of Germany and the political fear of the response by the Israeli public.

A short time after this discussion, the question was raised again in the cabinet at two meetings, on December 27, 1950 and a week later on January 3, 1951.[18] Sharett did not participate in the first meeting as he was in the United States. Director General Walter Eytan, who presented the foreign ministry's position in

16 Golda Meir headed Mapai's mission to the conference of the revived Socialist International in Zurich, June 1946, where she publicly declined to shake hands with the German SD leader Kurt Schumacher, who had been detained in a Nazi concentration camp from 1933 till the end of WW II.

17 Minutes of meeting, Israel Labor Party Archives.

18 See documents no. 4 and no. 5.

coordination with Sharett, proposed that the government open direct negotiations with the German government. He admitted that this was a difficult decision, but there was no alternative, and gave two reasons for the foreign ministry's position: first, although Germany was not yet a sovereign state, it was making giant strides towards this status, and second, this was a step that John McCloy, the US High Commissioner for Germany, supported. Even Chancellor Adenauer "viewed it as important," and was "prepared to pay a very large sum in order to attain moral peace, so to speak, for Germany."

Eytan's words aroused opposition from a number of ministers who vehemently took issue with him. Minister of Transport Dov Yosef (Mapai) said that he opposed any direct negotiation with the Germans and stated that a friendly nation should be requested to negotiate on Israel's behalf. He suggested appealing to Norway. Minister of Education and Culture David Remez (Mapai) voiced a similar position and suggested that the UK, the US or a Scandinavian country submit a proposal on our behalf to Germany. Minister of Labor Golda Meir (Mapai) also opposed Eytan's proposal claiming that, "it is inconceivable that a delegation from the State of Israel sit in a German government ministry and speak with German government representatives." In her opinion, the State of Israel should present its claim to the four occupying powers, and "should the powers, accept, so will we." But if they do not, direct contacts will not help, and the knowledge that Jews are negotiating with the Germans will be spread, "and then go and explain that this is not contact, that it is not recognition, that it is only trade relations."

Minister of Agriculture Pinhas Lavon (Mapai), too, voiced his opposition: A permanent delegation is in fact "the establishment of diplomatic relations and de facto recognition," he said. On the other hand, Lavon said, "I am in favor of sending a delegation to the occupation authorities because they are about to end the occupation of Germany, bringing Germany back into the community of nations, and I think that the State of Israel can approach them and say, it is your duty to deal with this matter." The most vehement opposition came from Minister of Religious Affairs Yehuda Leib Maimon, a member of the United Religious Front. "I doubt that we can achieve anything from direct negotiations with the Germans," he claimed, "and even if we do, will it be worthwhile?" He went on to determine categorically: "In my opinion we must not have any connection with the Germans, for we are in a war against the Amalekites from generation to generation. They murdered six million Jews. Shall we talk with these murderers? The government of the Jewish people, the Government of Israel, must declare that we will have no contact with them. Their murderous deeds will not be expiated, neither by millions of marks nor millions of pounds. There is no more to be said about a delegation to Germany." He went on to oppose not only direct contact with them but also the proposal to negotiate with them through a third party.

At the conclusion of the meeting on the 3rd of January, two motions were presented. The first was to open direct negotiations with the Bonn government and to this end send an official Israeli mission to Germany. This motion did not gain a majority – five ministers voted for and five against. The second motion was that "the representatives of Israel approach the central governments of the occupying powers on the matter of ensuring compensation from Germany and restitution of the Jews' property". This did gain a majority. Thus the government assigned the foreign minister a mission that he himself opposed.

Delaying the Inevitable: the Two Notes
In accordance with the government decision the foreign minister sent two notes to the occupying powers. The first, sent on January 16, 1951, dealt with the question of individual compensation, while the second, sent on March 12, 1951, dealt with the issue of reparations to the Jewish people in general.

Sharett presented his position with regard to the notes at the cabinet meeting on February 8, 1951,[19] some three weeks after the first note was sent. He emphasized two points that had not been expressed in his previous remarks and noted the connection between the reparations claim and the absorption of mass immigration, a point that was to later play a decisive role in the reparations affair. He called for prominence to be given to the fact that "we have absorbed more than half a million refugees, we have absorbed them into Israel, but their absorption still calls for massive investment, and we still have to absorb immigrants from Iraq, Egypt, North Africa and Romania." The second point was that our duty to recognize Germany was related not to the claim for reparations, but rather to two other facts: the existence of the State of Israel, and Germany rapidly becoming a reality that could not be ignored. Recognition of Germany, Sharett emphasized, was no simple matter. It had to come only after the German government provided "not only payment to the Jewish people, but also a declaration of conciliation with the Jewish people." However, after these terms have been met, "decency obliges that we accept and not reject them."

On March 12, 1951, a note was sent to the occupying powers in which the State of Israel presented itself as sole representative and heir of the millions of Jews who had perished in the Holocaust and demanded the imposition of reparations of $1.5 billion from both East and West Germany. Foreign Minister Sharett, who signed the note, appeared the next day in the Knesset plenum to "bring to the attention of the Knesset, and also to the attention of the public in Israel and abroad" of the existence and content of the note.[20]

The same day, before the Knesset debate, Sharett appeared before the Knesset Foreign Affairs and Defense Committee.[21] His words in this forum were far more detailed than those he voiced in the plenum. He touched, inter alia, upon the moral-ideological aspect of the issue. Although "material compensation can in

19   Document no. 5.
20   Document no. 7.
21   Document no. 6.

no way atone for the crimes and deaths," he said, "it is inconceivable that the German people continue to enjoy the spoils while rehabilitation of the victims, those who were saved and remained alive after the Holocaust, are a heavy burden on that same Jewish people." Sharett further determined that "the survivors are owed rehabilitation; and since the majority of the victims have found refuge here, we contend that compensation is due, first and foremost, to Israel."

Not everybody accepted Sharett's position; he argued mainly with the leader of the Herut Party, MK Menachem Begin. Begin did not reject outright the claim for compensation from Germany, but argued that the claim "can only be one: to restore the material property that was plundered," and therefore a claim of $1.5 billion was insufficient: "In my opinion it is a grave mistake to demand that Germany recompense the victims in the State of Israel, and that we specify what will be done with the money for the plundered Jewish property. Do we need a further explanation to justify this claim? Is humanitarian justification for compensating the victims necessary at all? If we assess the plundered property at $6 billion, we should demand $6 billion, and what we do with the money is our affair."

In his reply to Begin, Sharett drew a distinction between a claim that "would most likely appear reasonable to public opinion" and "one that must sound fantastic."

At the committee meeting Sharett argued, as he had in the cabinet meeting about a month previously, that the total boycott of Germany was a policy that could not be maintained. "Germany is a fact of life," he said, and Israel, a sovereign state aspiring to become part of the international arena, could not conduct itself as though Germany did not exist. A policy of boycott and ostracism could be continued for a generation or two, "to erase the question of relationship with Germany from the agenda of the generation that experienced and witnessed the horrors," but, in fact, "we encounter Germany wherever we go," and thus a boycott policy was doomed to failure. "We shall be with them everywhere, while at the same time our attempts to prevent Germany's admission to international bodies will lose any significance whatsoever."

The Political Arena on the Eve of the Reparations Decision
In the municipal elections held throughout the country on November 14, 1950, Mapai suffered a severe defeat. Although they were "only" municipal elections, the surprising results caused turmoil in the political arena, and it seemed to many that Israel was on the brink of a political upset. Indeed, the second government since the state was established fell. Elections to the second Knesset were set for July 30, 1951. The Mapai ministers who formed the majority in the government were preoccupied with the election campaign, and this caused delay in taking decisions on three critical issues: the scope of immigration, the economic situation, and reparations from Germany. In order to facilitate a decision on reparations, there was a need to present the highly-charged dilemma of direct negotiations with Germany to the Israeli public. However Mapai did not want to provide effective

ammunition both to the Left and the Right in the opposition with the crucial general elections imminent. Only at the end of 1951 did the third government, headed again by Mapai, take a decision on these issues: it was decided to limit immigration, to implement the "new economic plan," and to open direct talks on reparations with the Bonn government.

Sharett's Position Regarding Direct Contact

In April 1951, close to submitting the two Israeli formal notes before the occupation powers, Sharett received several memoranda from a number of senior officials from his office regarding negotiations with the Federal Republic of Germany. In response, he composed a brief on the subject to be circulated to all Israeli diplomatic missions.[22] In this document, he argued that, at first glance, the Israeli claim for reparations was perceived as "a figment of the imagination, due both to the unique character of the claim, being unprecedented in the annals of international relations, and to its financial magnitude, in excess of anything considered practical." But nonetheless it should be submitted for two reasons: first, because there are claims "whose failure is not in their non-achievement but in their non-submission," and this Israeli claim is a clear example of this; the second reason is that the note to the occupying powers is only the first step in a protracted and arduous process which, at the start, is perceived as clearly belonging to the realm of imagination but can still be realized. "We have possibly missed the boat," he wrote, but "on the other hand it is highly possible that we have not." Moreover, "contrary to initial impressions, we are possibly [submitting the claim] at the right time." The international status of Germany is about to change from an occupied country to one that is part of the Western bloc. It is at this particular juncture that there is a good chance of getting the powers to present the reparation terms to the Federal Republic of Germany. With regard to Germany itself, Sharett noted that now, "when it has almost reached its objective, I feel it would be beneficial to make a special effort to remove the obstacles from its path" as it is likely to accede to Israel's request.

Second, it was now possible to break the shackles of "the Yalta and Potsdam Accords regarding the compensation imposed on Germany" by the victorious allies. These accords, Sharett explained, "are a procrustean bed for us, and even if we had been recognized earlier as a partner to them, our reward would have been worthless and the whole business would not have been worth the disgrace." These accords "were founded upon two principles, which jointly and severally were inappropriate to our special issue." One was "to cover war damage caused to Allied countries" while "we are claiming compensation not for war damage but for the expropriation and destruction of property during the war and in the years preceding it." The other principle was that the scope of compensation should

---

22   "The Foreign Office, Informative Bulletin to Israel Legations," 17.4.1951, State of Israel Archives, FO files.

be adjusted to the level of Germany's annual revenue while we "are claiming compensation of a magnitude that cannot be covered by existing means of production, but which quite naturally must be imposed on current production and paid in installments over a period of years."

The third reason presented by Sharett was the situation of the German economy. "Had we submitted the claim earlier, we would have killed it with our own hands. Submitting it two or three years ago would have found the German economy in shambles." But now, "when the German economy is recovering and its production is soaring," there was a greater likelihood of obtaining real reparations.

The Road to Chancellor Adenauer's Declaration, September 27, 1951

This brief by Sharett contained a hint of his intention of paving a new road, a road leading directly to the Bonn government that he had already mentioned at the cabinet meeting on February 15, 1950. The first feelers in this direction were put out prior to July 15, 1951, the date on which the occupying powers had formally rejected the Israeli government's request, a rejection which was indeed expected.

The road was paved by the Israeli consul in Munich, Eliahu Livneh. On April 6, several days before Sharett wrote his brief, Livneh sent a confidential note to the Jewish member of the Bundestag, Jakob Altmaier, a member of the SPD opposition party. Consul Livneh proposed a meeting between representatives of Israel and the German chancellor during the latter's visit to Paris. "The aim of this secret talk will be to clarify the possibility of future negotiations between the two countries, their subject and structure." Two days later, on April 8, Altmaier replied that he had presented the Israeli request to Chancellor Adenauer who decided to meet with two representatives of the State of Israel. According to Altmaier, Adenauer told him: "I can well understand the Israeli need to hold these talks on neutral ground [...] For me, this matter is not only one of foreign policy. It must be presented as a genuine human need connected with amity and good relations between the German and Jewish peoples."[23]

Sharett reported on these developments in a coded cable to David Horowitz, Director General of the Finance Ministry, who was in Washington at the time. He wrote that an approach had been received from Bonn regarding a direct meeting, including a certain proposal from Adenauer. "Instructions have been issued to find out if Bonn indeed accepts our claim in principle, and if so to arrange a meeting with Adenauer in Paris for early clarification." Sharett stated to Horowitz: "In the event that the meeting is arranged to take place after your arrival in Paris, you will participate in it, but we thought it prudent not to delay it lest A.'s visit is cut short and we miss the opportunity." Clearly, this message demonstrated the importance Sharett ascribed to the meeting. He presented the rationale for taking the German channel: on the one hand there was a clear feeling that the occupying powers would reject our request: "In view of the lack

---

23   Y.A. Jelinek (ed.), *Zwischen Moral und Realpolitik*, Tel Aviv 1997, pp. 155-157.

of confidence in a positive response from the powers, we thought we should not turn Bonn down if it approaches us," and on the other hand, there was a need to find a special way of demanding compensation and not "to become part of the Allies' overall account," since our own account "is separate and special and we shall not be budged from this position."

On April 19, 1951 a secret meeting was held in Paris between Chancellor Adenauer, David Horowitz and the Israeli Ambassador to France, Maurice Fischer. In the course of the meeting, Adenauer expressed his readiness to open direct contacts with representatives of the State of Israel, but Horowitz and Fischer set two conditions for this: public acknowledgement by Germany of the German people's responsibility for its crimes against the Jewish people, and acceptance of the Israeli claim for reparations in the sum of $1.5 billion. The chancellor immediately agreed to publicly acknowledge the German people's responsibility for crimes against the Jewish people, and said that he could see no serious difficulties regarding the size of the compensation demanded by Israel.

For the Israeli government this was a step of paramount importance: it needed the public expression of remorse to sway public opinion in Israel prior to breaking the taboo on direct negotiations with the Germans. On September 27, 1951, one day before his first visit to the United States, Chancellor Adenauer presented his statement to a ceremonial session of the Bundestag in Bonn. Endorsement of the statement by the deputies – not by raised hands, but by rising – was a decisive step on the road to direct negotiations.

During the period following the Paris meeting in April and before Adenauer's statement in September, Sharett and the Foreign Ministry's senior staff were engaged with the question of how to convince the Israeli public and world Jewry to accept the dramatic turnabout from total boycott to direct and official contacts with the Bonn government. In June 1951 a meeting led by Sharett and Horowitz on this subject was held at the foreign minister's home.[24] Horowitz began by saying: "We have made one mistake, and it is that we started our diplomatic activity before ensuring the support on the home front or, in other words, Jewish public opinion." Most of his remarks focused on the American public position since, in the end, he said, "it is the American taxpayer who will have to shoulder the burden" of financing German reparations to the State of Israel. Horowitz went on to clarify: the reparations are likely to increase Germany's balance of payments deficit, and the Americans, as part of their struggle against the danger of communist gains in Europe, are trying to maintain a high standard of living in Germany while the Germans themselves are exploiting this American propensity and are not reducing their balance of payments deficit. Therefore, Horowitz argued, Israel must highlight the dynamic recovery of the German economy. He

---

24 "Summary of meeting at the foreign minister's home, Jerusalem, 18.6.1951," State of Israel Archives, FO-2417/2.

presented two concrete proposals: "Convening a special World Jewish Conference" and organizing "a World Jewish Petition."

The majority of the participants supported the idea of a conference, but opposed the proposal for a petition. Sharett vehemently rejected the petition idea. "A petition is no more than a demonstration that will not yield concrete results," he said. On the other hand, "the idea of a Jewish conference is an important one, and its feasibility should certainly be investigated." It was at this meeting that the preliminary initiative emerged for the Claims Conference that took place in New York on October 25, 1951. Sharett subsequently emphasized on various occasions that the initiative for this conference was an Israeli one. On the eve of the opening of the conference he spoke about it at a cabinet meeting: "It was our initiative. The Jewish organizations did not rise to the occasion. No Jewish organization thought that there was a need to enlist the Jewish people in this matter."[25]

October-November 1951: On the Verge of Decision

Chancellor Adenauer's statement opened a new chapter in the story of the attempt to achieve a majority in the Knesset for negotiations with the Germans, a chapter that lasted for some three and a half months from the date of the chancellor's statement until the Knesset vote approving the government's proposal, which gave a green light to direct negotiations with the Bonn government. This period can be divided into two sub-periods.

The first period led up to Dr. Nahum Goldmann's meeting with Chancellor Adenauer in London on December 6, 1951. The government's willingness to open negotiations was conditional to the German commitment to the sum that would form the basis for negotiations. At the time the government did all it could internally to disguise its intentions and to obviate a public debate. At his meeting with Goldmann, Chancellor Adenauer promised that the financial basis for negotiation would be $1.5 billion, the sum stated in Sharett's note of March 12, 1951. At this juncture the second sub-period began. Germany's undertaking removed the final obstacle – the government was now willing to open negotiations, and from that date onward the struggle to obtain a parliamentary majority shifted into high gear.

During this period Sharett was the government's leading spokesman on this subject in public forums, and thus became the central figure in all matters pertaining to preparing public opinion on the negotiations. Apart from that, he was aware that this was a fateful decision on which the government must not fail: "If the Knesset approves a decision that the State of Israel must not negotiate with Germany, it will be removed from the agenda. It would be both a very bad and hasty decision," he said.[26]

During the first sub-period, Sharett's principal role was to present to the public the government's complicated position. He first presented it to the public

25   Document no. 9.
26   Document no. 11.

at a press conference in Tel Aviv on October 26, 1951, one day after the cabinet meeting at which the subject of reparations was discussed. The press conference was called as part of the government's efforts to persuade the Israeli public to support negotiations with Germany, and Sharett tried to have his cake and eat it, too: he did not conceal his support for opening negotiations, but he evaded a clear commitment on the government's readiness to open contacts with the Germans. In reply to a question on this, he said that the government had decided "to do everything necessary to obtain reparations," and no new decision had been taken since then.[27]

A week later, in a policy statement to the Knesset, Sharett again addressed the issue, and on this occasion, too, his words reflected the government's complex position. He stated the government's willingness in principle to enter into negotiations with the Bonn government, saying that the submission of Israel's claim for reparations from Germany offered the possibility of "an injection of substantial funds for the building of our economy."[28]

During the second sub-period Sharett acted to persuade the Israeli public of the justness of the government's position in the face of attacks on it from both Right and Left, and furthermore he urged the government, some of whose members feared a parliamentary defeat and the public's angry reaction, to reach a decision quickly.

January 1952: Sharett in the Knesset Debates on Reparations

January 7, 1952 saw the opening of one of the stormiest, longest and most dramatic debates that the Knesset had ever witnessed. It had begun earlier that day with Sharett presenting the issue of direct negotiations to the Knesset Foreign Affairs and Defense Committee. Significantly, this was the first time that the subject had been discussed in a forum which included representatives of the opposition. Sharett reviewed the main points of the developments leading up to the negotiations, highlighting a number of them. He noted that from the outset the possibility of direct negotiations with the Germans had not been rejected outright. When the notes were sent to the occupying powers, he said, it was already clear that "even if we achieve results with the help of emissaries and envoys, or the powers' assistance, direct contact between us and the Germans on the form of payment is unavoidable. Every step we take is bound up with the country's vital interests, and in no way can we rely on an emissary who will not know how to demand terms and ensure their fulfillment."[29]

He mentioned two key events leading up to negotiations with the Germans: Chancellor Adenauer's statement, whose main thrust, in his opinion, was the fact that the initiative for negotiation was German, not Israeli; and the Goldmann-

---

27 *Haaretz*, 28.10.1951.
28 Document no. 12.
29 Document no. 17.

Adenauer meeting in whose wake "the government decided that it should conduct negotiations, and it is this decision that will be brought before the Knesset today."

Sharett clarified that the payment of reparations did not constitute forgiveness or atonement. "Nothing will be forgiven. Nothing will be forgotten for generations to come, perhaps for eternity." Apart from that, the reparations, he said, would not change the government's negative attitude towards Germany in the international arena. He also noted that the negotiations "will not be conducted in Germany. The intention is that they will not be on German soil, but neither will they be in Israel. They will take place in a European country."

At first, Sharett was supposed to open the Knesset debate, but in the end it was decided that Ben Gurion would do so. Sharett would conclude it. Sharett's speech, delivered before the vote on the government and opposition motions, concluded three days of debate in the course of which dozens of members addressed the plenum. It was a long speech, almost uninterrupted by interjections.[30] Shalom Rosenfeld, parliamentary correspondent of the Ma'ariv newspaper, described it as follows: "For an hour and a half, Foreign Minister Sharett stood at the microphone and in his fluent language fired darts of controversy at his adversaries, while defending negotiations with Germany."[31] Although Sharett spoke as a representative of the government, he expressed, to a very great degree, his personal position. He spoke from the heart and his words expressed the essence of his worldview, not only the specific issue on the agenda.

The speech contained practical and moral-ideological elements alike, and it is doubtful if they could be differentiated: his practical arguments contained ideological aspects while the ideological ones contained practical elements. In this speech Sharett expanded on his remarks to the cabinet almost two years earlier, in February 1950, when he spoke of the essential contradiction between the desire to totally boycott Germany and the desire to obtain "compensation from those malefactors for what they perpetrated against us."[32] This motif was manifested in several ways. In his opening remarks, Sharett referred to his statement to the Knesset of March 13, 1951, in which he read out the government's note to the occupying powers, and said that in the debates regarding the issue of reparations, "a very high degree of agreement that the claim for reparations is just and right" was evident. If there was any argument it revolved around question of the timing, whether we had missed opportunities, whether we had not missed the boat. There was almost no argument on the question of whether these reparations are our due or whether we were – or are – duty bound to claim them.

Later in his speech Sharett asked what would have happened had the occupying powers replied that "we are prepared to exert pressure on Germany and impose this upon it." If that had been the situation, he answered, Israel would

---

30   Moshe Sharett speech on 9.1.1952, document no. 18.
31   Shalom Rosenfeld, "The Parliament Took a Decision," *Maariv*, 19.1.1952.
32   Document no. 1.

still have had no choice other than entering into negotiations at a certain stage; for no one "deluded himself into thinking that, successful as we were, all our labor would have been done by others, down to the smallest detail. It is one thing to demand help, enlist pressure, when you too are prepared to execute your task. A different thing altogether is to impose all the trouble on others, to keep your hands clean and escape into the mists of supreme moral purity."

He went on to expound on a number of reasons for negotiations. One was "Let not the murderers of our people become their heirs" – we're talking about "vast amounts of property which, but for the slaughter, who knows how much of it would have flowed into this country to make its deserts bloom and to finance the ingathering of the exiles." Now it is "destroyed, plundered, vanished," and "if it is still possible to restore part of it, is that forbidden? Is it not our duty to take it and bring it here?"

Sharett even indirectly linked the reparations with immigration to Israel: "Just as we do not lock our door – not only do we not lock our door, we open wide our gates to every Jew who comes to us with only the shirt on his back after all his property has been plundered from him – thus we must open wide our gate and with our own hands return that property whose owners did not live to bring it themselves, for they were murdered. Today we are an independent state," he went on, "what kind of a proposal would it be on our part when the heirs of the Nazi regime sit down in a neutral capital to conduct negotiations with representatives of an independent Jewish state whose very appearance embodies the total defeat of the Nazi plot?"

Sharett's speech was one of the highlights of the prolonged and anguished debate and, in the end, with a majority of more than half its members, the Knesset authorized the government to open negotiations with the Bonn government. In his journal, Ben Gurion summarized the three days of the Knesset debate in these words: "On Wednesday the government's position was passed by a large majority and with a moral victory. The conclusion of the debate by Moshe [Sharett] was exemplary."

Summary

What was the connection between Sharett's position on reparations and negotiations with Germany and his overall worldview, and to what degree did this position express his personality and public path?

In the clear position he adopted in the prolonged debate, two elements that characterized Sharett throughout his public activity are clearly evident: the first is viewing Zionism as "a return to history's Vale of Tears" while the other is his tendency to consider matters, even difficult and emotional events, employing rational criteria and his revulsion of anything suggesting populism or spurious emotionality. In the view of historian Israel Kolatt, the origins of this element lie in the years Sharett studied in England (1921-1925) where he was educated to take "a methodical, lucid and empirical approach."[33] This education enabled Sharett to process everything throughout his life, even ideological truths, "in his methodical and organized mind."

Sharett's rational approach did not clash with ethical positions or moral values. As far as he was concerned, the disparity was between rationality and spurious romanticism - being carried away by illusions and mysticism. This disparity was clearly manifested in the matter of negotiations with Germany, but also in other issues he dealt with as well, for example, the partition of Palestine that was on the agenda in all its force in the summer of 1937, following the publication of the Peel Commission Report.

Sharett's position on both these issues derived from the same source: the profound belief that even emotional issues must be judged by the scalpel of cold logic, and the no less profound belief that aspiring towards sovereignty mandates the taking of difficult and unpopular decisions. In a speech entitled "Partition as the Lesser of Two Evils and a Golden Opportunity" which he delivered in August 1937 at the 20th Zionist Congress, Sharett voiced a number of arguments favoring partition, arguments he might have used to defend his position favoring direct negotiations with the Federal Republic of Germany. The similarity is apparent in the very presentation of the situation: "The choice facing us today is not between two goods, but between two evils." In deciding between the choices we do not have to make the more difficult one, "but we must not flinch from the difficulty," we must choose "the way of the greatest progress, and this way is possibly the hardest and not the easiest." He expressed his opposition to what he termed "that Zionist mysticism that prevents us from reaping the benefits of the opportunities actually presented to us." Although this mysticism has "deep roots in the soul of the people," he asserted that, "it is the enemy of Zionist fulfillment." And apart from that, the choice of partition does not derive from "a psychosis of defeatism" but from a resolute decision that our main task is "to enlist all the forces, but what are we to do if the historical development takes a different path from the one demanded by the troubles of the Jews?"[34]

*

Moshe Sharett, as foreign minister and prime minister of Israel, was the leading figure in Israel's relations with Germany. His positions and views on this charged subject symbolize the terrible drama that unfolded at the time: the transition from total boycott of Germany to contacts and negotiations which took place only a few years after the annihilation of European Jewry.

---

33   Israel Kolatt in Yaakov Sharett (ed.), *A Statesman Assessed ("Shoher Shalom") Views and Viewpoints about Moshe Sharett* (Hebrew), Moshe Sharett Heritage Society, Tel Aviv 2008, p. 329.

34   Moshe Sharett, *Making of Policy, The Diaries of Moshe Sharett*, 1937 (Hebrew), Am Oved, Tel Aviv 1971, p. 268.

[1] Direct Contact With Germany Is Inevitable

Cabinet Meeting, 15.2.1950

Minister Eliezer Kaplan (*Chairman of the meeting while Prime Minister David Ben Gurion is on vacation*): The Cabinet has decided that in principle we approve or encourage claiming compensation from Germany by individuals and permit the transfer of the money in the form of goods, on condition that the goods are purchased with these funds. Since there was a question of allowing payment in hard currency, the Finance Ministry was given permission to determine the quota.

Two issues have transpired: First, that it is impossible to attain large scale compensation without negotiating with the German authorities. We thought that after the American Occupation Authority in West Germany published a memorandum on the question of compensation, individual Jews would start claiming what is due to them, but that cannot be done easily. On the part of the Germans there was a gesture of granting about ten million marks, but it became clear that they were waiting for someone to negotiate with them.

Second, while it was impossible to obtain large sums, and we are discussing small and average sums, many Jews from Israel and other countries are doing business with Germany. There are even those who purchase goods with their own money and not with compensation, and the goods are then shipped to Israel by immigrants as their personal possessions. Trade is routine. Official means must be organized for these transactions, too. I have been informed of cases in which people wanted to import goods from Germany in the guise of transferring capital from Switzerland.

The proposal is that we agree to a government representative entering negotiations in this sphere of compensation. Should it transpire that we are talking about very large sums, we shall make the appropriate arrangements, and should it be evident that the sums are not large, then this should not be undertaken officially. Some estimate that we must not think about ten million dollars a year, but $50 million, since theoretically Germany owes the Jews huge sums. Another danger is that if this continues for a long time, the money could be lost during that period. We could save it all, or the greater part of it, if this continues for not more than two or three years.

Minister Moshe Sharett: I certainly approve the direction in which the minister of finance presented the question and his conclusion. I think we will have no choice other than making direct and official contact with the German government. This means that we must go open-eyed into a political storm at home and abroad. We shall find ourselves again in approximately the same debate we had during the famous "transfer",[1] but even more so. Meanwhile, all are aware of what happened during the years of the Holocaust, and that the issue has become considerably graver. I think it is vital to take this road even though it might entail a much more intensive internal clash than in the days of the "transfer," precisely because of what has happened, and because there is now less reason for foregoing what could be achieved, and also because of the great absorption needs created by the ingathering of the exiles.

There are several questions we are faced with. First, there is the question of interests, which on the face of it are definitely personal: Jews who immigrated to Israel left property behind in Germany. In fact, they abandoned that property. They can now obtain and realize it. Second, there are Jews who were incarcerated in the concentration camps and survived. According to a new law enacted in West Germany, compensation is due to them for the time they were detained. It can be argued that these are personal claims, and let those individuals get whatever they can. This, in my opinion, is an untenable position for any government to take, especially for our government. Any citizen of our state who has a claim from another government has the right to appeal to his government for help. It is inconceivable that the government could be oblivious to the interests of a single citizen, all the more so when such citizens are numerous. If Holocaust survivors arrived here with only the clothes on their backs, and if they can now obtain scores or hundreds of pounds [in compensation], then we cannot remain indifferent towards these citizens' claims as if their problems are not our concern.

There is another, no less serious, matter: the problem of property of people who perished and have no kinsmen left – the property of absentees and of Jewish communities that were destroyed. In many cases this property can perhaps be saved only by the Jewish people, and as we see it, the State of Israel can act as that inheritor.

In Israel two different slogans prevail side by side. Evidently, the man in the street is unaware that these slogans are contradictory. One slogan is: "No contacts with the Germans whatsoever; anyone touching the profane becomes profane; total boycott!" And the other: "Compensation from the Germans is due; compensation is due to the Jewish people from those malefactors for what

---

1   See Introduction, note 4.

they perpetrated against us." People do not realize that it is impossible to have both. It is impossible to obtain compensation from the Germans if we do not have contact with them. I have come to the conclusion that beating around the bush in this matter will not be beneficial. Any attempt to evade reality will on no account be advantageous.

What do I mean by contact? Suppose we find a way in which it is not a government representative who negotiates with them. Well, this too means contact. It is impossible to transfer a house with its foundations and walls and doorways from Germany to Israel; rather, it has to be sold and something must be purchased with the money. Those German marks must be transferred to the market in England to obtain English currency, or to Belgium to obtain Belgian francs, or Swiss francs or even only French francs, or perhaps American dollars. None of these actions can be done without contact. We cannot shut our eyes and not see the necessity of contact. On this matter we cannot be of two minds.

A study of the situation has proved that without official contact, compensation is out of the question. Our officials have clarified the problem. There are all kinds of local restrictions and prohibitions in Germany. It is vital to deal with this matter with the American, British and French authorities in their occupation zones, and possibly also with the Soviet authorities – if this can be done at all in the Soviet zone – there is certainly no prohibition in place in this regard. But there is a national government in Germany now, and the occupying powers act through it. Since it is possible that in various matters the occupying powers will follow a stricter policy than the German authorities, it stands to reason that we will be unable to avoid seeking the assistance of the German authorities to apprise the occupying powers of the German position.

What do we really want? If we want to stay pure, if it is all the same to us whether we obtain something or not, we can refrain from entering negotiations regarding all these matters and be content with what we can extract from Germany. But that will be a minuscule part of what was stolen. We cannot place ourselves in the position of being simon-pure from the sidelines. I will not feel unclean if we try to save Jewish property. We can face the public and say, "What moral law prohibits taking from the thief or robber what was stolen or robbed and which is still in his hands?" We must exploit every effective means to this end. This does not mean recognition of Germany. It does not mean establishing diplomatic relations with Germany.

This effort of returning plundered Jewish property will not be accomplished by an angel, nor by a seraph, but by the State of Israel. What moral right has the State of Israel to employ other states to do this, as if those states are permitted to, and Israel is not? There are probably some who will make such proposals. I foresee such a trend already. It is my staunch opinion that these are hollow options.

Minister David Remez: I say we must take action without any hesitation and only through official channels. If individuals start acting alone they would only entangle matters and undermine our efforts to conduct the matter officially.

Minister Dov Yosef: I am in favor of extracting whatever is possible from them, but I still disagree on the method. It is not essential to make direct contact for this purpose. The foreign minister's analogy is not relevant here. When dealing with a thief or a murderer, you bring him to a court of justice (*Minister Moshe Sharett: If you can do it by yourself – by all means*). I will not go and talk with Germans. They are so profane that I do not want to ask them for anything. I would only wish to destroy them, to annihilate them.

It seems to me that there is an internationally accepted method in such cases. We see ourselves as still being in a state of war with the Germans. There are situations in war in which one side needs some arrangement inside enemy territory, and for this purpose we can be served by a third, friendly, state. We could ask Uruguay, or any other friendly state, to negotiate our needs. We could direct the operation, but the friendly state would officially contact the German government. Of course, we need to find a state willing to represent our interests. (*Minister Moshe Sharett: What you are saying is similar to the imagined wall in Shakespeare's A Midsummer Night's Dream*). I propose appealing to a friendly state to represent our demands.

Chairman Eliezer Kaplan: I propose authorizing the Ministries of Finance and Foreign Affairs, together with the prime minister and in coordination with the Jewish Agency, which has acted in Germany on behalf of the Jewish people so far, to establish direct contact with the government of Germany. It should officially negotiate the release of the funds in Germany, the payment of claims and the realization of the claims monies, and inform the public of this.

It was decided:

Despite Minister Dov Yosef's opposition, to authorize the ministries of finance and foreign affairs, in coordination with the prime minister and with the Jewish Agency, to secure the payment of compensation and the fulfillment of claims from Germany by means of direct contact with the German government. The public must be provided with appropriate explanations in this regard.

[2] Shall We Boycott Germany Forever?

Cabinet Meeting, 30.10.1950

Minister Moshe Sharett: There is the question of Germany. The governments of the United States, England and France have informed us that they have decided to terminate the legal state of war between their countries and Germany. They are not rescinding their authority as occupying powers, but they have rescinded their own laws regarding the state of war with Germany and request that we join them in this.

In addition, we have received a special request from the Western powers that we support Germany's candidacy to the International Wheat Council. Their suggestion is that we abstain from voting, for only yesterday we were knocking on the doors of the nations of the world to support our request for membership in the UN, and now we must not oppose Germany's request.

There is another aspect of the question: for months now, any action by us in the matter of Germany has been delayed by lack of cabinet decisions. The public is complaining. The newspapers are also saying that we are missing our last chance due to the government's inaction in presenting Germany with a claim for compensation. All we have done in the face of the judicial change about to take place in West Germany – a change that does not put an end the occupation – is to have approached the three governments of England, America and France and requested that this change not adversely affect us, that it will not hinder our claiming compensation and being assisted in this matter by them. We have received a positive response from England, although they admitted that they are pessimistic regarding our chances, but in principle they have agreed to assist. We are awaiting responses from the United States and France. But there is a deadlock and inaction on our part on adopting a definite line and initiative. This imposes a very great responsibility upon us.

Three great powers have approached us in a matter pertaining to another great power which, in fact, is the fourth power of the West. The Foreign Ministry seeks to obtain approval of its position: as long as Germany does not conciliate and repay the Jewish people, we shall not accept any demands forwarded by the German people.

Prime Minister David Ben Gurion: Has the government of Israel ever submitted a claim for compensation from Germany?

Minister Moshe Sharett: We have never reached a decision on this matter.

Prime Minister David Ben Gurion: We cannot demand something from Germany without investing something ourselves. As the saying goes, an Arab believes that he can win lottery without buying a ticket.

Minister Moshe Sharett: Germany can offer us compensation. It must be aware of this problem weighing on its conscience. However, for the purpose of our response to the current approach of the powers, there is no need for us raising any new contention. Are you suggesting that we first demand compensation?

Prime Minister David Ben Gurion: We have demanded nothing from Germany, yet we are saying all the time that our claims have not been met.

Minister Zalman Shazar: I suggest we do not connect these two things. There is the matter of the compensation we are demanding. (*Prime Minister David Ben Gurion: We have not made a demand yet.*) I suggest that we do not make our response conditional on whether we demand compensation or not, whether we receive it or not. Our attitude towards Germany does not depend on it. And it does not depend on it if there is anti-Semitism of one kind or another there, Nazism of one kind or another. It does not depend on whether they pay us compensation. This is not compensation to the Jewish people. There is a huge account for the atrocities perpetrated at Auschwitz. Payment of money is a separate matter. There are people who need to receive their money, and we should demand it, but our account with Germany will not be settled by this. Until we are sure that the de-Nazification process has reached a satisfactory stage, we will not vote for Germany even if we are the only ones to abstain.

Minister Moshe Sharett: There are positions that seem reasonable, but, in fact, cannot be maintained, or in any event cannot be maintained for long. We cannot pursue a totally negative policy towards Germany, a policy of ignoring Germany. Germany exists. Their population is tens of millions. There are, for instance, international health matters. Do we think that should an epidemic break out in Germany it will stop at the border? Will we be able to say that Germany should not be a party to an international arrangement of health matters indefinitely?

Had the war ended with the eradication of Germany from the face of the earth, the problem would have been resolved for us. But opposing Germany's acceptance to the International Wheat Council means that millions of people will starve, for where will they obtain wheat? Our negative position can be a temporary one, but it cannot be maintained for a protracted period. Or, take another example: a German consul arrives in New York. He approaches our consul. He wants to make a courtesy call. Our consul refuses. Some time later a consular gathering takes place in New York. The German consul who, naturally, is attending it, greets our consul and extends his hand towards him. What should our man do? Should he banish himself from every gathering of consuls? Similar situations occur time and time again.

The question is, can we see a possibility for some kind of settlement on the basis of compensation, or do we ignore these questions and boycott Germany forever? The State of Israel was never de facto at war with Germany since the State of Israel did not yet exist during the war with Germany. We inherited various laws created by the British during the Mandate years, including regarding a state of war with Germany. The war with Germany has ended. The British want to rescind these wartime laws. Regarding German property in our country, we made our own law.[1] The remnants of the wartime laws are an anomaly for the State of Israel. If we are to follow the line of thought suggested by Minister Shazar, we can maintain that as long as there is no settlement with Germany, we shall not rescind the British Mandate state of war legislation; we shall not grant Germany relief." Will the anomaly remain? Let it remain. However, remnants of legislation enacted during WW II have no place in Israel's codex. A way must be found to resolve this matter.

What the prime minister says about us never having made a claim supports precisely what I contend – that we must reach a conclusion on this matter, that we must have a clear political line. I have discussed this matter with the minister of finance. All sorts of committees and subcommittees have been established for dealing with this matter, but no conclusion has ever been reached. I have raised the questions on several occasions and have done so again today. We must have a clear policy. In the meantime the note we received from the three powers still awaits our response. Indeed, the question of Germany's obligation to us has not been attended to. From an international standpoint Germany has an obligation to pay us compensation. This obligation has not become invalid because we have not submitted a claim, in view of Germany's responsibility for all those atrocities. At present, as a response to the powers, we should adopt the formulation I have proposed.

Minister Moshe Shapira: If we were one of the Big Five, enjoying veto power at the Security Council, then the question of Germany starving or not would have

---

1   German Property Law, passed by the Knesset on 26.6.1950.

depended on us. As it is, as one among dozens of UN members, the matter does not depend on our decision. For this generation, the generation of annihilation, there shall be no making peace with Germany. Were rabbis' stature as strong as it was in the days of the expulsion from Spain in the 15th century, were present-day Jews similar to those in the time of that expulsion, we would have declared a boycott on Germany. But today is not yesterday.

However, it is inconceivable that we, in our time, extend a hand towards Germany. This has nothing to do with demanding compensation from Germany as should be demanded from any murderer. We are entitled and obliged to claim compensation for the families and for the State of Israel, but we cannot establish ties with the nation that is responsible for the murder of six million Jews. Certainly there are difficulties. If our New York consul sees the German consul, he should not run away, but he should not make contact nor shake hands with him. There is no de-Nazification in Germany. There is Nazification there. The greatest murderers are being released from prison and their rights restored. The British and the Americans are participating in this process – and we are going to establish ties with them? The people residing in Zion and in the Diaspora will not understand us.

Minister David Remez: It is not yet time for fraternization. I propose that in the matter of Germany joining the International Wheat Council, we abstain. With regard to all the other matters of Germany's joining – we should oppose.

Minister Moshe Sharett: We have been approached on two matters: the matter of Germany joining the International Wheat Council and the matter of rescinding British Mandate laws pertaining to the state of war between Germany and the other allied countries.

Minister David Remez: Wheat is bread. I do not seek to starve a nation. But with regard to all other matters, the eradication of all signs of hostility between us and Germany is unthinkable. Joining something – no. The matter of wheat and health is a humanitarian issue on which we should abstain from voting. There is a historical state of war and hostility between us. As long as the wound remains open, we should not terminate this attitude.

Minister Yehuda Leib Maimon: I propose that we oppose both matters.

Minister Dov Yosef: The issue of wheat is not a humanitarian one. They can get wheat without joining the Wheat Council. They simply wish to get wheat on easier terms. We do not have to be so generous to them. I propose that we simply answer in the negative on both issues at hand. We shall oppose, and let the majority at the UN Assembly decide.

Minister Moshe Sharett: I propose opposing but elaborating our reasons for doing so.

Prime Minister Daid Ben Gurion: I reject going into our reasons. If we are making our positive response conditional upon compensation, we should demand compensation.

Minister Dov Yosef: I propose that we leave it to the foreign minister to formulate the answer on the basis of the meeting's deliberations.

Minister Pinhas Rosen: I generally accept the view that we should oppose both admitting Germany into the International Wheat Council and the rescinding of the laws whereby Germany is still our enemy.

On this occasion I would like to remind you of a question we are facing: West Germany is now permitted to join several international conventions, such as the Patent Convention on trademarks. We, too, are members of this convention. This obliges us, for instance, to register German patents here unless we say we are in a state of war with them. In any event, we face this question. Another question is whether this matter of state of war is beneficial to our economic situation.

Now, with regard to the general question, I support Minister Sharett's view that we must find the time to put the entire matter on our agenda because the Jewish Agency's handling of this subject is not taking us forward. I am also of the opinion that if the State of Israel, in its capacity as a sovereign state, does not get to the heart of the matter of compensation, the matter will not be advanced. But this question is somewhat connected with our having a mission or an official delegation in Germany, and then, as a state, we would conduct official negotiations with Germany. Since we have not wanted to do so, we have so far avoided considering this matter. However, demanding compensation from the murderers obliges us to act in a state-like manner.

It was decided:

To authorize the foreign minister to respond in the negative to the request of the three powers in the matter of rescinding the legislation determining that Germany is an enemy state as well as to the request regarding Israel's agreement to Germany joining the International Wheat Council.

[3] On Sending an Official Israeli Delegation to Germany

Cabinet Meeting, 27.12.1950[1]

Walter Eytan (*Director General of the Foreign Ministry*): About two months ago we received a note from the governments of the United States, England and France on the matter of terminating the state of war with Germany. The powers are about to terminate – insofar as this touches upon the legislation of those countries – the state of war with Germany. These powers are proposing to several states that they follow suit. Consequently, this request has raised anew the question of Germany for us. I am not discussing this note or a response to it now, but rather a more practical issue. In brief, what we at the Foreign Ministry propose is that the government decides on sending an official Israeli delegation to Germany to conduct negotiations on the compensation claims.

It is clear to the Foreign Ministry and also, as far as I know, to the Ministry of Finance and all other bodies that have dealt with the matter of compensation over the years, that Germany is obligated to us and that there is no other way of achieving this objective. All attempts at using an indirect approach, be it by mediators or by private agencies, have so far not achieved – and in our opinion will not achieve in the future – any serious result in this matter, and therefore we propose taking the daring step of dispatching an official Israeli delegation to Germany to conduct direct negotiations.

I have purposely not specified with whom to conduct negotiations since that is the essential question. I also have no desire to review the course of events because I think that the history is more or less well known to you. We should, in fact, have addressed this matter two years ago, or even in 1948, but at the time the country was occupied with other issues and opinions had not yet been formed on this matter. It is now very late in the day, but we can still deal with

---

1 Foreign Minister Moshe Sharett was attending the UN General Assembly in New York. Foreign Ministry Director General Walter Eytan's remarks in this meeting were made under the direction of the foreign minister.

these matters. In a few months' time, there will be no possibility of restoring the plundered property and of obtaining compensation.

So far these matters have been dealt with by many and varied bodies: the Jewish Agency, to a certain extent also private or semi-private organizations acting on behalf of American Jewry, and private attorneys acting on behalf of individuals in Israel and other countries. In fact, anyone able to claim property has traveled to Germany and realized what was due. However, whatever was restored in this manner is merely a tiny percentage of what is owing to us, and it dealt with individual claims only. In other words, a Jew residing in Israel who had property or personal claims in Germany went there, realized his property and wound up his affairs. In this way only a small number of Jews settled their personal accounts.

As you know, the political situation is that there is a German government, or actually two governments – one in the West and the other in the East – and each of the four powers maintains a High Commission. West Germany is currently not a sovereign state – sovereignty is in the hands of the three Western high commissioners. Germany is making great strides towards full independence and full sovereignty, and when it reaches that point it will be far more difficult to negotiate with it and achieve positive results. This change is likely to come about in the first months of next year, in any event during the course of 1951, and it is almost certain that by July of next year the Germans will have full sovereignty. We can see no way of dealing with these matters other than the dispatch of an official delegation. From the powers currently controlling Germany we can expect, if not enthusiasm, at least support for such a step. We know that John J. McCloy, the US High Commissioner, has been waiting for this step for some time and will give all possible support and assistance to this delegation. At the same time we know that Chancellor Adenauer views the matter of compensation as important for Germany, and, he is prepared to pay a very large sum in order to attain moral peace, so to speak, for Germany.

I realize that one of the inhibiting factors here, perhaps the most inhibiting, is the fear of public opinion in Israel in particular and that of world Jewry in general. It seems to me that there is no room for fear if the matter is explained appropriately, for there is here a possibility of obtaining what is due to us, what is due to all of Hitler's victims. There is also no question of quasi-recognition of the German government or anything similar. Sending a delegation is a practical, economic, financial step, the only possible step towards obtaining anything from Germany. From reports that have already appeared in the Israeli press we can even expect general support, although I would not say that there will not be some isolated opponents. You will perhaps recall that a year ago this matter was reported and discussed in the press and appeared to have been taken as a matter of fact. Our claims from Germany are vast and the government must take steps to realize them. Dr. Meron will now review the details of these claims.

Dr. Gershon Meron (*Head of the Economic Department, Foreign Ministry*):
Without a permanent, not temporary, delegation residing somewhere in Germany
and maintaining permanent contact with the authorities, perhaps only with the
present High Commission while it still functions – but who knows how much
longer these officials will be there? - without such a delegation we will be unable
to establish appropriate contact.

According to the latest news, the American government is inclined to permit
the transfer of capital from Germany, and that is vital. If the compensation claims
are worked out in some way, the main problem would be transferring capital. The
German economy is in an excellent state. This removes the pressure of constant
investment from America, and so there is a chance that they will allow the transfer
of capital.

Second, Chancellor Adenauer has stated that he wants to initiate a settlement
and, according to what we hear, he is sticking to that position. Now is the time for
someone to start talking, to explain our claim, even though, of course, there is no
way of knowing what the chances are of obtaining anything. This has nothing to
do with establishing diplomatic relations. We are talking here about the payment
of a debt. From an economic standpoint we must appear as the claimants and
collectors of money due to us. We have to break the vicious circle once and for
all. I do not know if we will succeed, but we shall certainly fail if we continue to
deal with this matter haphazardly. Time is on the Germans' side. I do not know
if the time has perhaps already passed.

The matter is urgent also from another standpoint. The Americans are seeking
to give Germany far-reaching powers. At present the powers' representatives are
supervising the German authorities, but according to information we received
only yesterday, the Germans are likely to receive their Supreme Court jurisdiction
regarding property restitution. So far the Germans have not had this kind of
authority. If it is in the hands of a German judge, that is, a Nazi judge, to decide
in the matter of a Jew's claims, the result is clear. This is the last power the
Americans hold, and there are grounds to assume that they want to transfer even
it to the Germans.

Then there is the question of reparations to the State of Israel. It is not written
in any law that this must be only a one-time sum. The Germans will apparently
seek some kind of arrangement. They will want to work out something with us.
It is difficult to define why, but apparently there is a desire in West Germany to
reach an arrangement with the State of Israel. We have heard this from several
parties. Yesterday we had a talk with Kempner,[2] who was a senior official in
Germany and the American prosecutor at the Nüremberg trials, and he stated

---

2   Robert Kempner, a Jewish-American attorney who was assistant U.S. chief counsel for
     the International Military Tribunal at Nüremberg. In the early 1930s he served in the
     German Ministry of the Interior. With the rise of the Nazis to power he was dismissed
     and exiled from Germany because of his Jewish background.

categorically: "If you want to take advantage of the last chance – send an official delegation like all the other countries did after WW I."

There is still the problem of East Germany. The chances of success there are almost nil, but we may perhaps assume that if we succeed in obtaining something concrete in the Western zone, then maybe the chances in the Eastern zone will be better.

Minister Dov Yosef: I do not know what we may obtain fro m Germany. There are not millions lying in a bank. If we do obtain something – how much is unclear but if we do – it is clear to me that we shall only dirty our hands. I would not take a thing from them. I would not want to dirty myself because of this money. Perhaps my attitude is childish, but that is my attitude. I know that the accepted attitude is that it is a good deed to take from them (*Mr. Walter Eytan: Hast thou killed and also inherited?*). I propose that we take whatever property we can but not bring it here. We can exchange it with South Africa or other countries. Let not German property be brought into Israel. I have already said that I oppose direct contact with the Germans. We should do what all other countries did during the war: ask a friendly state to represent them and conduct negotiations with the enemy. For instance, let us ask Norway to represent us. Our delegation will stay in Paris, maintain constant contact with the negotiators, and instruct them.

Prime Minister David Ben Gurion: What do you say to these Norwegians – why can't you conduct negotiations yourself?

Minister Dov Yosef: We say that we are still in a state of war with them. It won't burden the Norwegians. They can negotiate with the Germans. We have a psychological problem with it. It is impossible for us. I do not want to relinquish the property of Jews, but I cannot talk to them after what they did to the Jewish people. They did nothing like that to the Norwegian people (*Prime Minister David Ben Gurion: The Talmud says: "One's agent is as oneself"*) – I can send the Norwegians to speak on our behalf, but I myself cannot speak to Germans. I did not visit Germany after WW II. I cannot go there. I don't want to go there (*Prime Minister David Ben Gurion: I was in Germany after the war.*) Certainly, you went to see the displaced Jews there.

Minister Moshe Shapira: Regarding our recognition of Germany in any form we have already said: No. Here we are dealing with another matter: property. The Germans murdered Jews and they want to inherit them too. It is incumbent on us now to make an attempt to take this money from them. As far as I am concerned, there is only one consideration: is there a chance of receiving money, or is it very doubtful? If there is a chance then it is a mitzvah to take it. Why should they continue enjoying the money of Jews they murdered? And if I have to demand money from the Germans, clearly I must go there. If the matter is doubtful, if the raising of the demand stains our honor and only the stain remains, then I doubt if we should take this step. I would leave the matter to the foreign affairs and commerce and industry ministries. Let them decide whether or not to send an official delegation.

Prime Minister David Ben Gurion: In this matter, it is the cabinet which should decide.

Minister David Remez: One thing is clear to me: we must not send a delegation to Germany. At the same time it is also clear to me that if somebody – not the Germans themselves – told us on behalf of the Germans that Germany is willing to remove its stain, that it is willing to pay compensation, then we should decide to take it. In view of these two considerations, I think that if Britain, America or Scandinavia is prepared to mediate and to forward a proposal on behalf of Germany, I could sit down with the proposer, but we should not send a delegation just on account of something uttered once by Adenauer or in view of some reports about a mood prevailing in Bonn. Later on, everything might end with a double blow: our suffering and no concrete results. This we cannot afford. There is a historical enmity between Germany and ourselves, which as far as we are concerned is beyond repair. Establishing mutual relationship on the basis of compensation is impossible. Somebody else should endeavor and bring us a proposal on behalf of Germany.

Prime Minister David Ben Gurion: There is a cabinet decision on the matter. Indeed, several ministers were absent from that meeting of the Cabinet, including myself, but on February 15th the Cabinet decided, against Minister Yosef's opinion, "… to authorize the ministries of finance and foreign affairs, in coordination with the prime minister and with the Jewish Agency, to attain the payment of compensation and the fulfillment of claims from Germany by means of direct contact with the German government. The public must be provided with appropriate explanation in this regard."

Minister Rabbi Yitzhak Moshe Levin: We should announce that we are in a state of war with Germany and see to it that we receive compensation as a warring side. We should not claim anything from Germany. All the world's silver and gold would not compensate us. I propose, first of all, that all Jewish world organizations dealing with this matter be asked to participate in these deliberations. Why should we invite an additional attack on us? Why should we alone take it upon ourselves to decide on this matter? We are not the only party involved. We should avoid sending an official delegation to Germany, but at the same time we must do everything in order to demand the money.

Prime Minister David Ben Gurion: I would like to pose a question: The State of Israel did not exist during the war with Germany. Can it now declare that we are in a state of war with Germany?

Walter Eytan: That question must be put to the Attorney General.

Prime Minister David Ben Gurion: Is there any logic in the State of Israel declaring that it is in a state of war with Germany?

Walter Eytan: Had it been possible, we should have done so on the 15th of May 1948. I doubt if we should do so today.

Minister Dov Yosef: You can establish as a fact that you consider yourself in a state of war with Germany just as the whole Jewish people considers itself in a state of war with Germany.

Dr. Gershon Meron: Since we were asked in the American note whether we think that our state of war with Germany has come to an end, our answer should be simple: it is our opinion that the state of war has not ended.

Prime Minister David Ben Gurion: This note provides us with the opportunity to do what we did not do on May 14, 1948.

Minister Rabbi Yehuda Leib Maimon: It is simply beyond my ability to talk when I hear suggestions that the government of Israel should send an official delegation to Germany when the voice of our brethren's blood crieth unto us from the ground. I doubt if we will get anything, and if so, would it be worthwhile? In my opinion, we must not have any connection whatsoever with the Germans, for we are at war with the Amalekites since time immemorial. They murdered six million Jews. Shall we talk with these murderers? The government of the Jewish people, the government of Israel, must declare that we will have no contact with them. Their murderous deeds will not be expiated, neither by millions of marks nor millions of pounds. There is nothing more to be said about a delegation to Germany. Minister Remez says that others will come to our assistance. I do not think so. We would have to ask them to do it, and I am against this. If it is possible to declare that we are in a state of war with Germany, then we should. Let the Gentiles know that we cannot come to terms with the Germans after what they did to us.

Minister Pinhas Lavon: I am against sending a permanent delegation as proposed by the Foreign Ministry, for a permanent one would mean, in fact, the establishment of diplomatic relations and de facto recognition. I am in favor of sending a delegation to the occupation authorities because they are about to end the occupation of Germany, bringing Germany back into the community of nations, and I think that the State of Israel can approach them and say: it is your duty to deal with this matter. We are in a state of war with Germany and this duty is yours before you leave: you must see that the claim of the Jewish people and the claims of individual Jews are settled fairly In addition, this matter should be dealt with in London, Washington and Paris, since it is there that matters are being decided. I propose not to send a permanent official delegation. Let us send two or three authorized people to negotiate with the occupying powers. These people would also be able to negotiate with the occupation authorities of East Germany, submit our claim to them and ask whether or not they are prepared to do anything in this direction.

Minister Golda Meir: It is inconceivable that a State of Israel delegation sit in a German government ministry and speak with German government people. I presume that the Western powers have an interest in our making direct contact with Germany. This implies that the Germans are not considered a particularly distinguished group. The powers are about to establish a German army and terminate the state of war between themselves and Germany. For them, everything has been settled satisfactorily, but our negative position is seen as an uncomfortable hindrance. By sending an official delegation we would justify any action taken by the powers towards normalizing their relations with Germany.

We must submit our claims in the four capitals of the great powers. They are about to terminate the occupation. Should these powers accept our demands, so will we, and this will be implemented without direct contact with the German authorities. Should they not, direct contact will not help, but the fact that Jews are negotiating with Germans will be heard all over the world, and then try to explain that this is not contact, that it is not [diplomatic] recognition, that it is only trade relations. We must declare war on Germany. If that is impossible, we must announce that just as the Jewish people was at war with Hitler at a time during which the State of Israel did not exist, now we see ourselves as if the State of Israel existed and took part in the war, and we deem it inconceivable to end the state of war between us and Germany.

Prime Minister David Ben Gurion: We are facing two issues here. One is the individual claims of refugees or of Jews who have property in Germany. All measures must be taken to restore their property. The Germans are not entitled to such a gift.

There is another issue with which we have not dealt properly. We are indeed a Jewish State, but we do not represent the Diaspora. We represent only the Jews residing in our country. We are demanding that Jews wishing to immigrate to our state be free to do so. But there are Jews residing in Africa, in England, whom we do not represent. If England makes peace with Germany, there would be peace. If we do not declare war on Germany, there will be no war. I posed my question in all earnestness. Presumably, we will be asked, why have you waited for two-and-a-half years? Our answer is clear: we were engaged in a serious war, our War of Independence, albeit not with Germany.

I propose that we determine politically, officially and judicially that there is a state of war between us and the two Germanys. This will be legally enacted. Our law would prohibit Israeli citizens from traveling there. Should a citizen go there and come back, he will be punished. A German will be unable to come here even though he might be a Catholic bishop. I have given much thought to this question. Now the opportunity has presented itself. It will necessitate a Knesset declaration, not only in response to the note from the powers. In our response to them we shall include a declaration regarding the state of war. The Knesset shall declare it with all the judicial consequences, which will facilitate what Minister Yosef proposes, that we approach a friendly government to protect our citizens. Right now, hypocrisy is reigning there. There are laws according to which compensation is to be given, but owing to technicalities their promulgation is impossible. If we have a consul there, he does not reside in Germany. He resides with the Occupation Authority, for Germany is an occupied country. If we announce that we are in a state of war with Germany, the publisher of a well-known Israeli newspaper would not be able to travel to Germany and purchase printing machines with which he prints a newspaper that includes articles against our government making any contact with Germany.

I propose two things: let us find an effective way – even though chances are very slim – how not to leave Jewish property to Germany; the state must come to the assistance of those who claim money from Germany, but this should not be done through an official delegation. We should approach the American administration in Washington and they should know the matter is serious. Second, on this occasion we shall declare a state of war between Israel and Germany.

Minister Moshe Shapira: Are we going to decide to declare a state of war with Germany at the present meeting?

Prime Minister David Ben Gurion: If you propose that this issue needs further deliberation, then we shall not decide now.

Minister Moshe Shapira: I propose devoting further study to this question.

Minister Golda Meir: I am in favor of a declaration of war, but I want to consider the results – not the economic ones – that would ensue from this. Let us assume that there is a war between East and West tomorrow – what would it mean for us?

Prime Minister David Ben Gurion: There is no war yet. If there were, perhaps it will be easier for us if we are in a state of war with the two Germanys.

Walter Eytan: When I came here I did not intend to speak about a state of war with Germany. Since I have been presented with this new idea, I would like to say the following: (a) No decision must be made without first hearing a well-considered advice from the attorney general, since it touches upon various international legal complications and it is not a simple political decision. (b) This decision runs counter to the United Nations Charter, to the effect that a declaration of war, or of a state of war, is prohibited. I therefore suggest that in any event, the proposal be studied further. The powers' note should, of course, be answered in the spirit of what has been said here. I think that a negative response to the note should be sent. All the other conclusions derive from this negative response. We inherited a law from the British prohibiting trade with the enemy. We have not rescinded that law. The British, the Americans and the French want to rescind similar laws in their countries, and they are asking us if we are prepared to do the same – we say, No, we do not accept the proposal of the three powers, and that should be our response to the note. With regard to sending the delegation, the sums in question are enormous. They are greater than all the loans we have received, and are likely to receive in the future from America. This is not a question of waiving a tiny sum. It is a question of waiving vast possibilities. It is difficult to accept Dr. Yosef's proposal that it be implemented by a neutral state. I think it will be impossible to find any state that will accept this burden. There is absolutely no reason for Sweden, Norway or any other country to do this for us. It must be accomplished by us. We can either do it or not, but so long as it is not done centrally, intensively, nothing will come of it, and should we put it into the hands of another state without very competent supervision on our part, there is no chance of anything coming of it.

Prime Minister David Ben Gurion: The proposals are as follows:
(a) To send a delegation to the German authorities
(b) To do so through a neutral country;
(c) To announce through a declaration in the Knesset that a state of war between us and the two Germanys still exists. There is Minister Shapira's proposal not to decide today.[3]

It was decided:
To postpone the decisions until the next meeting.

---

3   See document no. 4 for negative juridical opinions on this issue.

[4] The Cabinet Decides to Send a Delegation to Germany

Cabinet Meeting, 3.1.1951[1]

Walter Eytan (*Director General of the Foreign Ministry*): I would like to add a few words to what I said here last week: all agree that sending a delegation to Germany, to function there under the auspices of the three Western powers of occupation, is the only way to deal with our demand for compensation if we do not want to forego what is due to us from Germany. The decision to send a delegation presents a chance to rescue whatever remains possible to rescue, for while the occupation authorities still exist, they will soon disappear and fundamental political changes will take place there. I must stress, therefore, that if we are to send this delegation, then this is almost the last moment to do so – it must be sent within a few weeks. In view of this situation I urge you to arrive at a "yes" or "no" decision today. The matter cannot be delayed: now is the last moment.

I would like to inform you that following the prime minister's idea of declaring a state of war between us and Germany, we requested judicial opinions from several legal advisors, including that of the Attorney General. Dr. Jacob Robinson, the legal adviser of our UN delegation, was clearly negative in his opinion.

Prime Minister David Ben Gurion: The Attorney General's opinion was negative, too.

Minister Pinhas Rosen: I support Mr. Eytan's proposal to send a delegation to the occupation authorities to conduct negotiations regarding our demands. We have been weighing this issue for several years and have not yet reached a decision. Jews have much property in Germany. I will never agree that in addition to all that we suffered we should give up their property there. This attitude is beyond my comprehension.

It must be clear, though, that only a small part of the Jewish property in Germany belongs to Israeli citizens, for the majority of rich German Jews

---

1   Foreign Minister Moshe Sharett is absent as he was still abroad. See document no. 3, note no. 1.

emigrated to the U.S.A. It is assumed that only 5 percent of that property belongs to Israelis, and that it alone amounts to $120 million.

Not attempting to rescue these properties is an absurdity. I was told that one of our ministers said that this money will contaminate us (*Prime Minister David Ben Gurion: Money has no smell, as the proverb goes.*); (*Minister Dov Yosef: I said that.*) Well, if Dr. Yosef said that, I am prepared to admit he is a greater idealist than I. Had I a personal claim for a property worth £10,000, I would not only have done everything within my power to obtain this sum but would also have demanded that my government help me submit my claim. I wonder if Minister Yosef himself would have given up such a claim. I have no idea whether the chances of a positive response to our claim are great or small, but the attempt to submit a claim must be made, and this can only be done by sending a delegation over there.

Mr. Kempner, Deputy Chief Prosecutor of the Nüremberg Trials, who is now visiting Israel, told me that if the claim is forwarded formally by the State of Israel, its chances of being accepted are good, and that if we miss the opportune moment and wait until the occupation regime is over, our situation will be much more difficult.

Minister Eliezer Kaplan: I support the Foreign Ministry's proposal of sending a delegation. Had we been able to punish Germany I would have understood such a move, but the only result of our refraining from any action will be that Jewish property worth tens of million of marks will remain in German hands. This is beyond me.

However, let us not delude ourselves. True, the proposal is to send a delegation for the purpose of negotiating with the occupation authorities, but, gentlemen, it should be clear today that sometime in the future our delegation will have to enter direct negotiations with the Germans if concrete results are to be obtained.

Minister David Remez: I would prefer acting through diplomatic channels without sending an official delegation. I do not want us to send a delegation and have it return insulted, frustrated and empty-handed. Only if we are offered a proposal of mediation will we be prepared to negotiate directly with the Germans.

Minister Golda Meir: I have already proposed that we should submit a claim in the capitals of the occupation powers – in Washington, London, Paris and in Moscow, too.

Minister Pinhas Rosen: As far as I know, Washington has not responded at all to our approaches in this matter.

Minister Yehuda Leib Maimon: I propose that we do nothing.

Prime Minister David Ben Gurion: Should we also forbid individual citizens submitting claims?

Minister Yehuda Leib Maimon: Private claims should be allowed. The government should do nothing.

It was decided:
(By a majority vote) Representatives of the State of Israel shall appeal to the central governments of the occupation powers with the demand of guaranteeing the payment of compensation and restoration of Jews' property in Germany.
(By a 5:5 vote) To reject the proposal of sending an official Israeli delegation to the occupation powers.

[5] On Individual Compensation and General Reparations

Cabinet Meeting, 8.2.1951

Minister Moshe Sharett: With regard to the matter of Germany: the cabinet is aware of the note we submitted on the settlement of payment for Jewish property. At the same time there are also claims for compensation submitted by individuals. I have taken particular care that our note should specifically state that individual compensation for Jews is unrelated to the question of the historical reparations that the German people owe us for all the mental anguish and suffering, destruction and plunder of property which do not come under the procrustean bed of an individual claim, such as one person's claim for his house, another's claim for his pension, or a third one's claim for imprisonment. We have stated that regarding the historical reparations due to us from the German people, we shall submit a separate claim.

I accept the considerations of several cabinet and state officials that the most appropriate moment for submitting this claim will be when the foreign ministers of the four powers convene to discuss the future of Germany. Whether or not this planned conference will take place is still unclear. If it is postponed indefinitely, or if it becomes clear that there is no likelihood of it convening, we will have to discuss submitting the claim without waiting for this international opportunity.

If the Four-Power Conference convenes, and settlements by Germany appears on the agenda – and there can be no doubt that the Western countries will press for more rapid progress on Germany's integration into world affairs – it will present us with an opportunity to submit our claim. The Jewish people comes along and says: "Wait, there is something else to be discussed first, and the question of Germany cannot be discussed until it is resolved." To this end we should enlist all the forces and influence at our disposal.

It is clear that we must submit a very substantial claim. I think it should be a most comprehensive one. In my opinion, the considerations governing our appeals for American grants do not apply here. We cannot approach the United

States without some chance of receiving a positive response, for a negative one would only demonstrate our failure. However, in the case of Germany I fear no negative result. We owe this very claim of compensation to our history, to our conscience, to our people, to the victims. We must not shirk from submitting this claim, and it would be immeasurably easier, and stands a greater likelihood of success, if we submit it to the powers rather than directly to Germany.

If we submit such a claim it may be said that it can be dealt with in stages and there is no need to determine everything in advance. But I want us to determine the matter in principle. If we submit such a claim and are invited to discuss it, and supposing they say, "Fine, your claim will be accepted" – then what? In my opinion the answer must be we can move on to arranging matters of our relationship with Germany. In other words, we cannot submit such a claim to Germany, even through others, and say that even if our claim is accepted we are exempt from settling our relationship with Germany; that we shall continue the war against the Amalekites forever. Why? Not only because I am keen that we do the right thing vis-à-vis Germany: it has done its share and we must do ours. It is clear that not only payment to the Jewish people, but also a declaration of reconciliation with the Jewish people must come from the German government. But if this happens, decency obliges that we accept, not reject it. Moreover, without it we will be pushed into a situation of meeting with the Germans without receiving a thing.

Had we opposed Germany's membership in the International Wheat Council, spoken against its acceptance and voted against it, only to see it accepted into the Council – would that have caused us to leave it? No. We are sitting there together with them. I have before me a letter from the International Students Association. We oppose Germany's acceptance into that association, but should it be accepted, will that cause us to leave the International Students Association? Generally speaking, Germany is turning the corner a lot faster, perhaps, than any other country and is occupying its place in Europe and the world; it will not be long before we are unable to move around in the world while avoiding contact with Germany, be it indirect or direct.

There are questions thrown at me regarding such contacts. Until now the occupying powers, even outside Germany, issued entry visas to Germany. But now a German consulate is functioning in London. Take the case of a Jew who goes to Germany carrying an Israeli passport, approved in a number of countries including Germany, and says he must visit Germany to wind up his affairs, and for this purpose he receives our approval. He reaches London and goes to the Home Office to obtain an entry visa to Germany. Until recently he would have been given the visa by the British and would be in the clear. Now the British will direct him to the German consulate, and then this fellow will go to our consul in London and ask, "Am I allowed, or prohibited, to go to the German consul?" The government of Israel approved his journey to Germany – is he now permitted to obtain a visa from the Germans, or does he give up the idea of going to Germany?

Or take another case: The Israel police have begun receiving communications from German police authorities on all kinds of routine matters in which there is inter-force correspondence. A great many matters are subjects of such correspondence without these matters reaching the Foreign Ministry such as that of an escaped criminal whose photograph is sent by the German police to the archives of other countries. There are some cases in which a reply is naturally expected. We receive a letter from the German Polizeiamt [German ministry of police]. Are we permitted to reply? Until now we could have replied: "Correspond with the British or American authorities," but that is rapidly becoming a fiction. An element of reciprocity is involved here.

At present we have a consul in Munich. He sends people who approach him not to the German authorities, but to the occupation authorities. But those institutions may soon be disbanded: should we take him out of there? Should we ban travel by Israelis to Germany? We certainly shall not. The occupying powers are withdrawing; we have no relations with Germany. Who will then protect the rights of the Israeli individual there?

This is an imbroglio with no way out. We can hold out for a short period, but not for long. We must therefore seek a fair and honorable solution: if our claim is met by Germany, we need to normalize our relations with it.

It is now clear to me too that if we submit a reparations claim to Germany, the issue of compensating the Arabs [Palestinian refugees] is likely to be raised by the Americans and others. They will say: "You are now demanding compensation, but you are also being sued for compensation – are you going to settle this?" We shall answer that the two matters are dissimilar – what Germany perpetrated against us is unlike what happened between us and the Arabs, but the fact remains that Arab people were uprooted from their homes, and we agree, within a certain framework, to pay compensation, and therefore I have said that perhaps we might have to arrange it through American aid and perhaps through the receipt of compensation from Germany, and perhaps through both. In general terms this may appear to be arrogance on Israel's part: it received a loan from the Bank for Export and Import, an Israeli bond issue in the United States was approved by the administration, it is demanding an American grant, it is demanding $500 million or who knows how much from Germany. I have specified the sum of $500 million; this is a small percentage of German exports.

I would not be deterred from posing the issue at hand. I think that we must present what we are doing in the correct light. We should underline the fact that we have absorbed more than half a million refugees into Israel, but their absorption still calls for massive investment, and we still have to absorb immigrants from Iraq, Egypt, North Africa and Romania. There was a point when registration for immigration in Bucharest was stopped and was only carried out in outlying towns, but registration in Bucharest has been renewed, the age range has improved, so that immigration from Romania is in full flow. The plan for raising the sum of one billion dollars was initiated. But one billion is not simply a slogan to impress others; it is required for a real need. We are talking of $1 billion from the US, but in fact we need $1.5 billion.

I think we must move forward towards announcing our claim from the German people. There is, of course, a complication with the Jewish organizations. We have read scathing criticism of us in the papers. The government of Israel was criticized for not submitting the claim through the Jewish Agency, for not enlisting American public opinion, and it was said that this entire action is worthless. Dr. Goldmann is going to see General John J. McCloy, the High Commissioner of the American zone of occupation in Germany. I have cabled Dr. Goldmann – since he is considering coming to Israel at the end of the month, it would be preferable if he postponed his meeting with McCloy until he is on his way back from Israel, and could consult with us first rather than hold it on his way here. It seems to me that we must move forward on this matter and embark on an initiative in the name of the Israeli government. Matters could become complicated without consultations and then nothing will get done. We must inform the various [Jewish] institutions that we are taking this action, and we must enlist their support, but for various reasons this must be an initiative of the Israeli government. There is no comparison between the efficacy of a step taken by the state and steps that may be taken by all kinds of Jewish institutions, including the Jewish Agency, with all due respect to its importance. Mr. David Horowitz has stated that our note has already begun to take effect in Germany. There have been questions and inquiries. There has been criticism of our over-zealous activity at UN headquarters at Lake Success. Let us assume that there is some defective reasoning behind this activity, but there are also reasons to praise it, including the matter of Germany. The fact that the Germans are aware that the State of Israel is a force to be reckoned with at Lake Success is also most beneficial.

The Israeli government has submitted a memorandum to the occupying powers demanding that they do not evade their responsibility for our current interests in Germany. I propose that we now move forward to the second stage and approach the four powers with the Jewish people's claim from the German people. The political and diplomatic efforts must be directed towards the Four-Power Conference.

I take this opportunity of presenting the question of whether we should link this with the matter of our compensation to the Arabs and say, "If we obtain compensation from Germany it will enable us to pay generous compensation to the Arabs." If we have claimed compensation from the Germans, we are not ignoring our obligation of compensation to the Arabs.

Prime Minister David Ben Gurion: I asked Mr. Horowitz how much he thinks we can get as compensation from Germany. He said $1 billion over ten years, not in cash but in goods. This is not more than three percent of German exports. We are talking here of compensation to the Jewish people. Individual claims are a different matter. If we could receive this $1 billion over ten years in the form of iron, wood, chemicals, machines, railways, etc., we would have solved half of our import problem. I see no reason to doubt this plan.

It seems to me that we can sum up the main issue. There must be consultations with the Jewish Agency, the World Jewish Congress, the Joint Distribution Committee and others. After these consultations we shall formulate our request to the four powers on the matter of the Jewish people's claim for compensation from Germany for the six million victims, apart from the individual claims.

It was decided:

The foreign minister will hold consultations with the Jewish Agency and other public bodies on the matter of a further approach to the central governments of the occupying powers on the matter of ensuring compensation from Germany to the Jewish people and the restitution of Jewish property.

[6] Compensation Claim From Germany; Release of Nazi War Criminals

Knesset Foreign Affairs and Defense Committee Meeting, 13.3.1951

Chairman Meir Argov (*Mapai*)**:** At the last meeting, MK Peretz Bernstein raised the question of compensation from Germany. I brought this question to the foreign minister's knowledge and he told me that he is prepared to provide details on this issue to the committee, as he is about to make a statement to the Knesset on this question.

Foreign Minister Moshe Sharett: Over the last twenty-four hours we have taken two steps, both related to the matter of compensation. One was towards the government of the United States in particular, by sending a note to the American ambassador here. The note expresses our protest against the policy adopted by General John J. McCloy in the commutation of sentences and release of a considerable number of principal Nazi criminals. This was done not by relying on reports published in the newspapers – I do not wish to say that the reports are incorrect, but that is not a firm basis for dispatching an international document – it was done on the basis of McCloy's own report. McCloy's report, officially published by the United States authorities, reached us ten days ago; our own note was composed on its basis. Today's papers carry a condensed version of the note; the full text will be handed to members of this committee later today.

This is a matter relating to a specific and special subject: the release, acquittal, commutation and remission of Nazi criminals adopted by the United States authorities in the zone in Germany for which they are still responsible. Quite naturally the note was submitted only to the United States as the party concerned. We expressed in it the profound frustration of the government and people of Israel in view of this policy. We compared the spirit of the report with the spirit of the Nüremberg Trials, and elaborated what this means for the future of justice in the world. The note contained both an expression of regret and deep and grave concern; it also included a clause on the seven convicted persons who were not pardoned, but whose sentences have not been carried out. In an oral addendum, strong emphasis was placed on these seven convicted persons still waiting for their sentences to be carried out, not because we are a people seeking blood and vengeance, but because this touches upon the core of world justice and is also necessary in order to deter future genocide.

Unrelated to this document, yesterday we submitted to the four powers – the United States, England, France and the Soviet Union – an extensive document on reparation claims for the State of Israel.

It is my intention to deliver a statement in this regard to the Knesset this afternoon on this subject, and I would like to convey to this committee a somewhat shorter but more detailed report since on the matter of reparations and procedure I am able to tell you more than to the Knesset. I shall read the contents of the document in the Knesset in full; here I shall do it in brief.

In the middle of January we submitted a note to the four powers in which we discussed the questions of restitution of Jewish property and individual compensation. In the note we dealt with those issues for which there are laws in force, to one degree or another, in West Germany. The subjects of these laws are compensation claims of individuals for personal damages, personal injury, detention, property expropriated and not returned, and various other individual claims. At the time we made no new demands but rather submitted a demand for reparations regarding several specific matters. There were two main issues on which we demanded that the central government, not the *Länder* [states] governments,[1] be bound, and expressed our reservations regarding the transfer of executive authority in these matters to the German authorities before the required procedure is ensured.

In that note we stated that all these claims do not close the account between us and Germany and that we reserve the right to submit another note that will discuss the reparations problem. There is a difference between "restoration," "indemnity"and other matters. We have termed the former "compensation" and the latter "reparations." There is the question of German reparations to the Jewish people, and on this matter we are about to submit a special claim in the second note. In other words, we have drawn a distinction between the clearance of personal accounts and the closing of the collective-historical account we have with Germany.

We submitted the second note yesterday, timing it in view of the present stage of preparations for the Four-Power Conference. We did not make our claim conditional on how it is dealt with at the conference, but submitted it as a definitive claim. If the powers, by their good grace, decide to release Germany from any compensation payment for themselves, we say that compensation, nevertheless, is still our due. We do not connect our claim with any existing division of compensation among the powers. Should they deem it necessary to include us in this matter, that is their business; that can be negotiated. We are not formulating the claim in this way; it stands by itself. Still, if our intention was

---

1   The governments of the states comprising the Federal Republic of Germany.

not merely to utter a heartfelt cry and to add one more document to the already rich body of literature dealing with the Holocaust and cleanse our conscience – if the intention is to make an effort to achieve something – there is a question of timing, of when the issue of Germany is dormant and stagnant, and when it becomes animated and active. Our reasoning was that it is better to submit this note at a stage when the issue of Germany is on the agenda anyway, all the more so when it is proposed as something that cannot be removed from the agenda. The aim of the Four-Power Conference is to terminate whatever remains of the postwar occupation regime and to restore Germany to the community of nations; thus now is the time to voice our claim.

It is clear that submitting the note must be followed by exerting heavy pressure. Thus we are now entering a phase of action in the relevant capitals, first and foremost Washington, but also London, Paris and Moscow, although the chances of achieving anything in this matter with the Western powers and with Russia are highly unequal. In America, England and France we have embarked on a campaign to enlist the press and public opinion, first and foremost Jewish public opinion, to our cause. This is not happening in the USSR, where Jewish public opinion is not heard, and there is no possibility of influencing the press – the press there is part of the state machine. In Russia we are limited to contact with the government, while in the West there is room for wide action and influencing public opinion. This dichotomy between the open and closed worlds is well known.

We shall take this action together with submission of the note, and accordingly we have already established contact with the appropriate Jewish organizations in America and England.

An additional remark: This claim is addressed to the great powers, not Germany. We do not promise Germany anything in return for these reparations; we do not promise that if it is accomplished we shall forgive and establish relations. We say it is our due. We are prodding the Western powers to assist us in this matter. Our purpose is, first of all, to obtain from them an admission of the justness of this claim so that they make it part of their plans. The chances of this happening are unclear. While I shall not say this in the Knesset so as not to outwardly weaken the claim, I must admit here that it is rather difficult to be optimistic in this matter. We deem it incumbent that we must make a maximal effort towards achieving our aim, but at the same time it is our opinion that if our claim is not accepted, our initiative should not be considered the failure. It would have been, had we not submitted the claim, even though implementation is clearly important.

I shall read the note in its entirety in the Knesset, and that will be its first publication. I could have handed the note over for publication and delivered only a speech in the Knesset. However, it seems to me that it is better that the document is first heard in the Knesset. In the note we take Germany to account and refresh the world's memory of the Holocaust; we do not assume that the world remembers everything – one could write a whole book about it, and we are doing it in five or six pages – but we thought that the best thing would be to cite quite a long passage from the Nüremberg verdict accepted by the four powers – what the trial found, what the Germans perpetrated against the Jewish people – it is a very detailed and very disturbing passage, for it contains details of how men, women and children were victimized.

We submit this note saying that the damage caused to the Jewish people in Europe – to property, of course – is conservatively estimated at $6 billion. This is an estimate reached by the World Jewish Congress Research Institute; there can be no doubting the seriousness of their research, and there is no point in starting again from the beginning. They are conversant in these matters; they added one figure to another and reached a total of $6 billion. We say that material compensation can in no way atone for the crimes and deaths. There can be no atonement for the torture and death. There can be no atonement for the destruction of cultural values. But it is inconceivable that the German people continue to enjoy the spoils while restitution of the victims, those who were saved and remained alive after the Holocaust, is heavily burdening that same Jewish people. The survivors are owed restitution, and since the majority of the victims have found refuge here, we contend that compensation is due, first and foremost, to Israel.

Second: Our state is the only one in the world entitled to make a claim in the name of the Jewish people. Do not look for a clear and absolute legal interpretation here, for this claim is not founded on conventional concepts. We constitute a special and extraordinary phenomenon: we have our own justice system and legal concepts. We say that there is a Jewish people. The damage was caused to that people as a whole. Six million souls, men, women, children, perished because they belonged to the Jewish people. When the victorious nations convened to discuss and obtain compensation, the Jewish people was not represented. Now the situation is different. Now there is a state – its embryo, the Yishuv of Palestine, existed previously. It fought, its sons and daughters fought in WW II, it always perceived itself as responsible for the Jewish people and its people took on that responsibility body and soul. It is now the claimant and it is claiming its due.

We have calculated that together with the immigrants still to come, the State of Israel will have absorbed half-a-million victims, Jewish refugees from Nazi-occupied countries in which Nazism destroyed Jewish life. We are submitting a claim for $1.5 billion. We estimate the damage caused to the Jewish people at $6 billion – and on the basis of this estimate we are demanding reparations in the sum of $1.5 billion, which they owe for the expense of restitution.

There is a view that we will not achieve results in this matter without contacts with Germany through the Bonn government and that others will not do it for us. At present the Government of Israel has not established hard and fast principles in this matter, it has not contacted the Bonn government and is not contacting it. We do not know what the future holds, but we think that when we submit a note to the powers for the first time, we must bring to bear all possible influence and pressure on them. We should not make their responsibility lighter by making direct contact or by an announcement that we seek a direct approach to the Bonn government.

We shall probably have to consult further on this matter of direct approach, but the time is not yet ripe. We must first achieve the maximum possible effect from our approach to these governments, ensuring that our matter is discussed at the Four-Power Conference. We must do our utmost to influence and exert pressure during the conference deliberations.

MK Menachem Begin (*Herut*)**:** I shall begin with the matter of the war criminals. I am sorry that the note ends with an expression of regret. When he raised this issue before the Knesset,[2] our faction member MK Aryeh Ben Eliezer made a concrete suggestion that the government demand the extradition to Israel of these war criminals who participated in the extermination of Jews. I am aware that according to the agreement concluded between the great powers during WW II it was determined that German war criminals would stand trial in the countries in which they committed their crimes, and I am aware that the formal legal aspect here is questionable. On the other hand, in my opinion there is no doubt that there is a legal element in this demand. The Nazis annihilated Jews in numerous countries, not just in one, or in other words, the committing of the crime cannot be delineated by the borders of a specific country – they committed crimes in Europe, and it may be said that they committed crimes in large parts of the world by incitement to racial discrimination that also occurred in America. Once the matter of specific borders falls, there is a basis for a legal demand for extradition, and the country bound by unbreakable ties to the victims is entitled to demand that those people, who committed crimes against its citizens' brethren be brought to a court of justice within its borders.

With regard to the pardon and release of criminals there is a precedent in the case of General Alexander von Falkenhausen, who was unconditionally released by a court in American-occupied territory, and six months later, as a result of the Belgian government's demand, was extradited to Belgium, stood trial and was sentenced. In other words, we, too, are entitled to demand, not only from a moral but a legal standpoint, that people exonerated by a denazification court, or by a court in occupied territory, be extradited to the State of Israel to stand trial here. Whether this demand will be met is another question. Here I must allude to the words of the foreign minister, that there are claims whose failure is not in their non-achievement but in their non-submission. This applies, first and foremost, to the demand I am talking about. I do not think that in the face of the inordinate release of Nazis, the State of Israel and its government can make do with an expression of regret, but a note such as this must include a concrete

2   On March 7, 1951. See *Divrey HaKnesset,* vol. 8, pp. 1297-1298.

demand that if the four powers do not wish to deal with them, they should be extradited to Israel, stand trial, and the court will judge them.

I propose that the committee pass a resolution on this matter and convey it to the government. I would like to express my regret that on matters such as both the first and second notes, the government did not deem it necessary to consult this committee. Ultimately, this is not a matter of partisan politics. It is a grave matter that touches the heart of every Jew, and it would have been better had there been a meeting of the Foreign Affairs and Defense Committee before the two notes were sent, and the foreign minister would have heard the committee's recommendations. That did not happen (*Foreign Minister Moshe Sharett: The committee knew that we would submit such a note. The matter was publicized.*) This must be axiomatic, that at least on a matter such as this there be a prior discussion and not an ex post facto one. But that is water under the bridge.

I have not fully understood – and if I am mistaken I ask the foreign minister to correct me – if the demand for compensation is with regard to everything the Germans inflicted upon us, or just for the plunder of property. This, from my viewpoint, is a fundamental difference. We shall be committing a grave sin if we demand monetary reparation for what the Nazis inflicted upon us (*Foreign Minister Moshe Sharett: Not only are we not demanding it, but we are saying that there is no compensation for it.*) The demand can only be one: to restore the material property that was plundered by the Nazis. The account of human life is completely different and there are no reparations for it. If the demand is for the restitution of the plundered property, then I must express my great amazement that we are demanding only a billion and a half when the damages have been estimated at six billion. As we are speaking of six million that perished, this seems incorrect. In my opinion it is a grave mistake to demand that Germany compensate the victims in the State of Israel, and that we specify what will be done with the money for the plundered Jewish property. Do we need a further explanation to justify this claim? Is justification on humanitarian grounds for the compensation of the victims necessary at all?

If we assess the plundered property at $6 billion, we should demand $6 billion, and what we do with the money is our affair. The demands of Jews and of public bodies can also be included, as well as a collective demand for full payment for the plundered property. With regard to the calculations and accounting, that is a different phase. The impression will likely be that first of all we are reducing the overall estimate, which I am not sure is exaggerated. There is no doubt that this property is estimated at billions of dollars. We are submitting a demand that sounds like a big one, and then, immediately afterwards, in order to receive part of it, we stop at only part of the sum due to us in accordance with justice and fairness. This is gives a bad impression. The assumption could be that the sum of a billion-and-a-half is exaggerated, and it will be a bad thing if we give the impression that we are haggling. We must demand payment for the plundered property without any further explanation of what will be done with the money in Israel. I ask that the committee discuss my request to recommend to the government that this wrong be rectified and that our demand from Germany should be payment of all damages.

Foreign Minister Moshe Sharett: The debate has covered a very wide area[3]. I would very much like to clarify several fundamental points, but it is getting late and I do not know if I will be able to discuss each proposal in detail, although I would be happy to do so.

A clear distinction must be drawn between the scope of the matters discussed in the first note and those discussed in the second. This is not simply a matter of convenience or because of the sheer magnitude of the material. It seems to me that several members have discussed the two notes without distinguishing between them.

There is the question of individual claims. This could be because a person was in a concentration camp and is due compensation for every day of his imprisonment; it could be because his property was confiscated and now he is laying claim to it; it might be that the property was not confiscated but he wants to sell it and invest the proceeds here, not there; it might be because he was physically injured or because his bank deposits were confiscated; it could also be community property – this is one aspect regarding which there are laws in West Germany, which to some degree are satisfactory and which are enforced to one degree or another.

Numerous Jewish organizations, a body called JRSO [Jewish Restitution Successor Organization], the Jewish Agency and the Joint Distribution Committee, the World Jewish Congress and other bodies are already entering this arena. That is not to say that Israel has no say on these matters; it is entitled to demand amendments and improvements. However, Israel appears here as the representative of its individual citizens' interests; it cannot appear on behalf of masses of individuals throughout the world, for these people will say, "Who appointed you?" There are American citizens who do not want the State of Israel to represent them. It could also be a German citizen, residing in Germany, who has an account to settle and does not want the State of Israel interfering in his affairs. Any initiative by Israel in matters not concerning it will generate conflict with institutions and opposition by individuals, as a result lead to the weakening of its status.

This is not the case in the second sphere, dealt with in the second note. Here the State of Israel stands alone. Inasmuch as a collective inclusive, claim on behalf of the Jewish people is submitted, the State of Israel will rouse no competition. First of all, nowhere else in the world is there such a concentration of Jewish responsibility. We need to inculcate the moral-political awareness

---

3   After MK Begin, seven members of the FAD Committee took the floor.

that Israel is the body authorized to submit demands in the name of the Jewish people. There is no other State that can submit such a claim, that can employ diplomatic channels and which can exert a degree of pressure. The second note deals solely with the second question, not the first. Questions regarding the first question could have been raised in the committee when that note was submitted on January 16. Two months have elapsed since then. I do not oppose calling a meeting dedicated to clarifying on what JRSO is, what is the state's position on this question, what is the relationship between the state and the Jewish Agency, what has been achieved and what has not. However, I shall have to summon experts to illuminate these issues.

I shall therefore not address the first issue, but only the second. Our approach to the second issue derives from two points of departure. The first is moral, the second practical. Our aim in this matter is not only to proclaim our right and duty to voice our claim, so it is heard the world over and convinces all that our claim is morally justified and that it should be inscribed to our credit in the annals of history. I do not belittle this moral aspect of our claim. In fact, as you will gather from the wording of the note, it attempts to emphasize it. But that was not our only intention. The intention was to achieve a concrete, maximal result.

As I have already said, our claim is definitive; it is not conditional upon any outside factor or circumstances such as whether the Four-Power Conference convenes or not, nor upon any reciprocal move on our part, such as establishing diplomatic relations with West Germany or forgiving the German people. No. Our claim for reparations is not dependent on any previous or future development. However, since right from the beginning we had a concrete aim in mind, the submission of the claim was accompanied by several fundamental considerations regarding the sum to be demanded. It may be argued, as I have already – and it gives me pleasure that MK Begin accepts my formulation – that there are claims whose failure is in their non-submission, but if the intention is to achieve something, then there is a world of difference between a claim which would could be perceived as reasonable by public opinion, and one that must sound fantastic; in this situation one can only be guided by intuition. There is also the issue of substantiating the claim. If the State of Israel voices a claim from Germany of only $1.5 billion, no one will say that a claim of $1.5 billion is too modest. It is a very substantial sum.

If the powers are going to raise the question of the sum, we shall point out that a billion-and-a-half dollars amounts to West Germany's exports for 1950. Possibly, they might say in response: "You want Germany to give you a whole year of its exports? It subsists for a whole year on that." One cannot ignore such an eventuality. Regarding the sum to be claimed, there is also the question of coordination between ourselves and other Jewish organizations which should not compete with us. If we demand the entire sum we will be inviting competition, for it will include what is due to individuals and what organizations are attempting to obtain. If it is to cover compensation costs, it would include the restitution of survivors emigrating to America. There is already a great deal of friction between us and the Jewish Restitution Successor Organization. They can also argue that they are dealing with various individual claims and oppose our entering this realm. What is the conclusion to be drawn in view of all this? That we should first convene a meeting of the Jewish organizations and reach an agreement with them to appear on their behalf – but if the State of Israel appears on behalf of those organizations it would weaken its own position.

Second, my own experience has taught me that reaching an advance agreement with Jewish organizations is a hard nut to crack and takes an eternity. We should demand aid and support from Jewish organizations because their opposition and competition would certainly limit our achievements. Evidently, this makes claiming the entire sum impossible.

Third, it may be argued that from the practical standpoint it is regrettable that we have waited until now, that we should have submitted the claim the morning after the declaration of the state, the problematic international situation at the time notwithstanding. However, if the claim is presented as a moral one, it can be submitted any time.

Fourth, there is the question of the timing our submission of the claim. Perhaps we were mistaken in this, but it seems that now, at this juncture, prior to the Four-Power Conference, the time is ripe.

And finally, if this were only a moral issue, there would have been no difficulty linking it with an effort to arouse the press and public opinion abroad and to enlist various personalities to exert pressure on our behalf. However, if we want to accomplish this, we must submit a reasonable claim acceptable to these organizations abroad.

My answer to members of this committee who posed the question of the form German payments will take is that obviously a state can only pay compensation in goods. How did Germany pay compensation to the Allies after WW I? Only through exports. Even if it does not pay in goods, it has to sell goods so that it has the money to give. Therefore, our note stated that part of the sum will undoubtedly be paid in goods. This means that goods would be imported into Israel and that some of those goods would be sold on the world market – by Israel – in order to obtain either currency or other goods. There is no other way. However, there is no question that this would mean the establishment of commercial ties with West Germany.

One of the obstacles we shall have to surmount is that of the monies Germany admits are due to individual Jews, for what can we do with German marks? We can only convert them into goods. The American authorities object to this. They say: should Germany sell goods for dollars, they should go the USA, since it is the USA that has rehabilitated Germany. That is one of the reasons we approached the powers. It is one of the reasons for my optimism in this matter. We have been deliberating this issue with the Americans, and I am confident we can reach a positive outcome

In response to questions raised by members of the committee, I would now like to devote a few minutes to a description of the background to Germany's integration into the international political arena – how it is being accomplished and what problems we face as a consequence. This process is already taking place, and we are already encountering and sitting shoulder to shoulder with Germans. Germany is a member of the International Food and Agriculture Organization of which we also are members, and we regard our membership highly. We objected to Germany's acceptance into this body. We voted against it but we were in the minority. The majority accepted them. They came in – we did not leave. We sit together at the same table. Germany is also a member of the International Wheat Council, and we hold our membership in it in high regard – obtaining wheat and ensuring that we are not being discriminated against pricewise is of vital interest to us. At the time we raised our voice against Germany's acceptance into this body. We voted against and again we were in the minority. They came in – we did not leave.

Germany is presently knocking on the doors of two UN institutions endowed with moral significance: the UN Economic and Social Council and UNESCO. Israel is not a member of the central council of ECOSOC, but it is a member of its important sub-council – the Social Council – and we viewed our entry into it as highly beneficial for we can learn a great deal there. Germany is knocking on the door of this body, and I have no doubt that it will be accepted – and, if so, we shall not leave. Germany can gain membership in any UN body of which we are members. It is presently also seeking admission to UNESCO, which requires a two-thirds majority. We shall speak and vote against its admission. I hope we succeed, but I fear there will be a majority in favor and consequently we shall be sitting with Germany in this very highly valued institution, established for international cooperation in the spheres of education, science and culture.

There are numerous other international organizations to which Germany seeks admission, such as the International Students Association. Our branch has decided to campaign and vote against its admission, but Germany will certainly be accepted. Shall we leave? No. We want to isolate Germany, not become isolated ourselves. But by pursuing an ostracizing policy we are risking that.

The part of my speech at the General Assembly devoted to Germany can be construed as a demonstration of our isolation, for it was the only voice of warning against Germany; judging by the response it was a voice crying in the wilderness.[4] Afterwards, I was approached by the French and the Yugoslavian

---

4   The allusion is to Moshe Sharett's speech in the General Assembly, Sept. 27, 1950, in which he called for the admission of Communist China into the UN and opposed the admission of the Federal Republic of Germany.

delegates, and others, who said "Well done" – but not one of them dared open his mouth on the podium. We must not flinch from taking similar steps whenever questions of morality arise in matters touching upon the life of the Jewish people. However, in view of Israel's interest in international cooperation, are we to leave any international body if Germany becomes a member? This would obviously be senseless.

There is currently a German consul general in New York. If he sends a note to our consul general there, asking for an appointment, our consul may respond in the negative, but all other members of the consular corps in the New York do meet with him. There are gatherings that our consul general must attend; there are also consular corps business meetings at which various rulings are determined – should Israel relinquish its place at them in view of the German presence? It cannot.

A further example: Our consul in Zurich was elected doyen of the consular corps. For the consul of Israel to be elected doyen of that body was a big honor for us, for this means that not only is Israel's stature respected, but the consul's personal standing is highly respected, too. His honor is Israel's honor. He has elevated Israel's stature, and that is quite exhilarating. However, the doyen of the consular corps cannot boycott any other member of the corps. Should the German consul have a complaint and seek satisfaction from the doyen, the doyen cannot reject him. The ultimate result is that an Israeli holding a high diplomatic office receives the German consul as he does all others.

We can continue following this policy of ostracizing for a generation or two, thus erasing the issue of our relationship with Germany from the agenda of the generation that experienced and witnessed the Holocaust horrors but, in fact, we encounter Germany wherever we go and in practice we are not boycotting it. We shall be with them everywhere. We must realize that our attempts to prevent Germany's admission to international bodies on moral grounds is bound to lose any significance whatsoever, while in return for our unavoidable compromise on Germany's admission into the family of nations of which we are part, we shall receive nothing – Germany will gain admission gratis. If this is the way the wind is blowing, then at least while it is not too late – while Germany's authorities are still sensitive to this issue – we should exert pressure on them so they know that if they want to achieve further progress in this process of their integration into the family of nations, they must pay, they must compensate the Jewish people. There is a lever at our disposal here for obtaining something. This is what we shall tell the powers, and the Germans will realize it themselves.

A few remarks on the question of war criminals. I cannot accept the Herut proposal, which was also expressed in the Knesset – I was absent from that session – that we demand the extradition of the Nazi criminals into our hands for the same reason I would oppose demanding the entire sum of $6 billion: it is a tremendous demand. The same applies here. We must always consider what is construed as reasonable. If we demand: "Those whom you have decided to hang – hang!" that is one thing; if we demand their extradition so that we could hang them – that is an entirely different matter. I do not think this claim had anything to do with reality.

I was asked why a statement on this matter of German war criminals should not be included in our note. That was our intention at the outset, but after further consideration we came to the conclusion that the matter of reparations, historically and practically, is so important that nothing should be added to it.

Chairman Meir Argov (*Mapai*): I put to a vote the proposal to request the government to also deliver a statement to the Knesset today on the matter of the release of the Nazi criminals. The second proposal is to do so at the nearest opportunity.

The vote:

In favor of expressing a protest in the Knesset today regarding the release of Nazi criminals – three votes.

In favor of doing so at the nearest opportunity – the majority.

It was decided that a protest statement on the release of Nazi criminals be delivered on another occasion.

MK Menachem Begin (*Herut*): I would like to make a two-point proposal:

The Government of Israel will demand from the German occupation authorities the extradition to the Government of Israel for trial of the war criminals who took part in the annihilation of Jews.

These war criminals will stand trial before an Israeli court, even in absentia.

Chairman Meir Argov (*Mapai*): I put MK Begin's proposal to a vote and also the proposal to remove it from the agenda at this stage.

The vote:

In favor of MK Begin's proposal – two votes.

In favor of the second proposal – the majority.

It was decided to remove this proposal from the agenda at this stage.

Chairman Meir Argov (*Mapai*): To sum up: A statement will be made today in the Knesset on behalf of the government on the matter of the note demanding compensation from Germany. The Speaker will announce a debate on the statement to take place next week.

[7] Demand for Compensation From Germany
Statement by the Foreign Minister

Knesset Session 237, 13.3.1951

Speaker Nahum Nir-Rafalkes *(Mapam)*: The foreign minister has the floor for a statement.

Foreign Minister Moshe Sharett: Mr. Speaker: On January 16, 1951, through its authorized representatives, the government of Israel, submitted to the governments of the United States, the Soviet Union, the United Kingdom and France, a note on compensation and restitution of property that Germany is obligated to Jews. The note addresses the payment and restitution due to Jews as individuals in which regard there are specific laws in the various zones of West Germany. The note also states that meeting all these individual claims does in no way repay the heavy debt imposed upon the German people vis-à-vis the Jewish people.

The government stated that it retains the right to raise, in a special note, an issue not covered by the existing laws – the issue of reparations owed by Germany to the Jewish people in its entirety for the plunder of property and confiscation of assets of masses of Jews throughout Europe – the same Jews who were slaughtered and who have no heirs to claim the restitution of their property or payment of compensation for their damages.

This second note was submitted yesterday to the four great powers, and I am honored to bring its contents to the attention of the Knesset and the general public in Israel and abroad.

This document puts an unprecedented claim onto the international agenda. In it the government of Israel demands to impose on Germany reparations in the sum of $1.5 billion, only one quarter of the value of plundered Jewish property. This claim is submitted in the knowledge that the German people in its entirety is responsible for the killing and plunder perpetrated by its previous regime against the Jews of Europe, and that this responsibility must be imposed on both parts of the German people, now divided between West and East.

These reparations are claimed by the government of Israel, as it sees the State of Israel as holder of the rights of the slaughtered millions, and is fully entitled and bound to demand satisfaction for them in its capacity of being the sole sovereign embodiment of the people who, as a consequence of being Jewish, were annihilated. The reparations claim has been calculated according to the financial burden shouldered by the Israeli people, and Diaspora Jews throughout the world, for the restitution and absorption of the half million Holocaust survivors who have settled or will settle in Israel.

The note reads as follows:

The claim of the Jewish people against Germany is without precedent. In the history of the world there is no mention of an act of slaughter and plunder of such tremendous magnitude as that perpetrated by the German people against European Jewry. In the space of a few short years in a campaign of systematic extermination, entire communities were eradicated, communities that had existed more than a thousand years. More than six million Jews were put to death by torture, starvation, killing and mass suffocation. Many of them were burnt or buried alive. No mercy was shown to young or old. Children were torn from mothers' arms and thrown into the crematoria. The elderly were hunted down and transported to the death camps. More than four million Jews perished in Poland and the occupied area of Russia alone. From Germany itself and all parts of occupied Europe – Norway, Denmark, Holland, Belgium, France, Italy, Greece, Bulgaria, Yugoslavia, Romania, Hungary, Czechoslovakia and Austria – trains packed with Jews were sent to the extermination centers month after month. This slaughter is one of the most horrific episodes in the history of humankind.

In the wake of the murder came the plunder, also of great magnitude. According to a conservative estimate, the Nazis in Germany and other European countries that fell under their rule stole Jewish property worth $6 billion. This sum includes the collective fine of one billion marks imposed on German Jewry following the riots organized by that country's government in November 1938, and also the fines, confiscations and other discriminatory taxes levied on German Jewry by the Nazi authorities. The Federal Government of Germany has accepted responsibility for this by viewing itself as the inheriting entity of the Third Reich.

This vast campaign of genocide and plunder of property was the climax of the process of persecution and repression that began on the day the Nazis came to power in Germany. The verdict of the principal German war criminals at the Nüremberg Trials defined this campaign as "a consistent and systematic human horror conducted in the greatest magnitude." The excerpts from the verdict cited here will serve as a description of the persecution of the Jews, from the establishment of the Nazi regime to the end of WW II.

The verdict reads as follows:

"With the Nazis taking power, persecution of the Jews increased. A series of discriminatory laws were enacted which restricted the posts and professions available to Jews; restrictions were imposed on their family life and civil rights. In the autumn of 1938 the Nazi policy on Jews reached a point whereby they were totally excluded from German life. Riots were organized, synagogues were burnt down and destroyed, shops were looted and prominent Jewish businessmen were arrested. A fine of one billion marks was imposed on the Jews, authority was issued for the confiscation of Jewish assets, and ordinances were promulgated restricting the movement of Jews to certain neighborhoods and times. Ghettos were set up throughout the country and on the orders of the security police the Jews were forced to wear a yellow patch on their chest and back. The imposition of the one billion mark fine and the confiscation of Jewish deposits began when arms expenditures led the German treasury into dire straits, so that the government was forced to cut the arms budget.

Persecution of the Jews in Germany, although harsh and repressive, cannot be compared with the policy adopted in the occupied territories during the war. At first this policy was similar to that adopted inside Germany. Jews were required to register, they were forced to live in ghettos, to wear the yellow patch, and were used for forced labor. Then, in the summer of 1941, plans were made for the Final Solution of the Jewish problem throughout Europe. This Final Solution meant extermination of the Jews. As early as the beginning of 1939, Hitler threatened that this would be one of the consequences of the war, should it break out. Then a special Gestapo department was established to implement this policy, one headed by Adolf Eichmann as chief of Department B-4.

The plan to exterminate the Jews entered its implementation phase a short time after the attack on the Soviet Union. Special squads – *Einsatzgruppen* – recruited to break down the population's resistance in the rear of the German armies in the East, were assigned to exterminate the Jews in these areas. The *Einsatzgruppen's* efficiency is demonstrated by the fact that in February 1942, Heydrich[1] was able to report that Estonia had been completely purged of Jews, while in Riga the number of Jews had been reduced from 29,500 to 2,500. In total, the *Einsatzgruppen* operating in the occupied Baltic states killed more than 135,000 Jews in three months. The *Einsatzgruppen* did in no way act without coordination with the German armed forces. There is clear evidence that their commanders enjoyed the cooperation of military commanders. These horrific acts were a direct consequence of the policy determined in 1942. Part of the Final Solution was to gather Jews from all parts of occupied Europe into concentration camps. Those able to work were put to forced labor in the camps. Those unable to work were put to death in the gas chambers and their corpses incinerated. Certain concentration camps at Treblinka and Auschwitz were designated for this principal objective. Regarding Auschwitz, the court has heard the testimony of Hoess,[2] who commanded the camp from May 1, 1940 to December 1, 1943. He estimated that in the Auschwitz camp alone during that period, 2,500,000 souls were exterminated and a further 500,000 died of sickness and starvation. In his testimony Hoess described the selection of the victims for extermination as follows: 'Those able to work were sent into the camp. Others were immediately sent to the extermination facilities. Young children were exterminated without exception. Women would often hide their children beneath their dresses, but when we discovered them they were, of course, sent for extermination'.

Hoess also described the actual killing process: 'Killing the people in the death rooms lasted from three to fifteen minutes, according to the weather conditions. We knew they were dead when the screaming stopped. We would usually wait for about half-an-hour before opening the doors and removing the bodies. After the bodies had been removed our special squads would remove rings and extract gold teeth from the corpses.'

Blows, starvation, torture and killing were an everyday occurrence. In August 1942 the inmates of Dachau were subjected to cruel experiments. The victims were immersed in

---

1   Reinhard Heydrich, head of the security forces of the S.S., later head of the Gestapo and the *Einsatzgruppen*. In 1940 he initiated the Wannsee Conference in which the plan for the Final Solution - annihilation of European Jews - was laid. Assassinated by Czech underground fighters in 1942.

2   Rudolf Höss, a S.S. high-ranking officer. In March 1946 was extradited to Poland, put on trial and sentenced to death.

cold water until their body temperature dropped to minus 28° centigrade, when they would expire. Experiments were also conducted in pressure chambers to determine the body's reaction to high altitude, and also to determine how long a human could survive in freezing water, and other experiments with poison pills, contagious diseases, and sterilization of men and women using X-rays and other methods.

Testimony has been heard on how the victims were treated before and after they had been put to death. Testimony was heard on how the women's hair was shorn before they were killed and the hair sent to Germany for use in mattresses. Clothing, money and valuables of those killed were also sent to the appropriate bureaus for further use. Gold teeth and fillings were extracted from the mouths of the corpses and sent to the Reichsbank. After the corpses had been incinerated, the ashes were used as fertilizer. In some cases, experiments were conducted on the use of body fat for the soap industry. *Einsatzgruppen* roamed Europe in search of Jews for the Final Solution. German delegations were sent to satellite states such as Hungary and Bulgaria to arrange transports of Jews to the extermination camps. We know that up until the end of 1944, 400,000 Hungarian Jews were executed in Auschwitz. Testimony was taken on the evacuation of 110,000 Jews from part of Romania for extermination. Adolf Eichmann, assigned by Hitler to implement the plan, estimated that this policy brought about the killing of six million Jews, including four million that were killed at the extermination facilities."

There can be no atonement or material compensation for a crime of such immense and horrifying magnitude. The Jewish people has lost a third of its number. The majority of European Jewry has been destroyed: of every four Jews in Europe, three were murdered. Any compensation whatsoever, no matter how large, cannot be compensate for the loss of human life and cultural values, or atonement for the suffering and torture of men, women and children slaughtered in every conceivable inhuman manner. When [Karl Hermann] Frank, one of the principal defendants in the Nüremberg Trials, confessed: "A thousand years will pass and the guilt of Germany will still not have been erased," all that can be done is to obtain reparations for the heirs of the victims and to provide reparations to the survivors. Jews were killed, but the German people continues to enjoy the spoils of the slaughter and pillage perpetrated by their previous leaders. Of this we can say: "Hast thou killed and also taken possession?" We cannot raise the dead, we cannot ease their suffering, but at least we can demand that the German people be required to restore the plundered Jewish property and pay for the reparations to the Holocaust survivors.

From the outset, Israel has played a dominant role in the absorption and rehabilitation of the survivors. With the outbreak of Nazi persecution in 1938, the Jews of what was then Palestine came to the aid of German Jewry. An incessant flow of German Jews – a flow that increased with the fall of Austria and Czechoslovakia and when the Jews of those countries joined the flight – found its way to Palestine. In the interim between the establishment of the Nazi regime and the outbreak of WW II, more than 75,000 refugees from the countries under that regime in Central Europe settled in Palestine. During the war years too, despite the restrictions imposed by the British Mandate authorities, immigration of Jews from Europe did not cease. Heroic efforts were made to rescue Jews from the countries that fell under the tidal wave of Nazi occupation or from countries threatened by that danger. At the end of the war the Jews of Palestine risked their lives and future to bring the survivors of the great slaughter to a safe haven. When the State of Israel was finally established, its first act was to open its gates to the survivors from the countries of killing and destruction.

Between 1939 and 1950, close to 380,000 Jews were brought to Palestine, later Israel, from the territories of the Nazi regime and occupation. Together with the Jews who immigrated from Central Europe during the prewar years of Nazi persecution, this figure rises to 450,000 souls. The majority of survivors came with only their exhausted bodies. Their property had long since been looted. Many of them were incurably crippled – human beings whose health had been irreparably damaged. Israel alone was prepared to offer them refuge.

Unlike other countries in which immigrants are easily absorbed into a developed economy, Israel has been compelled to make special efforts and devote huge public funds for investment and maintenance in order to create living possibilities for its immigrants. The economic structure of the young state was dedicated at the outset to serving this vital objective. Although great assistance has been received from Jews abroad, most of the expenditure bound up in receiving and absorbing the immigrants was shouldered by the people of Israel. Heavy taxation has been imposed and a regimen of strict austerity has been introduced; the people accepted all this with love in order to provide a roof and subsistence for the new settlers. It is no exaggeration to demand that the German people, which is responsible for this calamity and which holds as before the economic assets taken from Jews living and dead, be required to pay for reparations for the benefit of the survivors.

At the end of the war, when the triumphant Allies convened to allocate the compensation due from Germany, the Jewish people did not yet possess legal status in the family of sovereign nations. Therefore, although from a moral standpoint its claims were stronger than those of any other nation that suffered under the Nazis, at the time it had no voice. The time has come to rectify this wrong.

Israel is the only country authorized to speak in the name of the Jewish people – six million Jews were murdered solely because they belonged to that same people. The State of Israel was initially established to provide a home for all persecuted and expelled Jews. This responsibility has always been furfilled by the people of Israel, body and soul. In the war against Nazi Germany, sons and daughters of the Jewish community in Palestine fought in national units that were part of the Allied forces. The Jewish Fighting Brigade of the British Army, manned by Palestinian Jews, played a part in the final defeat of the enemy on the Italian front, and after the war ended played an active role in supplying aid and succor to Jewish survivors in various parts of Europe.[3] The recognition by the United Nations of the Jewish people's right to re-establish its state was reparation for all the evil acts perpetrated against this people through the ages which reached their climax in the Nazi campaign of annihilation. When the State of Israel was founded it immediately took upon itself the burden of absorbing and rehabilitating the Holocaust survivors. For all

---

3   The Jewish Fighting Brigade, formed out of the three infantry battalions manned by Palestinian Jews who volunteered to serve in the British army, fought the German army in WW II on the Italian front. Following the end of the war, the Brigade was stationed in northern Italy and later in Holland and Belgium from where its soldiers took upon themselves, without permission of the British High Command, to take care of the Holocaust survivors residing in the displaced persons' camps in Austria and Germany. Units of the Jewish Brigade were instrumental in organizing and in illegally transporting tens of thousand of Jewish Holocaust survivors to several ports on the southern coasts of Italy and France from where they illegally sailed to Palestine on ships purchased and commanded by the Haganah (the clandestine military organization of the Yishuv). This vast enterprise, encompassing several European countries, would not have been realized without the Jewish Brigade's presence in Europe. As the head of Jewish Agency's Political Department in 1933-1948, Moshe Sharett was instrumental in enlisting of Palestinian Jews into the British army and in prodding of the British High Command first to form the three Palestinian infantry battalions and then to establish the Jewish Brigade.

these reasons the State of Israel views itself as entitled to claim reparations from Germany as compensation for the Jewish people.

On the one hand, the sum to be claimed must relate to the damages inflicted on the Jewish people by the Germans, and on the other, to the expenses incurred in the resturation in Israel of those who escaped the Nazi actions or survived them. The government of Israel is unable to obtain accurate details of the Jewish property confiscated or plundered by the Germans which, as aforementioned, is authoritatively estimated at six billion dollars. The government of Israel can only base its claim on the sums already expended and which will be expended on the settlement and absorption of Jewish immigrants from countries that were under the Nazi regime. Their number is estimated at 500,000 and their rehabilitation will cost one-and-a-half billion dollars. This sum is roughly equivalent to the value of West Germany's exports for 1950 alone – exports that are likely to increase significantly in 1951 with Germany's continued economic recovery. Should these payments be arranged over a number of years and transferred in part in the form of goods, it should not be assumed that payment of compensation in this sum will be beyond the ability of the German people. No arrangement of the German compensation issue can be considered fair from a legal and moral standpoint if this minimal claim on behalf of the principal sufferers at the hands of the Nazi regime is not taken into account. Any progress towards restoring Germany to its place in the community of the world's nations is unthinkable so long as this fundamental debt remains unpaid.

Thus the wording of the note.

Payment of the reparations claimed by the State of Israel in this note will not absolve the German government of the responsibility imposed upon it to fully indemnify the Jews, the victims of Nazism. It will only constitute a contribution towards clearing the account between the German and Jewish peoples. The justness of the claim submitted by Israel is definitive and not conditional upon circumstances of time or the international situation. The government of Israel states that the Four-Power Conference which is about to convene shortly must discuss the reparations claim and impose it upon the German authorities. At the center of this conference will stand the issue of the final settlement of the relations of the powers with Germany. The government of Israel cannot imagine that the gates of the civilized and peace-loving world be opened to the German people whose hands are not only bloodstained but are also still holding the plunder. There is a day of reckoning – and that day has come.

Speaker Nahum Nir-Rafalkes: In accordance with the decision of the Foreign Affairs and Defense Committee, a Knesset debate on the foreign minister's statement will be held next week.

MK Shmuel Dayan (*Mapai*)**:** I propose to the Knesset: Whereas, having heard the contents of the note, we are emotionally unable to proceed with mundane matters. We postpone the debate on the next item on our agenda.

Speaker Nahum Nir-Rafalkes: I declare a fifteen minute recess.

[8] Mitigation of Nazi War Criminals' Sentences; Compensation Claim from Germany

Knesset Sessions 242, 26.3.1951; 245, 2.4.1951

Speaker Nahum Nir-Rafalkes (*Mapam*)**:** We now move on to Item 5 on the agenda, a debate pertaining to Germany. The foreign minister has the floor.

Foreign Minister Moshe Sharett: Mr. Speaker, the government has submitted a protest to the United States government regarding mitigation of the sentences of the Nazi criminals by the American authorities in Germany. A statement on this step, taken by the foreign ministry on behalf of the government, was published in the press. This matter was also discussed in the Foreign Affairs and Defense Committee. It expressed the wish that our protest note submitted to the United States would be reviewed thoroughly in the Knesset. I gladly respond to this wish with the following statement:

In its note to the United States ambassador in the matter of the pardon and mitigation of sentence of Nazi criminals in Germany, the foreign ministry has relied on the official report published by the United States high commissioner in Germany.

On the basis of that report's contents, the government of Israel, on its own behalf and on behalf of the entire nation, expressed to the United States its profound pain regarding the high commissioner's decision to approve the revocation and mitigation of the sentences imposed by the military tribunal in Nüremberg on a large number of the principal war criminals. The government has noted that these sentences were imposed following a trial for crimes unprecedented in human history, both in their scope and inhuman character alike. The victims of these horrors were men, women and children who were slaughtered simply because they were Jews, and the slaughter was carried out with calculated brutality that cannot be described in human language. There was hardly a family in this country that did not lose a relative in this terrible slaughter. The note determines that the Jewish people can only view this act of conciliation towards the worst of the German people as desecration of the memory of the holy martyrs.

The note goes on to say that the bitterness aroused in the hearts of Israelis and among Jews throughout the world by this astonishing decision was further exacerbated by the reasoning published in that same report. In that document the high commissioner justified the leniency shown to the Nazi criminals with the most puzzling reasoning: "an unstable mental state resulting from nervousness," "the fact that the guilty party did not bear the principal responsibility," the guilty party's age, and also the "limited participation in the criminal act." The aforementioned are direct quotes from the published report. The high commissioner himself says of the "death squads" – those who murdered two million people with their own hands – that they committed acts of murder on such a vast scale that it is beyond the grasp of the human mind. Yet he still found grounds for numerous mitigations of sentence, reasoning that the acts committed by these criminals were "of a scope significantly less" than those of others.

The government of Israel note relies on one specific trial in which the accused were noted judges, public prosecutors and government officials. The high commissioner's report states that they were all "anxious to ignore every principle of justice and law in order to advance the harshest political and racist principles." In his report, the high commissioner admits that he "found it hard to find justification for leniency in any of these cases." But still, "for reasons such as limited responsibility" he mitigated the sentences of some by half, ordered the release of others, and, for reasons of health, freed one who had been sentenced to life imprisonment.

As a particularly appalling instance, the note mentions the treatment of SS personnel and concentration camp staff. Included in this category were the murderers of Jews in the Auschwitz camp and the destroyers of the Warsaw Ghetto. Here too grounds were found for the wholesale mitigation of sentences and detention orders – which at the outset were for long periods – for the time that the guilty parties had already served in prison, mitigation that meant immediate release.

With regard to the execution of hostages by firing squads, the high commissioner's report states that many of these executions were carried out against hundreds of people who had no part whatsoever in attacks against German army personnel. In these cases too numerous sentences were mitigated, again because the criminals involved bore lesser responsibility than others. With regard to two of the most despicable in this group, which the military tribunal sentenced to life imprisonment, the high commissioner decided that as both were elderly and "are possibly afflicted with physical illnesses making a further medical examination desirable in order to determine whether they should be released on medical grounds," such an examination should be carried out.

Of numerous other instances worthy of mention, the memorandum notes one further example from what is known as "The Ministries' Trial" in which the defendants were senior officials who filled important roles in "the diplomatic implementation of a genocide program." This is the case of one man, SS General

Gottlob Berger, described in the report as Himmler's close aide. The report states that he was active in a plan known as Operation Stubble in which children from the eastern territories were sent to arms industries' training camps, and that he also took part in other extermination activities. The report states that according to the military tribunal's verdict, there is no doubt that "this defendant is guilty of numerous criminal acts and cruelty" and that "his very collaboration with Himmler gravely incriminates him." And yet his sentence was remitted from twenty-five to ten years, mainly because "towards the end of the war he actively intervened to save the lives of Allied officers and men and others who were held hostage prior to their execution." The foreign ministry note highlights the significance of this mitigation of sentence: a despicable criminal who was an active participant in the slaughter of millions of Jews gained a substantial mitigation of his sentence because he realized that the Nazis had lost the war and therefore hastened to establish an alibi for himself.

Finally, the note relates to the statement in the report according to which the high commissioner has already reduced the sentence of Ernst von Weizsäcker, Director General of the German Foreign Ministry, and taking into account time already served, thus ordered this man's release. The foreign ministry notes that it was von Weizsäcker who gave the German foreign ministry's official sanction to the transportation of French Jews to the death camps in Poland.

The note further states that only with regard to seven of all these criminals did the United States civil and military authorities in Germany uphold the death sentence. The acts of these seven are so horrific that there can be no possible grounds for any mitigation of sentence. Yet these sentences too, whose appeal was denied by the highest legal authorities of the United States, have yet to be implemented, and today they are the subject of a new appeal in the American courts.

Following that summary of the mitigations and pardons, the note goes on to an assessment of the direction in which the United States High Commission is acting in its occupation zone in Germany. It states that the Nüremberg Trials were an important juncture on the road towards a regimen of protecting human rights. They were founded on the principle that there are fundamental rules of human behavior which no country or government is entitled to break without paying the price, and that individuals found guilty of breaking them are personally responsible and cannot escape trial by claiming that they were following orders from above. The Nüremberg Trials were conducted while paying the most scrupulous attention to the defense of the accused and in accordance with the principles that are part and parcel of civilized humankind. They have erected a significant barrier against future war criminals and perpetrators of genocide running wild. Now comes the action of the American authorities in Germany which to a great extent turns the tables on this great achievement. Evidently, political considerations were advanced here ahead of legal and moral principles.

A potential perpetrator of genocide will not be deterred from his evildoing by these mitigations of the Nüremberg sentences.

On the basis of all the aforementioned, the government of Israel has expressed its profound concern to the United States government regarding the virulent conciliation towards Germany revealed in this unjust and dangerous leniency towards the Nazi criminals.

MK Yitzhak Ben Aharon (*Mapam*)**:** Members of the Knesset, we concur with the concern expressed by our government to the United States government regarding its responsiblity for the release of Nazi war criminals. It is hard to find words to express this protest. But we are puzzled by our government's tardiness in sending this note. Some two months elapsed until it found the words to express the feelings of its citizens to that government which is now making itself an accessory to the renewal of Nazism and the return of the criminals to the political arena in Germany itself.

It is not difficult to guess what was behind the foreign minister's vacillation and why several proposals on our part were needed until the government actually pronounced its grave concern. We cannot understand why this approach did not at least take the form of a clear protest, and why the government was satisfied with cold diplomatic language in this instance. One feels this cold and humiliating language even more so when it comes from a representative of the State of Israel.

The foreign minister's astonishing composure and the dry diplomatic wording are inappropriate to our common pain, which undoubtedly fills the hearts of our foreign ministry people as well. One senses a most delicate consideration in part of the wording of the foreign minister's statement and most particularly in its strange conclusion regarding the United States government. This evening we must discuss two matters together: the claim for reparations, or more precisely, restitution of what was plundered and stolen, and the claim for revocation of the release and return of the guilty parties either to prison or the gallows.

Even the reparation claim has come very late. At a meeting of the Zionist Executive Committee about a year ago, we were told that government and Jewish Agency representatives had had informal contact with the governments in West Germany for the purpose of examining the feasibility of compensation from these governments.

Even then we had the opportunity of warning against this approach to the problem. We knew that nothing more than being dishonored in the eyes of that murderous people could be achieved. We demanded then – and have demanded on various occasions since then in various state institutions, including the Knesset Foreign Affairs and Defense Committee – that direct contact with the governments of Germany cease. Negotiation with the various local German governments and most certainly with the central government of West Germany is unthinkable; we most certainly should not have contact with them for they have been appointed, in accordance with the authority granted to them by the Western powers, to revive Nazism and its entire regime. In its first steps that regime has embarked on unfettered anti-Semitic incitement in Bavaria and other parts of Germany. How can you not be ashamed of speaking with them?

Members of the Knesset, not one of the victorious nations waived payment of reparations by Germany for the material damage and destruction caused by the Nazi war machine in Europe and throughout the world. The four occupying powers exacted from Germany materials and means of production to the value of hundreds of millions of dollars. Even today the Western occupying powers are taking from Germany some half-a-billion marks for occupation expenditures. And we, who have taken the rehabilitation of the survivors of our people upon ourselves, have to stand in Washington like beggars at the gate and ask for grants and gifts, with all that that implies from the economic standpoint and from the standpoint of relinquishing our economic independence, waiving the same means that they themselves are taking from that same Germany and to which we, first and foremost, are due.

You are dependent not only upon the goodwill of the United States government but also upon that of the Bonn government. We can read in the papers today that the "poor" government of West Germany – after the United States government has invested a quarter of a billion dollars in its rehabilitation – is on the verge of bankruptcy. That same Germany gorged itself immediately after its defeat and during it while we tramped starving and exhausted through the cities of Germany and on its roads; it gorged while the victorious nations, including France and England in the West and the masses in the Soviet Union and Poland, bled as they beheld the terrible destruction of the labor of generations. At the same time this Germany was living well, and what it did not produce itself it received from the Americans and the British.

I stand astonished in face of our naïve, non-political approach in this matter. With all due respect, it is unthinkable that our political representatives be satisfied with an expression of feelings and a cry of pain. The question today is a political one of the highest order, and we must be fully aware where the real front of the denial of our rights and claims is; we must know who is denying us and why we are being denied, and we must draw conclusions from this situation. We cannot sit still when the government's policy is leading us into this dark alley.

The British press tells us that we have missed the boat. We have missed the boat, they say, since in 1945, 1946 and 1947 British policy granted us time to formulate our claim, to form the country's representation in order to submit our claim before the world. Then, after the Nazi slaughter, we were faced with the necessity of defending ourselves from an attempt at destruction by British policy here in this country. We missed the boat because in 1947, 1948 and 1949 we did not manage to submit the claim, for we were engaged in a life-or-death war with the puppets of British foreign policy that were equipped, armed and thrown against us. We missed the boat – they did not! They did not miss anything, neither the obtaining of compensation nor the revival of the Nazi beast. They did not miss forgetting the sacrifice of the Jewish people and its state, the only historical heir of the destruction of this people. They hasten to make peace with West Germany. They hasten to re-establish the Nazi machine. They hasten to restore independence to the Nazis. They have no time. And we have missed the boat…

It seems to me – in any event, this is our feeling – that nobody can fail to be shocked by the extent to which our official foreign policy has lost, even in this matter, the ability to maneuver and the freedom of independence in our affairs. One cannot fail to be shocked by the degree of accommodation in the formulation of our claims, and the weakness of our appearance before the deciding bodies on these questions of vital importance. Can you not see even today to what extent your stance on our rights has compromised us?

We feel that under no circumstances is the State of Israel entitled to enter negotiations with German political representatives. We think that as long as our elementary right for compensation has not been satisfied, the State of Israel cannot continue to conduct proper relations with these powers in whose hands and at whose discretion reside our participation in reparations payments. It is these powers who prevent imposition of peace, who are granting independence and all other benefits to the German people. And I say, the plunder and robbery accumulated there is several times greater in its value than any grant we might receive as a charity gift from the United States government, and for this gift of charity you will be compelled to waive the validity of our rightful claim.

We cannot but discern a worsening of our international political situation as a consequence of the impact made by the State of Israel's attitude towards the world's progressive elements, including the socialist ones headed by the Soviet Union. The potentially disastrous political consequences have been revealed precisely on this grave occasion. I believe that you also already know that you are at the beck and call of the Western powers and totally dependent on their goodwill. You have knowingly waived fostering friendly relations and mutual aid with the progressive socialist world and thus prevented the state from availing itself of its assistance. (*MK Yona Kesse (Mapai): Why didn't the Soviets give us compensation sooner? Do they have to wait until we submit a claim?*) I think that they do not have to be any hastier than the government of Israel's foreign minister, hastier than the representatives of the Jewish people.

I am hearing for the first time that we expect a foreign nation to voice our claim and our cry while the official representatives of the people keep silent. (*From the Mapai benches: Let the Soviets pay!*) It is the custom of the Mapai members to reach the boiling point whenever the name of the USSR is mentioned in a positive light. Why all this sensitivity and excitement? I feel no psychological or ideological difficulty when I demand my part from the occupying powers, including the USSR, and I do not understand this particular sensitivity you display when you are facing the fact that the powers from which you seek aid are defending the murderers of our people, identifying with them and preventing us – and you know that this is the naked truth – from obtaining reparations. They were even the first and foremost factor in preventing the reparations arrangement and ensuring our rights in the final accounting with the Germans. Why cover up this shameful fact for which the American representatives in Germany are responsible? Your conduct throughout this affair – the belated submission of the claim, your manner of speech, how the claim is presented, the political obfuscation of the significance of the refusal and rejection by the Western powers – was all erroneous.

I determine that in your note to the occupying powers and in the wording of your "concern" regarding the release of war criminals, you have clearly demonstrated your total dependence on the goodwill of the Western powers. You are not fighting at the front of the political war as openly and aggressively as the situation dictates. You continue to ignore the connection between your foreign policy and the denial of the rights of the Jewish people vis-à-vis Germany. Blindfolded, you do not see the situation into which you are maneuvering the State of Israel in its struggle for its claims because you have directly linked it to the Western powers, to Germany's allies, down to the point of negating your independent, firm stance on behalf of our elementary rights.

We demand that the Knesset not be content with the two notes submitted to the great powers. We propose that the matter be sent back to the Foreign Affairs and Defense Committee for formulating appropriate decisions. In the committee, we shall propose obliging the government to terminate all contacts with the governments of Germany, obliging the government to present the claim from the UN podium and through direct contact with the occupying powers in order to obtain payment of our material claims as part of the reparations to be imposed upon Germany or which have already been imposed on it. And should the occupying powers reach the conclusion that they have obtained the maximum possible from Germany, then they should allocate us part of the assets they had divided between the victors in payment of our material claims.

We propose that the government not be content with this feeble protest on the release of the war criminals. We demand the drawing of political conclusions: to see clearly, and in good time, this global political direction of the Western powers and its significance for our future in this part of the world and with regard to the entire Jewish people.

A country that releases Nazi criminals will not be Israel's ally. Release of Nazi criminals is only one of the symptoms, just as non-intervention in the plunder of property from the Jews of Iraq is but one symptom of the regime being prepared for the entire Jewish people and for us in this world. From this we must draw a conclusion regarding this country's international orientation and quickly restore its political independence. And this will only be possible if we can rely on the friendship of the Soviet Union which we have won in the past – only then we shall be able to restore to Israel the friendship of the progressive forces that you maliciously rejected with your own hands. This is a question of life for us, to be able to rely on their friendship in our war of defense against the forces that release Nazi criminals, that are reviving the Nazi regime and preparing for the entire world a new, despicable alliance between Western capitalism and the Nazi, European-fascist beast. The State of Israel must be freed from this alliance and dependence, and to save us from the consequences of this alliance, the foreign policy of the government of Israel must undergo a radical change which will restore its faith in itself and the friendship of those forces with which only strong, friendly relations can assure us of the hope of defending ourselves. We call upon the people to awaken in the face of the most grave and dangerous consequences that this policy towards the West is bringing down upon us and the entire world.

MK Eliezer Livne (*Mapai*)**:** I deeply regret that this debate, which should have expressed the unified feelings of the independent Jewish people in its own country – a people which must also be independent in spirit – has shamefully exposed attitudes of voluntary dependence and servitude. There is spiritual servitude that is worse than contractual servitude; a binding contract can be broken and destroyed, but if the spirit is subjugated to foreign ideologies and stratagems, how can those subjugated free themselves? In this debate we must draw a distinction between the murderers' guilt and the obligation to return the assets plundered, and not mix them at all. They are two different categories: political and spiritual-moral.

Blood has no price tag. About 458 years ago the Jews were expelled from the Greater Spain at the end of the 15th century. The edict of Ferdinand and Isabella, issued at the time of the expulsion, stated that within a number of months the Jews would be allowed to take all their property with them: gold, money, precious metals and stones, and anyone harming them on their way to the border would be sentenced to the ultimate penalty. But the Jewish people have not forgiven the Spanish people and Spain for the crimes of the expulsion and the Inquisition. If we consider the number of souls (and not only numbers are the deciding factor) – how many Jews were murdered by the Inquisition – then it is nothing compared to what was done in the center of modern humanity in the 20th century. The Jewish people must learn from this that "progress" does not resolve our problem among the nations and does not make the terror of exile any easier. What has happened in recent years, who knows? – I do not want to utter the words – who knows if it was the last time? If this is what we have come to with the development of society and culture, technology and science, if this is "progress" over five hundred years, if civilized humankind in its entirety was mirrored in the German concentration camps in the Ukrainian steppes and in the forests of Byelorussia, then where does the conviction that this is the last time come from?

With regard to this crime there are no absolute saints although there are those who are less guilty and those more. The foreign minister cited the case of the Nazi criminal Berger whose sentence was commuted by two-thirds; he spoke of the other criminals in West Germany whose release is sought as their health is failing. But are they the only ones? Are there not in Soviet captivity a Nazi field marshal and a great Nazi general – I refer to Field-Marshal Friedrich von Paulus and General Walter von Seidlitz [both taken prisoners on the Stalingrad front] – who have not been brought to justice? Have they been tried? Have they been charged with the extermination of Jews? Were they arrested and punished in a place where a forceful, harsh regime exists that knows how to arrest, punish and wreak vengeance?

The Jewish people is protesting to the United States for its conciliation towards our exterminators even at a time when it is our friend and we need its help. We shall not sell our independence for any money and any help. But if our voice is to be raised in protest, let it be raised against them all, West and East alike. If anyone has released criminals in West Germany, there is also someone who has not imprisoned them at all in East Germany; if there is someone that has not meted out appropriate punishment, there is someone that has not punished many of the biggest murderers. Our accounting is not absolute, it is independent of political stratagems. We must be united on this; anyone among us who is not at peace with his feelings and moral demands renounces his ties with the Jewish people, and not only the people in this country but the Jewish people for all time.

Something important has changed since we established our state. Up to 1948 the Jewish people were unable to punish the murderers of its sons and daughters and repeatedly stated, "vengeance is not mine." In this sense, too, the establishment of the State of Israel constitutes a fundamental change. Now there is justice, judgement and punishment. Even if we do not know at this time how punishment will be meted out and how justice will be done, the nations of the world must hear from this humble house, from this small city, from the representatives of this tiny state, that they have not forgotten and will not forget. The murderers will be punished. The killers will be brought to justice. The establishment of the State of Israel is a decisive factor with regard to the status of the criminals, torturers and murderers. What was possible prior to 1948 is no longer possible. The state of lawlessness regarding the murderers of Jews is over. Let the murderers in East and West, leaders and officials, generals and soldiers, know that the accounting for their crimes has not been closed. Crime awaits its punishment. And even if it is late in coming, it will come.

Moving from moral stocktaking to accounting of property, if not even one Jew had been murdered in Germany, its satellites and occupied territories, we would have demanded compensation in full. And we need not mention the blood of any Jewish child in order to demand full compensation from them for the robbery and plunder. They have murdered and also taken possession. The obligation to repay in full what they stole needs no further explanation.

In the matter of claiming compensation from Germany too, the attitude of all parties involved is more or less the same. We have yet to hear of official support for our compensation claim, either from the West or the East. Perhaps time is short and a government is a slow-moving machine, but in several countries we have read of support for our claims in some important newspapers which perhaps do not voice the government's opinion but do express the view of large sections of the public. This support has been expressed in the British, American and French press and also in the Swiss papers. I am not saying that what the papers say is binding upon the governments, but it shows that something is moving in the feelings and conscience of the nations; unfortunately, however, not in all of them. From the great power that MK Ben Aharon so fulsomely lauded, we have so far not read in any of the papers, in dozens of languages, a single word of support for the Jewish compensation claim.

We are possibly at fault for submitting the claim only now after most of Germany's compensation payments – through the transfer of factories and export of goods – have already been paid, and since then, attitudes towards Germany from all sides have also changed. Not only have the Western Allies ceased demanding machinery, materials and factories from Germany. The Russian and German communist press is lauding the fact that the USSR is rebuilding East Germany. All branches of the Soviet press are declaring an "eternal alliance" between the two nations, the Soviet and the East German. The presses in both countries are competing with each other as to which is contributing more to the buildup of East Germany. The West is also possibly building something in West Germany, but it is hard to say that the Soviets are so fastidious with regard to the renewal of Germany's military capability. I am no expert in military matters, but they say that the development of vast uranium mines in Saxony is related to the army and armament.

Had we demanded compensation earlier, at the time when both blocs claimed restitution from Germany, when Germany needed world opinion on its side for its return to the family of nations, it possibly would have been more prepared to compensate us and the victors' support would have been greater. But those employing this argument must remember the great controversy that in the early 1930s raged throughout the Jewish world regarding the tranfer of Jewish wealth from Nazi Germany. Those same people who for years insisted that we not claim any such compensation – and I know that on the Knesset benches there are important members, the representatives of respected parties, who even today oppose this claim for compensation – cannot propound both arguments at one and the same time: on the one hand to complain about the tardiness of the claim, and on the other to argue against submitting it. If we should have submitted the claim earlier, then those guilty of the delay are greater in number than those who are now attempting to appear as accusers.

I think that the claim is practical, or, in other words, there is a likelihood that part of the stolen property will be restored. It is precisely because of this that we must take note of a fundamental matter: today's Germany does not identify with the Germany that inherited the robbery. West and East Germany – we make no distinction between the two with regard to their obligation to pay compensation. In this regard East and West are completely equal. If East Germany hastens to pay compensation, it will inadvertently gain a moral advantage. There will be no one in Israel who will not commend that Germany which will be the first to pay. If there are members of this House who possess the power to influence East Germany, the German Democratic Republic, call it what you will, then blessed be their efforts. But we are claiming compensation from all those who inherited its territories and assets from Nazi Germany, and they are not only East and West Germany but all the countries that received a part of territory from the Greater Germany of 1938. The members of this House will surely recall that there is one absolute figure according to which the sum of reparations was calculated – the one billion marks taken from the Jews by Greater Germany in November 1938. All the territorial heirs of that same Germany are duty-bound to restore that plunder. Who are the heirs, or, in other words, what was Germany of November 1938? It included East and West Germany, the Saar region, the Sudetenland, part of East Germany that was annexed to Poland, and other territories annexed to different countries.

All "inheritors" must pay, whichever regime may be in power. The property account is unrelated to the account of lives. The difference between those who murdered and those who only inherited is vast; it is beyond comparison. But those who inherited by way of annexation must also restore the inheritance to its rightful owners. Inasmuch as the Jewish people determines its attitude towards the nations of the world not in accordance with political interests – and they do exert influence intentionally or unintentionally – it will highly value those nations that out of conscience hasten to pay compensation for the plunder. It is according to this kind of conduct that the Jewish people's attitude towards the various parts of Germany and towards states that annexed German territory and inherited plundered assets will be determined.

I would be happy were we unified on this matter, as a self-conscious people should be, were we able to differentiate between partisan stratagems – with all due respect – and objective considerations of international relations. The account is crystal clear; it represents national-historical interests and an ideological-moral stance. This regrettable debate should not have taken place in the Knesset.

MK Mordechai Nurock (*United Religious Front*): Honorable House: I welcome the foreign minister's appeal to the great powers, the Allies, in the matter of

restoring the property stolen by the murderous German people, and particularly
with regard to the release of the war criminals. For many years I have demanded
from this august podium, at the Zionist Congress, at the Zionist Executive
Committee and at the World Jewish Congress, submitting an appeal to the
occupying powers that direct contact with the nation of murderers be avoided.
Regrettably, unofficial attempts have been made, both by the State of Israel and
by the Jewish Agency, to establish direct contact with that profane country. In
the government's note we have exposed the shame of Germany but too late. We
have, in fact, missed the boat for submitting compensation claims to the great
powers. The proper time was at the end of 1947 when the occupying powers
decided to intervene in the matter of compensation for property that had been
either plundered or destroyed. Moreover, the powers' attitude towards Germany
at that time was different than it is today, for nowadays both East and West seek
to justify the German wrongdoing, citing numerous reasons, and seek to restore
Germany to the community of nations.

There is no room here for comparison with postwar reparations negotiations
when victors are sitting at the same table with the defeated. Here we face something
the world has never witnessed before: the murderers of one-third of our people.
Here we are haunted with the memory of the martyrs. Here the honor of our
people is at stake. We must declare to the whole world that our appeal to the
occupying powers has nothing to do with forgiveness, but only with the restitution
of the plundered property. I demand a clear answer from the government to the
effect that this will not lead to direct contact with the murderers or to them paying
us reparations in the form of goods – products of that accursed land that is soaked
with the blood of the martyrs. If there is to be direct contact, it will serve as an
opening to extending our hand in forgiveness to the murderers. In this manner
we shall permit any Jew to negotiate with the Germans, as was stated by our sages:
"If the mighty have succumbed, how shall the weak emerge unscathed?" It would
be better to waive such reparations and preserve Israel's honor as a nation. This
is a question of the honor of the Jewish people and not one of sentimentality, as
some realpolitik exponents mistakenly think.

In the Middle Ages the Nazis' ancestors, the *Raubritter*, robber barons, killed
people and atoned for their sin with money, the *Ablasszettel* paid to the Church.
We cannot accept compensation from the murderers and forgive them, however
indirectly, for their sins. That would be an indelible stain. The State of Israel must
defend the honor of the Jewish people.

There are those among us who say that not all the German people are guilty,
that only a small gang is guilty. This is incorrect. How can we extend our hand to
a German? If it was not him personally who perpetrated the acts of murder, then
it was his brothers and sons, his relatives and kinsmen who spilled the blood of
one-third of our people, and among them one million, two hundred thousand
children who could have bestowed honor and glory on the Jewish people and

all humankind. Not a single scientist, writer or artist in Germany lifted a finger to save our people. Worse, German scientists elaborated methods for the total extermination of the Jewish people. Are we now to become a modern Shylock?

The murderers took everything from us – but not our honor. By making direct contact we ourselves will defile our honor. Every Jew in the world would contribute the equivalent of compensation, if only to avoid direct contact with Germany. When the Jews were expelled from Spain and were allowed to leave that country unharmed, a Jewish foot did not tread the soil of Spain for hundreds of years. And now, after that horrible catastrophe, we take it lying down and perhaps are about to establish direct contact with the murderous German government. We sanctify the memory of the Warsaw Ghetto fighters. Is direct contact with the murderers in the spirit of those fighters? Did they leave behind them such a spiritual will and testament that we should trample on their graves and sit at the same table with their murderers? Is this appropriate to Jewish national consciousness? It would be a great crime.

We cannot compare this with the transfer of the property of German's Jews from Germany to the Yishuv in Palestine in the early 30's. Then Jews had not yet been murdered in Germany, and the transfer was of Jews and their property to our country.

Whereas in 1933 the World Jewish Congress announced, on my initiative, a boycott on Germany, then that boycott must be maintained even more so today. We are told that at long last we shall have to establish diplomatic relations with the German government. This is not so. Members of the Knesset, there was a small, backward nation in Europe – Lithuania. When the Poles, their closest neighbor, took Vilnius, the historic capital of Lithuania, the Lithuanians desisted from any contact or negotiation with Poland for many years until they finally did so by force of arms. And should we, the sons of kings and prophets put aside this national insult? It shall not be!

Mr. foreign minister, I bind you to an oath. There are those who win their moment of glory. You can ensure your place in the history of our time. Future generations will hold your name in high esteem if you stand fast in defense of the honor of the Jewish people.

MK Menachem Begin (*Herut*): Mr. Speaker: I must draw the attention of the members to the two final sentences of the note sent by Mr. Sharett to foreign ministers Messrs. Acheson, Schuman, Morrison and Vishinsky. And these are the two sentences: "Furthermore," our government writes, "no arrangement of the German compensation issue can be considered fair from a legal and moral standpoint if this minimal claim on behalf of the principal sufferers at the hands of the Nazi regime is not taken into account." And further, "It," that is, the government of Israel, maintains that "Any progress towards restoring Germany to its place in the community of the world's nations is unthinkable so long as this fundamental debt remains unpaid."

The members of this House know, or will admit, that even with regard to the law there is great importance attached to the interpretation of what the wise men of Rome called "implicitas," or as our own sages put it, "a negative rule implies the affirmative," and vice versa. With regard to a diplomatic note, its entire value is perhaps not in what it contains, but what it implies. And what is implied in the two sentences I cited earlier? The first states unequivocally that this government does not oppose the return of Germany into the community of nations, that this government even places a condition, and that condition is what it terms in the original language of the note: "The rehabilitation of Germany among the community of nations." And what is the condition? Money. $1.5 billion. If we receive it we shall agree to a discussion on "The rehabilitation of Germany among the community of nations." Thus it is written. And it is not by chance that I quoted the original English, for words, members of the Knesset, have a source and also a tradition. Etymologically the word rehabilitation means a return home, and so it is also used in the sense of restoration to normal life, but traditionally rehabilitation means the restoration of honor, in other words, the government of Israel has announced to the Americans, the British, the French and the Russians, to the whole world, that it will concur with the restoration of Germany's honor as a people among the community of nations if "this fundamental issue of compensation is put into effect."

Our honorable colleague Rabbi Nurock stood on this podium and said that with this note we have exposed the shame of Germany. No, we have not; we have brought shame upon ourselves.

And what does the second sentence say? It says that the government of Israel does not oppose handing over full governance to the government of Germany; it only places a condition on the establishment of an "independent Germany" or "free Germanys": the payment of $1.5 billion to the government of Israel. But this sentence goes even further. Let us assume that the powers accept Mr. Sharett's qualification. Let us assume that full governance will be transferred to Germany with the condition that the government of the independent Germany pays compensation to the government of Israel. But since the note itself proposes that the compensation payment process will continue over a number of years ,and since this year full authority is to be handed over to the government of Germany, it turns out that the government of Israel has made it clear to the Americans, the Russians, the British and the French, and to the whole world that the government of Israel is prepared to establish direct contact with independent Germany – that in the course of the coming years it will conduct normal relations with Germany in order to receive that payment.

Rabbi Nurock stood on this podium and beseeched Mr. Sharett to swear lest he execute what he, Rabbi Nurock, called a national crime, lest he establish direct contact with Germany. Mr. Sharett has still not sworn the oath that Rabbi Nurock demanded that he swear, and therefore on this matter I cannot blame the foreign minister for swearing a false oath. But I am afraid Rabbi Nurock did not correctly read this sentence. Had he done so, he would not have asked the foreign minister to swear a false oath, for in this note the government of Israel publicly states that it will enter into direct contact with independent Germany in order to receive this compensation of $1.5 billion.

The government's note has two parts. The first is a horrifying cry over spilled blood, the second is a horrifying and cold accounting. The account is very precise. What reasoning did the foreign minister not use to persuade the gentiles that they must pay compensation to the State of Israel at Germany's expense? He told them that we are absorbing immigration and that we have imposed a heavy burden of taxation upon ourselves; he informed them that we are living under a regimen of severe austerity; he told them that we shall absorb half a million survivors of the German murder. And in the name of the millions of victims of that murder our government demands a quarter of the Jewish property plundered by the Germans. And I ask, why have you done this to the Jewish people? How could you demand just one quarter of the Jewish property plundered by the Germans? By what authority? What does this accounting imply?

For the sake of argument, let us assume that the two-legged Teutonic beast had accomplished its fiendish plan and exterminated the Jews of Europe to the last man, and we would not have absorbed a few hundred thousand survivors, would we then not have had the right to demand compensation, the right to demand the restitution of the plundered Jewish property? That question, thank God, is theoretical with regard to the survivors, but it is not theoretical regarding the question under discussion. Is it only the fact that we have absorbed and saved several hundred thousand Jews that gives us the right to demand the restitution of Jewish property? By this demand you have announced that you are leaving three-quarters of the plundered Jewish property in Germany's hands.

I am not contending that had you presented a claim for full restitution of the plundered Jewish property you would have received it. But even the foreign minister cannot say one word to us to the effect that we have a concrete chance of obtaining the Jewish property as he has demanded. The gentiles are in no hurry at all to undertake compensation payments due to the Jews, as certain Jews are in a hurry to undertake payment of compensation that is not due to the gentiles. To be sure, we have also been tardy. Very tardy. We have been tardy not only because the Revolt only bore fruit – the removal of British rule – in 1948. We were tardy for another reason: more than a year-and-a-half ago, at a meeting of the Foreign Affairs and Defense Committee on May 5 1949, I suggested to Mr. Sharett that he claim restitution of the Jewish property plundered by the Germans, restitution of the entire Jewish property. Mr. Sharett said then that this matter is not new to the government and that the government is earnestly discussing it. The government must tell the people why it has been discussing this "not new" matter "earnestly" for almost two years. We are late!

Although I have no proof that had we submitted the claim two years ago it would have been met, by submitting a claim for $1.5 billion, while the assessment of the Jewish property is $6 billion, you have made it clear that you are waiving the claim for three-quarters of the plundered Jewish property. Why have you waived this claim? In whose name have you waived this claim? Will you go to the gentiles and quote the words of the prophet, "Hast thou killed and also taken possession?" and, at the same time, affirm that three – quarters of the plundered Jewish property will remain in perpetuity – in whose hands? Perhaps we will not obtain the money due to us. The question is in whose hands have you left this property? In the hands of your fathers' murderers! In the hands of those who strangled your children! How could you do such a thing to this people?

There is, however, another part in this note, and as I said it is all a cry over the spilled blood. Mr. Sharett has read the text here and we have heard how the Germans burned our fathers, drowned our mothers, smashed the heads of our babies against rocks, made mattresses from the hair of our sisters, soap from our brothers' bone marrow. After this bloody narrative, a Jewish government comes and announces that talks may take place on the restoration of honor to Germany as a member of the community of nations if they pay us $1.5 billion. Woe to us, for this note mixes blood with money.

I had assumed that the government would do something else, that it would take the narrative of blood out of the financial note and transfer it to the note in which our government attempted to determine its position regarding the release of the Nazi criminals. This would have been only natural; it would have been an honorable act. For then we would have again told the world how these murderers acted, and we would have asked: "Are you going to release these murderers?" However, the Government of Israel acted differently, and how did it present the release of the Nazi criminals? Mr. Sharett expressed his "concern" to Mr. Acheson over the release of the Nazi criminals. Is not this word "concern" routine in every diplomatic note? Were there no stronger words in the note sent by the British foreign minister to the Persian government on the nationalization of oil? Is this the statement of the Government of Israel on the release of the Nazi criminals, the SS officers, the perpetrators of Jewish destruction who exterminated millions?

I would like to ask the members of this House: why is it impossible to accept MK Ben Eliezer's proposal and demand from the occupying governments the extradition to Israel of our brothers' exterminators? Belgium, Czechoslovakia, Poland, Yugoslavia, Holland and France demanded the extradition of the Nazi criminals who committed crimes against their people. They will tell us that in accordance with the powers' decision, Nazi criminals are brought to trial in the countries in which they committed their crimes. I am aware of this decision, and yet I would argue that there are grounds, not only moral but also juridical, for extradition to Israel since these criminals murdered and exterminated Jews beyond the borders of any country that existed in WW II or which exists today. Can it be that just because the criminals crossed a country's border they shall escape punishment? Just because France will not demand the extradition of a criminal who murdered in Belgium, or vice versa, we should not demand to bring to trial those that murdered six million Jews? Those victims were potential citizens of this state. Why is it possible to construct a juridical case for demanding financial compensation in the name of the half million survivors and the six million victims, and why is it impossible to construct the principal juridical case and demand, in the name of the six million victims and the half million orphans and bereaved, the extradition of the Nazi criminals to this state of which those millions, had they not been exterminated, would have been citizens, in order that the criminals stand trial?

Indeed, I have no proof that our claim would be met. But have countries waived their demand for extradition in much less important matters simply because they assumed that their claims would not be met? Second, since when, I ask, has justice been annulled if the criminal escapes trial either by himself or with the help of others? We must establish a special court in Jerusalem to try the Nazi criminals who took part in the extermination of our people, and we must also try them in absentia. All the nations that the Nazis maltreated have established special courts to try these criminals; and we, of all nations, should not establish such a court! And should the court sentence the Nazi murderers to death, then we shall declare, not only as Jews but also as lovers of freedom, that if any person, Jew or gentile loving justice and liberty, puts an end to their lives – then all of us, as citizens of a sovereign state and as free men will stand behind him, defend him, offer him every assistance. For all the people of the world should know that from the day on which the new Jew appeared – the fighting Jew who they thought was dead and buried forever, and who has learned the simple truth of life and death, or, in other words, has learned that there are things more precious than life and more terrible than death – from that day onwards the extermination of the Jewish people will never be forgiven or forgotten, and the hand of Jewish justice will reach the exterminators of our brethren. Otherwise, despite the establishment of the State of Israel, how could we live with ourselves in this cruel world?

But how can we teach the gentile world and Jewish youth not to forget and not to forgive extermination if those terrible phrases contained in the note are not erased?

I therefore demand that the government or the Knesset decide and publicly state that the phrases implying that the State of Israel recognizes the restoration of Germany into the community of nations be annulled. This is not for our sake, nor only for the sake of our children's future. It is our obligation to those whom each of us left behind there, to the father and mother and the little child who were slaughtered together, and we know not where their ashes are and will never know. Let us pray in our hearts that the announcement annulling those terrible phrases will also erase them from memory.

MK Moshe Sneh (*Mapam*): Mr. Speaker: It is precisely because any debate on Germany opens in the Jewish soul wounds that will never heal, precisely because this debate has aroused turbulent feelings in the hearts of us all, precisely because this debate embodies different worldviews, differences in the vision of the future of the world and world peace – we must subdue our emotions when we touch upon this tragic issue.

What is the issue? German militarism has constituted a permanent focal point of aggression since the early twentieth century. German fascism, Nazism, committed the crime of genocide and the murder of six million Jews with particular brutality.

With the victory of the anti-fascist alliance over Germany, the democratic world has sought a solution to the problem of Germany. The victorious powers, the Soviet Union, the United States and Great Britain, jointly determined the solution accepted by democratic opinion the world over: first, to uproot German militarism – the demilitarization of Germany. Second, to uproot German fascism – denazification. And there are two aspects to denazification: the imposition of a new regime upon Germany that will continually educate the German people towards democracy, respect for the other, respect for man, for another people and its rights, for peaceful relations; and the merciless punishment of the Nazi war criminals.

The entire democratic world has accepted this solution, for it was clear that Hitler's doctrine, in theory and in practice, should be completely eradicated even within the people from which Hitler came. However, what do we see today? Not all the occupying powers are upholding what was laid in the foundations of the Yalta and Potsdam accords. Instead of the demilitarization of Germany, the Atlantic powers decided at the Brussels Conference to initiate German rearmament, to rebuild, in a different form, the Nazi army. Instead of denazification, a neo-Nazi government has been established in Bonn and in the West German regional governments – a reactionary government, a government aspiring to vengeance. Instead of punishing the Nazi war criminals sentenced to death, to life or long terms of imprisonment, twenty-one murderers, avowed criminals, have been pardoned, and pardons are being prepared for the other seven who even the beneficent American High Commissioner, McCloy, did not have the courage to pardon. This policy of reviving Nazism is an integral part, a purposeful instrument of the imperialist policy that is preparing a third world war. It is only in preparation of aggression that Nazism is being revived.

At the Paris conference of foreign ministers, on which all humankind pinned its hopes, Soviet deputy Foreign Minister Andrei Gromyko fought for four weeks, in twenty sessions – for what? For placing the disarmament of Germany, the prevention of German rearmament, high on the agenda. Was this endeavor of Gromyko's in the interest of the USSR alone? Is it not the struggle of all peace-loving peoples, for the sake of all the haters of Nazism and fascism and war in the world, and last but not least, for the sake of the Jewish people? Can there be any comparison between the USSR's demand for German disarmament and the refusal of the Western powers to discuss this proposal? No, it is impossible – if one wishes to abide by the truth. Can any comparison be made – from the standpoint of denazification, of uprooting the fascist, reactionary, militaristic education of the German people – between the regime established in Bonn by the West and the anti-fascist regime established in East Germany? No, it is impossible – if one wishes to abide by the truth. Can we compare the pardon and release of Nazi war criminals in West Germany with the conduct of the governments of the Soviet Union and of the People's Democracies that implemented all the severe verdicts meted out to Nazi war criminals? No, there is no comparison. The Davar newspaper recently published a report to the effect that "from one Austrian prison one thousand war criminals were released, including Julius Kampitsch, a former Nazi governor who was sentenced to twenty years in prison." The Soviet representative on the supervisory committee, General Sviridov, demanded that the Austrian government be instructed to cease the release of war criminals before they have served their sentence. His proposal was rejected by the representatives of the three Western powers And that is but one of numerous examples.

Mr. Speaker. The Jewish people face the terrible threat in form of the revival of Nazism and fascism. And not only in Germany. Listen to the fears of Australian Jewry with the opening of their country's gates to one hundred thousand German-Nazi immigrants; listen to the fears of the Jews of Argentina, a country where German and Hungarian Nazis have been honored with key posts in all the country's walks of life; listen to the news about Nazi generals and officers being sent to Middle Eastern armies, to our closest neighbors. You, members of the Knesset, are ignoring this danger facing the Jewish people in the Diaspora, facing our very existence and security in this region of the world, because you have joined the Anglo-American bloc – a bloc directly responsible for the revival of Nazism and fascism.

Our party's support for Soviet policy falls in line with the interests of the Jewish people, for it is a policy directed towards the uprooting of German militarism and fascism and ensuring world peace. Therefore our support for Soviet policy is born out of independence and freedom. Your support, members of the majority, of the Atlantic powers' policy runs counter to the interests of the Jewish people with regard to German rearmament, the release of Nazi criminals, the preservation of world peace. This support of yours is therefore born out of dependency and submission.

Despite the disagreement between us regarding the crisis and the way out of it, we think that the parliament of the Jewish State must unite on the following fundamental claims: obtaining reparations from Germany through the occupying powers, without making contact and without conducting negotiations with the Bonn government and the German regional governments; voicing of a strong protest against the pardoning of the twenty-one Nazi war criminals by the American high commissioner; submitting a demand to annul the arbitrary act of pardon and to implement the verdicts against the sentenced war criminals without mitigation of sentence or pardon. In this spirit we shall submit our draft resolutions to vote.

MK Meir Argov (*Mapai*): Mr. Speaker. I am extremely appalled by the debate's character today, and not due to the difference of opinions and positions taken but because of the attempt to divide us in this House on the question of the attitude towards the Jewish blood spilled by the Germans. There is no greater crime executed against Israel's history, against morality, against Jewish feelings than the making of such an attempt. Perhaps this attempt was made unintentionally, but it was made by Mr. Begin.

No Knesset member, nor any party represented here, has a monopoly over the blood, over the pain, over the murder. All of us present here have dead relatives annihilated in the Holocaust. There is no house in our country where you will not find a dead person. Nobody, not even a respected rabbi, is entitled to appear here as if the blood pains him more than any other. We are all orphans. We are all saying kadish. We are all standing by these graves, and we should have been united in expression and language at least on this matter.

I have no desire whatsoever to argue with communist, anti-Zionist Knesset members, who dare teach an Israeli minister a lesson regarding what Jewish blood and Jewish morals mean. But I shall argue with those colleagues who spoke here, that nobody can question their sincere feelings regarding Jewish blood and the magnitude of our disaster.

When MK Begin took the floor and attempted to analyze the whole note by concentrating on just one phrase, it was, if not to use harsher language, an injustice to truth. Nothing is more dangerous than picking one phrase out of an entire, most serious speech – be it a more appropriate or less appropriate phrase – and analyzing it out of context. I, too, would like to cite from the note, which I now hold before me, several phrases, and I shall not ignore that one cited by MK Begin. It states: "There can be no atonement or material compensation for a crime of such immense and horrifying magnitude." By saying this, the government of Israel has not implied that if it receives $1.5 billion this would constitute compensation for the blood spilled. It said precisely, Mr. Begin, that it would not compensate the spilled blood, the suffering. Why didn't you cite this phrase? Is it absent from the note?

I would like to read out another phrase: "Any compensation whatsoever, no matter how large, cannot be reparation for the loss of human life and cultural values, or atonement for the suffering and torture of men, women and children that were slaughtered in every conceivable inhuman manner." And to continue: "The German people must be required to restore the plundered Jewish property and pay for the rehabilitation of the Holocaust survivors."

Here is another phrase which I wonder why Mr. Begin has skipped: "The sum to be claimed must relate to the damages inflicted on the Jewish people by the Germans, and on the other, to the expenses incurred in the rehabilitation in Israel of those who escaped the Nazi actions or survived them." The foreign minister, then, has not waived those compensations which are claimed by Jewish communities, companies, institutions and tens of thousands of individuals who have survived. You, Mr. Begin, are aware that not all the Jewish people is concentrated in Israel. You know something about the internal divisions characterizing the Diaspora. We wanted to prevent the historic "Who made thee a prince and a judge over us?"[1] You must know that in 1939, when talks were held on rescuing the Jewish refugees from Germany, thirty-nine delegations represented our people. You are aware of this great trouble of internal division. Why, then, are you wondering that the government of Israel took care to prevent internal strife which can only disgrace our people externally? It was stated that the Government of Israel is not prejudicing the rights of those individual Jews that are claiming compensation; it demands this right for those who immigrated to the State of Israel. And you also know that the government of the Soviet Union views murdered Soviet Jews as Soviet citizens and thus it doesn't think compensation for them is due the Jewish people or the government of Israel, and the same goes for the governments of Belgium and France – they are claiming that compensation for their Jewish citizens should be handed over to them. You are aware of this matter, so what is this demagogic questioning of "why are we claiming only a billion and a half?" Why not see reality as it is and recognize the difficult complications emanating from our situation?

Furthermore, you cited the phrase "No arrangement of the German compensation issue can be considered fair from a legal and moral standpoint if this minimal claim on behalf of the principal sufferers at the hands of the Nazi regime is not taken into account," and "Any progress towards restoring Germany to its place in the community of the world's nations is unthinkable so long as this fundamental debt remains unpaid."

Well, this phrase was not directed towards the Jewish people or towards the government of Israel. It was directed towards those powers that are not asking you, me or the government of Israel, how Germany should be dealt with. You

---

1   Exodus 2, 14.

are aware that they are rehabilitating Germany, helping the establishment of its government, rearming and equipping it, releasing Nazi criminals. In face of all this we are saying: if you are doing that – then at least pay compensation before you conclude the matter of your own compensation.

You, Mr. Begin, said that the government of Israel, by the contents of its note, has paved the road to the acceptance of Germany into the family of nations. You should have mentioned the foreign minister's announcement at the UN General Assembly at Lake Success where he was the one and only speaker out of sixty nations, including the Soviet Union, who declared that Germany should not be granted membership in the UN. Has that declaration been erased from your memory? Can you draw from that declaration such a distorted conclusion that the government of Israel is going to recognize Bonn's Government or conduct negotiations with it and send a delegation there?

Had the government of Israel wished to be practical, so to speak, it would have had no difficulty with finding the necessary address. In fact it ignored this address intentionally. It sent the note to the four powers, not to Germany.

We are not divided regarding the spilled blood, nor in regard of our demands and the compensation issue or our attitude towards Germany's crimes. MK Begin's words caused us great harm by presenting us as divided on these issues.

And one comment to MK Sneh: I will not tell you with great relish that what is permissible in Russia is also permissible in the West, and vice versa. But for the sake of truth let me remind you of the announcement made in August 1947 by Marshal Sokolovsky, commander of the Soviet Zone of Occupation in Germany, to the effect that the full rights of all former rank and file members of the Nazi Party are to be restored. In this matter of recovering the rights of murderers, the Soviets preceded the West. They, East and West are indeed learning from each other. Let us not justify them. We have our own history and our own sense of justice.

Speaker Yosef Sprinzak: The debate on German matters is now concluded. I hope that the foreign minister will be able to make an answer by the end of this week.[2]

---

2 The foreign minister did not respond to the various speakers in this debate as he was unwell. His next appearance in the Knesset on the matter of Germany would be nine months later.

[9] Israel Enlists the Jewish Organizations

Cabinet Meeting, 25.10.1951

Minister Moshe Sharett: The last item in my report is the matter of reparations. I would like to inform the cabinet that we are currently engaged in an effort to clarify, indirectly through some Jewish people, the Bonn government's position on reparations – whether they seek to acquit themselves with a few million or whether they realize that this is about hundreds of millions of dollars. I hope that within a few weeks we will know something in this regard. We are not at the point of making a decision yet, but it should be clear to the cabinet that we will face a decision on entering negotiations with the Bonn government once it becomes clear that they are ready to talk business, for there is no other way of advancing this matter. If we have submitted a reparations claim, it is not to record our claim in the annals of history but to achieve concrete results, and we must be prepared for such negotiations.

Second, a conference of Jewish organizations on the subject of reparations opens in New York today. We initiated this conference. One step was submitting the claim – a claim for collective payments. No Jewish organization had submitted such a claim in the name of the Jewish people. When we submitted the claim, several organizations paid it lip service but there was no opposition. In the course of this matter and prior to Adenauer's speech,[1] we saw a need to reinforce this claim with both Germany and the powers. In order to gain support for the claim, we proposed convening a conference of the world's Jewish organizations.

It was our initiative. The Jewish organizations did not rise to the occasion. No Jewish organization thought that there was a need to enlist the Jewish people in this matter.

---

1   On 27.9.1951, in a statement to the Bundestag in which he acknowledged the Nazi war crimes perpetrated against the Jewish people, Chancellor Konrad Adenauer announced his government's readiness to pay compensation, and to that end enter into negotiations with representatives of world Jewry and the State of Israel.

It so happens that this conference, which we initiated before we knew of Adenauer's speech, is convening after his speech. At our initiative the Jewish Agency invited the Jewish organizations to this conference and they all accepted. Even the American Jewish Committee (AJC) will attend. The organizations have been invited to the conference to have their say and to explain their positions. As this conference is convening in light of Adenauer's speech, in which he categorically stated that they are prepared to discuss "Mit den Vertreter des judischen Staates und dem judischen Volk" ['with representatives of the Jewish state and the Jewish people'] – Germany is prepared to discuss payments with them – this has clearly whetted the appetite.

We held a closed, unpublicized meeting with the main Jewish organizations in America in preparation for the conference. It was convened by the Jewish Agency and was attended by the Agency, the Zionist Council, the American Jewish Committee, the American Jewish Congress, Bnei Brith, the American Jewish Labor Committee and the Jewish War Veterans.

There is the question of whether there will be negotiations. There is a willingness for this, but there is also the question of having one delegation appear vis-à-vis the German government or two. It is clearly desirable that there be only one delegation, that of the State of Israel. A joint delegation comprised of the State of Israel and non-governmental organizations from outside Israel is inconceivable. It is impossible for the state, inconvenient for the organizations or some of them like the AJC or the British Jewish Board of Deputies. Dr. Nahum Goldmann's first thought was that while negotiations take place between the two countries, an advisory committee of Jewish organizations would accompany the state's delegation, and contact be maintained between the State of Israel and the non-governmental organizations. This was not accepted by the organizations. The Jewish Agency, too, did not accept this position. Now Nahum Goldmann and others think that there should be two delegations working in tandem. Germany must know that it has business with both the State of Israel and world Jewry.

I argued long and hard with them. I tried to propose an arrangement of division of authorities, a division of labor between the two delegations. And I said, it is out of the question that two claims for collective payments be submitted to Germany, one by the State of Israel and another by world Jewry. The claim for collective payment must be in the hands of the State of Israel. It alone should appear in this matter. Apart from that, there are additional details: restitution of property, compensation payments to those affected – and here there are both legislative and executive matters. These matters, too, must be dealt with, and the organizations will undertake to deal with those claims. They will not demand money. They will demand rapid and orderly legislation and execution.

I must report to my colleagues that I did not succeed. My views were not accepted by those present; their opinion – including that of the Jewish Agency – was that the delegation appearing on behalf of world Jewry should also submit a payment claim, but they are prepared – and the Joint Distribution Committee (which did not take part in the meeting) is apparently also ready to accept this, to undertake that the monies they receive will all be channeled to Israel, but not necessarily to the Government of Israel. I proposed that only we would demand money and that they would demand arrangements for the benefit of the Jewish survivors in the Diaspora, for only we can demand arrangements for the benefit of survivors who are our citizens. When I say that I did not succeed in this matter, I mean that they did not budge and are intent on demanding money.

I spoke to Nahum Goldmann in New York for half-an-hour. I argued that appearing before the Germans with two monetary claims is, first and foremost, a disgrace, and that even from a financial standpoint it is neither worthwhile nor good since the Germans could play one party off against the other. They can tell us: "Had we known that we were concluding negotiations with you alone, we could have given you more, but you know that tomorrow the representatives of the Jewish people can appear and demand money from us again" – and to the representatives of world Jewry they could say: "We must give the lion's share of the money to the State of Israel; what can we give you? Only crumbs." Goldmann claims the opposite is true. The organizations promise that the money they are going to get will be chanelled to Israel, and perhaps they will have to set aside a very small percentage for needs outside Israel (*Minister Golda Meir: How will the grounds for the claims be divided between the two parties?*) The grounds for the claims can be divided. The note we submitted stated that the State of Israel has absorbed half-a-million victims of Nazi Germany. This is a most effective rationale for convincing both the Germans and the powers. The State of Israel affirms that it has given refuge to half-a-million victims of the Nazis; but unlike in America, where each of the immigrating Holocaust survivors had to fend for himself, we have absorbed them by a collective effort of the people of this country. The state has mortgaged its future, it has borrowed money and absorbed the victims of the Nazis. The property of these people and others is still in the hands of the plunderer, the plunderer must return it.

What other grounds of basing our claims are there? There is property with no heirs. It is hard to say that all the property without heirs belongs to the State of Israel. There still are other Jews in the world. Our attempt to appear as the sole representative of the Jewish people was not accepted at this meeting. There is no likelihood that it will be accepted in a different set-up, for then, first and foremost, we would have to give up on the participation of the American Jewish Committee and the American Jewish Labor Committee.

I do not know how protracted the discussions with the Jewish Agency and the World Jewish Congress are going to be, since if we insist on the State of Israel being the sole representative of the Jewish people, the Jewish Congress would lose its raison d'être. Neither will the Jewish War Veterans agree that the State of Israel will speak on behalf of the Jewish people. We contended that it is the only country the Jewish people has. That is a fact. However this position was rejected by the American Jewish Committee. We wanted them to take this matter of reparations to the US State Department. They did not want to do that. They did not want to identify themselves with our note on the State of Israel representing the Jewish people. Eventually, they did take it to the US State Department but only after a verbal and written exchange.

Meanwhile, there is the conference in New York. I had a meeting with Jewish Agency representatives Israel Goldstein and Morris Buckstein. After I argued with them, Buckstein accepted that this conference will not set hard-and-fast rules on this matter. A decision on who will negotiate with the Germans does not have to made because it is not known yet whether or not they will participate in the negotiations, and there is no need to determine today what claims they will advance. But a forum will be established to act in the name of these organizations and it will issue instructions to the various participating organizations to act in agreement with the State of Israel. We, of course, want to determine in advance which way matters will go.

According to the conference's planning, most of the sessions will be held behind closed doors. At the end there will be an open, declarative session attended by the press. A declaration will be made stating that our account with the German people has not been closed; the German people must pay for what it inflicted on the Jewish people. The speakers at this session will be Dr. Nahum Goldmann, Ambassador Abba Eban, and one or two other speakers from the non-Zionist elements. A program of action will be announced at this session. This document still has to be formulated so that it will be worthy of publication and impressive. The conference will convene for one day or a day-and-a-half.

[10] Review by the Foreign Minister Followed by a Cabinet Debate

Cabinet Meeting, 28.10.1951

Minister Moshe Sharett: I would now like to report on the Conference of Jewish Organizations in New York, which has ended. You have all read the newspaper dispatches. I have received a telegram from our New York Consul General Arthur Lurie with his first impressions following the conclusion of the conference. He writes: (1) "Matters were dealt with seriously and responsibly, and worthy of note was the absence of demagoguery on issues that might be so exploited. (2) Following a debate, consensus was finally reached between all the groups, including Agudat Yisrael, and this should be viewed as a laudable achievement. (3) This was an important step towards the formulation of public opinion and the creation of a framework for a more practical discussion of the details of the issue. (4) The idea of parallel claims is still extant, but there need be no concern that it will be a serious problem, and in any event the precedence of Israel's claim was accepted without question. (5) All praise is due to the skill with which Nahum Goldmann ran the conference." (*Prime Minister David Ben Gurion: He also displayed this skill at the Zionist Congress*[1]).

We have here a draft resolution that opens with calling the German people to account for their horrific acts. There are a number of clauses taken from our note, for in view of the already formulated document they evidently did not want to rewrite it. It says that there can be no compensation for the destruction of the life of a nation, cultural assets and so on, nothing can atone for the agonies of death. It further states that the elementary principle of justice and human decency obliges the German people to restore at least the plundered Jewish property in order to compensate the victims and their heirs and participate in financing the absorption of the survivors.

In this regard, the conference relied on the note sent to the powers by the government of Israel as well as on the statement made by the West German chancellor on September 27, 1951, ratified by the West German parliament,

---

1   The 23rd Zionist Congress, August 1951, Jerusalem.

which admits to the crimes committed and obliges the German people to pay compensation. This statement will be judged by the speed and scope of its implementation. In this regard the conference notes that the East German government has neither recognized such responsibility nor expressed its readiness to atone for the destruction caused. The conference asserts its complete support for the claim submitted by the government of Israel regarding the restoration to health of the victims of Nazi persecution residing in Israel. A second and third clause demand meeting the remainder of the claims and that Germany take legislative and executive steps in this regard.

The conference appointed two ad hoc committees: one to determine policy to be comprised of representatives of all the organizations and the second, an executive committee comprising twelve members appointed on a personal basis.

I am aware the Knesset will convene next week. It faces currently an accumulation of burning foreign policy issues: defense of the Middle East, the [American] aid grant of 1951/52 and 1952/53, reparations, direct or indirect negotiations with Germany, the [UN General] Assembly matters. There will doubtless be a demand for a debate on foreign policy matters, and it is desirable that the cabinet be ready for it.

It was decided:

To request the convening of the Knesset for next Sunday for a statement by the foreign minister on foreign policy problems.

Prime Minister David Ben Gurion: Not all the political issues mentioned by the foreign minister are problematical. There are issues on which we have already made a decision. These do not necessitate taking new positions. The matter of reparations is not a problem. Nothing new has happened on the matter of reparations.

Minister Yitzhak-Meir Levin: Regarding reparations from Germany – in my opinion it has not been decided yet to enter negotiations with the German government. This government has not made such a decision and neither did the previous one.

Minister Moshe Sharett: It is true that no decision has been made to enter into direct negotiations with Germany. I do think that such a step calls for a government decision. I am not sure that we have reached the point where we have to decide. I reported that we are clarifying Germany's intentions, whether it means business or whether it has acquitted itselves with the payment of a paltry sum. We shall not sell this matter for a mess of pottage. One or the other: either nothing will come of it or we shall succeed. In the meantime we have advanced on both internal and external fronts. We have enlisted Jewish forces. We have brought Germany to admit its crimes and its readiness for collective payment. This is an unprecedented undertaking.

However, should something come of it, and I am expressing my personal conviction here, then it could ultimately be accomplished only through direct negotiations for numerous questions will come to the fore. Whom will they pay? How will they pay? Even after an agreement in principle has been reached on the sum, there is the question of transferring it – what goods, what do we need, how will the goods be transferred? Perhaps it would be worth our while to take certain goods from Germany and sell them to other countries in exchange for goods from those countries. And there are further questions. There is the question of a Jewish delegation that will sit in Germany and determine how we receive the compensation. Any thoughts of it being forbidden to talk with Germany are absurd, not from an ideological standpoint but from a practical one.

The Jewish people are in fact negotiating with Germany. Nothing came of the indirect negotiations. If that is the position, we should not have submitted the reparations claim. We should have waived it. Having submitted the reparations claim, conclusions must be drawn.

I would like to bring another matter to the cabinet's attention: we are a state! If indeed we are, we cannot ignore the existence of other states. All Israeli writers publishing articles opposing negotiations with Germany are living in a Diaspora reality, not the reality of statehood. We have attempted to isolate Germany in the international arena – the result was that we isolated ourselves. It had no effect. While participating in various international bodies we conduct discussions with Germany, we vote together with Germany, we vote against Germany, we act together with them. (*Minister Golda Meir: It is still a good thing that we voted against them.*) I am not saying that we should not have voted against them.

I would like to ask you, Rabbi Levin: we have a consul general in Switzerland who has just been elected doyen of the consular corps. As doyen he has to protect the interests of all the consuls in Zurich, including the German. Let us assume that the German consul approaches him seeking protection. Will he not protect his interests? If not, then he should not be doyen of the consular corps for that is why he was elected.

We are now approaching the final stages during which we can put a price on our reconciliation with Germany's return into the community of nations. We could, at the very least, make it conditional upon receiving millions and millions of dollars for the plundered Jewish property. Or we could be a party to the process of Germany's return into the community of nations without it paying us even one penny.

Prime Minister David Ben Gurion: I would ask the cabinet members not to argue about reparations from Germany. We have nothing actually new before us; on the other hand, other political matters demand immediate attention.

Minister Peretz Naphtali: I somewhat disagree with the opinion that the question of Germany and the reparations is not urgent. In a certain sense it is because we must do everything to accelerate contact and settlement since any delay, in my view, is to the German government's advantage and not to ours.

Minister David Zvi Pinkas: With regard to the reparations – I think that Minister Naftali is right when he says that the matter is urgent for us. I know the government's position, and I want to say just one thing: these talks must be held somewhere, but certainly not in Israel. We will not invite Germans here for political talks, and they cannot be held in Germany either, but in a neutral location, let's say Paris.

Minister Moshe Sharett: That is the intention, either Paris or Switzerland, but it is not yet time to decide where the talks will be held since we do not know if they will be held.

Minister Moshe Shapira: I recall that we received information before Adenauer's statement in which it was said that we are talking about a specific sum. I would like to say that as long as we do not clearly hear from the people close to him what that sum approximately is, there is no room for a meeting even in Paris.

Minister Moshe Sharett: That there is no room for negotiations is clear. There might only be a meeting to clarify the sum.

Minister Moshe Shapira: We must know this in advance. We should not compare America with Israel. Let us not forget that in Israel there are 500,000 Jews from countries ruled by Hitler. They have gone through the Holocaust. There are not only emotions, of course. There is also the accounting. We must explain to the public that we must act according to the principle of "Hast thou killed and also taken possession?" We must obtain the plundered inheritance of the victims. By making an intensive effort we shall succeed in explaining this to our public, but it is unthinkable that we enter negotiations and later discover that the Germans are talking about five or ten million dollars a year. First of all we must know what sum they are talking about (*Minister Moshe Sharett: Certainly.*) Regarding our basic problems, it would seem that the State of Israel was born into hard times (*Minister Eliezer Kaplan: The Jewish people were always in a difficult situation.*); (*Minister Moshe Sharett: We chose an uncomfortable place and an inconvenient time.*)

Minister Golda Meir: A word about the reparations. I know it is not relevant at the moment, but even so, before negotiations start we must know that we cannot and should not relinquish what is due to the Jewish people. But is it so difficult to understand that there are Jews who are repelled by the very thought of contact with the Germans?

Prime Minister David Ben Gurion: I do not believe that there are more than a few.

Minister Moshe Sharett: Let us assume that we did not have only one small Jewish brigade in the Second World War, but that we participated in the war in great force and were part of the army that occupied Germany. We would have had "our own McCloy" there – would he not have negotiated with the Germans every day? Would anybody have said that a Jewish army should not be an occupying army in Germany?

Minister Golda Meir: That links up exactly with what I wanted to say. I said I realize that we must enter direct negotiations. Yet one still feels a sting of pain. Everyone knows that that this feeling comes from a pure heart, and just as Minister Sharett said – in different circumstances we could have been there in the occupying army. I asked for the floor to say that we must be careful in our manner of speech with them. In my opinion, the manner of speech is very important when we come to negotiate with them. If we do negotiate, then in my opinion the Foreign Ministry must ensure, and it knows how, that whoever speaks with any of the Germans, his manner of speech should not be that used when meeting with friendly countries, and that they should feel it.

Minister Levi Eshkol: What if they nominate people [for the negotiations] who were decent all the time? The Almighty is capable of everything.

Minister Golda Meir: It is immaterial. A German is a German.

Minister Ben-Zion Dinur: I would like to say a word about the reparations. This is a very important matter. This is, at long last, the first time in the history of the Jewish people that reparations are being paid to Jews. We must also look at it from that viewpoint. It is a fact. Why not mention it? Jews have been killed throughout the generations. The murderers never paid. There never was any compensation – they killed and also plundered.

Minister David Z. Pinkas: When we were independent we received reparations. At the time of King Saul's wars we received quite a lot of reparations.

Minister Ben-Zion Dinur: If there were no State of Israel we would not have received a single penny. Nobody would have entered negotiations with us as a stateless people. They might have given us alms. It is only because there is a State of Israel that we will possibly reach negotiations on reparations. When presenting the issue we must stress that there is another matter here, not that we are forgiving them. There is a different historic situation: there is a State of Israel, and it demands compensation. We must explain this unique fact to the general public, and this explanation is highly important because this issue is fraught with emotions. In my opinion, this explanation is vital.

[11] The Cabinet Prepares for the Knesset Debate
Cabinet Meeting, 4.11.1951

David Horowitz, Financial Adviser to the government: I assume that the state's balance of payments will amount to $300 million, and we do not have the resources to finance it. I think the American grant for the current year is guaranteed, and the same goes for next year's grant, but these will not suffice. There is one source of financing which I believe is sound and I have already made it known to the cabinet: reparations from Germany. I think there is a chance of receiving hundreds of millions of dollars through this channel if we act energetically. Accordingly we will receive $400-500 million during five to six years, that is between $70 and $1,000 million a year. These assumptions rest on quite well-based rumors. I do not think this is dependant on establishing diplomatic relations with Germany, but it will involve negotiations.

Let me add that either we clinch this matter of reparations within the next few months, or we miss out on the whole matter for good. Urgent action is necessary.

Minister Yitzhak-Meir Levin: What are the sources of this information?

David Horowitz: My information comes from indirect contacts with people close to the highest authority. I think it is well-founded.

Minister Moshe Sharett: We have no information regarding Adenauer's agreement to these sums. There are insiders in Bonn who are talking about this amount. They tell us that additional pressure should be brought to bear on the chancellor on this matter.

Prime Minister David Ben Gurion: A delegation of people calling themselves "Israeli men of letters" visited me in my office, and the poet David Shimoni read aloud a decision reached at their meeting: no forgetting, no atoning, and so on. I told them that all Jews would agree with that, but the question is, should we tell the Germans: now that "you murdered, you will also inherit," or should we receive a significant part of the inheritance? Not one of them said that we should go back on our claim. When the question of who would conduct the reparations negotiations was broached, an argument ensued regarding the issue of a wise policy of state vis-à-vis a Diaspora attitude. I said we are a sovereign state and our attitude must be one of wisdom. They contended that the State of Israel should not be seated together with the Germans. I asked: "Who should?" They said: "The Jewish Agency." I retorted: "Here again is the principle of using a Shabbos Goy.[1] It is unthinkable for a state to behave in this way. Either this is done by the state or not done at all!"

We must be prepared for the Knesset debate today regarding the reparations issue. I assume the opposition will submit a no-confidence motion. I think that perhaps we should put through a motion that the Knesset has taken notice of the government's announcement regarding the reparations claim.

Minister Moshe Sharett: If the Knesset should today resolve that the State of Israel should not conduct negotiations regarding reparations, this would be a very bad and rash resolution. It is my opinion that there will not be a debate on reparations today. In the Knesset I will say that we should wait and see how this matter evolves, and that initially this matter should be deliberated in the Foreign Affairs and Defense Committee. When the time is ripe, the matter would be brought up before the Knesset for debate and decision. Our only practical move should be to bring the issue before the Foreign Affairs and Defense Committee.

---

1   A non-Jew employed by Orthodox Jews to tend fires, turn on and extinguish lights or perform other similar services which Jews are forbidden to do on the Sabbath.

[12] Israel's Claim for Reparations from Germany

Knesset Sessions 14-15, 4-5.11.1951

Speaker Yosef Sprinzak: Foreign Minister Moshe Sharett has the floor.

Foreign Minister Moshe Sharett: Mr. Speaker, members of the Knesset, in recent weeks and months there have been a few new developments in several of our spheres of activity and interest in the field of foreign policy. In accordance with the cabinet's decision, I will now deliver a brief review of these developments.

The likelihood of a flow of substantial resources for building our economy, in addition to the American aid grant, could be realized if Israel's claim for reparations from Germany would be met. The first positive response to the note submitted by the State of Israel to the four occupying powers on March 12, 1951 – the note I had the honor to read in the Knesset – was the statement delivered by the chancellor of the Federal Republic of Germany in the House of Representatives in Bonn on September 27, 1951. This statement, which was unanimously ratified, contained an admission of the horrific acts committed by the Nazi regime against European Jewry in the name of the German people, although an attempt was made to present the majority of the German people as innocent of this charge. The statement also expressed willingness to impose reparations on the German people for the property plundered and the material damage inflicted, and to this end to enter into negotiations with representatives of the Jewish people and the State of Israel. The government of Israel is presently awaiting real proof of the Bonn government's readiness to shoulder collective payment for the plunder of Jewish property appropriate to the extent of the plunder, and on the basis of the claim submitted by the State of Israel.

The note submitted to the occupying powers stated: "There can be no atonement or material compensation for a crime of such immense and horrifying magnitude." It further states: "Any compensation whatsoever, no matter how large, cannot compensate for the loss of human life and cultural values, or serve as atonement for the suffering and torture of men, women and children who were slaughtered in every conceivable inhuman manner."

These phrases were reiterated in the declaration issued by the Conference of Jewish Organizations that took place ten days ago in New York. The conference was convened at the invitation of the Jewish Agency and was attended by some twenty international and national Jewish organizations. The delegates came from the United States, England, Canada, Argentina, South Africa and France. It was, in fact, a comprehensive representation of the major Jewish communities of the free world. The sessions were led by the chairman of the American branch of the Jewish Agency, Dr. Nahum Goldmann, and Abba Eban, the Ambassador of Israel in Washington, took part. It was declared that all the organizations represented wholeheartedly supported Israel's reparations claim and demanded that other Jewish claims from Germany, including claims for the restitution of property and the payment of compensation to individuals, heir-organizations and so forth should also be met. This important conference was characterized by a spirit of Jewish unity, political responsibility, and devotion to Israel.

I would like to prevent any misunderstanding. A question was raised in the Knesset's Foreign Affairs and Defense Committee on the reparations claim's method, whether it necessitates negotiations, what kind of negotiations, and so forth. I replied that in my opinion this question is not relevant at this time. When it becomes relevant, there will be a discussion. In my review at the committee, in view of recent developments I reported several relevant facts regarding our negotiations for reparations. It was not my intention to raise this question for debate. If the question is whether or not to submit a claim for reparations, then the claim was submitted several months ago; if the question is what kind of negotiations should be conducted, the government is not bringing it before the Knesset. When this question is put before the government, it will not take any final or binding decision.

MK Aryeh Ben Eliezer (*Herut*): The Foreign Affairs and Defense Committee, in the presence of the foreign minister, made a clear decision to the effect that the question of Germany will not be included in today's political debate but will constitute a separate issue to be discussed by the Knesset.

MK Israel Rokach (*General Zionists*): Will there be a separate debate?

Foreign Minister Moshe Sharett: When the time is right.

MK Yitzhak Raphael (*Hapoel Hamizrachi*): There will certainly be another opportunity, when the time is right, to voice our opinion on the issue that has vexed the entire Jewish people for some time. There is nothing more just than claiming compensation from the nation of murderers. As a people whose place is among the victorious nations, and one which suffered more than any other people in the world war, we are entitled and even duty-bound to claim compensation and reparations. We shall assert our claim on the property of our brethren for the purpose of materially assisting our brethren. Vast amounts of Jewish property, public and private, have remained in that country, whose surviving Jews have left it, and the 30,000 Jews who are still there will soon leave it, too. There is no room, nor will there ever be, for negotiation between representatives of the Jewish people and the nation of murderers! The people of the Torah has not forgotten its hatred of the Amalekite – the people of the Torah will not cease thinking, not even for one moment, about the catastrophe brought down upon it by a fiendish nation united by the spirit of defilement which characterized all Germans, from East and West alike, in carrying out the horrifying plan of our people's annihilation. The Knesset will have the opportunity to express the horror of the Jewish people residing in Zion towards the Germans, and the profound hatred rooted in its heart towards those unclean people, when the time is right for a debate on this issue, as we have heard today from the foreign minister.

Now we must ask not only for caution at every step taken on this sensitive and delicate matter but also great caution in any statement made in order to obviate a mistaken impression likely to be received by the public. We must ask the government that anything it may do in this regard – and it has much to do so that we may obtain the assets of our brethren to save those brethren waiting in their tens of thousands to be absorbed and rehabilitated – will be done with the approval of the Foreign Affairs and Defense Committee and in accordance with the Knesset's decision.

MK Aryeh Ben Eliezer (*Herut*): Even though the government has not yet entered into formal negotiations with the German government on the question of reparations and compensation, the fact is that preliminary contacts have been made and clarifications have already been discussed. These "clarifications" are in fact negotiations, and on this matter I would like to say that neither this House nor any other Israeli state institution has authorized the government to enter negotiations.

MK Shmuel Mikunis (*I.C.P.*): The foreign minister has elegantly by-passed the question from which the blood of six million Jews is dripping – that of Germany. In his effort to justify his negotiations with the neo-Nazi Bonn government, he cited the fact that under the direction of a few Jewish agents of the State Department, a conference of Jewish organizations was convened in the USA and "unanimously" supported Adenauer (*Foreign Minister Moshe Sharett: Who are the people you are calling foreign agents?*) – Nahum Goldmann was a British agent and now is an American agent! (*Speaker Yosef Sprinzak: In this House it is unacceptable to defame a Jewish and Zionist leader trusted by all of us. I ask MK*

Mikunis to retract his words) – I cannot retract true facts in which I firmly believe. I am saying that Churchill is a warmonger, that Truman is Hitler's heir! Am I not allowed to say the truth on this podium? It's my right! Am I forbidden to criticize Nahum Goldmann who is an American citizen? (*MK Yitzhak Rafael: He is a Jew and he is a Zionist! That is what he is!*) – He is a Jew? There were Jews also in the Judenrats! Are you going to prohibit me from criticizing them?

Speaker Yosef Sprinzak: Your time is up.

MK Yona Kesse (*Mapai*)**:** When deliberating the issue of reparations from Germany, we must draw a distinction between the genuine emotions of Jews who recoil from conducting negotiations for compensation with the German government, and others who criticize us not so much out of Jewish-Israeli emotion, but due to other, partisan accounts.

With regard to the Jews, in whose emotions and sensitivities I firmly believe, I would like to say that they are doing a great wrong in this matter to the government and to our national honor if they, through their opposition, create the impression that the reparation claim is linked with forgiveness and atonement for the German people. This is not true. We seek to restore the plunder, the Jewish property that was taken from us, and we do not seek it because we are avaricious but because we do not wish to leave in German hands the vast amount of property taken from our slaughtered brethren, and we seek to make it into a source for the building of the State of Israel: the settlement of its wildernesses, the absorption of immigrants and the development of this country's natural resources, so that we can advance the nurturing and building of our political independence. We shall not talk of forgiveness and the settling of our historical account with the German people. It cannot be atoned for, and should atonement be asked for, we will not grant it. I am confident that when we hold a special debate on this issue, the Knesset will categorically state that we cannot forgive the acts of slaughter and murder, and that for generations to come the German people must labor long and hard to prove that it has uprooted the forces of defilement and destruction that brought about our great national catastrophe.

We must avoid creating an outward impression that there are those among us who are sensitive and those who are insensitive towards this matter – those who remember the murder of the six million and those who have forgotten it. Why create an impression that we are divided on this tragic and terrible issue?

We obviously fear lest the statement made by the chancellor of the Bonn government is not sincere, and we shall certainly examine to what extent the Bonn government is prepared to restore the plunder. If the German people seek forgiveness, it must first restore all the plunder, and we shall not fall into the trap of some stratagem that will enable the German people and its government in any way to evade, culpability for the grave crimes they perpetrated and their condemnation by the Jewish people. But I ask: by what moral right do Mapam and the Communist Party condemn entering into negotiations on compensation with the German government? I have recently learned that a Mapam delegation is soon going to East Berlin to attend the Communist International Trade Union Conference – members of that delegation are going to Berlin, not Bonn. They are going to the city where Hitler and Himmler and the other murderers resided, the city in which the decision to exterminate the Jewish people was taken. Is it permissible to travel to East Germany? Are their hands not stained with the blood of Jews? Is it because Stalin has given them his seal of approval that these Germans are considered better? In this House I have heard the Communist MK Vilner say that for him Otto Grotewohl,[1] by virtue of being a Communist, is more important than a Jew who is not a Communist.

I do not know whether or not negotiations with Bonn are possible, but one thing is clear: on our part there is no difference between West and East Germans. Esteemed Mapam and Communist members of the Knesset, I harbor deep suspicions that while you attack us and suspect us of being prepared to compromise with the Nazis – you yourselves will hasten to reconcile with the German people residing in the Soviet sphere of influence. You say that Stalin has uprooted Nazism in East Germany and that the Germans of East Germany would not have done so without him; if so, why do you view them as better than the Germans of West Germany? Please do not speak about Jewish honor and do not accuse us of besmirching that honor. It is you who are willing to worship idols – the idols of Soviet communism – not us.

MK Mordechai Nurock (*Hamizrachi*): Respected House, The constraints of time compel me to touch upon one issue only, that of our relations with the nation of murderers. Never since the day the sovereign Knesset of the State of Israel was established have we faced such a grave problem. Although we have heard, with great satisfaction, our foreign minister's statement that the government has not made a decision regarding direct contact with Germany, and that in any event it will present its proposals to do that to the Knesset at a later date, I am deeply concerned lest the New York conference surprise us with a *fait accompli*, and therefore I am duty-bound to address this problem.

In this very House we decided to have an annual remembrance day for the one-third of our people that was destroyed with extreme cruelty, according to a specific plan set out by the German Amalekites, the perpetrators of anti-Semitism for over hundreds of years – and now we seek to honor the memory of our martyrs by sitting at the same table with their murderers? The entire German people are guilty of murder. Any contact and negotiation with the murderers of our people is, in any event, the beginning of our forgivness. It is a desecration

---

1   Otto Grotewohl (1894-1964), one of the leaders of the German Communist Party. From the end of 1949, prime minister of East Germany's government.

of the memory of the martyrs, and it constitutes grave harm to the honor and morals of the Jewish people.

We will receive no money at all but become a distributing agent for German goods, goods from which Jewish blood still drips. Reparations will require the establishment of a German legation in our country and of our legation in that unclean land – in effect, marking the termination of the state of war with the murderers and the establishing of diplomatic relations with their country. Consequently, we will open our gates to commerce between Jews and the murderers. What is permissible to the state and the Jewish Agency is also permissible to individuals.

As early as 1948 I demanded here, at the Zionist institutions and at the meetings of the World Jewish Congress that reparations be paid indirectly through international means by the great powers as part of the peace treaty with Germany, by appealing to the Hague International Court or to other important United Nations institutions. At the time, relations between the victorious powers and Germany were completely different. Now they are all trying to purify the unclean and use them as cannon fodder against the East, and this only six months after our country approached the powers – an approach that was made after considerable delay. The feelers sent out two years ago by the Jewish Agency and later by the State of Israel towards Germany through senior Israeli officials have brought down the barrier and caused us both moral and material damage.

Foreign Minister Moshe Sharett: Honorable Rabbi Nurock, are you not aware that the Jewish Agency has a permanent delegation in Germany which is constantly negotiating with the German authorities regarding the restitution of Jewish property? And not only the Jewish Agency, but other Jewish organizations are operating there, too? A whole gamut of Jewish organizations is engaged in this activity. Is this a secret to you? Are you not aware of this? Why have you not raised your voice against it?

MK Mordechai Nurock (*Hamizrachi*)**:** From a moral standpoint, this is a national disaster, a great and unprecedented spiritual-moral catastrophe for the Jewish people. The murderers exterminated one-third of the nation's body, they plundered everything from us but not our honor, and now we ourselves are offering them the honor of Israel and the soul of the nation.

When the Jews were expelled from Spain they were permitted to leave unharmed, yet no Jewish foot trod the soil of that country for centuries. All the more so after the extermination and torture of our times that has no precedent in either the annals of nations or in the annals of the Jewish people which are soaked with blood and tears. In the Middle Ages the ancestors of the accursed Nazis, the "robber barons," attacked travelers, killed them and stole their possessions, and then obtained from the Church, in return for payment, documents of expiation and forgiveness. Now the Jewish people are handing documents of expiation to the murderers of its parents, brothers and sons! The Yiddish poet Leivik Halpern quite rightly asked: "What is the price to be paid for a Jewish child who was burned and for a mother who was burned?" I totally reject any denial that reparations through direct contact are not leading to expiation.

There is no comparison here with the "transfer" agreement of 1933 when we faced the question of saving the Jews of Germany and bringing them to Palestine, and that was before the murder. Incidentally, then too, in 1933, it was decided at a conference prior to the World Jewish Congress in Geneva, following the initiative I forwarded together with Dr. Stephen Wise, to announce a boycott of Germany, and that was before the brutal murder during the war. We extol the memory of the Warsaw Ghetto fighters who saved Jewish honor through their heroism and showed the human beasts that the Jewish people will not be led like lambs to the slaughter and can die an honorable death. Is it in the spirit of our heroes that only six years after the slaughter we are prepared to sit at the same table with the murderers?

The Bonn chancellor's declaration is pure hypocrisy needed for external use with regard to Adenauer's visit to the United States. "Reparations within the bounds of possibility," as if reparations are a donation. "Equal rights for Jews domiciled in Germany." That statement is nothing but a calculated political ploy to make the world forget the terrible crime and mislead public opinion.

Intellectuals in Israel and abroad, leading Hebrew and Yiddish poets and writers, particularly in the United States, have issued a bitter protest against entering direct contact with the murderers. The "realists" say that the opponents' approach is quixotic. They forget that man does not live by bread alone. No nation can survive without a vision and moral values. The "dreamers" of "Zion Lovers"[2] brought about the Basel Plan,[3] the Balfour Declaration and the establishment of the State of Israel while the "realists" viewed them with derision.

We cannot compel those who hate us to love us, but we have the power to compel them to regard us with respect. Members of the Knesset, we must consider what the gentiles will say, that we have sold our birthright, our self-respect. And why should our children say: "Why have you defiled the memory of our heroes and martyrs?"

I propose that we appeal in this matter to the United Nations. The Jewish people fought in the last war with the victors. Our demand is that the United Nations demand restitution of the plunder in our name. They will understand us. We can also formulate a petition from the entire Jewish people with the signatures

---

2   An organization of Russian Jews, founded in Czarist Russia in 1881, with the aim of establishing Jewish settlements in Ottoman Palestine.

3   A plan promulgated by the first Congress of the World Zionist Organization convened in Basel in August 1897. The plan called for establishing a homeland for the Jewish people in Palestine.

of millions and submit it to the United Nations. That would be a victory for morals, justice and integrity.

And from our government, the Jewish Agency and all the Jewish organizations we demand: please avoid any direct contact with the murderers! Preserve the honor of the Jewish people! The eyes of the Jewish people are upon us, and perhaps even the eyes of past as well as future generations. If reparations depend upon direct contact, we should forego them. Remember and do not forget that history will hand down its verdict on us. We should ensure that we do not shame ourselves in the eyes of the future generations.

MK Eliezer Livne (*Mapai*)**:** Mr. Speaker, Members of the Knesset, the trouble with this matter is its late appearance. There are two basic views on this issue in the Jewish public arena. It seems to me that views on this matter are divided in most of this House's factions. There are those who say that we must not enter negotiations with Germany, thus claiming that compensation is forbidden; and there are those who say that we must obtain compensation even if it involves direct negotiations with Germany. The compromise reached between these two opposing schools of thought was to postpone the issue, and this postponement was not constructive. Had we claimed reparations a few years ago, when Germany did not have a central government and Germany's popularity was still at a low ebb in the eyes of the two global rivals, we would have been stronger than we are today. We would not have had to negotiate with the German government and we could have determined the appropriate form of reparations. I now fear that the question of reparations has become so complicated that its solution would be by far more difficult.

In any event, one thing should be stated very clearly: just as reparations are not compensation for the blood that has been shed, they cannot be a prelude to our establishment of diplomatic relations with Germany. We have not declared a boycott of Germany because Germany owes us a great deal of money, money that was plundered from us. We have declared a boycott because six million Jews were murdered by Germany.

If we receive a portion of the plundered property, the blood of six million Jews would still separate us from Germany. I would like it to be clear to any German government that payment of compensation will not take us one inch closer to establishing diplomatic relations with Germany. It is still too soon. There is no sign whatsoever that the Germans have repented. I have some knowledge of that people, and I do not see any signs of internal revulsion or remorse proportional – even somewhat – to the magnitude of the crime. This is one of the most fateful questions to be faced by Israel. It could indeed suffer a serious failure here.

Moral values carry some weight in international relations. In any event, our claim from Germany has moral force, for we have no occupying forces or means of economic pressure to use against it. Moral factor is the only force on which we base our claim for compensation; and its foundation will be undermined and the very basis of the compensation claim would be desecrated if the memory of the victims – and their murderers – does not burn within us day and night and guide our human and political conduct.

I would suggest that we relate to German statements with utmost circumspection. Good taste did not prevent the German chancellor from announcing, in his first statement on the subject, that they would not pay a great deal of money. West German officials have admitted, or at least paid lip service to their guilt; the other part of Germany remains silent to this day – it is evidently not guilty at all.

We have some slight recollection of recent European history. Even when the Germans promised to pay a great deal of compensation after WW I, they in fact did not pay and avoided paying by various pretexts. And now, when they announce in advance that they do not intend to restore the full sum of the plunder, what ground is there for optimism? Humane-moral reasons and political-economic reasons alike require us to act with the utmost caution. I say this as a supporter of the reparations claim. We must obtain reparations, but not at any price. Our honor and moral backbone are more precious than reparations.

MK Yizhar Harari (*Progressive Party*)**:** Members of the Knesset, on the matter of reparations we were assured by the foreign minister that there would be a debate before a decision is made. Since opinions on this matter are divided morally in our faction, we have decided not to impose party discipline. I would like to suggest that in this debate each of us, Knesset members, should express his own personal viewpoint.

I have read in the papers, and I hope it isn't true, that our representatives are saying that receiving reparations from Germany will enable our government to pay compensation to Arab refugees residing in Arab states. I would request complete separation between compensation to the Arabs and the reparations from Germany.

MK Abraham Deutch (*Agudat Yisrael*)**:** As far as reparations from Germany are concerned, it is clear, and this was voiced by almost all speakers here, that all the silver and gold in the world would not atone for the slaughter of one single Jew by the Nazis. The question facing us is, are we allowed to receive the money plundered from us? It seems to me that it is too early to voice a cry here since we do not know at all with whom we should negotiate, what form these negotiations may take and whether our demand will be accepted.

Let me cite one phrase expressed by our prophet Joel: "For I will cleanse their blood that I have not cleansed, for the Lord dwells in Zion." Our sages commented on this phrase and said that while the silver and gold plundered by the nations would be taken back by the people of Israel, the spilled blood would not be atoned for. The Lord who dwells in Zion certainly knows when and how he will take vengeance for the blood.

MK Benjamin Mintz (*Poalei Agudat Yisrael*)**:** Our decision carries with it one significant reservation: we are not moving towards peace with the German nation of murderers. We have not and will not forget what Amalek has done to us. There will never be peace between us and the German people, neither with its Western nor with its Eastern part, for the hands of both are stained with the blood of our brothers and sisters. But this should in no way be construed to mean that we are willing to leave the plunder in the hands of the robbers only because, in addition to the plunder, they murdered their victims. We shall claim reparations and channel them to the building of our country; this would be our great revenge against the human beast that sought to exterminate us in this generation. With the reparations extracted we will expand our building here, and in spite of Nazi plans fortify and increase this generation of Jews and its great enterprise – our state.

MK Yitzhak Ben Zvi (*Mapai*)**:** Mr. Speaker, Members of the Knesset, at the beginning of my remarks I permit myself to comment on one point to which the speaker, the foreign minister, devoted but little time and spoke of incidentally, but on which many other speakers focused. It is the question of our relations with Germany. Although as we have been assured this question will be the subject of a special Knesset debate, I would like to make two comments in view of what has been said here and steps already taken on this matter.

The opposition among our public to any contact with the present German government derives from understandable moral reasons, and it is understandable to all of us. It is manifested within political parties, Knesset factions, old-timers as well as new-comers. We are all in the same boat, and there is no need to explain and elaborate. There is also no need to explain that Nazism is our enemy and it is despicable and unclean not because it is Fascist. Even if it were liberal or socialist – and there have been such phenomena – we would perceive it as our enemy and a defiler of humankind to the same degree, and our attitude towards it would be the same. Neither the German people nor this German government should be absolved of responsibility.

However, the question facing us is whether we should also demand compensation; should we, therefore, or should we not have contact with the Germans? And on this I would like to make one comment.

The fact that Nazi Germany exterminated one-third of our people, six million, and millions from other races – the plunder and the persecution – these facts have no expiation. They cannot be expiated by any compensation, but that does not mean that we should waive the remainder of our just claims. We can and should obtain two things: exemplary punishment and compensation. The punishment does not completely depend on us. However, as to waiving compensation –

I think that those who propose it are mistaken. They are mixing two different issues and are not serving their people well. There are matters in the domain of the individual; no one is allowed to interfere here and advise the individual to waive personal compensation. Were it in our power, we would have taken a share by force, but as we cannot do that we shall do it another way.

We cannot decide for the individual, but there is also the matter of the people as a whole. The people were robbed. Murdered individuals left no heirs, and the Jewish nation is their heir. There are buildings, there are public assets in Germany which were owned by Jews who perished. The state that is concerned with its development and with strengthening its population does not, in my opinion, have the right to give up claiming restitution. With regard to the question of direct contact, we have a government that knows how to conduct itself. The question of what and how we should claim is one that should be put into the hands of our executive branch.

But there is another issue unlike this one that does not derive from purely Jewish considerations, and that is the differentiation made between East and West Germany. Evidently, some of those among us who do not only reject any contact with West Germany, but also oppose claiming reparations from it, are willing to sit together with Germans at festivals and all kinds of conferences in East German territory. Are Germans divided into two types? Are there good and bad figs, with the good figs concentrated in the eastern basket? Here, in this matter, I do not discern that concern for Jewish interests which I pointed out in the first part of my speech.

MK Israel Rokach (*General Zionists*)**:** Members of the Knesset, in these deliberations we have heard in this House, to my great consternation, the words "Chancellor of the German government." I think that during the last three years these words were not pronounced even once within the walls of the House representing the Jewish people. It was not gladdening to hear a hope expressed that the monies received from Germany would ease the economic situation of the State of Israel – I admit to a cold shudder upon hearing my foreign minister talk in this vein regarding the people who attempted to destroy us. To hear, pure and simple, that the economic situation of the State of Israel would be eased if we make indirect or direct contact with the government in Bonn, which in my opinion is Nazi as well, or at least guilty of the same wrongdoing and crime perpetrated by its predecessors, was not appropriate.

Speaker Yosef Sprinzak: The various factions have submitted draft resolutions. I will allow the proposers to read them out to the House if they so wish.

MK Yosef Sapir (*General Zionists*)**:** Our draft resolution regarding the foreign minister's statement is as follows: The Knesset resolves to hold a separate and special debate next week on the issue of reparations from Germany in which it will determine its position on the issue. Until that position is determined, the government will not initiate or act on this matter.

MK Moshe Sneh (*Mapam*): The Mapam faction proposes: The Knesset rejects any possibility of the State of Israel entering into negotiations with the Bonn government, which would mean indirect recognition of that neo-Nazi government; the Knesset opposes the government's foreign policy and expresses no confidence in it.

MK Aryeh Ben Eliezer (*Herut*): I have the honor to present the declaration of the Herut faction summing up the political debate: We reject any possibility of negotiation with the German murderers of our people and demand that the government of Israel avoid taking any step in that direction. The Israeli delegates to the United Nations should protest the participation of observers from the murderous German people in the General Assembly and demand their removal. Germany has no place in the community of nations.

MK Shmuel Mikunis (*I.C.P.*): The draft resolution of the Israeli Communist Party is as follows: The Knesset vigorously rejects negotiation in any form whatsoever with the neo-Nazi Bonn government which is reestablishing the Nazi army under the command of Hitlerist generals and is releasing war criminals – the arch-murderers of Auschwitz and Maidanek – in order to prepare for new aggression threatening the extermination of millions of Jews and members of other peoples. The Knesset rejects with revulsion Adenauer's hypocritical statement and demands the immediate cessation of negotiations with the Nazi murderers of our people. They desecrate the memory of our six million victims constitute an assault on the people's sensitivities and cause grave harm to our national honor. The Jewish people will never be in the same camp with the Nazis.

By its agreement to annex the state to the militant Middle Eastern bloc, the Ben Gurion government has agreed to place the State of Israel, its strategic positions and its economic and military potential at the disposal of the militant Atlantic bloc which is preparing a new world war against the peace-loving nations headed by the Soviet Union. Since the Ben Gurion government is in fact conducting negotiations with the neo-Nazi Bonn government, while agreeing de facto with the establishment of the Nazi army by the militant Atlantic bloc, and since these steps jeopardize Israel's security and independence, placing it in the hands of the imperialist warmongers and positioning the government in the same camp as the Nazis – the Knesset resolves to express no confidence in the government.

MK Meir Argov (*Mapai*)**:** On behalf of the coalition factions, I present the following draft resolution: The Knesset acknowledges the foreign minister's statement and proceeds to issues on its agenda.

Speaker Yosef Sprinzak: I put the no confidence resolution of Mapam to a vote.

Result of the no confidence vote:
For – 16; Against – 63
The resolution was rejected.

Result of the vote on the General Zionist's resolution:
For – 18; Against – 74
The resolution was rejected.

Result of the vote on the second clause of the Mapam resolution:
For – 18; Against – 52
The resolution was rejected.

Result of the vote on the Israel Communist Party resolution:
The resolution was rejected.

Result of the vote on the coalition factions' resolution:
For – 60; Against – 36
The resolution was passed.

[13] The Reparations Agreement with Germany

Central Committee of Israel Labor Party (Mapai) Meeting, 13.12.1951[1]

Chairmen Meir Argov: We have invited our Knesset faction members, the secretariat of our party branches abroad, our members at the Histadrut [the Federation of Labor in Israel] executive, and correspondents from our party to this meeting of the central committee of our Knesset faction. I would like to emphasize that while so many of you are here, all those present are obliged to avoid any leaks of content to the outside world. No reporting in the press will be allowed other than a formal communiqué issued by the party Secretariat.

David Ben Gurion: Members of the central committee will remember that the government informed the Knesset of the note it submitted to the four occupation powers in which it demanded $1.5 billion dollars from Germany as compensation for plundered Jewish property in addition to the restitution of property to individual heirs.

When a note is submitted to Russia, it is impossible to know what happens to it. The situation in the West is different. America's attitude towards our note was generally negative, for they assumed they would have to shoulder the burden of reparations, and the attitude of Britain and France was not too keen. We could appeal to public opinion, Jewish and non-Jewish alike, in these three countries. Possibly, the three Western governments did exert some pressure on Germany, even though they did not inform us of any steps taken. Then came the famous statement by Chancellor Adenauer in which he admitted the German people's responsibility, although not its guilt, and agreed to pay compensation. When we submitted our claim, we realized that we would contact the Germans directly if we knew beforehand that our claim would be accepted. Otherwise we would not have submitted it.

Meanwhile, a campaign against direct negotiations was initiated in certain newspapers. A delegation of men of letters approached me some time ago and

---

1 Foreign Minister Moshe Sharett was not present at this meeting as he was abroad.

its members expressed their opposition. I told them that the question is whether or not Germany should be the murderer and the inheritor as well. I asked them: should we not secure the plundered property for the heirs who have survived as well as for the Jewish people? They said yes, but that this assignment should be carried out by an emissary, not by the State of Israel. I retorted that I disapproved of this being done by a Shabbos Goy.[2] If this action is to be executed, it must be by us. We shall not introduce the Shabbos Goy custom into our state.

According to available, authoritative information, the German government is prepared to discuss the State of Israel's claim with representatives of world Jewry and of Israel. You are certainly aware that the Conference of Jewish Organizations in New York unanimously decided to support the claims for payment of compensation to the State of Israel and to the Jewish people. Undoubtedly, a noisy Knesset meeting on the issue of direct negotiations is awaiting us, and the cabinet would probably be able to discuss this matter as early as next week.

However, according to the government's promise to the Knesset, no step in this direction will be taken before it is brought before the Foreign and Defense Committee, and I assume that the opposition in this committee will demand bringing the issue before the Knesset. Therefore, we must first discuss this question here and determine our position.

Our cabinet members will propose conducting direct negotiations. Whoever is sent abroad for this purpose will negotiate in the name of Israel's government. I do not assume we will receive the entire $1 billion, but the Germans agreed to negotiate on the basis of this sum. Not all of this sum, but most of it, would be transmitted directly to the State of Israel, and much of the rest, which will be given to the Jewish Agency and the Joint Distribution Committee, would be channeled to finance their activities in Israel. We must now discuss if this is to be done or not.

Yosef Sprinzak: I would just like to raise a question which stems from my fundamental opposition, right from the beginning, to conducting negotiations, directly or indirectly: is it really necessary that our party should be inscribed in history as the main force responsible for Israel entering direct negotiations with Germany? Why not let each of our Knesset members determine a position regarding this issue on an individual basis? I hope our party will not be inherently connected with the reparations issue.

Meir Dvorzhetsky:[3] I must admit that I came to this meeting as someone who mourns for his father. It seems to me that our government's proposal to enter direct negotiations with Germany is a corollary of a painful process taking place

---

2   Document no. 11, note no. 1.
3   Dr. Meir Dvorzhetsky, a Holocaust survivor who succeeded in escaping from the Vilnius Ghetto.

in our public life. While strolling on Tel Aviv's streets one sees numerous German books on sale; one notices that an exhibition of Heidegger's books was opened in Jerusalem this week; after the end of WW II Yehudi Menuhin played his violin to a German audience, not to Jewish camp survivors, and yet is welcomed in our country. I could not abide his performance here and turned off my radio. A few years ago I could see a picture of Israeli mayors sitting together with German mayors at some convention abroad, drinking coffee and smiling at each other. If I had been given a file containing Ben Gurion's speech and a pencil with the words "Made in Germany" on it when I was a delegate to our last party convention, if Israeli writers attending the last international conference of PEN were not given any material against German writers who cooperated with Hitler, if Adenauer visited London and Paris, and Jews did not demonstrate against him in the streets – then all this would not point to an atrophy in our memory of what has happened to our people.

It is not easy to say, "Do not take money!" And especially on this rainy evening when one can picture the dire straits of our new immigrants in their tent camps. That part of me which is alive says: "Hast thou killed and also taken possession?" However, there is also a part within me which was killed, and it says "Hast thou forgotten and taken possession?" Once the Bible is cited, let me remind you of another phrase regarding the Amalekites to whose king the Prophet Samuel said: "As thy sword hath made women childless, so shall thy mother be childless among women." [4] If you ask me what is my wish regarding the German people, I would say, A mother for a mother, a father for a father, a child for a child. My soul would rest in peace if it were possible to kill six million Germans for six million Jews. But if we cannot take revenge, at least we can spit in their faces for the entire world to see, in spite of all their payments, which could certainly help us. However, if we say, "Let us take the money and build our country with it," then our hands are tied.

I am already closing my eyes in an attempt to avoid seeing how an Israeli minister, or any other Israeli representative, sits together with Adenauer at the same table to sign the reparations agreement. I don't envy the Israeli. What would his feelings be at that moment?

Then, after the signing, the Germans will deceive us. They have always deceived the entire world. Within two years Adenauer would be no more, and those who will rule after him will say that they are not responsible for his doings. This is why I say with a burning heart, even though we are going to negotiate with the best of intentions, we are about to make a historic mistake. It is not in my power to convince you. My language is too poor to achieve that, but I beseech you: do not make such a mistake!

---

4   Samuel 1, 15:33.

Yona Kesse: I can sympathize with Comrade Dvorzhetsky. But I tested myself and did not discern an atrophy in my memory. I think that any dream of taking revenge against the German people is an empty dream. Worse, anybody enmeshed day and night in this kind of wishful thinking is only destroying himself by succumbing to impotent anger. We shall not take revenge against the German people. No nation has done that, including those who also suffered under them. This has nothing to do with retaining the Holocaust's memory for ever.

I would like to ask Comrade Dvorzhetsky, suppose we could have conquered Germany in WW II, would we have then slaughtered six million Germans? Would we have then slaughtered one million German children? (*An un-identified MK: Yes, precisely!*) Are we allowed to give up reparations because this involves sitting together with Germans? Would not this, historically, be one of the greatest acts of revenge ever taken by the Jewish people? For what was Hitler's plan? He wanted to uproot the entire Jewish people, but we are now sitting together with Adenauer as a people who defeated that plan.

The reparations will enable us to absorb several hundred thousand Jewish immigrants, and any strengthening of the State of Israel is an act of revenge against Hitler and against all anti-Semites.

I am in favor of conducting direct negotiations, since I do not believe that gentiles would negotiate for us. Comrade Dvorzhetsky reminded us of the Amalekites. There was some sense in the Biblical saying "Remember what Amalek did unto thee – thou shalt blot out the remembrance of Amalek from under heaven; thou shalt not forget it."[5] There was a time when the Jewish people could do that. However, nowadays we are witnessing how Diaspora Jews marry German women. And during my visit to the displaced persons' camps in Germany, I saw for myself how Jewish couples engaged German girls as nannies for their babies. This phenomenon has nothing to do with receiving reparations from Germany. As far as "Thou hast killed," we are helpless to reciprocate, but as to the second part of that phrase, "… and also taken possession," the claim of reparations will remain relevant for years to come. I would not oppose receiving the check from General McCloy, but if this is impossible, let us negotiate directly with the Bonn government.

Eliezer Lidovsky:[6] As we all know, Hitler came to power not through a revolution, but through general elections in which 40 million Germans voted for him. We all know the results of his plan regarding the Jewish people. How is it that five or six years after the end of WW II, not one representative of the German people has yet publicly admitted the guilt of the German people and offered compensation to the Jews? What has suddenly happened that prompted Adenauer to utter his solemn statement? It certainly did not come about as a result of pressure emanating from within the German people. These people have remained exactly

---

5   Deuteronomy, 25:17,19.
6   A Holocaust survivor.

the same as before. I have no faith in them, but I feel that if they pay us they will do so in order to get something back from us in return. We too shall have to pay, but once we do that we will sit together with them on numerous international bodies, and I wonder how we will be able to prevent this process.

As a Jew and as a human being I ask, what certainty is there that we will receive what they promise us? Our agreement to enter into negotiations with Germany for receiving compensation means that we compensate them. I oppose granting them this. I appeal to members of our central committee to keep off this road which the Germans expect us to take.

Melech Noy: Our debate is generally conducted on an irrational, emotional plane, which makes it difficult to advance rational arguments. Nevertheless, some logic must be taken into consideration, and logic makes it clear that avoiding direct negotiations, instead of harming the Germans, will harm us. We have been harmed enough by others; why should we harm ourselves?

We must be careful lest we fall prey to a racist approach in such matters. The Swiss, too, are a German-speaking people. Well, then, are we going to ban the German language? Such a collective approach is wrong. I cannot forget a story I was told by one of our party's delegates to a recent socialist youth congress in Scandinavia. Our group of delegates decided they would avoid contact with the German youth there. When a German girl, a member of that delegation, approached our delegates and started talking to them, they simply shunned her and she became hysterical. It was only afterwards that they learned that her Socialist father was put to death by the Nazis in a German concentration camp. The entire congress vehemently deplored the Israeli behavior.

And I ask, if we say "No" to direct negotiations, what impact would it make worldwide? Would the world experience shock, and as a result draw some negative conclusions regarding the Germans? In view of what we know, nothing of the sort will happen. Let me remind you that during the war years, when news regarding the Holocaust started trickling through, there were Jews in Palestine who turned off their radios saying they were not able to listen to reports of Nazi atrocities.

If we succeed in receiving reparations through emissaries, would this be more kosher? Would not everybody know that such negotiations were carried out on our initiative? If we evade direct negotiations, would this be considered moral by the outside world?

Reparations would serve as concrete admission by the German people of what it has done to the Jews. If the reparations agreement is implemented, it will be inscribed forever in the annals of the German people; otherwise there would be nothing to testify to the crimes of the Holocaust and inscribe it in their history.

Arieh Sheftl:[7] I would like to apologize for being unable to discuss this question of reparations unemotionally since it arouses in me numerous memories from another world. In his speech, Chancellor Adenauer said that his government is prepared to conduct negotiations with representatives of the Jewish people and the State of Israel. If the interest of the German people, six years after the Holocaust, is to conduct negotiations with the State of Israel, I say that our historic interest obliges us not to conduct direct negotiations.

There are three aspects to this question: emotional-moral, logical-judicial-political, and "is-it-bad or good-for-the-Jews?" I contend that all three end up with "it-is-bad-for-the-Jews."

Let us not deride the emotional-moral aspect, for it is this aspect which led us to the establishment of the State of Israel. Let us not be too realistic. We all know why a bride enters the marriage ceremony, but it would be obscene to spell this out. We all know why, five years after the end of the war, Germany wishes to "marry" into the United Nations. We should not act as best man at the ceremony. Germany will become a UN member anyway; nobody will consult us on this matter, but by conducting direct negotiations we will open international doors for Adenauer, we will grant him rehabilitation. I well remember how in the Vilnius Ghetto, when the temperature in winter went down to 39° below zero, when Jews died in the streets from cold and hunger, the Germans brought us clothes which had belonged to the thousands of Jews they had murdered and said: "Please, take them, put them on against the cold!" But the ghetto representatives refused to take the clothes which were soaked with their brethren's blood. I was present at that event. My friend Dvorzhetsky and several rabbis were there too. We said "No," because we knew that the Germans wanted to photograph us putting on those clothes and thus demonstrate their humane behavior to the outside world. There were Jews who rushed to get those clothes and even exchanged blows with each other while fighting over them. They were photographed and the pictures were later published in the German press. Our response to the Germans was indeed irrational. Another case of irrational behavior occurred when the war was over: people started digging out corpses of Jews from the fields of Treblinka to find gold rings. Jewish leaders appealed to the Polish government and asked that this atrocity be stopped, and indeed Treblinka was fenced around and the gold remained buried in the ground. That was an irrational step, but a moral one.

As to the judicial aspect, let me remind you that neither the Russians nor the Americans conducted negotiations with the Germans regarding compensation. They came as victors and took away assets as well as scientists. Should only Jews negotiate compensation with the Germans as equals? The same as the Arabs refuse to negotiate with us regarding compensation for their refugees, so should we not sit together with the Germans. After WW I, because of the annexation of Vilnius by Poland, tiny Lithuania refused to have any contact with Poland for

---

7   A Holocaust survivor who succeeded in escaping from the Vilnius Ghetto.

20 years – and the Jewish people are prepared to receive the money due it only by direct negotiations? Why not let others conduct such negotiations for us? Let a Shabbos Goy do it.

A Russian proverb says: "The wolf is not afraid of the dog, but it does not want to be barked at." Nothing can prevent the historic process of the German people returning into the family of nations, but they don't want us to bark.

The Germans deceived the world after WW I and deceived again during WW II. They contended that if they would be compelled to pay compensation, this would pave the road for a Bolshevik triumph in Germany. We can sign agreements with them too, but tomorrow they will cease paying, contending that if they continue compensating us, Germany would be impoverished and as a result become a Communist country. Whatever happens in our stormy world within the next year or two, we should not give the Germans a kosher certificate which at the same time would constitute testifying to our failure. Should our party be instrumental in obtaining this document? Better remain a Shylock than become Judah Iscariot, for we were slaughtered and annihilated as Shylocks, not as Judah Iscariots.

Eliyahu Dobkin: I fail to understand how waiving our demand for money plundered from our people by the Germans can be interpreted as taking revenge on them. It is Jewish money, not German. What revenge is there in giving it up? Opposing direct negotiations is, in fact, opposing receiving compensation, for we will not find a Shabbos Goy to negotiate on our behalf. Nobody but us cares about the plundered Jewish money.

How is it that there are people among us who started debating the issue of direct negotiations only at this late stage? The truth is that we have been negotiating directly with the Germans for the last three years, although about smaller sums. An Israeli consul resides in Munich. A representative of our ministry of finance functions in Germany. Two Jewish Agency representatives have been negotiating in Germany for two years now – they have already received money from four regional states, $5 million from one, $6-7 million from another; and they are about to receive $12 million from the State of Essen. How come that now, when the sum claimed is $1.5 billion, the principle of direct negotiations is suddenly contested?

Meir Argov: I do not dare judge any Jew who experienced life in the ghettos of Poland. But I do claim the same right as our Comrades Dvorzhetsky and Sheftl to pronounce my views. I too was bereaved: all the members of my family were murdered. Nobody here can claim a greater right in this debate.

Eighteen years ago a similar debate took place inside the Yishuv of Palestine. Comrades Dvorzhetsky and Sheftl were not living here when Haim Arlosoroff,[8] head of the Jewish Agency's Political Department, was dubbed as the main "traitor" for concluding an agreement with the Nazis regarding the transfer of property of German Jews to Palestine. Undoubtedly, we shall soon be tarnished as "traitors" for the reparations agreement.

As far as I know, we are presently witnessing the first instance in our people's history when Jews are able to react to slaughters not only by angrily grinding our teeth, or by saying prayers around graves, but by claiming restitution of plundered Jewish property. The Russians claimed compensation, as did the Americans, the British and the French – are we to remain the only people avoiding what is due us?

If reparations from Germany were conditional upon our establishing diplomatic relations with the Federal Republic of Germany, the opponents would have had a case, but this is not so.

The State of Israel faces constant dangers. It must prepare for war. The reparations will enable us to purchase arms to defend ourselves – why is this not justified? Why should direct talks be forbidden? We shall sit face-to-face as victors with the Germans, posing an ultimatum. Why should this act be seen as humiliating when it demonstrates Jewish pride?

In view of the seriousness of the issue, our party's Knesset members should not vote individually, each according to his conscience, when the Knesset discusses the question of direct negotiations. They should vote according to the decision that we make here at the end of our discussion. We must act as a party, not as group of individuals.

Haim Yahil: Individual Jews have been receiving money for years now, thanks to German laws allowing restitution of their property in Germany, and individual compensation has been paid to German Jews for three years, all as a result of insistent pressure exerted by German-Jewish organizations, supported by organizations of the State of Israel, aided legally in Germany by the representatives of the Jewish Agency and the Joint Distribution Committee. The only voice

8   Haim Arlosoroff (1899-1933). Born in the Ukraine and grew up in Germany. Immigrated to Palestine in 1921. An important leader of the Zionist labor movement. Member of Mapai. Headed the political department of the Jewish Agency in Jerusalem from 1931. Concluded an agreement with Nazi authorities in 1933 permitting German-Jewish emigrants to Palestine to sell their property and transfer its worth in goods to Palestine. The Transfer Agreement was fiercely attacked by right-wing parties throughout the Jewish world as a desecration of the honor of the Jewish people. When Arlosoroff was mysteriously murdered in Tel Aviv in June 1933, it was believed by many, especially by members of the left-wing parties, that he was assassinated by extremist members of the right-wing Revisionist Party, then headed by Ze'ev Jabotinsky. The murderers remain unknown to this day.

heard against taking any individual compensation was that of the poet Leivick Halpern. His opinion was rejected. Why then waive general reparations to the Jewish people? What positive results can be achieved by a policy of rejection?

I reject the comparison made here by Comrade Sheftl between the refusal of Jews from the Vilnius Ghetto to accept clothing from their murdered brethren and their refusal to receive reparations. The lives of the Jews in Vilnius were in the hands of German murderers. They were liable to be put to death at any moment. They were forced into a most humiliating situation and proudly refused to put on those clothes. The State of Israel is indeed a small country in comparison with Germany. But it is an independent entity. Its existence is not conditional on any outside power. It is equal to Germany in stature.

I do not believe we are psychologically capable of taking revenge. No revenge proportional to what has been done to us is possible at all. I was in post-war Germany. I felt guilty for refusing to give alms to a starving German boy. We cannot take this road. Our only historical revenge is to be found in the survival of our people and in the establishment of a sovereign Jewish entity after the Holocaust. Our revenge lies in our very existence, not in the fact that German compensation is paid to Jews as individuals but in the fact that representatives of the German government, of the people that tried to destroy the Jewish people, will have to sit at the same table with representatives of the state of the Jewish people. Historically, there can be no revenge greater than that. What a triumph it will be when Germany signs a formal agreement, reached by negotiations, not by force, to pay reparations to the Jewish people!

But it seems to me that another historical revenge is also possible. It must be hoped that it will be attained when, at some time in the future, a German generation arises that will be appalled by the evil deeds perpetrated by its ancestors.

I doubt the wisdom of labeling all Germans as Nazis, including those who truly wish to atone for Nazi crimes and correct whatever can be corrected. By sitting together with Germans for the purpose of attaining reparations, we are not losing our dignity. We are erecting a statue testifying to our national honor and to the evils of Nazism.

Binyamin West: I think the claim of reparations is justified, but I am afraid we were tardy and missed the appropriate moment for submitting the claim. Had we done so three years ago, we could have been part of the victorious allies. Now we are facing the danger of attaining nothing and at the same time defiling ourselves. Meanwhile, we have been witnessing a revival of Nazism. In our neighborhood Germans are participating in organizing the Arabs against us. German ex-officers, technicians and engineers are active in the countries around us. We should not ignore these facts while debating the issue of reparations.

We shall certainly not leave the UN because of Germany's membership. But direct negotiations with Germany when results are rather doubtful, while German professionals are helping Arab armies re-organize, is a totally different question.

In view of such an uneasy situation, I think it is better that reparations are negotiated by a Shabbos Goy, and if such an emissary is not found, let us waive this claim altogether.

Pinhas Lavon: With all due respect to individual experience, in the name of which Comrade Sheftl or others are debating, the matter we are dealing with should be discussed at the national-historical level, not the individual one, and, if so, we must avoid becoming intoxicated by hollow expressions. I am afraid that this Jewish talent of becoming intoxicated by words has survived and is still in evidence here. The word "revenge" is fraught with significance when it is not hollow. Otherwise it is just a slogan. Had we been faced with two alternatives: annihilating 40 million Germans or accepting reparations, I think I would have preferred annihilation. However, this choice is nonexistent today and shall be for generations to come. "Revenge" is a meaningless word at present. It is devoid of any substance, morally as well as practically.

The words "national honor" also need some analysis. My dear friends Dvorzhetsky and Sheftel, WW II was not the first time Jews as well as others were slaughtered. Fifty years ago the Armenian people was slaughtered, and their blood was as dear to that nation as Jewish blood is dear to us. But why go back to past history? We are enjoying good relationships with Poland, Hungary and Czechoslovakia. Poland has enriched itself on the corpses of over three million Jews; it thrives on the assets accumulated by slaughtered Jews. Poland maintains a consulate in Tel Aviv, and I guess there is also an Israel-Poland Friendship Association. Nobody contends that our national honor is harmed by this. Jews were slaughtered everywhere, time and time again, and not even one murderous people saw fit to sit down with our people and offer compensation. Moreover, Russia, Poland and Czechoslovakia received reparations on account of the murdered six million Jews who were their citizens. What was the Jewish people's share in those reparations?

My friends Dvorzhetsky and Sheftl, I permit myself to admit that my emotional reaction is opposite to yours. It is the first instance in history that our people's spilled blood is not being entirely ignored. This is a revolutionary change, never witnessed before in our past. Surely, Adenauer is guided by political interests as well, but for heaven's sake, what is the basis of international life. Pure moral precepts? The very fact that a people numbering 80 million, a people all other nations are now courting and seeking in friendship, feels an obligation to atone in some measure for its crimes, is this not a revolutionary change? Moreover, is this change accidental? No, for evidently it came about since a concrete Jewish revenge has been partially attained by the establishment of the

State of Israel. Had there been only Jewish communities around the globe, the question of reparations would not have arisen. It arose only because, in addition to the survival of our people, we have succeeded in creating a totally new national entity – a state. It was this revolutionary change which has brought about the historical revolutionary change of Germany's willingness to pay us reparations.

I wonder what is considered national honor or national dishonor. Was there more national honor in the times of the Spanish Inquisition? Is there more national honor in a Jew leaving Poland with only two suitcases in his hands? Where is dishonor in the fact that our people have overcome the attempt to kill them off and compelled the Germans to find a way of atoning for its wrongdoing? Is this not honoring us?

Had our people found themselves today in the same situation as in 1930 or in 1800 or in 1600, when no atonement was sought and no national representation of our people existed, we would have been looked upon by all as a miserable and unwanted nation. The picture of the clothing episode in the Vilnius Ghetto, described here by Comrade Sheftl, is the very opposite to our situation now. That terrifying story is an often-repeated episode in Jewish history, while the matter we are dealing with now embodies the revolutionary change which has taken place in our history.

I think the people of Israel and the State of Israel are entitled to conduct these negotiations for German reparations with full pride and self-assurance, and with no feelings of our national honor being harmed. The revolution that has taken place in our national life obliges our comrades who survived the Holocaust to overcome that experience and discuss the issue at hand from a national-historical standpoint.

David Ben Gurion: I would like to say to our two comrades, Dvorzhetsky and Sheftl, that I share their pain, not their emotion. I categorically reject their emotion, because I do not want to go back to the ghetto and to its fraught emotions. Our accounting is that of an independent people which must invest much work to maintain and build up its independence.

The main debate is between two attitudes: that of ghetto Jews and that of citizens of an independent people. I do not want to run after a German and spit on him. I have no interest in running after anybody. My interest is to stay where I am and build my home. I will not go to America in order to demonstrate against Adenauer. I will go there for the purpose of advancing Israel's interests. I will not ostracize Germans because by doing so we ostracize ourselves. We shall not cease mailing letters abroad because Germans are part of the international mailing system, for we are not living in a ghetto but in our state – and a state cannot do without mail.

Instead of sitting together with Adenauer, can we send 100 divisions to Germany and tell our soldiers: "Take!?" No. But even if we could, I would do so first of all in Iraq – but that, too, is impossible. We cannot do everything. Even the Russians and Americans cannot.

A state endeavors to strengthen its wellbeing, its security, its economy. It does not occupy itself with spitting at somebody. Citing the Biblical phrase "Thou shalt blot out the remembrance of Amalek from under heaven" is senseless. For if the Amalekite people survived and established universities, Jews would have gone to study in those universities. How can a modern state pursue a policy according to such senseless phrases?

I see no national honor in demonstrative spitting. I see national honor in the existence of the State of Israel. I see national honor in taking out 50,000 Jews from the dark and horrible Diaspora of Yemen. That is national honor! I despise finding honor in spitting and demonstrating. When we lived downtrodden in ghettos, we found solace in spitting at non-Jews, but not directly at their faces. We did it behind the closed doors of our homes. I reject this kind of national honor. I ran away from it when I was nineteen-years-old and went to Palestine, and you shall not take me back there.

We shall not isolate ourselves from the outside world, and this world includes the German people with its Nazis and murderers and hangmen and the ghettos they established. And we cannot leave this world. We will be sitting together with Germans in the International Communication Agency. We will be sitting together with them when they become members of the UN and of the International Labor Organization, because we are living on Earth – but we will do this as a free people. When it is necessary, at the right time, we will say to the Germans what we think about their deeds, but I wonder whether we should repeat it day and night, for if we do, it will lose its impact and the world – including Diaspora Jews – would become fed up with us. Let us leave this to a new Jeremiah, if ever he appears.

The reparations are owed to us. True, reparations were due to us before – they were due 20 years ago after the pogroms in the Ukraine, they were due after the massacres of Khmelnitzky and of the Crusades, but nobody paid attention to us. Now for the first time we may possibly receive what is due, although perhaps not all. These sums are due to us and we must take them. Were I able to take them directly without sitting with Germans for even one minute, but just by entering Germany with jeeps and machine guns, I would have done so, but since that is impossible, I will accomplish this in a saner way. For this property is ours. Why give it up?

Those who oppose receiving reparations for political reasons are doing so with the purpose of enfeebling the government, but the end result will be the enfeeblement of the state. They do not care if the state is harmed as long as the government is weakened. Our party members who oppose reparations must be aware in what company they find themselves – they are walking hand-in-hand with Herut on the Right and with the Communists on the Left.

People who live inside a ghetto are living outside reality. They live in the realm of the "End of Days," thus consoling themselves that while the gentiles are enjoying their states and power, a day will come when the Messiah appears – when all gentiles lie dead and we shall inherit. We have been toying with this faith for 2,000 years, and perhaps it helped us survive. But now, as a state, we must live in this very concrete world. Comrade Dvorzhetsky has no right to give up the possibility of Israel absorbing hundreds of thousand of Iraqi and Rumanian Jews. An individual Jew can waive what is due him personally; he cannot waive what is due to the Jewish people. He has no right to waive it even if our present economic situation were stable – and it is not – for we must look forward to bringing more Jews to our country. Moreover, our situation is not so cheerful. Tomorrow we might be slaughtered here. We do not want what has happened in Europe to be repeated. We do not want the Nazis and Arabs to come and slaughter us, and spitting at the face of any German will not guarantee our security; it will not suffice to prevent such an eventuality. In order for this not to happen to Comrade Sheftl and my children, we must acquire guns, and no proud gesture of waiving what is due to us will fulfill our needs. The Jewish people cannot waive this debt. Herut and the Communists can, for they – and those toeing their line – do not share in shouldering the burden of securing our existence.

We are facing a decisive Knesset vote on the right of the Jewish people to demand what is due to it. Our party's Knesset members do not represent themselves alone. They are emissaries of our movement. They have no right to enfeeble the Jewish people, to enfeeble the state, to enfeeble this government.

Meir Mandel: Our people have survived for 2,000 years in exile by clinging to the religious and spiritual values which it has in abundance. Indeed, being stateless left it no other alternative. This situation has dramatically changed before our eyes. It was a positive change, for we have achieved sovereignty. But it was also a negative change, for we have no more traditional and religious values which bind us all and guarantee our people's continued existence. We can continue existing only if we succeed in maintaining the new state's framework, but this framework might fall apart if concrete resources, not miracles, are not available to guarantee the well-being and the security of those living here as well as of those who are expected to come and join us tomorrow. In view of all this I am convinced that our party and our government must decide to receive reparations by any possible means.

Ben-Zion Dinur: There are three aspects to the issue at hand: moral, national and political. As to the moral question, I fail to understand the contention that direct negotiations with Germans are an immoral act. If someone murdered my parents, if I am one of those whose whole family was destroyed and its property looted, why can't I claim back my property and take it from the murderer's hands?

Why should I not indict him? Isn't avoiding this claim immoral? Morally, is one allowed to let the murderer get away with the property of those he murdered? Of course, there can be a harsher punishment for the murderer, the biblical punishment "Thou shalt blot the remembrance of Amalek from under heaven." However, we know that this was not attained even in those times, to say nothing of the present.

The Germans admitted their crime. They openly agreed to pay reparations. The question at hand is not our demand for reparations or not but determining their dimensions.

Now, as to the national aspect, we should be aware that Jews always wanted compensation after they had been plundered; however, they did not dare to demand it. It was only in the 19th century that in some cases they appealed to the courts of justice with such demands, but only rarely were they satisfied. And they never demanded compensation from governments. To those opposing direct negotiations on the grounds of national honor, I would like to mention a book written by a Jew sometime after the 1788 pogrom in the Ukrainian city of Uman, in which he wrote: "Lost was Israel's honor. We are worse than cows. When a cow is driven to the place of its slaughter, it is mooing, but what are we doing? We are returning to the very places where our blood was spilled. Would a cow do that?" Is that honorable?

The very fact that there are Jews residing today in Germany is indeed dishonorable. But is demanding compensation from the Germans dishonorable? On the contrary, if we give up, if we waive demanding it – that would be dishonorable, a national sin. Can others harm us and not pay? Is there no justice and no judge?

Politically, we should realize that if we do not demand compensation, the gentiles would not think that we have waived it because we felt it would be a dishonorable act on our part. No, they would say that our minds are set only on taking bloody revenge. What would German Christians who opposed Nazi evildoing think in the face of our refusal to take compensation? They would say that this testifies to our refusal to make peace. Demonstrating our refusal to take compensation will merely enhance hating, us not only in Germany, but in other countries as well. It is incumbent on us at present, when we are engaged in building our country, to avoid provoking hatred and enmity towards us. Let us, at this juncture, strengthen ourselves by receiving as much compensation as we can.

Kalman Schwartz: I am in favor not only of conducting direct negotiations; I do not see any possibility of for long evading the establishment of diplomatic relations with Germany. (*Meir Dvorzhetsky: A German ambassador will be stationed here and would not be murdered?*) Comrade Dvorzhetsky, my veins, too, are not filled with ice water. I shudder too, remembering what had been done to my own family. Let us not compete with emotions. I reject forgiveness. I reject forgetting,

I reject atoning – nothing can purify a monster. Hitler's years shall be forever inscribed in our people's history. But I say: history's court of justice apart, and the flow of life apart; nobody has the right to demand ostracizing the Germans in the name of the dead who were murdered by Hitler – this is nothing but irrational spiritualism.

I would like to ask, why stop at ostracizing Germans? Were not the Ukrainians active in the massacre of Jews in occupied Poland and the Ukraine? What about the Lithuanians and Latvians; it is well known that they more than readily murdered Jews at the service of the Nazis? Why was Poland selected to be the extermination's arena? What about the French who participated in hunting Jews? I dare say here – I know it might compromise me – that there are no good and bad peoples. The behavior of any people is molded by its leadership; each generation toes the line of its leaders. Few were the communists in pre-war Poland; now Poland is full of Communists, and the same goes for Czechoslovakians, Bulgarians, Romanians and Albanians.

Undoubtedly, it would have been a good thing had we been able to prevent or postpone Germany's acceptance into the family of nations, but just as we cannot rule wind or rain, so we cannot dictate the future of Germany. It will not be long before it is accepted. Those among us who think in terms of angrily ignoring Germany, those who would jump at any opportunity to curse Germany, should not nurse any illusions that this kind of attitude on our part will be one-sided, that Germany will accept such a behavior openheartedly. Anger and hatred will breed anger and hatred. Whoever is not living in an ivory tower surely realizes who is going to win more international influence if we compete with Germany – a most powerful country numbering 80 million – in the field of hatred.

Yosef Sprinzak: I would like to make it clear, in view of ideas about revenge and ostracizing Germans advanced by opponents of reparations, that I reject both revenge and ostracizing. I would have no qualms sitting with Adenauer in any international organization. However, I am against receiving money for anything related to the six million. For generations our people have maintained the oath of Spanish Jews expelled from Spain, never to return there. Maybe that was only a myth, but nevertheless it became a cherished national symbol. If we receive reparations, if we accept money related to the six million, we shall forfeit our historical account with Germany, and I am thinking not only in terms of today's State of Israel, but in terms of our generations to come. I do not want it inscribed in the annals of our people that we took compensation from Germany, the same as I reject the Bible's instruction that whoever rapes a girl must pay compensation to her father. I think that is morally absurd.

Herzl Berger: While it is quite easy to argue the reparations issue with the opponents of the Right as well as of the Left, it is not quite so with opponents such as Comrades Dvorzhetsky and Sheftel. Still, as I see it, theirs is a battle of retreat. Why indeed? Because if you examine the world's present situation, you will realize that our initiative to isolate Germany has already been defeated. As a rule, in any international meeting in which Germans take part, we protest against their presence, and justly so, but then they are formally accepted, and we continue our membership only to repeat this cycle over and over again. Consequently, our repeated failures, unaccompanied by leaving any such organization, can only be interpreted as succumbing, and so it is time to ask what we are gaining by such inevitable failures. I think this fight of ours is a battle of retreat not only on the international level but for the Jewish people as well.

A test case is perhaps the pencil made in Germany, mentioned here before by Comrade Dvorzhetsky. That pencil might have been imported by an Israeli kibbutz whose members received individual compensation in Germany and purchased it with that money they realized. Or perhaps they were brought in by a recent immigrant who realized property in Germany. That immigrant may participate tomorrow in a street demonstration against the state receiving reparations, but that demonstration will only prove that we are witnessing a battle of retreat.

But there is still more to it. In the aftermath of WW II we witnessed a new historic phenomenon: for a few centuries now, unlike in ancient times when victors used to kill off the leaders of their vanquished enemies, the vanquished were made to pay compensation. However, after the last war, leaders of Nazi Germany were sentenced to death at the Nüremberg trials. Our demand for reparations, and its acceptance by the German government, has introduced a new international principle. From now on, any state that goes to war will have to take into consideration that afterwards it would be compelled to pay compensation for atrocities perpetrated during the war it initiated. This precedent enhances the security of Jews all over the world, and certainly our state's security.

Beba Idelson: I think we should be careful to avoid the kind of scorn shown in Ben Gurion's speech. In principle I am in total agreement with Ben Gurion though his style hurt me deeply.

I detest all talk about taking physical revenge, as if this were a concrete possibility. Why is this necessary at all? I hope we will never need to carry out such atrocious actions as those inflicted on us. While I do not see eye-to-eye with those among us who contend that "not every German is evil," and I do not try to locate good Germans within the German people, I nurse no intention of hating them. What good can result from that? It is a well-known fact that in our midst there are hundreds of German women, married to our comrades. They are all mothers of Jewish children in this country, and we have never castigated them. It has come about and we have fully accepted this fact.

We are fully entitled to demand the worth of Jewish property plundered by the Germans. Consequently, those who nurtured the idea that somebody else would claim reparations for us were mistaken. Neither gentiles nor Jews of other countries should demand reparations. Israeli citizens, our government representatives, members of our party, should do that. Who else but our party should shoulder that burden? What other party shoulders the ingathering of the exiles but ours? Our members who will negotiate for reparations perform a holy task, though I do not envy them. We must take on full responsibility in this sphere and prepare ourselves for carrying out a campaign aimed at convincing the public of the righteousness of accepting reparations.

Dov Lipov: My position regarding reparations is negative. The reparations issue and taking revenge against Germany are two separate things. Had the Jewish Brigade been stationed in Germany, its soldiers would certainly have taken revenge; however the revenge issue is not relevant. Taking compensation is not an act of revenge. We would better stay out of the question of revenge and concentrate on the issues of Jewish national honor and of our people's historical memory.

There are several deep-rooted biblical phrases pertinent to our present situation, although Ben Gurion invalidates them. One of them relates to "…avenging of the blood of thy servants which is shed."[9] Another is the instruction: "Thou shalt blot out the remembrance of Amalek from under heaven; thou shalt not forget it." Such phrases are not meant to be taken literally. They are fraught with symbolic significance, and I am of the opinion that we should not invalidate such symbols just because we are a weak people, incapable of taking revenge by firing guns.

True, Germans nowadays are being morally rehabilitated by the world at large, but should we, a weak people, take part in this process? A German statesman said after WW I: "Before the war we organized our victory. After it we organized sympathy from the world." They did the same to us – first they organized the slaughter, afterwards they organized the sympathy. Let us not reduce the prophet's injunction: "Hast thou killed and also taken possession?" to the framework of diplomatic negotiations, for the prophet meant it to be a moral one. If there are good Germans, let them be ashamed, just as we are ashamed of what took place in Deir Yassin[10] even though there is no comparison between the two occurrences.

The contention that we should demand reparations because we achieved statehood is absurd. Let us not succumb to a "state complex." Jewish national honor and Jewish historical memory oblige us to refuse reparations – one cannot compare it with the "transfer" of the early 30s since that was before the Holocaust. At the time the Nazis only took money, not six million lives. Money and blood do not belong together. There is no place for peace and quiet on our part; we

---

9   Psalms, 79:10.
10 On April 9, 1948, units of the Irgun and the Stern Gang stormed the Arab village of Deir Yassin in the vicinity of Jerusalem and massacred some 120 of its inhabitants.

should see to it that the experience of the Holocaust strikes deep roots in the nation's historical memory. I think this will strengthen us more than money will. That our blood is not worthless could be proved only by physical revenge, by a blood-for-blood attitude. A money-for-blood attitude will not prove our blood is not worthless. We were told here that we need guns. I think we cannot accept guns in return for people's lives. Such an attitude will not enhance our morals; it will undermine the morals of our youth. One should not accuse opponents of reparations with harboring a ghetto mentality. Our comrades who fought the Germans in the ghettos were demonstrating political awareness by their fighting; otherwise they would have passively let themselves be massacred.

We all know that our situation is difficult and that our protests have no effect, but that does not mean that we should stop protesting. If we protest tomorrow against the internationalization of Jerusalem but to no avail, would we stop protesting? Sometimes protesting is a formidable moral weapon. Sometimes even the most irrational actions are in fact rational because they testify to resolve.

I propose that our party oppose reparations. The fact that the Israeli Communists oppose it does not make me one of them. They have their own reasons, I have mine.

Golda Meir: Four principles guide my approach to the reparations question. First and foremost, I would like to state that I hold a racist view: as far as I am concerned, all Germans are *a priori* Nazis; only later will I be prepared to find out whether this or that individual German is pure. I was not at all shocked on hearing the story of that German girl. I presume that she is a good person and that her father was pure, but what can I do when there is no room in my heart for being impressed by the hysterical German girl shunned by Israeli youth after all that has happened to our people? What about the hundreds of thousands of Jewish girls who perished in the Holocaust?

I remember meeting with Kurt Schumacher[11] during a socialist conference in Zurich in 1947. He appealed there for the acceptance of the German Social-Democratic Party into the post-war Socialist International, and made a great speech, full of pathos, in which he attempted to convince his listeners that not only members of the Socialist Party in pre-war Germany, but also all its present members were pure and innocent Germans. However, in all that long speech he did not devote one word to what happened to Jews at the hands of Germans. Luckily, the German SDP was not accepted into the Socialist International at that conference, thanks to our vote against, in spite of the pleading of the British, the French and the Belgians. Had we abstained, the Germans would have become members. Later Schumacher had the nerve to approach us and ask why we did

---

11   Kurt Schumacher (1895-1953) was first chairman of German SPD after WW II, member of the Reichstag 1930-1933. He was detained in a concentration camp from 1933 till the end of the war.

that to him. And I had to tell him – that innocent Social Democrat – that it was only because of his speech in which he forgot to mention all those Nazi crimes. No, I am not yet prepared to divide the Germans into "good" and "bad." As far as I am concerned, they are all one and the same. There were a few exceptional people amongst them, but I prefer mistakenly blaming a good German than to contend the opposite.

I think we have sinned much by not inculcating our youth with the history of German crimes against our people. I am afraid that there are numerous young Israelis whose knowledge about Germany is lacking because we have neglected teaching them. There is no reason to be ashamed of holding a racist attitude towards Germans. Not yet.

Second, I ask, since when has our labor movement and, in fact, the Zionist movement of which we are part, raised the flag of rationality? If we were rational, we would not be here today. Whatever we have achieved was attained by efforts seen by the wise and clever as irrational.

Third, "I feel as if I were there" is not tantamount to "I was there." One could say about all of us who were in Palestine during the years of the Holocaust that we felt "as if we were there," but nevertheless we were not. There is no comparison.

Fourth, much has been spoken here regarding national honor, but in my eyes this question is quite simple. We have always examined any Socialist Party abroad according to its attitude towards Zionism, towards the revolutionary struggle of the Jewish people for independence. A similar criterion should guide us in the matter of national honor, and it is this: there can be no Jewish national honor without the State of Israel. Jewish national honor everywhere around the globe would rise or fall in view of the existence or non-existence of the State of Israel. Look at American Jewry, numbering millions: it is a rich community, wielding great political influence; it has at its disposal everything one can wish for. Objectively, however, this community is devoid of Jewish national honor, and enjoys it only a result of some connection with our tiny state. Woe to the great American Jewish community if there were no State of Israel. National Jewish honor is not something abstract; it is a concrete matter, directly connected to a concrete geographical area – the State of Israel – and to its solid standing.

As to the reparations issue we are discussing, I must admit I attach no importance to what the outside world, what the gentiles, say. As I see it, there are two important things here, and I would like to mention them in the simplest way possible: we cannot debate the issue as if it were just a theoretical or moral one. We would deceive ourselves if we did. We are debating the issue on the certain, firm background from which we cannot extricate ourselves, and I mean the task of building this state which we are shouldering in the present complex situation. We cannot ignore the real considerations of our survival, and therefore we must ask ourselves straightforwardly: is the step we are about to take so wrong that we should avoid taking it, thus endangering progress in building up the country?

I think perhaps we suspect each other of not divulging the true severity of our state's problems. In view of our situation, I see the moral argument against receiving reparations as definitely wrong. I must ask myself: Hitler slaughtered six million Jews; have I a moral right to endanger even one more Jew? Let me remind you that the Jewish Agency's spokesman revealed this very day that it has curtailed immigration because of a lack of resources. Who amongst us is prepared to shoulder responsibility for deciding which of the Jewish communities threatened at present is to be rescued immediately and which is not? Surely, the Jewish Agency's executive took its tough decision not because it is anti-Zionist. It simply ran out of money.

Am I allowed, is any one of you allowed to give up the needed funds? Consequently, I can say that the people that slaughtered six million Jews owe me the opportunity to rescue every Jew who can be rescued. Germany owes me that. It is not a matter of mercy. It is a debt.

At the same time I have two fears. I fear that if we succeed in our negotiations with the Germans, our achievement might lead to forgiveness and forgetting. Therefore we must repeat day and night to our people that the reparations we are receiving come from the hands of murderers.

But there is another, deeper fear, and it pertains to the atmosphere of the negotiations. I fear that in order to facilitate negotiations we will employ over-agile, over-talented men. Such people frighten me to death. We should select for this delicate and complicated matter people who can guarantee that while coming into contact with unclean people, their integrity and dignity will remain intact. I cannot imagine that our representatives in the negotiations would shake hands with their counterparts and converse with them freely, for they are not being sent to a friendly party; they are going to represent a people of which one-third were slaughtered.

We must take money from wherever we can. We are now going to take it from very dangerous places, but while anxiously doing so in order to reinforce our state, we should be aware that we are collecting a detestable, repelling debt. It is a debt which must be paid. In view of our situation, not only should we not waive it; it would be a sin to waive it. And I say that this consideration suffices. There is no need to look for good people among the Germans. I have no need of any humanitarian philosophizing regarding Germans. I would very much like to warn the comrades who will represent us in the negotiations not to act in a spirit of enthusiasm which might distort the entire matter.

Peretz Naftali: I feel a moral obligation to pronounce my opinion. I will not touch now upon financial aspects, especially since my naïve confidence in the financial results of the negotiations is not great. I am speaking now of emotions. It seems to me that I need not emphasize here my family's account with Germany which is at least no smaller than that of anybody else. Nevertheless, I want to receive from Germany whatever is possible for the Jewish people and the State of Israel. But there is one thing I reject receiving, and that is Hitler's heritage, Hitler's doctrine, Hitler's racist ideology.

I must confess I was deeply hurt on hearing comrades say here that their ideal is the extermination of six million Germans – indeed, why not 40 million of them? What is the meaning of these words? They mean that while debating the issue of reparations we have adopted Hitler's racist doctrine.

If I say that all Germans are murderers and that I cannot shake hands with any German – to my mind, this is nothing but the embodiment of the racist doctrine. I would like to state here that there are quite a few Germans with whom I would willingly shake hands.

Let me cite an example, a certain gentile, thanks to whose willingness to risk his life I am sitting here among you. He resides in America, but he is German. There are others like him. It was said here that convening Israeli and German mayors together is a calamity. I am not acquainted with all the present German mayors; I happen to be acquainted with two: one is Ernest Reuter of Berlin who was incarcerated in a concentration camp, as was I. He was rescued by the British and then resided in Turkey until Hitler's suicide. He escaped from Hitler; he had to run away exactly like Jews had to. Should he be ostracized for that? The other is Max Brauer, a great friend of our state who is now Mayor of Hamburg. He escaped to America and worked there constantly against the Nazis until their final defeat.

Now let me say a few words regarding Kurt Schumacher who spent 18 years in a Nazi concentration camp and before that was a staunch warrior against the Nazis. It seems now I should approach him and say: "In the meantime I have accepted Hitler's doctorine. I cannot shake hands with you because you were incarcerated in a concentration camp of that accursed race…" I think this attitude is neither moral nor socialist.

I agree with Golda Meir that we must not ignore emotions. But human emotions may evolve along different lines, and I am of the opinion that we must see to it that emotions within our camp do not evolve along the lines of a racist doctrine but along those of socialism.

Chairman Meir Argov: We shall now take a vote on the question of entering into direct negotiations with the German government regarding reparations. Eligible for voting are members of the central committee, our party's Knesset faction and the Secretariat of our party's branches abroad.

The vote:
For entering direct negotiations: 42
Against: 6.

[14] The Israeli Claim is Accepted as a Basis for Negotiation

Cabinet Meeting, 16.12.1951

Prime Minister David Ben Gurion: I have two matters to announce, both of which are particularly confidential. One is, in my opinion, positive, the other extremely negative.[1]

The first matter regards reparations from Germany. You have been informed that the Chairman of the Jewish Agency executive, Dr. Nahum Goldmann, met with General McCloy in Paris. He discussed with him the matter of encouraging the German government to pay reparations to the Jewish people and the State of Israel. Following Sharett's conversation with Acheson, who expressed a negative attitude towards the reparations claim,[2] McCloy did not voice a negative attitude but promised to speak to the West German chancellor at the earliest opportunity regarding this matter. On December 6 Adenauer wrote to Nahum Goldmann regarding our reparations claim and concluded his letter by stating that the claim submitted by the government of Israel can serve as a basis for negotiation.

As we have been informed, Adenauer has not yet brought this to the attention of his cabinet. He will do so only this week, and therefore I ask all members of the cabinet to keep this matter confidential so that the German cabinet does not find out about it from the press. Once we know that Adenauer has informed his cabinet of this matter, we shall bring it to the Knesset Foreign Affairs and Defense Committee. We shall propose that the government enter negotiations with Germany on reparations. (*Minister Moshe Shapira: I would suggest convening a meeting of the coalition at which you should announce this matter.*) I am prepared to announce to the Knesset Committee and to the Knesset that we propose entering

---

1   "Extremely negative" matter was the American administration's request to Israel to dispatch a military force to South Korea.

2   Foreign Minister Moshe Sharett met with Secretary of State Dean Acheson in Paris on November 19, 1951 during the UN General Assembly meeting held there. The matter of reparations was the last one to be raised by Sharett in this conversation, and the same day he summarized it in a detailed report written in English (see Documents of Israel's Foreign Policy, Vol. 6, pp. 818-819).

negotiations with Adenauer on the Jewish people's claim, but we, of course, must first decide on this.

Minister Sharett will be with us next Sunday [30.12.1951]. He is leaving Paris on Saturday evening for the recess of the UN Assembly. We shall postpone the discussion until Minister Sharett's return.

[15] Negotiations Immediately –
The Opportunity Must Not Be Missed
Cabinet Meeting, 31.12.1951

Minister Moshe Sharett: With regard to reparations, the prime minister has already reported on the situation in one of our past meetings: (a) We have an agreement with the other side to publicly announce that the Bonn government has approached us and proposed negotiations; (b) it states that it accepts the claim formulated in our note to the occupying powers as a basis for negotiations.

We can now publicly announce these two statements. You are aware of Adenauer's letter.[1] The Germans request that it not be made public. Incidentally, one of their biggest problems at present is that they are under pressure from the United States, England and France to introduce sums for payment to the occupying powers into their budget. The talk is about 13 billion marks needed for financing Germany's participation in the defense of the West. They are apparently

---

1   Moshe Sharett is relating to Chancellor's Adenauer's letter from December 6, 1951, to Dr. Nahum Goldmann:

Dear Dr. Goldmann,

In connection with the declaration of the Federal Government in the Bundestag on 27.9.1951, in which I announced its readiness to open negotiations with representatives of the Jewish people and the State of Israel regarding compensation for the damage invoked in the days of the Nazi regime, I want to inform you that the Federal Government is of the opinion that the time has arrived to start these negotiations. I would like to ask you, in your capacity as Chairman of the Jewish Conference of Claims from Germany, to inform this to the Conference and to the government of Israel. I would like to state that the Federal Government views the compensation problem, first and foremost, as a moral duty and deems it that the honor of the German people obliges it to do whatever is possible to amend the wrongs done to the Jewish people. The Federal Government will pursue a positive attitude in this context towards the possibility of contributing to the buttressing of the State of Israel through transfer of goods. The Federal Government is prepared to accept the claims formulated by the government of Israel in its note of 12.3.1951 as the basis for these negotiations. Very sincerely, Adenauer

keeping this secret, although these issues will come to light and will benefit neither the powers nor us. They have informed us that they are bent on our claim being arranged. This was conveyed to us on Adenauer's behalf, and he requests that we understand the difficulties of this situation.

I would like to open my speech in the Knesset plenum with a brief statement on the facts and conclusions of the Foreign Affairs and Defense Committee. I will certainly be called upon to speak again during the debate, and I presume that the prime minister will also speak. We will have to reply to what we hear in the debate, either during it or at its conclusion. I do not want my speech to open the debate.

On Tuesday, January 7, 1952, after the highly important meeting of the coalition members, there will be a meeting of the Foreign Affairs and Defense Committee on reparations. I suppose that at this meeting I should speak at greater length on the negotiations between us and the Western powers about which the Foreign Affairs and Defense Committee has never been apprised. The committee should be informed of the responses we have received; we have received none from Russia. They may ask about the statement we received from Germany, whether it is oral or in writing, and if it is in writing, then what is its content, but the situation is such that we cannot convey its content, even in confidence, to the committee. On this issue I have considered long and hard about what to say. In my opinion it would be better not to tell the committee members about the letter, but rather to say that we have received information through official channels.

A factual comment: we have been informed that (a) Adenauer has informed his cabinet of this matter; (b) the wording of his letter will serve as a guideline for the German delegation to the negotiations; (c) they are going to appoint their delegation, or might have already done so, but in any event the name of the delegation's leader has been announced; (d) they expressed the hope that our delegation would not be excessively large.

Minister Rabbi Yitzhak Meir Levin: I must remind you that no discussion was held and no decision was made in the cabinet. There was only the prime minister's report in the cabinet meeting of December 16, 1951. I think that we should have a brief discussion here since we are aware of the delicate situation for all sides involved, and we are also aware of the country's economic situation – a drowning man must grasp at straws – and we must exploit anything that may be of help.

There are two sides to the coin. On the one hand we say: "Hast thou killed and also taken possession?" There is no forgiveness here. But this matter has another side too: Adenauer writes a letter and each time the Germans announce their intention of *Wiedergutmachung* [rectifying the wrong]. They think that they will do so by paying money. It is not that simple. Let nobody assume that by receiving reparations we will forgive, which is how they interpret it. (*Minister Moshe Sharett:*

So what are we to do?) We must decide yes or no. We are now hearing that the Germans are emphasizing their financial difficulties to us. What has that got to do with us? We remember Germany. In the previous war it borrowed millions from America and then went bankrupt. Two things might possibly happen: they will not give us the money, and negotiating with Germany will cause us grave moral harm. I do not know if we will receive money; I do not know if the money we will receive will save us. We must think long and hard before we decide. (*Prime Minister David Ben Gurion: You have had time to think. What is your opinion after having thought?*) I have been thinking day and night. I cannot vote in favor.

Prime Minister David Ben Gurion: I would like to take issue with two things that Rabbi Levin said. (a) He said we are taking action because of our need for money. I would not disagree with Rabbi Levin regarding the need, but that is not the reason. It is our due. We must not waive even part of the plunder owed us by the Germans if it can be claimed. Even if we were not in dire straits, that money must not be waived. (b) I disagree that there is moral harm in negotiating. We know that those opposing reparations are foolish followers of the Soviets, or hypocrites – and most of them are hypocrites – they write and type on machines purchased in Germany. (*Minister Yitzhak-Meir Levin: When I remember my murdered grandchildren I am unable to support this.*) When I remember my niece who was murdered there, mustn't I say, "Hast thou killed and also taken possession?" A moral harm would be caused if we forgive them. Will it be respectful of the dead and the murdered if we do not claim, at the very least, a significant part of the plunder? We are demanding its restitution to the Jewish people. It is the duty of the Jewish people not only because we are in such dire straits. We are duty-bound to do it. I do this with the same feelings you have, but a person should not be blamed for the harsh words he utters in his grief. That they might cheat us is possible, but that does not relieve us of the duty to make an effort to get what we can from them.

Minister Moshe Shapira: The cabinet must be aware of a future wave of vicious propaganda against us at home and abroad. This does not mean that we should cease taking our path, but the cabinet should be warned; it should stop keeping silent. We have an Information Department which provides no information to the public on this issue. Nobody is going to attack Jewish organizations abroad. All the criticism is going to be directed against the government of Israel. Mapam's daily *Al Hamishmar* today published an editorial under the headline "Last Warning." The members of Mapai Party may all be immune to propaganda and vote as one man, but the situation within the other parties is different; their members are not so immune to the vicious propaganda that has already begun to circulate. Those responsible for the Information Department should start working. Thank heaven, we have the radio, the press and public Forums at our disposal in which to inform the public. Let us be on guard.

Minister Ben-Zion Dinur: Anti-reparations propaganda is immoral since all those opposing compensation on the national level are at the same time individually endeavoring to get what is personally due them. Suddenly, an effort to obtain what is due to the Jewish people is considered immoral. In this regard, we must adopt an assertive position. We must not be on the defensive. Indeed, what we are witnessing here is not only an immoral stance but one of our common weaknesses: lack of sovereignty for 2,000 years has taught our people lack of responsibility. A strong position on our part is necessary here. We must attack this chutzpah and irresponsibility. Everyone does as he likes for his own benefit and no one asks if doing so is permissible, but when it touches upon the property of the Jewish people, he becomes a righteous saint. This is one of our society's calamities. The state must take the initiative and shoulder the task of enlightening the general public. Members of the cabinet should be active in this field week by week.

Minister Moshe Sharett: I would like to caution the cabinet against talking around in circles. We must come to a decision: negotiations yes or no, for we are liable to miss the hour of opportunity.

We have been criticized for the tardy submission of the claim. I reject this criticism, for had we submitted the claim two years ago it would have been unrealistic to claim $1 billion from Bonn. Now it is realistic, in view of their immense industrial output. It is significant that the Americans and the British are confident that very big payments can be imposed on them for financing the occupation armies. We cannot drag the matter on and on. We must enter negotiations immediately, without further delay.

Prime Minister David Ben Gurion: I propose that we decide to enter negotiations with the West German government on the payment of reparations on basis of the claim we submitted to the four powers.

It was decided:
(By eleven votes) that the Government of Israel will enter negotiations with the Federal Government of (West) Germany on the matter of reparations on the basis of the claim submitted to the occupying powers. The foreign minister will make a statement in the Knesset to this effect.

[16] Reparations: Permissible or Forbidden? Kosher or Non-Kosher?

Excerpts from a speech by Moshe Sharett, election meeting, 5.1.1952[1]

The State of Israel is saying: we are owed a debt by the country that exterminated six million Jews and plundered vast amounts of Jewish property. There is no repayment for the blood that was spilt. There is no forgiveness for the torture. But we must take the plundered property back from that country so that it does not remain in its hands but instead will be devoted to the building of the State of Israel.

The two political fringes, Left and Right, who do not shoulder the responsibility of building up the state, permit themselves to incite the people against the government that is claiming reparations from Germany. They seek to influence not the mind, but the embittered Jewish heart, and both are maliciously distorting the main question.

What is the situation today? The country is full of German machinery. Any Jew who survived and owned property in Germany is entitled to go there and claim his property. And if his house no longer exists and if he cannot identify his goods, he demands and receives compensation in German marks. He does not take those marks out of Germany, but purchases a machine or other goods with them, and imports them to Israel – to be used or sold – thereby increasing the assets in Israel which are our means of production.

Is this permissible or forbidden? Is it kosher or non-kosher? Any Jew, a "General Zionist" or a member of a Mapam kibbutz, who has claims against Germany, goes and claims his due and for that he is to be commended, for he is increasing the wealth of the State of Israel. But does this apply solely to an individual Jew who has survived? What about the property of the millions who were exterminated and who have neither relatives nor heirs? They too have an heir and savior. It is the State of Israel!

---

1   The speech was delivered during the election campaign to the local council of Beit Dagan on behalf of the Histadrut, dominated by Mapai.

What did Hitler want? He wanted to exterminate us, to trample upon our honor and erase our name. Well, he is gone and we fought and we are alive. We are members of the United Nations while Germany is still knocking at its door. But we have not completed our work. We live in order to build a solid, strong state, and for this we need all the Jewish property. Had the Jews of Germany and the German-occupied countries survived, we would have had the hope of bringing them to Israel – them and their property – and would have benefited from their help in building the homeland. But having been Hitler's victims, should we waive their property? We need it for the benefit of the masses of Jews immigrating to Israel with only the shirts on their backs, Jews who are penniless and must be given everything here – from a roof over their heads to clothing, from work and production tools to schools and clinics. The plundered Jewish property is devoted to the Jewish people who are building its homeland.

Jewish property was stolen and plundered, but if there is someone to whom we can submit a claim – if the debt is acknowledged and payment is promised – should we stand aloof? Would this not be a moral act, a Zionist, national act, befitting the Israeli labor movement?

Everyone knows that we need great resources for building our country. Everyone knows that we seek help from Diaspora Jews and the countries of the world, and especially from the United States, and we hope to receive help in the future as well – and here, too, Mapam is hindering the enlistment of help – but can we demand help from others if we waive what is ours, what is our due?

What is permissible for every individual Jew is permissible for the Jewish people, and for the State of Israel it is clearly a necessity.

[17] The Foreign Minister Reports to the Foreign Affairs and Defense Committee Before the Knesset General Debate Regarding Direct Negotiations

Knesset Foreign Affairs and Defense Committee Meeting, 7.1.1952

Chairman Meir Argov: In accordance with our decision, we shall now discuss the question of reparations from Germany before the Knesset debate on this issue this afternoon.

Foreign Minister Moshe Sharett: I can report very briefly on the situation. On March 12, 1951 we submitted a note to the four occupying powers in which, for the first time, a claim was voiced in the name of the State of Israel and in the name of the Jewish people, for collective payment for the plunder and destruction of Jewish property. We received a reply to this note from the three Western powers. To this day we have not received a reply from the Eastern power, although we have reminded it about this matter several times, both in writing and orally.

The Western powers responded as folows in almost identical wording, with slight variations, each according to its particular etiquette: it is not true that the Jewish people did not receive compensation. After the war it was decided that if any German gold was found and had not been converted into coins, it should be devoted to rehabilitation of the refugees, and German Jews' deposits abroad were also set aside for this, and on this account we received $20-25 million that were transferred to Jewish institutions. It is also not true that no aid was extended to the refugees. Various countries threw open their gates to victims of the Nazi extermination. The compensation account of the powers with Germany has already been drawn up, although it is not yet final, and the dates of the final settlement have not been set. In any event the powers cannot oblige Germany to make further payments.

That, more or less, was the reply. They added verbally that it should not be perceived as the last word. They further said – especially the Americans –

that since they are helping Germany, should Germany pay it cannot be at their expense. It can only be at Germany's expense, not theirs.

We replied to this note. We argued what we argued and proved the special character of our claim, which does not fall into the category of the Allies' war damage claims. We are not claiming war damages but damages for destruction and plunder of property. This plunder began before the war, it continued after the beginning of the war and is not necessarily connected with the war. The intention is not to obtain compensation from America but to obtain compensation from Germany, and the surprising recovery of the German economy and its increasing production prove that Germany can pay from its own resources without becoming a burden on the American taxpayer. We were told again verbally – in Washington and London – that without direct negotiations with Germany, they do not think we can advance our case. It was clear to us from the outset that possibly nothing will come of our claim, but this was not our intention; we did not submit the claim solely to pacify our historical conscience and to have it inscribed on tablets of stone for the sake of posterity, although that in itself was important. I have already stated that there are proposals whose failure is not in their presentation but in their non-presentation. However, I made it clear that if we aimed at concrete results, then even if we achieve results with the help of emissaries and envoys, or assistance from the powers, direct contact between us and the Germans on the form of payment is unavoidable. There are questions such as whether payment will be in currency or in goods, the quantity of goods and what kind, at what rates, and so forth. This is a very serious matter and every step we take is bound up with the state's vital interests. In no way can we rely on an emissary to demand terms and have them fulfilled.

All this was clear from the outset. When we first realized that all this meant direct negotiations, we did not flinch from this conclusion. I do not wish to anticipate this evening's Knesset debate. I will elaborate on this issue of direct contact there, but it was clear to us that it is no simple matter for us to propose negotiations. For while such a proposal will satisfy Germany - though it is altogether unclear if we will achieve any satisfaction - we have made it clear to these German authorities that we will not withdraw the claim and will hound them in the international arena at every possible opportunity.

The next stage was Adenauer's statement at the end of September 1951 in which he admitted the atrocities committed against the Jewish people. Although he attempted to clear the majority of the German people of responsibility for them, he did admit the obligation of the German people to shoulder the burden of the outcome; he accepted the principle of a collective payment in addition to the arrangements already in place for compensating individuals, and he announced the readiness of the Bonn government to enter into negotiations with representatives of the Jewish people and the State of Israel to settle this matter.

In the meantime, a conference of world Jewry – so to speak – was convened. It was attended by 20 Jewish organizations from countries in which Jews are free to organize and express their views. Iraqi Jewry, for instance, was not included. This conference was initiated and planned before any of us knew that Adenauer was about to make such a statement regarding reparations. The initiative for this conference began in August, Adenauer made his statement in September, and the conference was held on October 23-24, 1951 and addressed Adenauer's statement. The conference supported Israel's claim and declared that the claims of individual Jews must be met. The conference's executive committee, which met immediately after the conference, accepted the principle of direct negotiations should Israel enter into such negotiations. They had no intention of entering negotiations without us. They accepted the principle of direct negotiations but made the cooperation of the State of Israel a condition of the implementation of their decision.

We said to ourselves, this statement of Chancellor Adenauer to the world is not enough for us. We want to know first what they think, whether they are thinking of tens of millions or hundreds of millions; whether they accept our claim as a basis for reparations; whether they are prepared to offer something definite on negotiations and whether it is clear that it is their initiative. These conditions have been met. At the beginning of December a letter signed by Chancellor Adenauer was handed over to the New York Claims Conference and the State of Israel. In this document he made his September statement in which he announced that his government feels that the time is ripe to enter negotiations; that they view this as a grave material burden but also as a moral duty; that they accept our claim, formulated in the note dated March 12, 1951, as the basis for negotiations – the German term used was "Grund Lage," which means "on the basis of." Based on all this, the government decided that we should enter into negotiations, and it is this decision that will be brought before the Knesset today.

David Horowitz (*Director General, Ministry of Finance*): Before the formal answer to our note was given by the powers, we were told in conversations that our demand has a very strong basis, that it is almost unquestionable. However, contrary to press reports at the time, the Western powers, for several reasons, are not interested to act on our behalf. They said they have their own financial interests in Germany and have no desire to become involved in a conflict with Germany on our issue. In Germany it is primarily the socialists who support the idea of reparations, although generally they are not too happy about cooperation with the ruling parties.

MK Zalman Aran (*Mapai*): It seems to me that in its claim for reparations, the government should emphasize that the claim is directed at both West and East Germany. We have not heard that the reparations claim is also directed at

East Germany. They are the same Germans and the same race. I think that the government's announcement should be so worded that it seeks the Knesset's authorization to include the possibility of conducting negotiations. However, I understand from the government's announcement that it is not yet demanding authorization for entering negotiations.

Foreign Minister Moshe Sharett: As far as I know, there is no intention to request Knesset approval for negotiations at this stage. The government sees no need for it.

The prime minister will open the debate, not I. I assume that it will be clear from his statement that the government thinks that there should be negotiations, or that we should be prepared for negotiations. That does not mean that the government will seek a Knesset resolution to conduct negotiations. I do not think there is a need for it. From a certain standpoint it could also cause damage. What the government will request from the Knesset is its authorization to act in this matter according to its understanding, but it will be clear to the Knesset that the government views the possibility of negotiations as realistic and a matter for the near future.

[At this point five committee members posed questions to the foreign minister.]

Foreign Minister Moshe Sharett: I shall answer several questions. We know nothing of the Bonn government's intention to deduct any sum whatsoever on account of what has been paid so far to individuals, institutions or organizations. They will possibly do the math themselves: when they argue that we have exaggerated in our estimation of their payment capabilities, they will say that they have already restored or are about to restore property the Nazis had plundered. But we have taken this into account. In our note we stated that although certain actions of restitution in the sphere of compensation are already taking place, it does not settle the account. What Germany owes the Jewish people for property that has been lost cannot be set off and cannot be the subject of any form of accounting. We think, first and foremost, that Germany owes this to the State of Israel, if only because the State of Israel has rehabilitated 500,000 naked and penniless victims of the Nazi regime, and because the State of Israel is the Jewish people's only state. We have no intention of retracting this statement, and we estimate the cost at $1.5 billion. Certain Jewish organizations disagree with this statement but not with the practical conclusions. While they unreservedly agree with submitting the claim, they did not agree with the basis of the claim. Had we asked the New York conference for its agreement to this basis we would not have obtained it since there are Jewish circles that do not accept the concept of a Jewish people as a single world entity and the State of Israel as an asset belonging to the entire Jewish people. They are prepared to help the State of Israel but without ideological commitment in this respect. It was stated categorically to the Germans that aside from what you have paid and will still pay to individuals and organizations, we estimate the sum due us at a $1.5 billion, and this claim is now acknowledged as the basis for negotiations.

Here I should add the following: when we used the figure of $1.5 billion, we used it in respect to all of Germany, West and East alike. And it will be only natural if the Bonn government says: "We have accepted this claim as the basis, i.e., we have accepted $1.5 billion as the basis. Let us assume that East Germany is one-third and we are two-thirds. What we have accepted as the basis means that we have accepted $1 billion as the basis." It would be logical for them to contend this.

With regard to the rumor spread by the London weekly *The Jewish Chronicle*, that we consented they should reach agreement with us, the account will be closed and they would no longer pay compensation to any individual, let me say this is utterly false. What is correct is as follows: when the Bonn people considered this problem, an argument was advanced: "We know what goes on inside the Jewish people. There are all kinds of Jewish organizations that do not admit that the State of Israel represents them. What will happen if we complete negotiations with the State of Israel – that contends that it speaks on behalf of the Jewish people – and then these organizations submit collective claims? We should say that we will meet a collective claim only once, and we want to be sure that if we complete the collective account, that is the end of the collective account, and afterwards we shall not deal with additional and pre-estimated collective claims."

That is a logical stance. It may be assumed that Adenauer's letter to the New York conference, which recognized the Jewish organizations that carry some weight, and linked them with the State of Israel, was sent with this consideration in mind. Thus the German negotiators thought that if they negotiate with both the State of Israel and the Conference of Jewish Organizations together, success would be guaranteed.

Chancellor Adenauer's letter contains no hint of this rumor, but at a press conference in London he said that after the New York conference was convened it would be possible to negotiate with a unified body and not to deal with a new body of organizations popping up later saying, "You have settled with the State of Israel; now we submit a fresh collective claim." This version, to the effect that it makes the collective claim final, does not apply to individuals. On the contrary, in the sphere of individual claims the New York conference thinks that if it enters negotiations – and it will if we do – it will present all kinds of demands for legislative and procedural amendments regarding the restitution of private property, etc. There are various loopholes that they know must be plugged, and the issue of legislation and procedure must be dealt with, too. The sum that this legislation would enforce is not predetermined. We cannot know in advance how many Jews in Uruguay or Portugal are owed compensation for property in Germany.

As far as diplomatic and consular relations are concerned, we have no such relations with either West or East Germany. There is no intention to establish such relations and no intention to agree to a German initiative to establish them if such an initiative is taken. There are consular relations with the occupying authorities in West Germany. We applied for establishing a consulate in the East, but no response was received.

The negotiations will not be conducted in Germany. The intention is that they will not be on German soil, but neither will they be conducted in Israel. They will take place in a European country, a West European country, of course.

When comments from Germany began to be heard to the effect that "Adenauer has stated that he is prepared to conduct negotiations. Why aren't you ready?" We said: "That is not enough. They must clearly state how they intend to deal with the negotiations." As a consequence, we received Chancellor Adenauer's letter on behalf of the Bonn government. I am unable to show the letter to the committee. I have seen it. It is not long. It contains but a few paragraphs:

The basis is the September statement by the Bonn government saying that the Bonn government is prepared to discuss reparations with representatives of the Jewish people and the State of Israel;

The Bonn government feels that the time is ripe for negotiations;

The Bonn government views this not only as the resolution of a very important material matter but also as a moral duty;

The Bonn government views it as its duty to make a contribution to the rehabilitation of the State of Israel;

The Bonn government wishes to convey this statement to the Government of Israel and the Conference on Jewish Material Claims Against Germany;

The Bonn government states that it accepts the claim formulated by the State of Israel in its note to the occupying powers dated March 12 1951 as the basis for negotiations.

MK Eliezer Livne (*Mapai*): To the best of my understanding, the question of the German reparations is extremely grave and not procedural. It is perhaps the gravest issue placed before the Knesset since its inauguration. There are two hypotheses here, both are correct and possibly contradictory. The first is the practical conduct – not only the stance – of the Jewish people vis-à-vis the German people. I have to admit that for me this is the main question. The German people exterminated one-third of the Jewish people. Hundreds of thousands of

Germans took part in the acts of extermination. Millions of Germans knew about them. The death march of the Dachau inmates[1] was witnessed by millions of Germans. They exterminated the Jewish people not as soldiers at war but as a nation. Like the Amalekites, they murdered children and the elderly, the sick and disabled, out of a lust for annihilation. The stature of a people in history, and its stature in the community of nations, its honor in its own eyes and in the eyes of others is determined by two things, defined by the late publicist Asher Ginzberg as "The power of memory and the power of hope." Thanks to the power of our memory, we have not forgotten the destruction of the Temple for 2,000 years. In accordance with this event we determined our attitude towards the Romans, and they did not exterminate us like the Nazis. We fought them and revolted against them, but our attitude towards them is determined, to this day, by what they did to the Temple and the Jewish people. We have not forgotten the Spanish Inquisition, and the acts of the Spanish Inquisition were child's play compared to what Germany did to us. For centuries we did not return to Spain even though those expelled from Spain were allowed to take all their possessions with them.

We have not forgotten Khmelnitsky,[2] and those who did forget ceased to be Jews. And since we did not hasten to forget, this determined the character and the very existence of the people for 2,000 years. Because it forgot less and hoped more, the Jewish people are distinguished from other nations. I am not saying for better or worse, but this is how our people's character and existence have been determined to this day as well as its determination to return to this land. We would not have returned had we not remembered the destruction of Zion, had we not preserved our hatred of the Romans, of Vespasian and Hadrian. I admit that I am of mixed mind here for I admire the Romans' legislative talents, but as a Jew I determine my attitude towards the Romans as the people that destroyed the Temple, shattered the Kingdom of Israel, and brought about a dispersion lasting 2,000 years.

From an economic standpoint, we in this country are living in difficult times. I am far from ignoring economic matters. But there is something more important than economics, and in the final analysis it is that which determines economic competence: the spiritual character of a people. Belief and a sense of honor run an economy. Our pioneers knew how to be satisfied with little, to forego donations and to increase productivity under harsh conditions. A people's self-respect enhances its national unity. These are economic factors of the first order. Without Jewish faith, without a preparedness to suffer, without the power

---

1   In April 1945, in view of the advancing Soviet army, abut 7,000 surviving Jewish inmates of the Dachau concentration camp in south Germany were forcefully marched to areas in north eastern Germany. Many of them died on the way. Similar death marches of Jewish survivors from other camps were carried out as well.

2   Bogdan Khmelnitsky (1595-1657). A Ukrainian leader and national hero who led a revolt against the Polish kingdom during which about 100,000 Ukrainian Jews were massacred by his forces.

to remember and the courage to hope for recompense, Jewish pioneering would not have been born. That pioneering spirit provides more economic benefit than all the dollars in the world. From an overall national standpoint, I feel that a nation's spiritual image is the deciding factor; the spiritual image of the Jewish people returning to its land will be determined by its attitude towards the German people who physically exterminated six million Jews. And the German people have no remorse. What Antiochus[3] did not do to us, what the Romans did not do to us, what Khmelnitsky did not do to us, and also what the Amalekites did not do – the Germans did. Perhaps the memory of the Amalekites has been preserved for the purpose of warning us against Germany.

Will such an event as the Holocaust not determine our international conduct? If we forgive and forget, if we begin compromising and conciliating so quickly, how will our honor be perceived by the nations? And the money we will receive – can it be weighed against the moral downfall?

On the other hand, there can be no doubt that our claim is just and should be made. Furthermore, the fact that they have killed and also taken possession does not make them legal heirs and does not diminish our right to a claim.

I would therefore assume that there are two correct assumptions here: one is that the fate of our people will determine its attitude towards the German nation; the other is that we must claim reparations, and it is our duty to do so. If there is a contradiction between the two, then the first overrides the second. But I do not think there is an absolute contradiction here. Around this approach an attempt must be made to unite all our country's political parties whose conduct is determined solely by Jewish motives.

What is actually implied by these two ideological assumptions? We have no grounds for establishing normal diplomatic relations with Germany. The Bundestag, through Adenauer, announced that they view reparations as the beginning of conciliation and "normalization" of relations. This concept was alluded to in the unofficial letter quoted here. Had I seen significant signs of remorse in the German people I would have considered it, even though all my family in Poland was exterminated by the Germans. Had that people been dismayed to the very depths of its soul by the terrible sin it committed, had it, on its own initiative, punished the Nazi criminals in East and West – in the East they are found among the heads of its government, in the West they occupy less important positions – I would have said that we might decide in favor of conciliation. Perhaps it is too soon to hasten, but in principle it is permitted. I have devoted much thought to this issue. I have read the German press and spoken to people who came from there. I have, unfortunately, come to the conclusion that there is no real remorse for the crime they committed, and given

---

3   The Syrian-Greek King Antioch the Great (223-187 B.C.) captured Jerusalem in 168 B.C. and plundered the Second Temple. His forced Hellenization policy led to the Hasmonean Revolt by the Jews of Judea.

the chance to murder again, they will. Regrettably, I have no doubt about this, and it must determine my position regarding the Germans even if I have to waive $30-40 million a year. In this instance the honor of the Jewish people is tantamount to the chances of its physical existence – there are still Jews in Europe – and that honor is more precious than $30-40 million, which I know are needed so much. Indeed, there is something more precious than $30-40 million dollars in the Israeli balance of payments for 1952. From this we must draw several conclusions:

The German chancellor made a declaration on relations between his people and ours. It is impossible that the Knesset not declare our own attitude towards the German people which only a few years ago exterminated six million Jews. We must state clearly that there is no credible desire among the German people to stamp out Nazism on its own initiative. Therefore there is no basis for conciliation; there is no basis for normal diplomatic relations between us and them.

We should have a consulate on German soil only if the Allies rule there and it should be closed the moment the occupying powers leave.

No negotiations on any subject, compensation or no compensation, on German soil, and of course not on Israeli soil. I do not wish them to sully this soil, and receiving the Germans here is also fraught with other dangers.

Stating our position regarding Germany and voting against Germany at the UN must continue even if we are the only ones to do so. We shall not leave the UN or any other international body because of their participation. We shall not isolate ourselves because of them, but we shall not cease to give prominence to our position towards them. It is precisely now that we must clearly state to all mankind that we have not forgotten, that we do not feel that our people are safe in the Diaspora, that Nazism still exists. I must voice this position of mine with the deepest power of persuasion. Laying down this position is even more important than millions of dollars.

We are alone in our account with Germany. No other nation has such an account with Germany, not even Yugoslavia where the Germans exterminated 12 percent of the people. Our fate depends on the overt or covert Nazi resurgence, regardless of the Russian and American considerations. We must vote and speak out against Germany, even though we may be a voice crying in the wilderness. Any form of negotiation between us and them – I do not reject negotiations, although I do criticize some things that have been done – must be conducted as negotiations with an enemy. At present the German nation is a more dangerous enemy than the Arabs. The negotiations between us and the Arabs were conducted in the presence of a third party, UN representatives. I would like negotiations between us and Germany, should we reach that point, to be conducted with the participation of an international body. In other words, negotiations between enemies with no handshakes. No Israeli minister, no senior official should participate in these negotiations. Experts – yes, not only financial experts but experts on German psychology. I do not know if the Germans are astute in other spheres, but historical experience teaches that they are shrewd and astute in international financial negotiations. The directors general of our Finance and Foreign Ministries should not attend the negotiations, only experts. We should also exercise self-restraint in the economic sphere. We must not accept goods that will link our economy with theirs. If these limitations make obtaining the money more difficult, then let it be more difficult! We can accept only those materials or goods that will not involve us in permanent relations with them. No normal trade relations, no German agents or experts, not even traveling from here to there.

In view of all this it is very important that we obtain maximum hard currency. If this is difficult for them, let it be difficult. It was far more difficult for us when they exterminated six million Jews. If they do not want to pay reparations under these terms, we shall give up the whole business. We must reduce linkage between us and them as far as possible. Using this approach the issue might possibly not be concluded so quickly. So be it!

For what do the Germans want? This is a big international issue for them. A grave spiritual-moral struggle, fraught with far-reaching consequences for both sides, is taking place here. By this step they seek the erasure of the mark of Cain from their forehead. They are trying to create an atmosphere of compromise between Israel and Germany. They are interested in this atmosphere. And what are they giving us? They are trying to give us reparations, but not all at once. I shall not give my opinion on the overall sum they will offer, for my doing so might cause damage even if spoken in a forum of 20 people. I regret that the opponents of reparations are making statements in public that are beneficial to the Germans. I believe that what they will offer is far less than what has been mentioned here. But the overall sum is not so important for it will be paid over a number of years. The annual payment is what's important! And they, evidently, intend to extract everything from us – conciliation, "normalization," amicable negotiations – in the first year. And they will possibly stop paying in the second or third year. This is their ploy. However, even if the negotiations are postponed we should not view this postponement as a drawback. The money is not the answer to everything. But from a financial standpoint as well, our image may be more important than chasing after the estimated sum of money.

It is preferable to harden our attitude towards Germany now. The more we harden it, not only will we be taking the right road from a spiritual-moral standpoint – I admit that for me this is the main thing – but it will almost certainly be beneficial. The more the Germans feel that we are not reconciled, that we view their crime as great, the more likely we shall also obtain better results.

I offer these conclusions to all Knesset members whose decisions are based upon a Jewish touchstone. There is no social or class question here. We have before us a mainly spiritual-historical and political question. The increase of partisan considerations in this matter testifies to the low standard of our public morality.

I propose that the Knesset answer the Bundestag with a clear reply: no conciliation, no compromise, no basis whatsoever for normal relations between us and the German nation and any German government.

Second, that the practical matter of claiming compensation and its payment be handed over to the Foreign Affairs and Defense Committee which should determine the appropriate means of implementation, not contrary to the first assumption but resulting from it. When the committee discusses these appropriate means, I shall make proposals for implementation.

MK Peretz Bernstein (*General Zionists*)**:** It is no secret that I have long been in favor of reparations and the necessary negotiations, and I have taken the opportunity of reminding the foreign minister that I proposed trade relations with Germany as early as 1948. Then, the temporary government rejected my proposal for more or less the same reasons we have heard today from all the opponents. Within my own party, I am almost alone in this regard.

I must admit that I have not succeeded, as did MK Livne, in finding a mental compromise between the tendency to conduct direct negotiations and the psychological opposition to it. However, in my opinion there is a need for caution against illusions in this matter: if we conduct negotiations there will be a handshake. But there is another question, a moral one. I admit that I have not seen signs of remorse on their side. But are they not, in fact, making compensation conditional on some form of forgiveness, even if not saying so, even if there is no declared intention of arriving at the establishment of diplomatic relations by means of the negotiations? This might be an inevitable process which would be accomplished if not today, then tomorrow.

And now a number of questions to the foreign minister: Doesn't the acceptance of our claim in the sum we have stated impart a frivolous character to the entire issue? Had they responded immediately that the sum demanded was unrealistic but were prepared to talk about $100-200 million, then I would have said it was serious.

My second question is less weighty: to what degree will we remain dependent upon German production by receiving some products we need very much, what you term "investment assets," first and foremost machinery? Raw materials do not enslave but machinery does, for it means a continuous dependence on spare parts until the machines fall apart. In any event, it means dependence for the duration of 10 or 20 years.

MK Yona Kesse (*Mapai*)**:** I would like to say to my friend MK Livne that any attempt to explain, as he has tried, that accepting compensation does not mean conciliation is only serving those who advance the opposite position. I am aware of a current theory claiming that negotiations on compensation mean conciliation with the Germans. MK Begin or others say that; we don't have any such argument among ourselves. MK Begin said at a recent public meeting that accepting reparations from Germany is anti-patriotic, and that if it is decided to accept compensation then terrorism will ensue in the country. Is it patriotic to threaten the country with terrorism? And I do not want to say right now what the state will do if the use of such means is attempted. But that is not the issue. I have a Jewish feeling towards this entire matter, and I would like to refer MK Livne to the minutes of what was said following the foreign minister's statement in the Knesset on the note submitted with regard to reparations. You will find that much of what you stated was said by many of your colleagues. But I am amazed by this nationalistic attitude which leads one to declare before the entire world, as do several of our own parties, that if we conduct negotiations on reparations, it means conciliation with Germany. Adenauer himself does not make this assumption. Are they thus rendering a patriotic service to the state? I was under the impression that it was categorically stated to Adenauer that our historical account with the German people will not be settled with the payment of reparations. I also dare say that Adenauer understands that our historical account with the German people cannot be settled. But why pronounce these words here, in Israel, as if the policy of the Jewish people is to establish relations that smack of forgiveness with Germany?

I am astonished by what is being said here. A conference of 20 Jewish organizations convened in New York and decided to claim reparations while determining that this did not mean conciliation, that it is only a reparations claim, and here, such a storm is raging! The debate is whether there is conciliation or not, and not the technical question of whether or not to conduct negotiations. It was categorically stated that this is not conciliation, so why, therefore, all this rage?

I find it difficult to understand MK Bernstein's reasoning. Suppose the negotiations fail. What is more important from a political and moral standpoint: that if we respond negatively to Adenauer, this enables him to appear before the world as the righteous one since he proposed reparations to the State of Israel and was rejected? We are posing the German people a more serious test by compelling them to give us reparations than by rejecting Adenauer's response.

National honor has been spoken about here. That same German people with whom we want or do not want to conduct negotiations held a nationalistic view similar to that of MK Begin. We know what havoc it brought to the world in general and to the Jewish people in particular. It seems to me that had we been concerned about our national honor and the possibility of obtaining reparations, the entire population would have behaved as did Diaspora Jewry when they convened in New York and decided to conduct negotiations on reparations.

MK Yaakov Riftin (*Mapam*)**:** Several political factors accompany this issue, and I would like to point out the decisive one in my mind. I am quite convinced that there will not be a world war before West Germany is ready for it. If a world war erupts, Germany will revive an attempt to exterminate the remnants of the Jewish people. This is the point of departure for examining the issue that obviously America and England will not be prepared for a war in Europe without a German army. Accordingly, since the rebuilding of Germany is speeded up, the eruption of war will be speeded up, and if war is speeded up, the danger of the final extermination of the Jewish people, Heaven forbid, will be speeded up. In my opinion, this should be the decisive factor from the political standpoint and the Jewish standpoint. (*MK Peretz Bernstein: This process will be accelerated by receiving compensation?*)

My second point: Clearly, a meeting between Churchill and Truman is a more decisive factor regarding a future world war than the State of Israel's negotiations with West Germany. But it is still a significant factor. I think that normalization of Israel's relations with Germany would be an objective consequence of the negotiations. It is inevitable.

I think that the process I spoke of earlier is so dangerous and so terrible that the Jewish people and the State of Israel must do nothing to speed it up. I would say this even if I were optimistic with regard to negotiations, if I thought they would provide a decisive contribution to the country's economy. I am somewhat pessimistic on that. But even if I were more optimistic, I would think that the Jewish people and the State of Israel cannot conduct negotiations which will advance a process that is liable, in time, to try again to complete the work that Hitler began.

MK Yitzhak Ben Aharon (*Mapam*)**:** I am of the opinion that in different times, as we had done in the past, the government would not have decided such a question by a 51 percent majority. (*Foreign Minister Moshe Sharett: One could say that in normal times a minority front of 49 percent against would not have been achieved.*) I say a government that considers itself not only of the state but of the people could on regular issues certainly rely on a majority of 50.5 percent, but when deciding upon an issue of such historical and national significance, it would be a mistake to do so. I am of the opinion that the government should not be allowed to push through a decision by the present coalition majority. The question I am posing to the government is, can it take upon itself such a terrible responsibility of deciding this matter of direct negotiations by such a parliamentary majority?

I assume that no government would declare war and lead the people into a war by a majority of 51 percent. It would thus be endangering both itself and the state when half of the people are against it. I cannot imagine such a thing. There have not been many such cases in history. In this issue, which cuts deep into the realms of Jewish history, of the interests of the Jewish people and its future, taking a decision not according to the opinion of many, perhaps not the opinion of half the people, is tantamount to shedding all the responsibility and unity necessary in the life of the Jewish people.

In my opinion the government does not have this authority. It must ask the people for it. It is not enough to ask the Knesset and not enough to decide by a majority of a coalition that was formed for other purposes. I ask the government if it is prepared to transfer this question to a decision by the people, to a decision by referendum, for this matter is worthy of such a procedure.

I also think that the government's view that the fate and continued existence of the state depend upon the reparations is mistaken. We are faced here with an act that will go down in Jewish history. It will be taught and debated for generations to come. It will be a signpost in Jewish history like numerous other signposts in our people's past. At this juncture the government must act by a different, more decisive authorization than the one it had or has now.

I am astonished that colleagues such as the foreign minister and the government's economic advisor permit themselves to think that this Germany, which is on the threshold of achieving complete independence, whose government will within several months cease its dependence on any international body, will honor any scrap of paper signed by Adenauer, and that these two believe that during the first year of these reparations they will see any payment coming in. Moreover, while still being occupied, Nazi forces are returning to all the country's governmental posts. In other words, as far as they are concerned we are about to offer forgiveness for a mess of pottage which contains nothing concrete for our needs.

In conclusion, I would like to ask the government whether it is prepared to extricate itself, the people and the state by means of a national referendum? This situation created by terrible decision-making is being forced through by a coalitional, partisan and factional whip.

Chairman Meir Argov: Let not anyone among us dare to speak in the name of the spilled blood. Every one of us can speak only for himself. If this is not accepted as a basic premise, I can foresee the gravest consequences for the fate of this country. Nobody has a mandate to speak on behalf of the victims because no one has been appointed to do so.

And the second thing is the attempt being made here, not for the first time, and not only with regard to this fateful question, to make it appear as if the Knesset cannot decide. Had we asked the entire population at a given moment whether we should declare the establishment of the state, I am doubtful if we would have achieved a majority in favor of it. What does a referendum mean? Tomorrow people will go to the new immigrants and ask them if they are for or against Germany? The referendum question may well be formulated incorrectly. I know how a referendum is conducted. Can you prove to me that it is going to be a democratic procedure, and that there will be no demagoguery and no bloodshed involved? The government of Israel is responsible for the fate of this country. This Knesset, elected by the people, is the only body that can express an opinion. You are repeating here the attempt to declare that the parliament does not represent the people. You have not asked the people about it. This Knesset represents the people. The people have no other representation. Each party represents a different sector. It does not represent the people. The people are represented by the Knesset.

I think it a matter of national honor and pride to claim reparations from Germany, to sit at the same table and demand reparations. And I am no less a Jew than you, and I do not deny your Judaism by even ½ of 1 percent. I cannot measure your Jewish feelings and Jewish pride. But I repeat that in my opinion there is Jewish pride in approaching the murderer, sitting beside him and demanding reparations. What is happening here in our streets[4] I can only explain as some sickness; indeed, sometimes we behave like the mentally ill. Therefore, nobody can tell me that some members of the Knesset are patriotic and others are not. What is this attempt to say that the Knesset cannot decide? This Knesset has the authority to decide so long as the people do not topple it. Should the people elect another Knesset, that Knesset will either decide differently or in exactly the same way.

MK Mordechai Namir (*Mapai*)**:** A question has been raised here of direct negotiations being moral or not, in line with pure conscience or not. I think that pure conscience is a personal matter. I wonder whether a collective conscience can exist at all, but I am certain that pure conscience is not distributed along partisan lines.

I listened attentively to MK Livne's speech and got the impression that that he is warning against a draft resolution for signing a friendly alliance with Germany, perhaps not even with Germany but with Hitler himself. I will not deal now with his conclusions and general assumptions, but I would like to ask: what have direct negotiations and their outcome to do with the problem of forgetting? Forgetting or remembering historical events is not a matter of decision at all. In this matter decisions cannot help. Events are either remembered or not. Their remembrance is not dependant on decisions.

The name of Khmelnitsky was mentioned here. The Jewish people have never concluded that negotiations could never take place between the Ukrainian and the Jewish people. In fact, an attempt was made to conduct some kind of negotiations on behalf of the Jewish people, so to speak, with Khmelnitsky's heir – with Petliura.[5] Had there been negotiations with Petliura about compensation,

---

4   Several vociferous anti-reparations demonstrations were organized by opposition parties, mainly in Tel Aviv.
5   Semion Petliura, a nationalist Ukrainian leader, fought against the Red Army during the civil war that erupted following the 1917 revolution in former Czarist Russia. His forces murdered thousands of Ukrainian Jews. In 1921 he fled to France. He was assassinated

nobody would have opposed them. I have no idea whether the Polish people were so righteous; after all, it was in its territory that all those gas chambers were built. I visited a few of them right after the war, when the wounds were still fresh, and I did not hear that Jews were boycotting the Polish government. As for the Mapam Party, I doubt whether all its members criticized the Soviet-Nazi non-intervention pact of August 1939. There is not one European country that was not harmed by Nazi Germany. Not even one of them has boycotted Germany. I am convinced that the public rage we have been witnessing in recent week against direct negotiations has been staged. It represents a shameful exploitation of peoples' feelings and emotions.

MK Shalom Zysman (*General Zionists*)**:** As an individual I am in favor of claiming compensation, but there is a difference between the actions of the individual and the behavior of the public. An individual Jew can go to Germany and trade. Even a collective can stake a claim. But there is a difference between that and negotiations conducted by the State of Israel, which is the supreme embodiment of Jewish national sovereignty. I would like to say to the members of Mapai who are in favor of this that the question here is whether the supreme embodiment of national sovereignty should conduct these negotiations. While amongst ourselves we are talking about compensation for the plunder of property and damage caused to the Jewish people, in the outside world compensation will be perceived as a financial donation for the murder of six million Jews. It would appear that we are receiving a per capita tax. The world will see it as if we are receiving $10 for each murdered child. The Jew-haters will make this calculation with a pencil in their hands.

I would like to say that we must be consistent to the end here. We need any remedy possible to heal our economy. This healing is a most sacred purpose. But we are faced with the question of what is preferable. The Jewish people have a long account with the German people. What impression will this make on Jewish people all over the world and on our own youth? When I ask myself what is preferable, I cannot but be aware that there are impoverished people who would not allow themselves to do anything for money. Those who justify negotiations with Germany say that the objective is sacred. It seems to me that moral considerations must prevail here and are preferable to other considerations. (*Foreign Minister Moshe Sharett: Nothing prevails more from a moral standpoint than strengthening the State of Israel.*) The question is whether by doing this we build up the State of Israel or bring about a moral decline in the nation. Perhaps it is too early to judge. Perhaps the issue should be left for the next generation. The conclusion must be that the state and the Knesset must take a negative decision.

---

in Paris by Shalom Schwartzbard in May 1926. The Zionist leader Ze'ev Jabotinsky negotiated an agreement with Petliura in 1921 by which he agreed to establish a Jewish police force in the Ukraine for defending the local Jewish population.

Foreign Minister Moshe Sharett: I wonder why members of the committee saw fit to devote so much time and so much fervor to debating the issue here. I have nothing against debating here, but this was not the original intention, which was to conduct the debate in the Knesset. Thus I shall not go now into the core of the matter. I shall only make a few comments in response to certain views and criticism expressed here.

First of all, is it not clear to the other side that in exchange for the payment - if there will be one —there will not be a reward? Germany will not be rewarded in the sense of attaining forgiveness or forgetting. I think that this is completely clear. One of the people who came to us from Germany for clarifications was requested to inform Bonn that nothing will be forgiven. Nothing will be forgotten for generations, perhaps in perpetuity. Furthermore, we were informed by the US State Department on the basis of their contacts with Adenauer and the Bonn government, contacts which they are not bound to keep secret and without them knowing that we had submitted such a statement that the other side fully understands that it will receive no reward, political or moral, for the payment and that the State of Israel is not going to change its attitude towards Germany in the international arena.

My second comment: I do not know what the outcome will be. I am not a prophet. There are prophets among us who declare that nothing will come of it. I will not utter a decisive prophecy that I am sure we shall obtain the $1 billion to the last cent. I shall by no means say that. But I do not accept the certainty of those who say that we will not succeed. In the course of my life I have been partner to political initiatives that people among us decreed would not be attained and were impossible to attain, but the fact is that they came about. Once upon a time I heard irrefutable proof from MK Riftin that the establishment of the State of Israel was impossible. I did not then prove that it would happen. I said that we must demand it and fight for it. And we have seen that this is what came about.

When we submitted the reparations note, numerous people claimed that nothing would come of it and that Germany would not accept it. It has accepted it as the basis. I will not say that it will pay the entire sum, but it is possible. We have already seen one impossible initiative become a reality. Perhaps the other impossible initiative will become a reality as well. It depends on our effort and on their interest.

A third comment regarding a referendum: the issue of a referendum has not been discussed and decided upon by the cabinet. But if you seek my opinion, it is two-sided. First, I am personally opposed to a referendum. True, we are faced with an extraordinary issue here, but who determines the extraordinary quality of any given issue? If a precedent is set it could bring new procedures in its wake; in any event, it could elicit arguments for establishing a procedure or a fight for setting it. I view a referendum as an undemocratic procedure per se since it does not enable the electorate to familiarize itself with the issue at hand, to clarify it;

the electorate becomes prey to all kinds of demagogic stratagems and to making unbalanced or irresponsible decisions. Factually, I am certain that a referendum on this issue would reveal a large majority in favor of negotiations.

A final comment on the background. We have heard repeated arguments here that we have been tardy with the reparations claim. I would like to read two excerpts from a briefing I sent out to our legations in April 1951, with the purpose of providing them with proof of the practicality of the matter. I shall read out the part dealing with the problem of whether or not we were tardy:

> Regarding the question of choosing the suitable date for submission of the reparations claim in view of the process of Germany being accepted into the international community, it could be argued that the claim would have been more effective had it been submitted at the start of the "acceptance" process. However, upon consideration it seems to me that its efficacy is likely to increase towards the end of that process. There are grounds to assume that if the road to membership in the community of European nations were not long and laden with obstacles, Germany would not have displayed such great sensitivity towards clearing its debt to the Jewish people as it is likely to do now, when it has almost attained its objective, and it is worth its while to make a special effort to clear the final obstacles from its path.

It is also quite easy to refute the argument that we missed submitting our claim for compensation to the powers when they dealt with the problem of imposing payment of compensation after the end of the war. I continue reading the briefing:

> What does being tardy from the standpoint of reparations mean? Those who think so mean that had our claim been submitted earlier, it might have been taken into account in the division of compensation imposed on Germany at the time, and we would have received some part of the spoils taken from it. Today, now that we have appeared after that division, we are likely to come out empty-handed. Some are lenient and do not fill us entirely with despair; they remind us that the Western Powers' Reparations Commission is still deliberating in London to conclude the accounting, and we must hasten to become part of that circle of accounts so that we might salvage something for ourselves. Both sides are missing the point and do not grasp the essence of our claim.
> All these claims of missing the boat with regard to reparations, including the version showing lenience and giving us an extension, are essentially groundless. They are intended to bind us to the Yalta and Potsdam Accords on compensation payments imposed on Germany. But those arrangements are a procrustean bed for us; even if we had been recognized earlier as a partner to them, our reward would have been worthless and the whole thing would not have been worth the disgrace. In other words, the Yalta and Potsdam Accords were founded upon two principles, which jointly and separately were inappropriate to our special issue: first, the aim of the compensation was to cover war damage caused to Allied countries; second, payment of compensation was not imposed on Germany's annual revenue but on its existing means of production. If we rested the main points of our claim on these two principles, their incompatibility would be evident: first, we are claiming compensation not for war damage but for the expropriation and destruction of property during the war and in the years preceding it; second, we are

claiming compensation of a magnitude that cannot be covered by Germany's existing means of production but which quite naturally must accrue from current production and paid in installments over a period of years.

And here we come to the main refutable point in the argument on tardiness. Had we submitted the claim earlier we would have killed it with our own hands. Submitting it two or three years ago would have found the German economy in ruins, its production nil, the chances of its recovery unknown. In that situation, our claim would have been unavoidably reduced, and we could not have had the courage to specify the sum we are claiming today. Furthermore, with regard to the reduced sum we would have claimed, we would have been compelled to compete against all the other claimants, and there can be no doubt about the sorry outcome of that competition. We would have been forced to accept the little we were offered as clearing the account, for we would have forced ourselves into the overall international arrangement. It is precisely because of our restraint, because we took care not to enter into the general turmoil, that we can now present our claim as something separate and unique and to independently determine its dimensions, defined by the essence of the claim on the one hand and by Germany's current payment capabilities on the other. These are not subject to the general rates of compensation that have become obsolete.

Chairman Meir Argov: This meeting is now adjourned.

[18] The Reparations Agreement with Germany General Debate and Decision

Knesset Sessions 38-40[1], 7-9.1.1952

Speaker Yosef Sprinzak: The prime minister has the floor.

Prime Minister David Ben Gurion: Mr. Speaker, Members of the Knesset, as members of the first Knesset will recall, on January 6, 1951 the government of Israel submitted a note to the governments of the United States, the USSR, Britain and France regarding payment of compensation and restitution of plundered property to Jews by Germany. The note mentioned the payment and restitution owing to individuals and noted that meeting all these personal claims in no way concludes the German people's grave obligation vis-à-vis the Jewish people for the plunder of the property and confiscation of assets of Jews throughout Europe, those Jews who were slaughtered without leaving heirs.

Accordingly, on March 12, 1951 the government submitted a second note to the four allied powers. From a formal standpoint this claim is unprecedented in the annals of international relations. In the note the government of Israel demanded that reparations amounting to $1.5 billion be imposed upon Germany, both West and East, this sum covering only part of the plundered Jewish property. This claim was submitted out of the conviction that the entire German people, residing in West Germany and East Germany alike, were equally responsible for the killing and plunder perpetrated against the Jewish people in Europe. In the note the government made it clear that this responsibility was imposed upon both sectors of present day Germany. It also noted that the State of Israel, in its capacity as the sovereign embodiment of the Jewish people, was both entitled and duty-bound to demand satisfaction for the rights and property of the millions of victims, who were slaughtered and burnt in crematoria and gas chambers while

---

1   The debate, in which 30 out of the 120 Knesset members participated, lasted for three days.

their property was confiscated, stolen and plundered only because they belonged to the Jewish people.

Determining the reparations was based upon two basic assumptions:

a. Our duty to restore, to the greatest possible extent, the plundered property of Jews without heirs, and to take it from the murderers and those who came after them, in East Germany and West Germany alike, so that the murderer will not also take possession.

b. Our obligation, aided by Jewish communities throughout the world, to assimilate Holocaust survivors and absorb them in Israel and to utilize the restored property for this purpose.

The note stated that this claim is unprecedented since during the Holocaust the State of Israel did not exist and did not fight with its own army against Nazi Germany, although thousands of its sons and daughters volunteered for Jewish units in the framework of the British Army, first and foremost in the battalions of the Jewish Brigade which took part in defeating the Hitler regime.

It was also noted that there is no precedent for the acts of slaughter and plunder of such tremendous magnitude perpetrated against the Jews of Europe by the German people under Hitler's rule. More than six million Jews were put to death by torture, starvation, killing, and mass asphyxiation. Many were burnt and buried alive. No mercy was shown to the aged, women and children. Babies were torn from their mothers' arms and cast into the furnaces. Before the mass and systematic murder and during and after it, came the plunder which was also of vast, unprecedented scope. According to the most conservative estimate, during the period of Hitler's rule the Germans plundered Jewish property in Germany and the Nazi-occupied countries valued at some $6 billion. There are some estimates that reach even larger figures.

A crime of such magnitude cannot be forgiven by means of any material compensation. Any compensation whatsoever, great as it may be, cannot be commensurate with the loss of human life or forgive the suffering and anguish of men and women, children, the elderly and infants.

Yet the German people, even after the defeat of Hitler's regime, continue to enjoy, in the West and East alike, the fruits of the slaughter and the looting, the robbery and the plunder of the murdered Jews.

The government of Israel views itself as duty-bound to demand that the German people restore the plundered Jewish property; on the one hand, to restore that property of the surviving claimants and heirs, and on the other to restore the vast property that has no heirs to the State of Israel – committed to welfare of the Holocaust survivors and which so far has absorbed the vast majority of them.

Even before the establishment of the state, the Yishuv of Palestine played a decisive role in the absorption of German refugees who started to arrive following the outbreak of Nazi persecution in 1933. During the war the soldiers of the

Jewish Brigade were the first to encounter the survivors in the detention and death camps in Germany and Central European countries, and to raise their spirits by bringing them the message of our resourceful and fighting homeland.[2] Upon its establishment, the State of Israel opened its gates to all displaced persons and survivors of the countries in which the killing took place, and in the last two or three years, hundreds of thousands of survivors have reached a safe haven in independent Israel.

The majority of the survivors brought only their lives to Israel, for all their property had been plundered. A tremendous task has been imposed upon the government of Israel, a task which is also unprecedented in contemporary history and perhaps even throughout past generations: the rapid absorption of hundreds of thousands of immigrants who came with only the clothes on their backs into a young, poor country under Arab siege. The burden that this mass, impoverished immigration has imposed upon the state is beyond its capabilities and the Jews of the free world have assumed their duty to participate in this vast enterprise. Nevertheless, the burden upon the state is still great. Thus, not only does it have a moral right – even though this right has no formal precedent in the annals of international relations – but also a sacred duty to do everything within its power to restore at least a great part of the plunder to its rightful owners, so that the Nazi murderers' heirs in West and East Germany would not also become the heirs of the murdered Jews.

The government of Israel specified the sum of $1.5 billion as its claim from both sectors of Germany – although the plundered property's value was several times higher according to authoritative, expert estimates – because it is the minimal sum required for the absorption of half a million immigrants from countries that were under Nazi rule.

Payment of these reparations to the State of Israel does not absolve the German governments in the West and East from the responsibility imposed upon them to pay everything due for their plundered property to individual Jews living here with us or to their legitimate heirs. These reparations will be claimed by the representatives of world Jewry.

As I mentioned, the note was sent to the four occupying powers: The United States, the Soviet Union, Britain and France, and the claim was directed at both parts of present-day Germany, West and East. So far we have received no response from the Soviet Union, and the same goes for East Germany. We have received an official reply from the other three powers in almost identical wording. The replies were sent on July 5, 1951, some four months after the note was submitted.

In its note to Israel's ambassador in Washington, the American administration writes that the government of Israel is surely aware that the despicable crime against humanity perpetrated by the Nazi regime in the planned extermination and plundering of the Jews of Europe has appalled the American people and its government. The government of Israel must surely also be aware that from the

---

2   See document no. 7, note no. 3, on the Jewish Brigade.

beginning of the conquest of Germany, it has been the American administration's firm policy to bring to justice all those responsible for the planning and implementation of the crime and to rectify, as far as possible, the wrongdoing committed against the victims of Nazi persecution. The note goes on to say that the United States government gave shelter to thousands of Jewish refugees who fled Nazi persecution during the war, and at the end of the war it enacted special laws in order to open its gates to many of those who survived, penniless and bereft, because of the war and Nazi oppression. Together with Britain and France, it also made substantial contributions to refugee organizations and for refugees who had settled in Israel through the International Refugee Organization [IRO].

Although the Jewish victims of the Nazis, the American government adds, were not represented at the Paris Compensation Conference, a sum of $25 million confiscated from German deposits in neutral countries was allocated to the rehabilitation of Nazi victims, and it was then acknowledged that the majority of those victims were Jews; thus it was decided that 90 percent of that sum and also all the unclaimed property of Jewish victims in those countries would be earmarked for the benefit of the Jewish victims. The United States government does not think that these reparations given to Jewish refugees are sufficient compensation for their suffering. The United States government accepts the view of the government of Israel that no material compensation can be sufficient. But the American government notes that other peoples who suffered at Nazi hands also have no chance of obtaining reparations that can adequately compensate them. But the main point of this note – and the same holds true of the notes from Britain and France – is to clarify that according to certain agreements to which the United States was a party, it is not entitled to demand further compensation from Germany at this time, neither for itself nor for others.

The responses from Britain and France were in the same spirit. However, it should be noted that this formal reply does not exhaust the full and final position of these three countries, for there are not only governments there but also free public opinion that can exert pressure on their governments and on other nations as well. Jewish communities in these countries are free to voice their pain and their claims carry considerable weight, though it is not decisive. Public opinion in these countries – both in general, and more particularly Jewish – was not satisfied with the formal stance and platonic sympathy of their governments but demanded rectifying the wrong as far as possible, at least in the sphere of restitution. This pressure of public opinion led the German chancellor to announce at the end of September 1951, that the horrific crimes perpetrated against the Jews during the Nazi regime impose upon the German people the duty of compensating the Jewish people, and the West German parliament ratified his statement.

At the end of October 1951 at the initiative of the Jewish Agency, a conference was convened of Jewish organizations from the United States, Canada,

South Africa, South America, the countries of Western Europe, Australia, and world Jewish organizations such as the Jewish Agency, Agudat Yisrael, the World Jewish Congress, and so forth, in order to discuss Jewry's claim from Germany. In a resolution passed unanimously, the conference in fact identified with the government of Israel's note to the four powers. The conference also declared that the atrocities perpetrated against the Jews by the Nazi regime, their brutality and scope, cannot be forgiven and no material compensation can atone for them. No reparations – whatever they may be – can atone for the extermination of millions of Jews and the destruction of Jewish cultural values. Nevertheless, the conference of the Jewish people decided to demand that the Germans at least restore the plundered Jewish property, compensate the victims of the persecution, their heirs and descendants, and ensure reparations for the rehabilitation of the survivors as demanded in the government of Israel's note of March 12, 1951.

The conference declared that the West German chancellor's statement would be judged and assessed in accordance with his government's actions, and by the pace and scope of its implementation. The conference expressed its full and loyal support for the claim submitted by the government of Israel for reparations of $1.5 billion from West and East Germany. The conference also demanded that the claims of the remainder of the Jews of Germany be met, including the claims of Jewish individuals and organizations.

As a consequence of the pressure brought to bear by the New York conference, and due to the friendly intervention of government circles in Britain and other countries, a few weeks ago the chancellor of the Bonn government in West Germany undertook in writing, on behalf of his government, to discuss reparations with the State of Israel and representatives of world Jewry on the basis of the claim submitted by the government of Israel in its note of March 12, 1951.

The government of Israel and the entire Jewish people view the German people as responsible for the atrocities committed against European Jewry during WW II. Those atrocities will never be forgotten, and any government in Germany – be it in the West or the East – that does not make a firm, full and practical effort to rectify what can be rectified, cannot shed full responsibility for the Nazi crimes. The righting of this wrong must take place not only in the material sphere, the restitution of plundered property to Jewish individuals and organizations to the Jewish people and to the State of Israel. It is also incumbent on the United Nations – on all those nations loyal to principles of peace and human dignity – to see to it that the Germans do not evade their heavy responsibility which perhaps has no precedent in the history of mankind. At the United Nations General Assembly, presently convening in Paris, the Israeli delegation has expressed its anxiety and concern over the danger inherent in the rearmament of West and East Germany.

The government of Israel, together with representatives of world Jewry, views it as its duty to make every appropriate effort, without undue delay, to speedily restore the maximum quantity of the plunder to individual Jews and the Jewish people as demanded in our note of March 12, 1951. Let not the murderers of our people also be their inheritors!

Speaker Yosef Sprinzak: The Knesset Committee has decided to allocate ten hours to the debate on this item on the agenda. MK Elimelech Rimalt has the floor.

MK Elimelech Rimalt (*General Zionists*)**:** The government is asking for the Knesset's authorization to conduct negotiations, at this stage with the West German government, in order to obtain compensation for confiscated property, compensation that for some reason is termed "reparations." This question has engaged public opinion for many months. It has been causing much agitation, and the closer we came to the Knesset debate, and the Knesset demanded this debate, the agitation has intensified. I am sure that this question is also painful for those who support direct negotiations with Germany. I am sure that they too, the government and the parties asking us to authorize negotiations on payments, are doing so not without hesitation and not without an inner struggle. Under the present circumstances, the word "compensation" is more appropriate than "reparations;" the Hebrew word "reparation" has connotations of vengeance and reprisal. The debate on this issue is replete with pain, memories of a disaster, a catastrophe unprecedented and unparalleled even in our history, a history tainted with suffering and torture, a history of a people that time and time again experienced physical but not spiritual, destruction. It is vital that the debate be conducted in this House at the highest moral level of which we are capable. We must not debate the issue as saints versus villains, as loyalists versus traitors, as good versus evil. We must debate with our brothers, who in our view are wrong and terribly confused. Our people once possessed absolute moral criteria: the Torah, a spiritual heritage common to and binding upon all. And when there were disagreements on the interpretation of one item or another of that heritage, when the two items were sometimes contradictory, a "third version that decided between them" was always found, and the third version was accepted by all, its authority was not doubted or controversial. Today we do not possess one binding, authoritative, moral criterion, although in more recent times we have achieved such a criterion again, thanks to the Zionist movement and the values of national awakening it evoked, which not only endowed us with a common language but have also made us think in common terms.

And how paradoxical it is that with the establishment of the state, the embodiment of the yearnings of generations, we have apparently lost this criterion common to the entire people! For now, a third authoritative and decisive version binding upon all is hard to find, and hence our confusion. We must now conduct a serious, bitter and painful debate against the tragic backdrop of the Holocaust.

And tragic, too, is the fact that this issue was raised for debate at all, regardless of the good intentions of those proposing direct negotiations.

And another preliminary remark: we cannot avoid calling witnesses to this debate, silent ones, invisible ones, witnesses whose very appearance chills our blood. Let us not desecrate their memory, let us not turn the controversy and debate into a cheap partisan controversy, let us not make political capital out of it, for the pain is too deep, and the heart of each one of us is bleeding. Whether we want to or not, we shall turn these sessions into a painful remembrance ceremony such as this House has never before witnessed. Therefore, we must conduct a brotherly debate out of pain. We shall endeavor to convince you of our view, to arouse you, to shock you, to appeal to your conscience, to open the hearts of the Knesset and the people.

This will be a fierce debate for another reason: it will not be conducted by equal forces. Two main forces exist within every man's soul and apparently within the soul of every people. The first is the force of logic, of deliberation, of thought in accordance with rules that are reputedly common to all humankind; the normal civilized man relies on rational thinking in his everyday, practical life. The second force is irrational or emotional. Under normal circumstances, these forces operate in the lives of sane, healthy people on different spheres. Practical life is ruled by logic, by deliberation, while emotion rules in spiritual spheres such as religion, art, and so on. But sometimes, when these forces are mixed up and invade the other sphere, a tragedy occurs in the life of the individual and in the life of a people. If in instances where common sense should guide a person, emotional forces determine his path instead, or conversely, if in extraordinarily fateful moments, when the weak light of the torch of logic, of common sense, is inadequate and cannot show the way out of the labyrinth, then reliance on logic and cool reasoning may lead to tragedy.

In the lives of nations, too, there are moments in which cool logic is but a flickering lamp. Were all of man's thought processes outside the irrational, were they subject to rational logic, then it would be impossible to argue, for rational logic is objective and its reasoning clear and persuasive. But not all our thoughts are controlled by reason; to a certain extent our train of thought is subject to the irrational, and this may lead to conflict.

Regarding the issue under discussion: those in favor of direct negotiations, whatever their intention, argue from the standpoint of rational considerations, of "Have they killed and also taken possession?" They contend that Israel needs money, needs to strengthen the state, the same state that is the fulfillment of the yearnings of generations, so that if we can strengthen it with these reparations, receiving them could be viewed as justified, as retribution. That is how rational thinking goes. But those opposing direct negotiations cannot use this form of logic, for the background to the debate is an unprecedented, horrific historic event. Indeed, the Americans tell us that other people, too, were harmed and did not receive full compensation for what was looted from them. However, when we seek compensation for the plunder, we are thus shifting the debate to a dangerous area: to the generally accepted principle of imposing compensation for the plundering and expropriating. But our case is different. The plundering and looting of Jewish property has precedents in Jewish history. Which nation of the world has not plundered us? Rome, Byzantium… every nation that conquered and trampled on the Jews stole their money and then expelled them from their land. But this slaughter, this Holocaust, has no precedent throughout the generations. And the perpetrators were not a savage people of the Asian steppes, nor desert savages accustomed to slaughter and robbery. This was a civilized people, perhaps the most technically and materially advanced people in the world. University professors, educated professionals, the entire people, with all its talents, with all its diligence, with all its technological achievements – murdered, slaughtered an entire people. For what? What was the rationale, the logical reason? Not only did they take money; they took and they murdered. Germany's hatred emanated from a world of the darkest drives that are imprinted in the beast residing deep in man, it acted out of irrational, satanic motives, for in everything, in every thought and emotion, there are two sides: the negative satanic side and the good positive side. There can be no rational explanation for the phenomenon of people – educated people – maltreating children to the sound of a military band, dragging infants to be burned and slaughtered. Who among us has not seen the photographs taken by the Germans of piles of corpses from which, here and there, a dead man's fist was raised in a horrifying protest towards heaven? And in those photographs they were seen boasting of their deeds.

Was this crime rational? Can this phenomenon be categorized in the sphere of logic and rational debate? Is it surprising, then, if a reaction emerges against direct negotiations that goes beyond logic and cool deliberation? And since when has logic been the decisive force in our lives? Our entire history is often nothing more than a revolt against simple logic, for there are two kinds of logic: the logic that sees only the immediate present, and the logic that looks forward to the future. The Jewish people did not possess the first one throughout its up and downs: for 2,000 years the Jewish people yearned for and aspired to a land in which it lived for less than 2,000 years. All the years that our people lived in its land – from the days of the Patriarch Abraham till the destruction of the Second Temple – do not add up to 2,000 years. Apparently, the people could always have chosen the path of logic, to mingle with the gentiles during the periods of assimilation, when the assimilated Jew would have had the individual option of freeing himself from Jewish destiny. Zionism has taught us that the people will find no remedy in assimilation but only in national revival and a return to the homeland. But the national idea is only a recent chapter in modern history. In the Middle Ages the people could "manage"; it could choose the path of logic and escape its suffering. In the new era, however, any assimilated Jew could personally escape suffering. But there was something immeasurable binding him to his people, and that was the unique feeling embodied in Jewish destiny; there was something unfathomable that commanded him not to do what is "worthwhile," but to do what is "not worthwhile."

Look at what the Germans have done to us, as if, with a fiendish plan, they also sought to take the sanctity of martyrdom from us. Indeed, all of them – the holy victims – died in martyrdom, but what in fact is martyrdom? If one has the alternative of fleeing, of disappearing, of evading Jewish destiny and thus saving oneself but instead chooses to mount the gallows, then it can be said that a free choice of self- sacrifice has been made. But there is no martyrdom where there is no choice, if one is devoid of the choice of the moral act of martyrdom over a life of defilement. The evil Hitler left us with no choice. Nobody had a way out. There was no escape from fate. There was no possibility of being saved.

Having lost numerous lofty common principles of our Jewish heritage, what we have been left with – since "culture" cannot replace religion as a decisive principle, for it lives on others' values, on translation and imitation – is only a measure of reverence. We live in dread of our Jewish destiny, manifested in what is considered "illogical."

Behold what an evening this is for a Jew – the evening of the Kol Nidrei prayer on the eve of the Day of Atonement. What a holy moment for every Jew, even the most assimilated! But what is Kol Nidrei? It is an evening on which we go to the synagogue to listen to an almost judicial-formal declaration in Aramaic on the cancellation of obligations, vows, and so on. Does the content of the Kol Nidrei prayer justify its sanctity? No. But such are our lives, such are the foundations of our existence whereby we survived. Our national vision is not measured by its logic, and we cannot exist here in our country without a vision. Many peoples and countries were rich with assets, but material riches have yet to save a people devoid of vision, a people that has ceased to sanctify moral values, a people for whom moral values are worthless. That is why Zionists opposed the idea of solving the Jewish problem in Uganda[3] and the attempts to solve it in the Crimea,[4] and Birobidjan.[5] It was out of a profound irrational desire that

---

3   In 1903 the British colonial secretary's plan for settling East-European Jews in Uganda was transmitted to Dr. Theodore Herzl, President of the World Zionist Organization. The plan, submitted by Dr. Herzl to the 6th Zionist Congress in 1903 as a "temporary solution to the Jewish Problem" was later rejected by a vast majority of the delegates of the 7th Zionist Congress in 1905.

4   In the first half of the 1920s, a failed attempt was made to establish a Soviet Jewish autonomy in the Crimean peninsula, where some 40,000 Jews (6 percent of the population) were already residing.

5   In 1928 the Soviet government decided to allocate the Birobidjan region of Eastern Siberia for mass Jewish settlement, and in 1934 the region was declared a "Jewish autonomous region" in which both Yiddish and Russian would serve as official languages. The number of Jews that emigrated there did not exceed 50,000, and at its peak the Jewish population there constituted the fourth-largest national group.

we decided to fight for the establishment of the State of Israel in face of all the rational calculations.

And now we think that we can settle the account of generations accumulated with the German people through installments and payments. We think we can say: "We shall take this money, it is our due, but we are not conciliating with them, we will despise them, but we will take their money." In 1945, when the Germans were a defeated enemy, the victors could exact a price from them. It is a different situation today. Now, when the Germans are once again ruling the roost, when they are courted by many, we are in fact going to conclude a "gentleman's agreement" with them. But the Germans in the East and the West are one and the same, for people do not change in the course of a few years. A people, the majority of whom were murderers – and the few who were not either fled the country, or were detained in concentration camps – a people such as this does not change so quickly. And with these "gentlemen" we have to conclude a gentleman's agreement!

We, a proud people possessing a sovereign state, are going to sit together with them at the same table! They are dictating the negotiations to us, they who are not desert savages, and we shall sit at the same table with them, drink with them, shake many hands that spilt blood, the blood of our brethren and parents! The German chancellor is quite possibly not one of the murderers, perhaps he is set apart from the vast majority of his people, but what about his subordinates? I do not know what is happening in East Germany, hidden behind the Iron Curtain, but who knows how much time will elapse until the former Nazi General Otto Remer[6] succeeds Adenauer?

There is, of course, a difference between German cash money and its equivalent in goods. We will have to go and sell German goods in the outside world like hawkers. We will receive crates from Germany that might bear the slogan "Jude Verrecke" [Jew, perish] inscribed by an unknown hand. German longshoremen might send regards such as these to Israel. And what are their motives? Why do they want to pay? Perhaps the better ones amongst them seek to salve their consciences? Perhaps through compensation they seek peace and quiet, nights without nightmares of remorse? We should leave them to their nightmares, to their shattered consciences, to their mark of Cain. We must not relieve them of these horrors! For if history has meaning and justice, then that mark must remain so that they will not find peace, so that they remember what their people did, and shudder. But if we conclude a deal and say, according to our Jewish polemic acumen, we have taken the money but have not forgiven,

---

6   Otto-Ernst Remer (August 18, 1912–October 4, 1997) was a German Wehrmacht officer who played a decisive role in stopping the 1944 July 20 Plot against Adolf Hitler. The Socialist Reich Party, which he had co-founded in 1950, was banned in 1952. He was sentenced to 22 months imprisonment in October 1992 for writing and publishing a number of articles that were said to incite "racial hatred" by denying the Holocaust.

what will they say? They won't believe us. And the gentiles are familiar with the old rule: where there is trade, there are relations.

And what shall we say to our youth, to our children, our children in whom we have inculcated moral values, whom we taught that there are situations in which what might seem worthwhile can also be morally unacceptable? Can we prevent them from translating the money we shall receive into a per capita figure? My young son asked me: "How much will we get for Grandpa and Grandma?", for both of my parents were murdered. This is too grave and too painful for us. We did not want to reduce this bitter debate to partisan controversy, and you know that this is the way it will be.

And one more consideration, perhaps the most grievous of all: I do not know what we will get. Let us assume that we do receive compensation from them. Have we tried to measure at all what damage it will cause to our morals? We are a people endowed with something specific; there is a certain Jewish spiritual uniqueness, without which there is no hope of survival for either the state or even the Jewish people. This uniqueness has protected us down the generations and protected us against destruction. What will remain of our moral uniqueness if we remove all restrictions, if we no longer maintain the age-old prohibition concerning some things which we are "forbidden to enjoy?" Our people upheld such a concept, which was not only judicial but also moral. Are we now to endorse that everything enjoyable is permissible?

Let us not justify this matter of reparations with "Hast thou killed and also taken possession?" In that case the killing occurred because of the possession, because of money, and so in this case punishment should fit the crime and the guilt. But Hitler did not murder Jews for their money. He could, and did, extract their money without murdering. The German people murdered from their darkest drives. Perhaps this mark of Cain should remain forever for the world to see, for we believe that the world will not attain peace and quiet even if a compromise is reached between different social regimes, if the original sin of humankind against the Jewish people is not atoned for, if no guarantees are established, so that what happened in recent years will never recur in human history. Till that moment, the world must not find peace and quiet. However, we ourselves are helping in this artificial appeasement by salving an unclean conscience.

It was the Holocaust – this can be said – that brought about the establishment of the State of Israel, and for two reasons. It was established not only after we witnessed what could be perpetrated against us and led us to declare that there is no refuge, no choice, no salvation and no existence for the Jewish people without its own state; for tomorrow Maidanek is established here and the day after, somewhere else. That was the first logical reason. But there was another, subconscious reason: what shocked us all after we recovered from the first blow? It was a tragic thought that perhaps, Heaven forbid, there was no sense in the suffering, in the slaughter, in the catastrophe, was there no moral-historical conclusion to be drawn from this appalling Holocaust? Was it all in vain? Just for nothing?

During the War of Independence a profound insight took hold of us: that there was indeed some sense, some unfathomable rationale for all the indescribable suffering of the Holocaust: that it gave birth to the State of Israel, that it brought about the fulfillment of age-old yearnings. Let us not then turn our accounting with Germany into haggling over payments. Let us all listen not to the staged outrage, not to the shouting in the streets, for those voices are liable to silence the inner voice that each one of us must hear in his heart. All of us, those in favor and those opposing, hear that inner voice telling us: "Jews, what are you about to do?" At this moment the Knesset has no other way but to decide: No negotiations with the murderers! The account with them cannot be settled in this generation. And if we obtain payments, Talmudic rule says: "He who pays is not damaged," and that rule has a moral significance, not only a judicial one. There is no alternative but to decide that we shall not take money from bloodstained hands.

The country needs money, resources for its support. We should all make a concerted effort towards achieving this purpose, but not by the payment of reparations, for this money would not do us any good. The issue at hand belongs to the realm of faith. It is hard to argue over it with a bookkeeper's pencil, over a balance sheet, for this money is bloodstained and accursed. It shatters the moral backbone of each and every one of us and of the entire nation. It destroys the innermost spiritual core of our deepest subconscious.

Let us not add a further calamity to the day of tribulation, the tenth of Teveth,[7] which we mark tomorrow – the calamity of the final disintegration of the people's lofty moral values. The moral value that is beyond the grasp of logic is not measurable mathematically, by considerations of benefit or of opportunism. It is not justified by necessity. That issue should be erased from our national agenda! Let us free ourselves and the state from this nightmare, for as with any healthy body, once you impair its balance, that body will convulse and spasm and not find rest. The decision to accept payments is likely to impair the moral and spiritual balance of the people, destroy its moral force. It will cause unrest in the country. Let us not allow this.

In the name of the country's public opinion, with the support of all those silent witnesses to this debate who cannot be with us today, let us strike this issue from the agenda!

MK Yaakov Chazan (*Mapam*): Members of the Knesset, on November 5, 1951, a crucial debate on foreign policy was held here. The significance of the government's proposal announced on that day, and also of the decision made by

---

7   According to Jewish tradition, it was on this day of the Jewish calendar that the Babylonian King Nebuchadnezzar put Jerusalem under the siege which ultimately led to its fall and to the destruction of the First Temple. Religious Jews fast on this day.

a Knesset majority, was tantamount to relinquishing our political independence. That was as far as the outside world was concerned. Internally, it resulted in a deep political schism in the country, a widening political schism that is endangering our entire future.

Today, the continuation of that debate carries with it a much graver character. Today the government is proposing relinquishing our spiritual independence, the sale of our souls following the sale of our bodies.

In two instances we would have been able and entitled to deal with the issue of reparations from Germany:

    a.   Had the defeated Germany been ordered to restore to us everything it stole from us, in the same way as a payment was imposed on it by the victors at the end of the war;

    b.   Had we negotiated with a German people that had mercilessly eradicated and destroyed Nazism and the Nazis, and had atoned in this way for its crimes and expressed its willingness not for reparations, but for the restitution of all the property plundered from the Jewish people.

But what is the concrete situation?

    a.   The victors, our Western "friends," did not want to include us among the victors and did not include us among the recipients of the payment, and they did so with good reason.

    b.   The German people is not a people that eradicated Nazism, it is not a people that destroyed the Nazis. On the contrary: Nazism in Germany is on the rise again. Nazi Germany is being revived and our Western "friends" are nurturing that Nazism. They are reestablishing Nazi Germany and that Germany will again bring havoc to the world. It is with this Nazi Germany that the government of Israel intends to conduct negotiations, the basic meaning of which is negation of the heroic struggle of the Warsaw Ghetto fighters, betrayal of the hell of agony undergone by the Jewish people.

This is the appalling inner Jewish meaning of this intention. But what is the political content hidden behind this whole reparations issue? We heard a clear reply to this the day after Adenauer's first statement when Berlin Radio announced that we should not expect reparations of large dimensions. They – the Germans – are, as is known, a poor nation. But in my opinion that is not the main issue. In the final analysis, all that pertains to the past. The main issue now is that we Jews are in the same boat with the Germans, for we have been jointly commanded to save civilization from the so-called communist danger "that threatens to destroy Western civilization, to destroy us and your brethren" – thus Radio Berlin – and that and only that is the real meaning of Adenauer's statement. That is the appalling, true political significance of our agreement to conduct negotiations with them.

What is the government proposing? It is proposing something extremely odd, something that even a political tyro would not believe possible: to conduct negotiations with the German government – and not de facto recognition of the German government. An act like that has never before been staged by any state in the world, and has no chance of being accomplished by our foreign policy. This is squaring the circle. Negotiations with the Bonn government on reparations are, in fact, de facto recognition of neo-Nazi Germany. That is the main point. This is the appalling political conclusion inevitably resulting from these negotiations. It is becoming increasingly clear that a third world war will not be an atomic one, and consequently there is a need for present-time cannibals, murderers and Nazis, without whom a third world war could not be waged. The European nations do not want a world war. To lead them into such a war, a new camp of murderers, the camp that has already murdered once, is needed. Without it there will be no war. And there are only two candidates for these camps of cannibals: Nazi Germany in Europe and fascist Japan in the Far East. To these German murderers they want to give as a gift what they did not achieve by means of murder: they want to position them at the center of Europe, and the cost of the gift is the service of performing new global murder. The Western powers want West Germans to lead Europe against the Soviet Union. Are you willing to support this despicable act? We, the State of Israel, the sole heirs of the six million, for whom we once meant to pass a law making them citizens of the State of Israel – shall we justify this crime? Can you not see that this is the meaning of your current proposal?

If this proposal is accepted, it means entering into official negotiations with a government that is run by and large by former Nazis, and whose army is already Nazi. Moreover, the most terrible thing is that preparations are already being made for our joining the camp in which Nazi Germany will be the leading and decisive force. Our army, the Israel Defense Forces, will slide into the political abyss and will find itself in the same camp as the Nazi army, and the Nazis, who have already appeared in the vicinity of Israel as advisors to Arab states, will start coming here not as our bitterest enemies but as our partners; nothing could be more appalling. That, and none other, is the real significance of the government's proposal.

The government's concern for the state's economic and financial future is understandable. However no reparations will materialize. The Germans have already deceived the world once, they deceived the world that had the power to force them to pay, and they will not deceive us? Did they pay reparations after WW I? Have they not already begun to evade paying what they must after WW II? The same will be with us. We will receive some money but lose our integrity in return. How can we be caught so appallingly in that same web of deceit that makes us, the victims of Nazi murder, the sponsor of the Nazi return to the international arena? (*MK Yochanan Bader (Herut): Gas against Jews! That's it. That's how you'll win. The gas is outside!*[8]); (*Chairman Yosef Sprinzak: I ask the members not to interrupt a Knesset debate*); (*MK Yochanan Bader (Herut): We are in the Land of Israel.*); (*Chairman Yosef Sprinzak: Yes, we are in the Knesset of the State of Israel.*) The government's proposal will inevitably lead towards such a development. In the home arena it has already led to what we saw on entering the Knesset building today: it was surrounded by barbed wire. We saw many policemen preparing for battle. Evidently, the devil's dance has already begun among us. There will be no reparations, but on the other hand the destructive tensions within our society will deepen.

We are debating one of the most tragic issues of our lives, a problem that must surely deepen the chasm of alienation and hostility within our people, that must surely lead to ceasing to understand one another, and this at a time when it is impossible to live without some trace, be it the tiniest, of national solidarity. We lack the confidence that we live, despite everything, within a framework of shared moral values. The government's proposal endangers all that. The proposal means recognition of the Bonn government's legitimacy. It means that we are moving towards our integration into the camp in which the German army is the main force. It means that we shall march together with them in the new global march of murder. It means that we would be compelled to offer our hand to those who will again be the murderers of our people. Because, clearly, they will return to history's stage as they are today, as Nazis. And those who will give us reparations will murder us again. They will murder us everywhere they go, and if they come here, they will murder us here, too. These then are our new partners? Our party is most vehemently opposed to this, heart and soul. We shall vote unhesitatingly against this proposal. We will view it, even after it is adopted, as non-binding. We shall continue to fight it, and we will enlist the Israeli people against what we consider as one of the foulest situations could possibly are bring down upon us.

MK Yitzhak Raphael (*Hapoel Hamizrachi*)**:** Members of the Knesset, the debate taking place today is without doubt bitter and tragic, necessitating meticulous consideration and a serious approach. Only someone who has devoted much thought to this issue, an issue that has troubled him day and night, and who has examined it from all its aspects, is able and entitled, after he has examined it in the light of the love of Israel in his heart, to determine a pro or con position. A debate such as this calls for a calm and quiet atmosphere so that we can listen to each other, hear and also try to understand each other. My heart is open to the opponents' arguments. I have read their articles and explanations. I have thought

---

8   MK Yohanan Bader's shouting was triggered when he burst into the Knesset at that
     moment from the street, where demonstrators organized by the Herut Party were
     approaching the Knesset building, shouting and throwing stones while the police were
     dispersing them with tear gas (about the pandemonium that ensued at this point around
     the Knesset building and inside the plenum hall, see Appendix A.)

about, considered, and rejected their verdict. In a matter such as this there is no place for hysteria, especially when it is artificially inflamed.

An inner, practical approach, free of alien thoughts, is called for. We must discuss the facts as they are, facts that cannot be dissected by a partisan scalpel in accordance with factional allegiance.

The general atmosphere surrounding this debate, "the rage of the people" that is being organized through blatant inter-party competition, engenders flawed reasoning. We have the impression that not everyone is acting altruistically, and there is a gnawing doubt that narrow partisan factors are at work here. Who among the opponents of direct negotiations has an interest in presenting the proponents as seeking conciliation with the Germans? Why the rush to doubt the chances of reparations or belittle their scope? Does it strengthen our position vis-à-vis the outside world? The claimants of restitution of property plundered from our brethren and parents have clearly and categorically stated that even if it involves personal contact with representatives of Germany, it contains no step whatsoever towards settling the terrible blood account that we have with the sons of that nation of murderers, the offspring of Satan. Our heads of state and leaders have declared, and they reiterate this declaration time and time again, that eternal hatred exists between us, the survivors of that hell, and the people of Nazi Germany. That declaration is a vow for generations to come.

There are a few unrestrained, flippant and rootless Jews constituting a tiny marginal phenomenon who reside among Germans, enjoy their bread and wine, and even intermarry with them. They are destined to everlasting abhorrence. But our people at large will remember; a people like us does not forget.

Our reckoning, however, is much wider. It is not limited to West Germany alone, for the people of West and East Germany were joined together in the execution of those satanic crimes. Who are those among us who dare to take the liberty of differentiating between the perpetrators? The selective attitude of Mapam and the Communist Party, dividing the two Germanys according to political boundaries, should be roundly deplored. This attitude is rooted in bizarre considerations. It is not based on feelings of the Jewish heart. It is not governed by a concern for our national project and its success. This attitude is alien to us. Let not those who are defiling the State of Israel from far-away, foreign platforms turn suddenly into defenders of our national honor!

Even though I might disagree with the practical considerations of the opponents of negotiations, I do empathize with their negative attitude when it is pure and consistent. However, I think that initially there was a great deal of justice in the contentions of the proponents who demanded the restitution of Jewish property to us, their legal heirs, and who view claiming from an enemy nation and its realization as a duty and a commandment.

There is indeed much room for hesitancy, for a sigh, for pangs of the conscience. Were it not for the numerous needs of our people, the grave financial difficulties in implementing the task imposed upon us, it is doubtful whether the most enthusiastic of those in favor would be eager for direct contact with representatives of Germany, a contact fraught with numerous dangers and demanding great caution. The heart bleeds on seeing that the needs and their size tip the balance. Our burden of debt is onerous, but one should bear this willingly. Building up the country calls for sacrifices, physical and mental alike. The ingathering of the exiles is only just beginning, and we cannot slacken its pace. The Jewish communities in Moslem countries are groaning and suffering, living in shameful conditions and in danger of extinction, and crying out for help. Hundreds of thousands of our Jewish brethren await immediate salvation. The opportunities for immigration are dwindling before our eyes due to lack of funds and of means for treating ailing Jewish children before their immigration. Poverty is thwarting the implementation of rescue programs. And it must be said openly: if we had the money, we could bring down the walls behind which fine, young, healthy, loyal, pioneering people keep the national ember burning, and yearn for the day of their redemption. Anyone who has seen Jewish children wasting away from lack of treatment in the filth of the ghettos of Tehran and Isfahan, Casablanca and Marrakesh, in the villages of southern Tunisia and Algeria, knows full well that the onus of rescue stands above all, especially a rescue contributing to the building and development of the state. And as for the suffering of our newly arrived brethren here in the homeland in torn tents for homes, in the cold and wet without warm clothing, can we look at them with indifference? I have attentively read the "Order of the Day" issued by the Herut Party to its members, calling upon them to convene in Jerusalem for a "day of emergency," in which it was recommended that they "should prepare very warm clothing."[9] My heart was touched by this motherly concern of Herut for its followers, but are we exempt from concern for others as well, for the children and babies and the aged residing in the torn tents of immigrants' camps, who suffer from the cold not only for one "day of emergency" but day after day of emergency?

Our own people cannot provide us with what is both necessary and vital, and the nations of the world are hardly helping at all. While we are knocking on locked doors for help and understanding, shall we waive what is our rightful due, what was taken from us by force of arms? This is the time for fulfilling our obligations. We must overcome doubts and hesitation even when our inner feelings hold us back and deter us. We shall forcefully and loudly demand our due. We will submit our claim to West Germany and renew our claim from East Germany whose occupier, the Soviet Union, has so far not deemed it fit even to respond to our note. Sacred and noble is our aim, and to attain it we shall claim the inheritance of our brethren; noble as well are the needs to which it will be dedicated.

---

9   These instructions, issued in preparation for the Herut Party demonstration opposite the Knesset building on this day, were published in the *Herut* daily newspaper on January 6, 1952.

What we are claiming as a state, as the people's emissaries, is but a small part of what is due to us. And those who will claim in our name and in fact determine the means of payment should endeavor to reduce the payment period as much as possible so that our required contact with the Germans will also be short as possible. If we are to obtain the payments in the form of goods and industrial products, then we should choose what we need for our own use so that we do not become distributors of German goods in the world market. We should demand goods and industrial products that will not make our industry dependent on German spare parts. Germany has much to furnish us with. Let it be a one-time transaction. We need raw materials, chemicals, metal pipes, sheet steel, timber, prefabricated houses and so forth; all are vital for our development and the consolidation of our industry, and will not involve us with long-term trade with Germany.

I would also like to emphasize the importance of the tone we adopt in our negotiations. We should appear as claimants representing a victorious people, permeated with national pride, for our very survival as a people after such bloodletting proves our clear victory. Our representatives at the negotiations should not be of German extraction. Our people should speak to them through an interpreter. They should include Holocaust survivors who experienced the atrocities. In presenting our common interest, they will know what to say without displaying a spirit of conciliation and forgiveness. They should display national pride, as befits the government of a sovereign state that has only just tasted its independence, and of the Jewish people in the Diaspora, whose large and major organizations have given it their full support.

MK Menachem Begin (*Herut*)**:** Members of the Knesset, on March 13, 1951, Foreign Minister Sharett read us the note he submitted to America, England, France and Russia as to what he terms "reparations from Germany."

In the debate on that note, I attempted to share with all the members of this House the emotional shock I underwent on reading the following: "Any progress towards restoring Germany to its place in the community of the world's nations is unthinkable as long as this fundamental debt remains unpaid." These words are not open to interpretation. They are completely clear. They say that if the issue of compensation to the Jewish people is put into effect – then, in the government's view the restoration of Germany's honor as a nation among the community of nations is obviously possible.

My rival colleagues, at the time my words upset you, you created an uproar, you heckled me, you falsely accused me of falsely accusing the foreign minister that he was prepared to negotiate with Germany. Then old Rabbi Nurock appealed to the foreign minister not to commit the "national crime" of making contact with Germany. And now this government is going to go to Nazi Bonn!

Mr. Ben Gurion, you rebuked a member of the Knesset for going to Berlin, saying: "You went to Nazi Berlin." Is Berlin Nazi, and Bonn not? Does not the theory that East Germany is good and West Germany not lead to a theory that West Germany is democratic and East Germany Nazi?

Perhaps you will say that the Adenauer government is a new government, not a Nazi one? You must know who Adenauer is. I ask, in which concentration camp was he kept during Hitler's rule in Germany, into which prison was he thrown as a result of the Nazis' bloody regime? I ask, who are Mr. Adenauer's aides? The answer: approximately half of the staff in Adenauer's bureau were members of the Nazi Party. And with them – with the "experts" of Ribbentrop, with the "experts" of von Weizsäcker, with the murderers who prepared the ground for the extermination of millions of our brethren, telling the world that the news of the Jews' persecution was nothing but "grauel propaganda" [ghastly propaganda] – with them you are going to conduct discussions?

And perhaps you will say you can negotiate with that government which is prepared to give back part of the property because it does not bear responsibility for the murder? Let me remind you of the facts. Sixteen million Germans voted for Hitler before he rose to power. There were 12 million Communists and Social Democrats in Germany. Where did they disappear to? In the German army there were 12 million soldiers, millions in the Gestapo, the S.A. and the S.S. From a Jewish standpoint there is not one German who is not a Nazi and not one German who is not a murderer. And you are going to obtain money from them?

You argue that if we do not go and obtain the property from them, then we shall be leaving it in the hands of the plunderer. But now the figures have been publicized. At most you expect $300 million in Nazi German goods. You estimated the plundered Jewish property at $6 billion which means that you are going to get 5 percent of the plundered Jewish property while you leave 95 percent in the hands of the murdering robber. The difference is that if you do not go to Bonn, then the property remains plundered and Israel's claim still stands; but if you go to Bonn and sign an agreement with Nazi Germany, then by your agreement, by your signature, you announce on behalf of the Jewish people, in the name of the millions of victims, that 95 percent of the Jewish property is to remain in the hands of the murderer, in the hands of the thief. Who authorized you to do this? Who permitted you? Did those who are no longer with us give you such authority?

From whom are you going to claim the property? I will give you a simple example: Shimon set fire to the house of Reuven's father and Reuven's father died. What is Reuven to do? He can waive the house, for his father was burnt to death in it. He can go to court, submit a civil suit and claim the value of the destroyed house. But in what savage tribe can you witness the son of a murdered man going to the murderer and claiming the value of the house from him? But you, bereaved sons, orphans who have lost your fathers, are going directly to the murderer. Not to claim "indemnity", as you call it, for those murdered, but to obtain the value of the house in which your fathers were burnt to death. In what savage tribe can you witness such an abomination? Into what are you going to turn the Jewish people who for 4,000 years have both learnt and taught moral values?

You have laid the foundations for negotiations with Germany on the basis of Mr. Sharett's note. But there is also a second element of the bridge that Mr. Sharett crossed from Jewish Jerusalem to Nazi Bonn and that is Mr. Adenauer's own statement. It would be fitting if I read out that statement in the original, the language in which Mr. Adenauer is conducting negotiations with you, but the honor of this House – as long as it has not taken the fateful decision, fateful not only to me but to all of us, not for several years but for generations to come – is too precious in my eyes, so I will read it out in Hebrew. And thus said Herr Adenauer: "I state that the vast majority of the German people were revolted by these crimes. I state that the vast majority of the German people did not take part in these crimes." And Mr. Adenauer further stated that the German government would be prepared, together with representatives of Jewry and the government of Israel, to resolve the problem by rectifying the wrong – or in his own unclean language, *wiedergutmachung* – of the material aspect of the issue in order to facilitate a way of cleansing the soul of immeasurable suffering.

One Knesset member accused Mr. Sharett, and you, Mr. Ben Gurion, of having the text of the unclean note in your possession before Mr. Adenauer read it out to his Nazi advisers. If that is true, then woe to us all. You read it, you accepted a proposal whereby the majority of the German people were revolted by these crimes, and did not take part in them, as the basis for negotiations with the Germans. You accepted as the basis for negotiations a statement according to which this money will be given to you *Zur seelischen Reiningung eines unendlichen Leides* [for cleansing the soul of immeasurable suffering]. And if you did not read it, why did Mr. Sharett view this note as the commencement of negotiations? And if you read and approved it, then let the people of Israel know on what kind of bridge was contact established between Jewish Jerusalem and the Nazi Bonn government.

Adenauer's note was read by millions of Germans, millions of Americans, millions of Frenchmen. That note was well studied by the gentiles. All nations of the world have learned, this is the basis on which you will receive money in payment "for immeasurable suffering." How will we be pitifully looked upon, how will we be despised! To what depths have we sunk? Your reservations will be written in Hebrew – who will read them? The gentiles will be aware of one single fact: you sat at the same table with the murderers of your people, that you admitted that they are entitled to sign an agreement, that they are capable of upholding an agreement, that they are a nation – a nation member of the community of nations.

Not only did the gentiles hate us, not only did they murder us, not only did they burn us, not only did they envy us – they mainly despised us. And in this generation, which we call "the last of bondage and first of redemption"[10] – the generation in which we gained a position of respect, in which we came out of bondage – you, for a few million unclean dollars, for unclean goods, are going to deprive us of the little respect we have gained. You will set up a company called "Deu-Pal," short for "Deutschland-Palestine," and distribute German goods in France, England and America. You will be agents of the Nazis, distributors of German goods. How we will be despised in the world when a Jew, an emissary of the State of Israel, stands in his shop in Argentina and says: "Come and buy, they're fine goods, 'Made in Germany'." With this you are pulling the rug from under our feet; you are endangering our honor and independence. How we will be despised!

And against what international background is this taking place? Our talented ambassador in America used the phrase "the renewed Germany." Indeed, Germany is being renewed: 50 million in the West, and 25 million in the East. Their industry is booming. Nineteen million tons of steel a year – these are the achievements of "the renewed Germany." Churchill devoted half his book to describing the blindness and stupidity that led to Germany's rearmament and to WW II. Today he leads the march towards Germany's rearmament. Out of blindness, out of terrible fear, the fangs and claws extracted from it are being restored to the Teutonic wolf pack. And we are going to assist? Will we say that they are a nation, that they are entitled to conduct negotiations, that they will uphold an agreement signed by either America or Britain?

Mr. Ben Gurion, instead of speaking of the bankruptcy of the American Zionists,[11] if you had mobilized American Jewry to warn the American people of the danger facing it from the rearming of that wolf pack, then perhaps the situation would be different. Had that great Jewry risen and said: Germany will not be rearmed, perhaps the situation would be different. Perhaps this disaster could have been averted. But you joined forces with the assimilated Jews whose wealth has always been in inverse proportion to their courage and their loyalty to Zion. And one of the assimilated Jewish leaders said: "If the government has decided to rearm Germany, it's none of our business." These are your partners.

Woe betide us, for we are witnessing, five years after the end of the war, how the Nazi murderer has risen, how it is taking up arms. Today it is still talking smoothly with the Americans and French; soon, when it has the power, its true voice will be heard.

---

10 A phrase coined by the national poet Haim Nachman Bialik.

11 In numerous speeches he made since the establishment of the State of Israel, Prime Minister Ben Gurion contended that the Zionist Organizations in the Diaspora have lost their right to exist, for the Zionist aim has been achieved and thus real Zionists should immediately emigrate to Israel while former Zionists, who prefer residing abroad, cannot be defined any longer as Zionists.

Perhaps all these arguments are superfluous. Why this accounting, why the explanations? For there is but one account – the account of Jewish blood. There is but one argument: Jews, representatives of the government of Israel, are going to sit at the same table together with the German murderers. I shall therefore conclude my remarks with several appeals.

The first is to you, Mr. Ben Gurion. I appeal to you, not as rival to rival – as rivals there is an abyss between us, there is no bridge, there will be no bridge, it is an abyss of blood. I appeal to you at the last moment as Jew to Jew, as a son of an orphaned people, as a son of a bereaved people: do not do this! It is the blasphemy of all blasphemies in Israel; it is unparalleled since we became a nation. I am trying to give you a way out. As a rival I would not have given it to you, but as a Jew I will: go to the people; hold a referendum. Not because I suggest holding a vote on this issue; I do not think it is possible to vote on it. The votes have already been cast – in Treblinka, in Auschwitz, in Ponari. Jews voted there in their death throes: no contact, not negotiations with the Germans.

Go to the people!

You do not have a majority in the Knesset on this matter. Some of your own party's members oppose it, and I am proud that Jews, even though they are my opponents, even though they hate me, oppose these unclean negotiations. Some Hapoel Hamizrachi members oppose it, some Hamizrachi members oppose it, some Agudat Yisrael members oppose it. You are in the minority. True, you have forced them, you have intimidated them.

Go to the people! And should the people say "yes", then each of us will draw his own conclusions and perhaps say: "Surely the people *is* grass."[12] Perhaps all the sacrifices were in vain. But then you will be able to say: the people are behind me, 51 percent of the people are prepared to negotiate with them. But if the people say "no", you will not lose. After all, you are a democrat. You will bow to the will of the people. Why take this decision upon yourself? You do not have a majority. This is the way out. In God's name, I call on you: go, deliberate alone, back off, place this matter before the entire people and may God have mercy on us!

My second appeal is to the members of the Knesset who were elected by the country's Arab citizens. I would not, Heaven forbid, take your formal right to vote away from you. You have equal rights. I believe in equal rights. You have the formal right to vote on this matter, but I do draw a distinction between a formal and a moral right. This matter is ours, the blood of our mothers, brothers and sisters is mingled in it. Let us decide on this matter.

My third appeal is to the members of the religious parties. You went to the people in the general elections not in the name of this issue. You went into the elections in the name of the Jewish religion, the Jewish Torah. What has the Jewish Torah to do with negotiations with the Amalekites? With this vote you will expunge an entire, holy and sacred verse from the Torah: "The Lord will

---

12   Isaiah, 40:7.

have war with Amalek from generation to generation." How will the Lord fight Amalek if you, the defenders of the faith, vote for peace with Amalek, for receiving money from Amalek?

Today is the tenth of the month of Teveth, a day of remembrance for us all, and also the remembrance day for my father, and also a national remembrance day. (*Commotion in the hall, shouts from the Mapai benches.*)[13] I stand before you, members of the religious parties, as a believing Jew, the son of a believing Jew, and beg you: do not do this deed. Search your conscience, your belief. How will Jewish youth believe in the Jewish religion and Jewish faith when its spokesmen raise their hand in favor of negotiations with Germany? Therefore, at the last minute, deliberate together, discuss, have mercy on this people, do not abet this blasphemy which is unparalleled in our history since the [biblical episode of] "the concubine of Gibeah."[14]

And now, members of all sides of the House, I come to end of my remarks. I know that this is one of the most decisive moments in the history of our people. I say to you: there will be no negotiations with Germany. There will be no negotiations with Germany![15]

The debate was adjourned at 18.45 and reopened at 21.35

Speaker Yosef Serlin (*General Zionists*)**:** I hereby reopen this session of the Knesset. I was forced to suspend it after MK Begin did not accede to my request to retract his insulting remark to the prime minister. I hereby inform the House that MK Begin has retracted the remark, his insult to the prime minister, and also the sentence in which he said: "If he [MK Begin] will not speak – no one will."

I would like to take this opportunity of saying to the House that I regret – and I assume that I am voicing the feelings of all members of the Knesset – what took place during MK Raphael's speech and during MK Begin's speech and the shouting that sullied the dignity of the Knesset. And I appeal to the members of the Knesset: The debate is still before us, a grave and painful debate for both sides, so let us maintain our composure and the respect and the dignity of the House so as to enable the Knesset to conclude the debate, whatever its conclusion may be, as befits the Knesset of Israel and its members. I yield the floor to MK Begin for the conclusion of his speech.

---

13 At this point the Herut demonstrators outside the Knesset building attempted to storm it. Stones thrown by them shattered windows and fell inside the hall. One MK was lightly wounded.

14 Judges, 19:20.

15 At this point tumult erupted in the plenum, the climax of which was MK Begin shouting at Prime Minister Ben Gurion: "You are a hooligan!" which caused the session to be suspended.

MK Menachem Begin (*Herut*): I affirm the statement of the honorable Speaker.
I affirm it not as result of pressure, nor as a result of threats to remove me from the
Knesset – I view my removal from the Knesset as a marginal act in this particular
struggle – but because I still have a role to play here, perhaps my last, and I shall
play it to the end.

In 1919, several days before the Seder night, a tragedy occurred in a Jewish city,
a remote but a large Jewish city called Pinsk. An anti-Semitic Polish major took 34
Jews whom he suspected of Bolshevism, stood them against a wall and murdered
them. I was a youth at the time. I was taught a poem about that killing. I do not
remember all the words, but I still remember this sentence: *Besser kumt nicht zu der
seder nacht* – better you do not come to the Seder night. The world, different then,
was shocked by the murder of 34 Jews. Henry Morgenthau came from America:
a commission of inquiry was sent from England;[16] the Polish government, half of
which was anti-Semitic, set up a parliamentary commission of inquiry. And then,
based on the recommendation of that parliamentary commission of inquiry, the
Polish government suggested offering compensation to the bereaved families for
what had happened to their parents and brothers. And the Polish government
was not directly responsible for the murder. Major Luchinski committed it on
his own initiative. The Polish government dissociated itself from the murder and
offered compensation to the relatives. And then – thus states the book I have here
before me – the Zionist committee convened in the city of Pinsk, called in all these
bereaved families and told them: "If you accept compensation you will desecrate
and disgrace the memory of the martyrs. It will be said that the Jews sold the souls
of the martyrs for money," and on the same occasion, a protocol was written in
which it was stated that the spilt blood would not be sold for money; only if the
murderers were punished would the sin be atoned for. The statement was signed
by the heads of the families and sent to the Army Ministry, and thus the episode
was concluded.

And what was understood by the Pinsk Zionist committee will not be
understood by a government in the State of Israel? What was understood by
the Pinsk Zionist committee will not be understood by the Jewish legislature?
For had you succeeded in getting the Germans to sign, after signing a mutual
agreement with them, a statement such as this: "We, the Germans, who murdered
six million Jews, will give you $300 million over ten years, and we agree that you
continue to hate us. We who are responsible for the murder of the six million,
do not seek forgiveness from you." Had you managed to get them to sign such

---

16 Henry Morgenthau (1856-1946). Born in Germany. Emigrated to the U.S.A. in 1865.
    American ambassador in Turkey, 1913-1916, and in this capacity extended help to the
    Jewish community of Palestine. In 1919 headed a commission set up by President Wilson
    to inquire into the situation of Jews in Poland. In 1923 he was appointed head of the
    League of Nation's Committee for Refugees' Settlement. The inquiry commission sent
    by the British government to Poland was headed by Stewart Samuel.

a statement, the fact would remain, for you still are taking money directly from the murderers on the basis of a mutual agreement, on the basis of a compromise. You demanded such and such, they refuse to give the whole sum, they will give less, you will agree. An agreement will be signed, in full view, with the murderers. This then can only be blood-money.

I have come to warn, and I am warning: members of the Knesset of all factions, this matter cannot pass! If there is meaning in the words, "Sanctification of God's name," if there is content in the term, "Be killed and do not let it pass," this is the meaning and this is the content. This might be my last speech in the Knesset, and I cannot but say to you some very simple words, which certainly flow from a bleeding heart – perhaps they will enter your own hearts. We, Herut representatives, have sat with you in the Knesset for three years. We were a minority. You were the majority. You were elected as a majority. We accepted it. We did not come to this Knesset from wealthy homes, from a life of ease. My colleagues and I came here after a war that lasted for years against the British. We were hunted incessantly, rewards were put on our heads, detectives searched for us all over the country, we risked our lives 24 hours a day. We succeeded, the oppressor retreated, the state was established in a part of this divided country, we reached the moment of the first general elections.

But there was one other event that took place before the elections. Mr. Ben Gurion will recall it. On June 22, 1948 he ordered that I be fired on from a cannon. I was on board a burning ship, the *Altalena*,[17] I saw my comrades, my boys, my followers, fall, murdered. My boys, my followers, my brothers, members of the Irgun, had machine guns, mortars, rifles. I gave the order – in the face of the enemy – not to raise a hand, and they obeyed. And in this Knesset, for three years, the resolutions you have made aroused our deepest antagonism. Those resolutions left us extremely depressed.[18] Very sadly, we asked ourselves if we had failed in accomplishing our mission. Later, after those resolutions were passed, we went, my comrades and I, to those young men, whom you vilify – who readily sacrificed their lives and spilled their blood for their people and country –12 of them later mounted the scaffold and sang Hatikvah[19] until their last breath. I went to those young, battle-scarred young men and told them: this is our Knesset, it is our government.

---

17 The sailing of the *Altalena*, a ship carrying arms and volunteers from France to Israel in June 1948, was organized by the Irgun, the military organization of the Revisionist Party headed by Menachem Begin. Upon reaching the shores of Israel the Irgun commanders refused to hand over the ship's arms to the IDF authorities whereupon fire was opened against the ship by orders of Defense Minister David Ben Gurion, causing its explosion and sinking. The Irgun was immediately disbanded, and its members were conscripted into the IDF.

18 MK Begin refers to laws enacted by the Knesset for allocating financial support to disabled Haganah fighters, and to bereaved families of Haganah fighters killed in action in pre-state years, support which did not cover members of the Irgun.

19 A Zionist, and later on the State of Israel's national anthem.

The majority decides. Let us go to the people. Let us try and persuade them. If we do not succeed, what else can we do? This is our people. Afterwards I went to the Diaspora, I met with tens of thousands of Jews, they are witnesses, they will confirm what I said, and told them: be it this government, be it a different government – it is a Jewish government. Blessed art thou who has kept us in life, and hast preserved us, and enabled us to reach this day in which there is a Jewish government. The government is ours, the government is mine whatever its composition. That is what I said to the Jews of America, Argentina, Mexico.

That is how we have educated our youth. We accepted everything, even though we were deeply distressed. After 2,000 years of exile we wanted to educate this people towards a life of statehood, a life of freedom, a life of independence, a normal life. Do we, too, not have children? Do we, too, not have wives? Do we, too, not deserve a quiet family life? Do we, too, not have the right to live as free citizens in this country? We gave everything for its establishment. We received nothing – no military or police commands, not a share in government, not a position in the state machinery – nothing! We approached you and asked for recognition of the rights of those Irgun clandestine fighters as the rights due to discharged soldiers, and you refused; for two years you refused. The prime minister said that as long as this government is in power, it will not give them a penny, not a penny to the amputees, the invalids for life, the bereaved, the poor and shattered families. And we accepted that, too. Again we went to our youth and said: we will change their minds; we will persuade them; don't worry, this is our country.

That is what I taught our youth. That is what I learned from my father. But I learned something else, and I taught them that, too: there are things in life more precious than life itself. There are things in life more terrible than death. And this is one of those things for which we will give our lives, for which we will be prepared to die – we will leave our families, say goodbye to our children – and there will be no negotiations with Germany.

People worthy of the term took to the barricades for far lesser issues. On this issue of direct negotiations we, the last generation of bondage and the first of redemption; we, who saw our parents dragged into the gas chambers; we, who heard the rumble of the wheels of the death trains; we, before whom an old man was thrown into a river together with 500 Jews from Brisk in glorious Lithuania, and the river ran red with blood; we, before whom an old woman was murdered in a hospital; we, before whom all the events unparalleled in history took place, will we fear risking our lives to prevent negotiations with the murderers of our fathers? Were we not to rise, we would have to bury our faces in the ground. We are ready for anything, anything, to prevent this shame to Israel. I hope we can avert it.

In Zion Square,[20] I said to 15,000 outraged Jews who had gathered in the rain and cold: go, stand around the Knesset. Do not interfere with the Knesset's business. All the provocative accusations, implying that we thought of interfering with the Knesset debate, are false! I said: go, stand, surround the Knesset. As in the days of Roman occupation, when a Roman governor wanted to erect a statue in the Temple, Jews from all over the country surrounded the building and said: over our dead bodies. I said, let your silence cry out that there will not be negotiations with Germany. They were attacked with German gas grenades. And I say to you, gentlemen: woe is me that I have reached this point; happy am I to have been honored with it! There are still young people in Israel. No, these young people do not want wars, they do not want battles, they do not want to die. They want to live. They have the right to live. But the time has come when everything is thrown into the balance. Shall we not uphold this commandment? We shall. This is my last call to the Knesset: prevent a holocaust befalling the Jewish people. In the pits of Hell the voice of Satan was already heard – what else has he brought about after his destruction? The spilling of Jewish blood over German money! Why and for what? The money will be devalued, spent, it will disappear, and the shame will remain!

I know you have power. You have jails, concentration camps, an army, police, secret police, artillery, machine guns. No matter. On this issue all that power will shatter like glass against a rock. For a just cause we shall fight to the end. In these cases, physical force is worthless; it is utter nonsense. I am warning, but not threatening. Who can I threaten? I know that you will drag us into concentration camps. Today you have arrested hundreds, perhaps you will arrest thousands. No matter. They will go. They will be imprisoned. We shall be imprisoned with them. If there is a need, we shall be killed with them. And there will be no reparations from Germany. And God help us all to avoid this holocaust for the sake of our future and our honor.

Mr. Speaker, please note and please inform the state authorities that from 4 pm today, I, a member of the Knesset and subject to the law of parliamentary immunity, view that law as null and void.[21]

Minister Pinhas Lavon (*Mapai*): Mr. Speaker, Members of the Knesset, I permit myself to say that today we have witnessed the gravest act in the history of the Jewish people: it was a calculated attempt to attack the only Temple that the Jewish people in our time has, the Knesset of Israel. There have been instances in the history of our people when its Temple was burned down by enemies and

---

20 The Herut demonstrators who stormed the Knesset building had first gathered in nearby Zion Square where MK Menachem Begin had made a fiery speech before they started marching.

21 On 22.1.1952, the Knesset decided by a vote of 56 to 47 to suspend MK Menachem Begin from the Knesset until the Passover recess in March 1953.

foreigners. It will be recorded in the young history of Israel that the criminal attempt to intimidate the elected representatives of the people with physical terror, to prevent any possibility of them filling their role, an attempt intended – although the outcome was, fortunately, different – to create something similar to the burning of the Reichstag[22] – was all done by Jews in the name of the honor of Israel and Jewish history.

We have heard an extremely momentous statement. It is serious, it is an announcement of a planned revolt in the State of Israel. We heard, "This shall not be because I will not allow it." We heard the announcement of a challenge and a war against the freedom and independence of the State of Israel. We heard an announcement that we are returning to the days when any gang, whatever its motives might be, can impose its will on the state by force. That statement and that act which we have witnessed today tell us: the young Republic of Israel is in danger! Before the issue of reparations and after it, the crucial question will remain for all of us: how are we to live in this state and how are we to make decisions in it – by the will of armed sheikhs, or freely as a free people? Shall we decide matters as a free people or by the force of the gun? I used the words "force of the gun" intentionally, for these gentlemen, and I must say this plainly, are also presently engaged in incitement to murder. If you read what is written in their press, if you follow the speeches made at their public meetings, you will realize their words simply cannot be interpreted otherwise. At this present time, our first duty is to unite all those loyal to the state to root out this danger. Permit me to say just one thing to MK Begin: you are too puny to be a threat to the State of Israel. The State of Israel has enemies more numerous and stronger than you, and it may not be able to deal with them all. You may sow destruction and provoke disturbances, but the State of Israel has the power to deal with the source of this lawlessness.

The Knesset will decide on the question under discussion, and what it decides will come about. Arrogant and empty boasting may cause painful feelings and spread insults, but it cannot change this basic fact by as much as an inch: the Knesset's prerogative to make decisions. For once we relinquish this basic fact, the very existence and future of the State of Israel is denied.

Now to the subject of this debate: from MK Rimalt we have heard a comprehensive explanation to the effect that two factors are in play in man's soul – rationality and irrationality. I think that MK Rimalt will agree that in 1952 that is not a revolutionary discovery. But I would like MK Rimalt to accept two corrections to his basic premise. First, that we are not divided into people for whom everything works irrationally and others for whom everything works rationally. Emotion is common to all of us; it is nobody's monopoly. Not always does a hysterical scream testify to the genuine emotion of profound pain. On the contrary, a loud scream and hysteria are often a clear sign that the screamer is far

---

22   On 27.2.1933.

removed from genuine emotion and profound pain. We are all emotional, and yet we are all people who act rationally.

I would also ask him to accept a second correction. It is said that life remains an unsolved enigma, and yet we must live it rationally. When we convene here to debate a certain issue, it is not enough to impose a taboo upon us: "The matter is irrational and so my position is sacrosanct, and so do not touch me, and so let us not discuss the matter, and so let us hear no reasoning concerning it." No, MK Rimalt, with all due respect to your feelings and to mine, a rational debate must take place.

I must say this to the honorable members: in the debate so far there has been much competition in describing the atrocities that took place in Auschwitz and Maidanek and other places, and we are certainly going to hear more in this vein. Everyone has spoken, and will speak, in the name of his father, mother and so forth. Gentlemen, by what Jewish moral right are you turning the six million victims into a monopoly for a certain position? By what right? Were you given their authority? Did they tell you what they think? Who decides? It is the living who decide! The living decide according to their consideration, their understanding, their sense of human and national loyalty. We are the living. And when I say that we, the living, decide, I make no distinction and give no privileges to anyone including partisans and soldiers who fought against the Germans in WW II. No living partisan was left a will and testament with his dead comrade telling him what to do in this instance. No living soldier was given a moral authorization by his dead comrade telling him what his position should be on this matter. We must discuss this issue as a living people bearing responsibility for the past, present and future of Jewish life in general. On more than one occasion, the Zionist movement has been faced with grave questions in the sphere of relations with nations that are hostile, enemies and haters. Before the Zionist movement was established, the Jewish way of survival was very simple: outwardly by intercession, inwardly by composing prayers, issuing boycotts, silently cursing enemies, and so on. And there was value in prayers, there was great value in restraints and curses, too, for in the life of a helpless people, these were very effective psychological and moral weapons.

The Zionist movement faced this problem right from its inception: how to shape relations between the Jewish people lacking a sovereign state of its own but yearning to achieve it, and the gentiles and the Jew-haters. A case in point was the Herzl-Plehve episode[23], and the serious debate it engendered is well remembered. Now, decades after that episode, we can quite possibly sum it up and say that at the time Herzl was mistaken in taking that step, but from a historical-political

---

23 Vyacheslav Plehve (1846-1904), an anti-Semitic Russian statesman, was minister of the interior of Czarist Russia from 1902. He was thought to be responsible for the Kishinev pogroms of April 1903. Dr. Theodore Herzl met with him twice in August 1903 to obtain concessions for Zionist activity in Russia and support for the claims of the Zionist organization regarding Palestine.

perspective, it is quite possible he was right; his action embodied the nascent sense of the great change in relations between the Jewish people and the gentiles which resulted from the fact that contrary to the traditional Jewish way of survival through carrying on life in minority communities everywhere, a Zionist movement arose seeking statehood.

There was a second episode, the episode of Ze'ev Jabotinsky's[24] agreement with Maxim Slavinsky, Petliura's emissary. That agreement was concluded in 1921 or 1922, two years after hundreds of thousands Jews were massacred in the Ukraine. It was an event of disastrous magnitude. Perhaps the victims were not slaughtered scientifically by Hitler's method, but nevertheless the massacre was executed very thoroughly. And the agreement was signed not with some Adenauer but with the chief slaughterer. The agreement had nothing to do with reparations; it was about cooperation and mutual assistance. Had there been a minimum of historical honesty in our own political life, then the followers of the man who signed that agreement in particular should have taken a somewhat less extreme attitude in reacting to the matter we are debating now. Jewish public opinion at the time rightfully rejected the agreement with Petliura. There exists an interesting, thirty-year-old document that if it were read now, after hearing Mr. Begin's speech, we could assume that it was written only today. When Jabotinsky was summoned to the Zionist executive meeting which discussed his agreement, he said, and I quote: "The matter is irrational and so my position is sacrosanct, and so do not touch me, and so let us not discuss the matter, and so let us hear no reasoning concerning it. As to the agreement between me and Slavinsky, the Zionist executive's attitude towards him does not interest me now and has never interested me before, and I have no intention of taking it into consideration neither as a member of the Zionist executive nor as a private individual." Change a few words in this statement and we get almost a copy of Mr. Begin's declaration here: "This doesn't interest me and I don't deem it important. From four o'clock onwards, to hell with my immunity. But take care – I and I and I shall not let you do it." It seems history repeats itself rather exactly, if somewhat boringly.

There was a third event, and rather a serious one, that also split the Yishuv and the Zionist movement. It occurred early in the history of the Nazi ascent to power, when the question of the transfer of the property of German Jews to

---

24   Ze'ev Jabotinsky (1880-1940), a member of the Zionist executive from 1921 until 1923, seceded from the World Zionist Organization in 1935 and founded the New Zionist Organization (the Revisionist Party), which he headed until his death in 1940. In this capacity he was the commander of the clandestine military organization of the Irgun (the National Military Organization) which operated in British-ruled Palestine from 1935 until 1948. The Irgun did not recognize the authority of the elected national bodies of the Jewish community of Palestine (the Yishuv), in contrast to the Haganah, the clandestine military organization of the Yishuv, which became the IDF in May 1948 upon the establishment of the State of Israel. MK Menachem Begin, a disciple of Jabotinsky, headed the Irgun from 1942.

Palestine was debated. Most of us still remember that affair. I think that some of the figures involved in the present drama also took part in that one. But it is not only the figures that are the same. If we compare the speeches made then with those made today, you will see that there is no argument made today that was not heard then. The 1933 transfer was said to be a "blasphemy," "selling the Jewish people's honor for money," "giving Hitler an entrée into international society." And clearly, Chamberlain's appeasement policy and the Ribbentrop-Molotov Pact came about only because of the transfer arrangement to save Jewish property.

Almost 20 years have passed, and we can ask ourselves a simple question: assume for a moment that we had taken the path of those opposed to it and left the Jewish property we saved in the hands of Hitler's extermination machine? As a result, we would not have been able to absorb the wave of Jewish immigration from Germany that became a cornerstone of the process of building up this country. Whom would we have helped – Hitler or the Jewish people? The decision of 1933 was not an easy one for any of us. We did it because the spark ignited in the Zionist movement became a flame of recognition of the Land of Israel's centrality to the life of the Jewish people, recognition of our national duty even when we did not even yet have a state. It was a positive historic decision that built up the power of the Jewish community of Palestine, the Yishuv. And even though demands for a referendum were voiced then, no stone was left unturned by the opponents. Even though they claimed in the name of all past Jewish generations that we were going to destroy the foundations of Jewish morality, we can say today, with a clear conscience, that our decision of 1933 was a great and positive act from the national-political standpoint, from the standpoint of saving the people, from the standpoint of building up Jewish power.

In this debate there has been an almost inflationary use of arguments of conscience and morality, or to put it more precisely, of arguments on behalf of public morality. It would be worthwhile to examine this side of the coin, too. Forgive me if I speak bluntly again. We are not debating this issue for the purpose of exchanging pleasantries. I think that the combination of opponents to this vote in the Knesset symbolizes public amorality. The honorable Rabbi Nurock, with his particular reasoning and background, is sitting in one and the same boat together with MK Vilner; MK Vilner's judgment of the Bonn government derives from the single fact that it does not bow to the political interests of the Soviet Union. Had Adenauer accepted Grotewohl's suggestion and become chancellor of a united Germany, at least in the first year, MK Vilner would have had to prove in his newspaper and speech that Herr Adenauer had become a "progressive factor." This pro-Soviet argument is perhaps decisive for MK Vilner, but it cannot be so in the eyes of the Jewish people and the State of Israel. If, for parliamentary reasons, Rabbi Nurock is joining hands with Communist MK Vilner, and they are joined by Mapam's MK Rubin, and these three are joined by General Zionists' MK Rimalt, then I permit myself to say that this union is basically spurious for it covers up the gaping truths separating you; each of you has deep-rooted, different attitudes, reasons and positions on the current question, and nothing can unite those differences. (*MK Menachem Begin: Your union with the clerics is spurious too!*) Well, if we are talking of collusions, I think that from a standpoint of morals and conscience, it is an exemplary collusion.

Let us discuss Mapam's position for a moment. If I try to formulate it in simple language while ignoring the attendant phraseology, I must put it this way: towards East Germany – an attitude of forgiveness in advance, even if it doesn't pay reparations; towards West Germany – no contact and no reparations, with only one stand requirement: acceptance of the rulings of the Cominform.[25] Our position on West and East Germany is demands reparations from both and shows no forgiveness to either. Let me say this: if we accept the theory that anyone born German is a Nazi, then the fact that someone was painted red only a few days ago makes no difference at all. If the problem is a Jewish one, then from this standpoint the type of the ruling regime in any country makes no difference at all. The position you are attempting to foster bears no relation at all to Jewish interests. It derives from a worldview, from a social philosophy, from a political philosophy, but it has nothing to do with Jewish interests.

Only a few years ago we went through a world war. Before that war the Ukrainian people were brought up on the teachings of the Soviet Union, not for three years but for close to 30 years, but when the shock wave hit, what became of Soviet Ukraine? What did the Ukrainian masses do? The Ukraine was one of the European countries in which the greatest slaughter of Jews took place. We were slaughtered by Ukrainians, by the Ukrainian masses. Do you now want us to accept the view that if a "Social Christian" of the Adenauer type is a member of the East German government, with the background of this historical experience, then he becomes kosher? That thousands of Nazis and SS men serving in the governments or in central and regional state institutions in all the "Peoples' Democracies" are kosher and free of any obligations towards us? That we should demonstrate unlimited affection to them to whom we owe a pardon in advance while demanding reparations from that part of Germany which, though it states its readiness to pay, is automatically non-kosher? Why?

We are told that if we claim and receive reparations from the West German government, it will bring the German army into the European army. God Almighty, are you really so naïve? Do you think that the Jews of Israel are so naïve as to believe that this question of whether the Germans will or will not participate in the European army, and we have a certain opinion about that, depends on reparations to us Jews? Had the matter of attaining an international stamp of

---

25   Cominform, established in 1947: an information agency of the Communist Parties of
       the Soviet Union and of its East European satellites as well as of the Communist Parties
       of Italy and France,. This body was, in fact, an international communist organization,
       directed by Moscow. It was disbanded in 1956.

approval for that participation been dependent on reparations, then Adenauer's statement regarding it would suffice even if the State of Israel had rejected it. It is idiotic to assume that central issues in the international life of this crazy and conflicted world can be resolved by our position on reparations. We must decide on only one thing: what is necessary and what is just for the Jewish people, and what the State of Israel is entitled and duty-bound to demand from the German people in its capacity of being responsible for the fate of the Jewish people.

I would have understood had the opponents told us "not reparations but vengeance," for then this debate would have been appropriate, but all I hear are tirades. You say "vengeance" without anything behind the word. You say "Amalek," and nobody knows the meaning behind the word. "Vengeance" is a very concrete term. (*MK Menachem Begin: The vengeance would be very concrete!*[26]) Don't scare me and others with so many threats. I have a weak heart, as you know.

Much has been said about national honor. I regret that I must say that this, too, is a hollow slogan for national honor is nothing but words, a phrase cried out in the marketplace. National honor is an utterly insignificant word unless it is filled by concrete content. It is not artificial boasting that says, "See how honorable I am!" Honor is manifested in deeds. I ask myself, when we were expelled from Spain, what honor was in that? At the time of Khmelnitsky's massacres, where was the honor there? Let it be emphasized: this is the first time in the history of the Jewish people that the murderer feels a certain inner need to restore at least part of the plunder. This is the first time in the annals of Jewish martyrdom that the murderer and plunderer – and the reasons are unimportant – feels a need to restore part of what was taken from us.

With regard to national honor and concrete vengeance, I say national honor and vengeance would be attained if Germany, if the German people, would work towards clothing, rehabilitating, healing, and housing masses of immigrants in Israel; if the German people would have to work in order to assist in the economic consolidation of the State of Israel, for our vengeance and national honor will be manifested and fulfilled by increasing our power. All the rest are hollow declamations. If the entire Jewish people had not been exterminated in the Holocaust, if we have not lost all hope, then that is due to one thing only: the rebirth of the Jewish center of power, the State of Israel. To the question of historical vengeance, to the question of our historical national honor, there is but one answer: the accumulation of power, of more and more power, of more and more Jews, building a healthier people, a stronger state, so we will able to withstand any future tempest. The historic response to the plot to exterminate the Jewish people will be embodied in the emergence of our healthy people and strong state.

We will claim reparations with heads held high as emissaries of the Jewish past, present and future, loyal to the voice of the only true values of Jewish

---

26   See document no. 28, note no. 2, regarding the implementation of this threat.

history: the healing of wounds, the ingathering of the exiles, the strengthening of the state and its people.

Speaker Yosef Serlin: Members of the Knesset, this session is concluded for this evening. The debate will resume tomorrow at 6 p.m. We are adjourned.

Second Knesset Session 39, 8.1.1952

Speaker Ze'ev Sheffer (*Mapai*)**:** I hereby open Session 39 of the Knesset. We will now continue the debate on the government's statement on reparations from Germany.

Minister Pinhas Rosen (*Progressive Party*)**:** I would like to join MK Lavon in deploring yesterday's disturbances. We must be watchful that our young democracy does not collapse due to weakness, that it knows how to defend itself against those forces which are prepared to undermine its foundations in the name of the sacred freedoms of democracy.

It must be clear beyond doubt, and this must be clarified in the negotiations to be conducted in one form or another, that the sum of reparations should be reasonable. As we have heard from the prime minister, the basis for the negotiations will be the claim submitted by the government of Israel, and this is how it should be. MK Begin's contention that the basis for the negotiations should be Adenauer's statement is unfounded even though I think that the previous government was right to express its satisfaction with it.

With regard to the individual claims, it must be clear that the reparations would not come instead of them. The reparations must not undermine the individual claims which, if I am not mistaken, the prime minister said yesterday amount to $6 billion. In any event, the sum of the individual claims is not less than the sum we have claimed as reparations.

Yesterday we heard a song of praise to irrationality from MK Rimalt. A very beautiful song indeed. Every Zionist knows the value of irrational beliefs, for they play an important part in the life of every people, including our own. Didn't we fight rational assimilators and defend irrational Zionism? And those who immigrated to this country before Hitler, motivated by reasons other than pogroms, were not their motives certainly irrational? And the same applies to many who came here following the pogroms. Still, one cannot justify everything with irrationality.

I sometimes ask myself, how would another people have reacted in similar circumstances? You, members of the Knesset, all know that Hitler plotted to eradicate other people, although by different means: starvation, exile, sterilization, separation of families, and so on. And had that madman succeeded, he would have accomplished these evil intentions. Let us assume that he had perpetrated the mass slaughter of another people – an imaginary assumption, perhaps entirely fictional, but in view of what happened to us, any such assumption cannot be overly imaginary. And let us assume that, under similar circumstances, the German government said what the Germans are saying today. For what are the motives driving the Adenauer government to propose what it is proposing, or more precisely, to meet our claims? I think that two motives are in play here. First, they are ashamed; second, we have acquired the status not only of a state, but also of a people, and particularly for the United States. We can now functin as an influential and disturbing factor in the international arena.

In parenthesis, I would like to say to MK Chazan that yesterday I heard him making an extremely demagogic speech for the first time. The generalization he made regarding the simplistic definitions of Adenauer's government as "fascist" and present Germany as "Nazi" certainly derives from an irrational attitude. Irrationality can sometimes be very primitive. Savage peoples are utterly irrational, as is evident in their taboos. You, representatives of Mapam, are proposing that we take on a new taboo. But let me return to my theoretical assumption. Suppose the government of Germany approached another people that went through an experience like ours and said: "We are ashamed. We feel regret. We admit our collective guilt. We want to compensate you for the material and moral damages caused to you." And suppose this people, whoever it is, retorted: "No. We do not want to accept your goods," would this people still consider participation in negotiations an insult to their national pride?

Members of the Knesset, what do the opponents suggest? MK Lavon said yesterday that they are not even suggesting vengeance. I think they are suggesting that we foster feelings of hatred and vengeance. None of us is free of these feelings. In any event, I cannot testify that I am free of them, though I am not proud of them. But after taking the road of statehood, after acquiring the status of both a people and a state – a political status – I say that we cannot be satisfied with fostering feelings of hatred and vengeance. Today we are duty-bound by loftier commandments than "do not talk," "do not conduct negotiations," "do not forget." Key issues are imposed upon us today, superior in their sanctity and importance to all other duties and commandments including the commandment to hate and exact vengeance. MK Begin yearns for the time of the Pinsk Committee. But here lies the entire difference: we are living in a different time today and we cannot be satisfied with fostering feelings of hatred and vengeance. A loftier commandment is imposed upon us today, to build our country. Who has given you the right to waive what in everyone's opinion is our due? Does national sentiment oblige us to waive it because of the need to conduct negotiations? If it were true what MK Chazan said yesterday in a most simplistic generalization, that they are all Nazis, I would say this: it is precisely because they are Nazis that we must claim restitution from them. Had they at least changed, perhaps it would be possible to forgive their sins. In my view it is unimportant if these reparations are restitution of the plunder – although it is clear that it is truly restitution – but even had I viewed these payments as a penalty, a fine, I would not waive them, and I certainly would not surrender them to the Nazis.

The contention forwarded by some Knesset members, namely that when we appeal to the USA for grants we are behaving as beggars, seems very sick and strange to me. But strange as it is, I find it much more sensible than the contention that we waive reparations, even though the prime minister said this demand is unprecedented in international law, for demanding them is our natural, elementary right.

The Knesset has no right to waive one penny due us. We cannot view this from the standpoint of the Pinsk Committee but rather from the standpoint of statehood. Members of the Knesset, a state as such, must act rationally. We would not be able to hold our own in the international arena if we follow an eccentric line. We cannot behave as a stateless people such as the Pinsk community. We must build up the country and obtain all the money due to us. Let us not waive it. By what right can we demand support from others if we waive the reparations the Germans are prepared to pay us?

MK Zalman Shazar (*Mapai*)**:** Mr. Speaker, Members of the Knesset, where has this confusion of ideas that has beset us come from? It is indeed the confusion which disturbs me, rather than the opposition to the direct negotiations, or the hatred, the screaming and the staged demonstration and the scandal to which we were shocked witnesses. I shall waste no words about that hatred. I know where it comes from. I know that there are those amongst us for whom there remains only one of the 613[27] Zionist commandments. It is "Thou shalt hate everything this government does and which this country seeks to do." If that is the moral and Zionist standard, if that is the spring from which the soul of the opponents slakes its thirst, it should not be touched upon in this fateful and grave debate which must be very dignified. I find no sense in responding to those who have clung to this issue of reparations in order to turn it into a quarrel; they have found in it a succulent morsel wherewith they can nourish us and themselves for the purpose of inciting people against this young country, against the government of Israel, against all of us and our entire future.

But I do ask myself: from where did Satan come down to divide people who had once been close to one another? How did it come about that people I respect very much, people dear to me, people I always felt identified themselves with me; people who are my spiritual brethren – representatives of literature, of the arts, of high morals, men of the cloth, and people from the death camps and the ghetto uprising – how have they become so divided? Why and how have the ideas become confused and Satan come down to perplex and further confuse

---

27   The Bible lays down 613 commandments which all observant Jews must obey.

them, erecting a wall between us overnight until we no longer understand each other's language?

I would like to state at the outset that when I received the manifesto signed by intellectuals and Warsaw Ghetto fighters condemning direct negotiations,[28] I felt awed for a moment and, out of courtesy to my friends, rethought the whole matter lest I was mistaken; now I demand of them that when the Knesset makes its decision, when they see whose hand is raised in favor of approving direct negotiations, that they, too, hesitate as brothers should. And this with the same degree of common courtesy. They, too, should rethink the matter at hand and ask themselves whether perhaps they were wrong, lest this time they were mistaken in their judgment.

And when I seek a reason for Satan's successful intervention, I state categorically that this is part of the birth pangs of our new independence which is still a new phenomenon for all Jews of this generation. It is the painful cutting of milk teeth of this infant – the State of Israel – that will grow, live and discover its strength, and teething always causes the child pain. For this road of independence is indeed new, and because it is surprising and amazing, its deep significance was at first not recognized. It was blurred and distorted and filled with absurdities, totally unrelated to this experience of having a state of our own.

Members of the Knesset, Jewish historians have studied the history of one of the great calamities that has been part of Jewish history throughout the time of our exile, in the Middle Ages and afterwards: the phenomenon of expulsion. And they asked, why were the Jews expelled from England, Poland, Germany and other countries, city after city? In his book, *Die Letzte Vertreibung der Juden aus Wien* [The Last Expulsion of Jews from Vienna], Professor David Kaufmann asked, what caused this calamity to repeat itself throughout the period of European economic development? There were historians and economists who viewed the expulsions as a lawful part of that development. They asked, why is it that this nation, the Jewish nation, became the object of expulsion, which was in essence the plunder of Jewish property? And they answered, because the robbery went unhindered. Why did expulsion become a kind of refrain, down the generations, always accompanied by anti-Semitic hysteria and hostility and incitement, ending in expulsion? Why weren't other peoples expelled as frequently, and why were only the Jews subject to expulsion, to expropriation and plunder as something of a constant throughout the history of Jewish Diaspora?

---

28   At a gathering of intellectuals initiated by leftist circles in Tel Aviv on January 7, 1952, a manifesto condemning direct negotiations was composed and signed by 32 men of letters. The manifesto ended with the words, "We appeal to the masses of our people and to our government to stop this danger which is bound to bring on us not only disgrace but ruin. Let us not shake hands with Hitler's heirs!"

Do you know why? Because this people, residing in foreign countries, was unprotected and thus could be expelled and its property plundered because not one of the expelled and the plundered would come to lodge a claim. No political power in the world could arise and claim that this plunder must be restored even if the plunderer might be weak. A situation wherein a claim could be placed on behalf of a Jewish victim was unheard of throughout our life in exile. We did not experience that. We did experience rioting and self-defense. We did experience martyrdom. We experienced intervention and very bitter fighting, too. But not "reparations." This was a phenomenon known only to independent people. From the time of Titus onwards, Jewish history has not known reparations because we did not have the power to claim and receive them. Titus took the ability to claim reparations away from us. Our regained independence has made it possible for us to take this path. Even though many of our people still reside in the Diaspora and even if a tyrant were able to run wild in a hostile country, our fate would be different from now on because the State of Israel has been established, and it will demand satisfaction, it will demand justice. The curse borne by our people throughout the generations of bereavement has been removed with the establishment of the State of Israel. That is the entire meaning of the reparations – the historical, new, liberating meaning – and the State of Israel should be proud of it. The state, by its very existence, has restored to the Jewish people the possibility of claiming and receiving what is due to it. From now on justice can be done, for there is a claimant – the State of Israel.

For our generation in Israel, for us, all of us, even for the best of us, this is a new concept, a still unfamiliar concept. Our forefathers did not know about it. Neither could the previously mentioned Pinsk Committee have known about it, for it was unheard of throughout the Diaspora. This is not because our generation is better than theirs and not, heaven forbid, because past generations were worse than ours. Our people was not aware of this concept after the Kishinev pogrom in 1903 and again after the Petliura massacres in 1919. It could not have known it in an era when we did not possess a fleet or an army, or comprehend what representation at the UN means. We can rejoice for having finally attained what every independent people aspires to: the ability to speak in world forums. No wonder that because of the magnitude of this innovation, many people think that this step of entering direct negotiations with Germany is an "act of appeasement," or "bootlicking" or "going to the murderers" or something similar that might account for all the shock, the scandal, and the stormy debate.

Peoples who have been robbed speak of payments and penalties in spite of deep feelings of hostility toward the vanquished aggressor. Germany waged war against France, and, following the Treaty of Versailles, it paid penalties and reparations. With that German money many French regions were rebuilt. France demanded more and received less. Much of what was promised was not paid; still, Germany did pay a great deal. Did France stop hating Germany? Did any Frenchman even consider waiving what was due to his nation and cease demanding full payment from the vanquished enemy? Was any Frenchman – left or right, intellectual or worker – capable of holding that distorted view, a view, I dare say, characteristic of Diaspora mentality, that those reparations should not be accepted because they came from the hands of the Boche? They hated and took, they hated and built, they hated and were strengthened! For that property was theirs.

Why should we be told that reparations mean appeasement? From whom does one take reparations? Not from enemies? Reparations are always taken from enemies. How can one take reparations if not from enemies? After the enemy's conquest, after the victory, one takes reparations. Why are we being forbidden to do what nobody would dare forbid to any independent people? Is it because we were plundered less? Are we are less worthy? Or are we less needy?

Indeed, I am aware of another difference. And that difference also adds to this confusion. The historical drama came about in two different spheres: war was declared on the Jewish people by Hitler when the people was still stateless, and now the Jewish people are claiming reparations as a people already having a state. Thus the added confusion of ideas. Even had the reparations claim been the be-all and end-all of our defense against the gentiles, no theatre director could have staged it, for there is no substitute for a state.

Now we have attained this aim and the enemy's fiendish plot has not been accomplished. Had Jews not arisen and left the European exile and gone to America and to Palestine, then Hitler would have, heaven forbid, found not only the six million with his talons, but almost the entire Jewish people. Thanks to those who immigrated overseas, the American Jewish community of millions came about. Were it not for the early Zionist pioneers who settled in the Land of Israel, the state would never have been founded. But Jewish history foiled the plot of our greatest of all our foes before it reached fruition. Our predecessors and we, the emissaries of history, are the only ones in the world to have vanquished Hitler even before all his venom was exposed. We, by virtue of our emigration from Europe, created this mighty fortress that later became a haven of shelter, of mass immigration, of independence, with the ability to claim reparations. Indeed, for the first time we are now introducing into Jewish history the concept of reparations from our enemies.

Members of the Knesset, I hope that my words will not be distorted. No one should suspect me of not appreciating the importance of immigration and its absorption, of building new settlements, and of the needs of our young state. But not only because of these are we demanding restitution of the plundered Jewish property. The reparations we are claiming from Hitler's people and Hitler's descendents and Hitler's friends, from the entire German people – and I mean the entire German people, including even the opponents of Nazism – these reparations are rightfully ours. Let no one dare say that this is alien or unclean money. It is Jewish money. Jewish people, down the generations, saved it through the sweat of their brow, their initiative and creativity. It is good Jewish money and an anti-Semite foe plundered it. The State of Israel has risen to reclaim it.

This money has not been desecrated or soiled because it was plundered. On the contrary, it has become sanctified by the agony and blood of the victims, and it shall be purified by our will and power to reclaim our honor and our property. And it is purified twofold because we have spilt our blood here for our independence so that we would be able to claim reparations. Had I known that not a single penny of this money would be devoted to immigration, to settlement building and to the security of the state, had I known that not even one settlement would be built with it and that we would spend it all on the building of museums and theatres, I still would have said that we should accept it because it is ours and because we are duty-bound to teach the people of the world that the isolation of the Jewish nation is over and that the State of Israel has decided that from now on all our plunderers shall pay.

We are a unique state. We are the State of Israel, the state of its inhabitants but at the same time a state – and here lies our uniqueness, our sui generis – whose purpose is to save the honor, life, property and future of all the Jews in the world. We were made for this purpose. We must appear in the international arena as the protector of the Jewish people even though they may be in foreign lands. Therefore, today we are introducing a new concept into our Jewish struggle for survival: the removal of the stain of shame from the nation, the annulment of being an orphan nation; this has been achieved by the change that has taken place in the life of our people. We once were powerless – now our capability is greater by far. However, let it not be said that reparations can only be obtained when backed by an army standing at the ready. A state can also obtain reparations and restore plunder from a predator's hands when it is capable of exerting influence in the diplomatic arena.

The establishment of our state, after our having been a powerless people for many generations, has provided us with this capability to claim and to win.

MK Shmuel Mikunis (*I.P.C.*)**:** Members of the Knesset, the Jewish people are shocked and agitated over the government's negotiations with the Nazi government of Bonn. These criminal and base negotiations have inflicted serious harm to our national honor and rubbed salt into the bleeding wounds of our heart. Common sense and Jewish and human feelings revolt with all their strength against contact with the government of Hitler's heirs and disciples in Bonn. The people cannot accept the government's hypocritical and hollow arguments that are all guided by considerations of the coin. Considerations of this kind have nothing to do with the perspective of a peace-loving and independent people; they are the last refuge of the bankrupt rulers of Israel. The government is seeking the Knesset's authorization to extend its hand, in the name of the state, to the American puppet government of West Germany, to the Nazis in Bonn whose hands are stained with the blood of millions of our brethren, and who are bent on renewing Hitler's atrocities against the Jewish people and against all peace-loving nations. The government and its spokesmen in the Knesset are not ashamed and do not flinch from voicing their views from the Knesset podium, telling us that these Nazis will aid us in building the country by means of what they call "reparations." This is what they call "Israeli considerations" that are likely, so to speak, to bring about only "good tidings and salvation" for the people and the state.

Every intelligent person must ask himself, how did it come about that these so-called "Israeli considerations" are so harmoniously identifiable with the considerations of Truman, Churchill and Adenauer? Moreover, how did it happen that the initiative for negotiations between the government of Israel and the neo-Nazi Bonn government – which, according to the government spokesmen, stems from "Israeli considerations" – came from abroad and from circles that encourage Nazism and anti-Semitism? It turns out that something went wrong with these "Israeli considerations". They are nothing but a demagogic argument, aimed at smearing the consistent opponents of negotiations with Hitler's heirs as "anti-Israeli," and blindfolding the people and diverting attention from the national betrayal by the champions of these grave negotiations.

Only a few days ago *The New York Times* wrote that by virtue of "quiet pressure" from Washington, the government of Israel will enter negotiations with the Bonn government. It is well-known there has been "quiet" as well as not-so-quiet pressure from Washington for some time, but it has recently become more aggressive in light of the vital needs of the rulers of the United States, in light of their desire to accelerate the re-establishment of the Nazi Wermacht in West Germany.

This conclusive fact and the entire negotiations affair of the Ben Gurion government's representatives with the Bonn government over the past year, clearly demonstrate that these negotiations have nothing whatsoever to do with the true needs of the Jewish people and the State of Israel, that these negotiations derive from the criminal interest of the Anglo-American warmongers who are reviving Nazism in West Germany.

It is known that the rearming of West Germany is one of the keystones of the Anglo-American bloc's policy of preparing for war. They view the protectorate of Bonn as the main supplier of cannon fodder, the most important arms manufacturer for wars of conquest as well as the bedrock of anti-Soviet aggression in Europe. Their objective is to rapidly establish a Nazi army and rehabilitate West Germany's military-economic power.

But in this matter the warmongers have encountered the opposition of the people who have tasted the occupation and destruction of Hitler's predators. The rulers of the United States are looking for ways to break this opposition. One means of doing so is by conducting negotiations and the establishment of diplomatic relations between the government of Israel and the Nazi Bonn government. Truman and Adenauer's fiendish plan is to obtain a Jewish seal of approval from a Jewish government, from the Jewish people – Hitlerism's biggest victim – for Hitler's heirs to revive Nazism in West Germany.

That is the grave political and concrete significance of the negotiations between Ben Gurion and Adenauer. The government is attempting to obscure the gravity of its proposal and its destructive significance for our national interests for reasons of "practicality." Only a government alienated from its people, from its pains and aspirations, could act in the way that the Ben Gurion government is acting. The people contemptuously reject this "practicality" and the Truman-Adenauer-Ben Gurion plot to make it part of the sinister plans of reviving Nazism and the establishment of an army of murderers in West Germany.

The people of Israel and Jews throughout the world, together with all the people who suffered from Hitler's atrocities, are striving for a different aim – the aim of preventing war, of preventing the formation of Nazi shock troops for the purpose of waging a third world war. It is not Ben Gurion with the Nazi Bonn government in the guise of reparations that tops on our people's agenda but ensuring conditions that will prevent a recurrence of the Holocaust of Hitler's era.

If the Ben Gurion government were a people's government and not an American puppet, this despicable proposal would not have originated; it would not have promoted support for Adenauer's "democratization;" it would not have obscured what is happening in the Germany of the Bonn government led by the Anglo-American warmongers. Let the government not measure the people by its own yardstick. The people cannot be bought and led into the Nazi camp for thirty pieces of silver.

In light of the dangers threatening world peace stemming from the Anglo-American policy of aggression, the problem facing our people is to win on the moral-political front, for only that victory will also ensure material compensation. Like all other peoples, ours is interested in the fulfillment of the Potsdam Accords signed by the five great powers which are the political and legal basis for ensuring peace in Europe. These accords set out a historic plan aimed at preserving world peace; their basic points follow: (1) eradicating and uprooting Nazism, (2) eradicating German militarism and the total disarmament of Germany, (3) dismantling the German military-economic monopolies and cartels, (4) punishing the war criminals, (5) democratization of Germany in all spheres of political, economic and cultural life.

Who has already breached and continues to breach this vital agreement daily? Is it not the American "bosses" and friends of the government of Israel? Is it not the criminal Truman-Churchill-Adenauer partnership? The people of Israel know full well who upholds the Potsdam Accords. The people of Israel know that the government of the Soviet Union has fully upheld it in the Soviet occupation zones. It is the government of the German Democratic Republic and the anti-Nazi fighters led by President Wilhelm Pieck and Prime Minister Grotewohl; it is they who carried out the demilitarization, denazification and democratization of East Germany, with the aid of the Soviet occupation authorities. They enacted laws for the protection of peace and against racism and anti-Semitism, and they execute them effectively.

The Ben Gurion government, together with its Washington masters, has opposed this policy of ensuring peace and preventing the revival of aggressive German militarism. The foreign minister's rhetoric about "his concern regarding the rearmament of Germany" cannot conceal the fact that the government of Israel actively supports the warmongering policy of Truman and Churchill, the policy of the aggressive Atlantic Alliance, a policy of rearming Germany. It not only supports it, it has openly declared its readiness to join this criminal warmongers' pact. That is the reason for the dangerous phenomenon of the Ben Gurion government tumbling downhill towards Nazi Bonn. Here you have the reason for this fateful debate in the Knesset which has been enraging the people: proposing national betrayal by negotiating with Adenauer.

Members of the Knesset, the prime minister brought us the "good tidings" that Adenauer has given his written undertaking to implement "reparations." Certain government ministers and representatives of the American-Jewish millionaires are saying that Adenauer is a democrat and attempting to purify the Nazi beast. But the facts prove the opposite and refute their hypocritical propaganda. Adenauer, together with the Nazi Bonn government, is undertaking all these actions in order to revive Nazism in West Germany. Do we not know that they have already recruited 450,000 of Hitler's troops and officers? Under their aegis and on their initiative, only two months ago did not dozens of Nazi organizations in Germany celebrate the 13th anniversary of the torching of synagogues in Germany, accompanied by bands and choirs that sang the Horst Wessel song? Do not the Union of German Soldiers and other Nazi organizations openly and freely declare: "Hitler's gas chambers and concentration camps were efficient and valuable?" Who does the government seek to strike blind – the people who personally experienced all these atrocities, who went through Maidanek and Auschwitz, Treblinka and the Warsaw Ghetto? Can it be that to these people you are proposing entering negotiations with Bonn's government of Nazis?

You will not succeed. The people of Israel will never be in the same camp together with the Nazis. Our people will not join the criminal Truman-Churchill-Adenauer front which is planning an attack against the supporters of peace and the independence of nations against the Soviet Union and the people's democracies.

We Communists and all forces of peace and democracy in the world view the problem of Germany first and foremost as one of uprooting German fascism and militarism. It is on the positive resolution of this problem that world peace and peace for our people depend. Therefore, we wholeheartedly support the consistent anti-Nazi policy of the German Democratic Republic and the fight of the anti-Nazi forces within West Germany against the revival of the Nazi Wermacht by the Adenauer government.

Any negotiations with the Bonn government have no other meaning than at least de facto recognition of that government, a government of Hitler's heirs and of the disciples of murderous German militarism. Any such negotiations will provide encouragement to the forces of Nazism and revanchism in West Germany and a Jewish seal of approval for the rebirth of Hitler's troops. That is their concrete significance. For a token payment, Adenauer and his American masters seek a Jewish agreement for the continuation of Hitler's murderous tactics. They seek to bring Israel into the war camp of Hitler's heirs who are preparing a new world-wide Holocaust, one for the Jewish people in particular.

The government proposing this is sliding into the abyss of the greatest national betrayal in the history of our people. If it continues along this path, this government will go down in the history of this country as a Judenrat government.

The Jewish people aspire to peace and fights for it. The people want to ensure Israel's independence and its future as a free people. Our nation can attain these lofty aims by joining a common struggle with all the peace-loving people led by the socialist Soviet Union. The people reject any negotiations with the Nazi government of Bonn. We will demand a roll-call vote on this fateful issue. Each member of the Knesset will be personally responsible for his vote. The people of Israel will not forgive those who raise their hands in favor of negotiations with the Nazi government of Bonn, thus supporting a shameful act initiated by Truman, Adenauer and Ben Gurion.

MK Mordechai Nurock (*Hamizrachi*)**:** Members of the Knesset, I speak personally and not on behalf of my party. I thank my party and also the honorable members of the coalition who deemed it proper to give me a free hand.

First of all, I feel a need to express my deep sorrow over the unfortunate events we witnessed outside this honorable House. The elected representatives of the people cannot be influenced by threats and stones. We have, thank heaven, democratic parliamentary rule. Although I oppose direct contact with the murderers with every fiber of my being, I condemn taking such extreme and violent steps.

There is a great difference between public opinion, which we view as very important and precious, and organizing and inciting a mob. Our only guiding principle should be maintaining the dignity of the sovereign Knesset of the State of Israel.

What we feared most has indeed came about: the government of Israel is seeking authorization from the Knesset for direct negotiations with the murderers of our people, for sitting at the same table with the human beasts of prey who killed, burned and suffocated, in accordance with a specific plan and with terrible cruelty, a major part of the Jewish people and destroyed the most splendid and ancient Jewish communities. "But money answereth all things."[29] The government is using various pretexts in striving to justify its contact with the German beast. They say that this does not entail forgiveness and atonement. To my regret, this is but self-deceit and deception. At first they spoke of "compensation." That was later replaced by a more convenient term: "reparations." But everyone knows that they both embody the same thing – compensation or reparations through direct contact – the beginning of forgiveness and of Israel's de facto recognition of Germany.

Do not say our claim from Germany is just. Do not say "Hast thou killed and also taken possession?" The debate is not about that. It is about what Germany is claiming from us. In return, we are to establish, in one form or another, normal relations with Germany. This amounts to the same pardon given by the great powers not long ago to the worst of the war criminals.

And if anyone has any doubts, they are dispelled by the minutes of that solemn session of the Bundestag in Bonn, sent to me by Paul Lübe, President of the last Reichstag. Von Brentano,[30] who at the time participated in the inter-parliamentary conference in Istanbul and headed the West German delegation to Paris, interestingly stated in that session: "The degree of our regard towards the Jewish citizens will be determined by the degree of regard we seek towards ourselves." That is a clear answer to those who claim that there is no forgiveness and atonement. The murderers demand regard and respect from us. That is what is expected in exchange for the money. These are the notes of forgiveness and atonement, the *ablasszette* handed over by the Church to the *raubritter* – the robber barons of the Middle Ages. And what do the better ones among them, Adenauer and Lube, say? Adenauer promises equal rights to the Jews of Germany. Did you hear that? Equal rights! This is his remorse, his repentance and his response to the horrific Holocaust. And what did Lübe say? "We are united, especially with the Jews, who like us were born German. They gave us Heine, Mendelssohn and Rathenau."[31]

---

29   Ecclesiastes, 10:19.
30   Heinrich von Brentano, a jurist, headed the Christian Democrat Party in the Bundestag. He was later foreign minister of the Federal Republic of Germany.
31   Felix Mendelssohn Bartholdy (1846-1902), grandson of Moses Mendelssohn, was one of the greatest composers of his generation. Walther Rathenau (1867-1922), a German-Jewish statesman, writer and industrialist, was in charge of the German economy during and after WW I. In 1921 he became minister of reconstruction in the Weimar Republic and in February 1922 – foreign minister. Rathenau had long been the target of anti-Semitism. He was assassinated by right-wing nationalists in June 1922.

I believe that three years ago – and certainly before the establishment of the state – a solution could have been found. The great powers and the United Nations could have included our claims in the peace treaties so that we would not have had to come into direct contact with the murderers. I demanded this again and again, many years ago, in meetings of all of our people's highest bodies: the Knesset, the Zionist Congress, the Zionist executive, the World Jewish Congress. It is now clear that the government missed the most fitting opportunity to submit our country's claims to the International Compensation Commission in Brussels, which concluded its work in 1949. The argument that we had no authority to submit a compensation claim, as our country did not actually take part in the war against Germany, is groundless. Egypt, for instance, also took no part in the war against Germany, and Pakistan did not yet exist during the war, and yet these two countries submitted compensation claims. (*Foreign Minister Moshe Sharett: And how much did Egypt and Pakistan receive?*) Mr. foreign minister, it is the principle which interests me. The historic right of removing the barrier between us and the murderers undoubtedly belongs to the Jewish Agency, which was the first to send its representatives to that unclean country and establish a permanent office there, in the name of "Hast thou killed and also taken possession?" In so doing they took the moral weapon out of our hands and showed the murderers, the great powers and all the international bodies that the Jews are willing to maintain direct contact with the murderers. The representatives of the State of Israel learnt this from the Jewish Agency representatives and eventually did the same thing when they traveled to that blood-soaked country for preliminary contacts. Thus the leaders of our people gave individuals the go-ahead to trade with the Germans. Now they want to open wide the gates. And not only that: in recent years goods have been purchased in Germany – water pipes and railway lines – either directly or through a middleman from a neutral country, but with the full knowledge of where the goods originated. These acts have cleared the way to establishing contacts.

It was only six months ago that the government approached the great powers, but unfortunately we were too late. Three years ago the international atmosphere was different, and the attitude then towards the murderers was appropriate. Now they are being shown a welcoming face due to the intention of using them as cannon fodder against the Eastern Bloc. We have even come as far as to witness the pardon of the worst Nazi war criminals by the United States and Britain. In these circumstances we cannot expect the powers to do anything for us.

And now direct contact is proposed. It is an open secret that our government's work is done by proxy by one of the heads of the Jewish Agency, Dr. Nahum Goldmann, who three years ago claimed that our proposal to approach the great powers was both quixotic and ineffectual.

And here a word to my honorable friend, MK Lavon, about Herzl's action. I had the privilege of traveling with Herzl from the Russian border to Berlin following his visit to the Russian Minister of Interior Plehve. Herzl told me then: "I overcame my feelings of repugnancy and went to Plehve to save most of the functioning of the Zionist movement there." In truth, the Kishinev pogrom was child's play compared with the Nazi Holocaust, and Herzl did not demand compensation but approached the proper authorities for a permit for Zionist activity.

We are now facing a historic test of great responsibility. At this late hour it is my duty to sound a warning. Let us not forget that the entire German people, the fomenter of anti-Semitism throughout the centuries, is guilty of the Holocaust. West and East Germany alike share the responsibility. Where were the millions of socialists and communists who voted in the elections to the last Reichstag in 1933? They did not lift a finger.

Any direct contact is a desecration of the memory of the martyrs and the heroes of the ghettos and a severe blow to the moral dignity of the Jewish people. We will not receive money at all, but we will become a distributor of German goods from which Jewish blood is still dripping. And soon a neo-Nazi government will be formed that will abrogate all the agreements – just as the accursed "Fuehrer" did with regard to the great powers after we give our agreement to the recovery and cleansing of that unclean country now advancing the hypocritical slogan, "Peace with Israel," in order to serve its own interests.

From the moral aspect this is a national calamity, a great spiritual-moral catastrophe for the Jewish people, one never before witnessed. The murderers destroyed one third of the nation's body, they plundered everything from us, but not our honor, and now, with our own hands, we are offering them the honor and the soul of the Jewish people. We cannot force those who hate us to love us, but we can force them to act respectfully towards us.

Members of the Knesset, we must consider what the gentiles will say – that we have sold our birthright, our self-respect. Why should our children have to ask, "Why did you desecrate the memory of our heroes and martyrs?" In 1933, when we faced the question of saving the Jews of Germany and bringing them to Palestine, Dr. Stephen Wise and I took the initiative, and so it was decided at an earlier meeting of the World Jewish Congress in Geneva to announce a boycott of Germany, and that was before the brutal murders.

The Talmud recounts that during the Jerusalem siege in the Hasmonean war, the people of the city would lower every day a box of dinars from the heights of the city wall and a calf for the daily sacrifice at the Temple would be sent up in return. Once, they lowered the box of dinars and a pig was sent up instead. When it reached halfway up the wall, it dug its hooves into the wall "and the Land of Israel trembled four hundred parasangs."[32]

My brothers and sisters, the elected representatives of the Jewish people! Do not raise this profane pig to the top of our wall, the wall of moral Judaism so that it does not dig its hooves into the honor of the nation and make the Land of Israel

32   Suta Tractate, Minhot and Bava Kamma.

tremble four hundred parasangs. Remember, since its inauguration the sovereign Knesset of the State of Israel has never faced such a grave issue. The eyes of the entire Jewish people are upon us, and perhaps even the eyes of past and future generations. The cherished images of the pure and heroic martyrs stand facing us. Have mercy on the honor of Israel! If this matter depends on direct contact, then let us waive reparations. Do not bring "the hire of a whore, or the price of a dog"[33] into the House of Israel. We demand the avoidance of any direct contact with the murderers. That will be our revenge. Remember and do not forget that history will be our judge. Jewish spirit will triumph over matter. May we not be ashamed before our future generations.

MK Yosef Sapir (*General Zionists*): Mr. Speaker, Members of the Knesset, while it is true that every problem should be discussed rationally, it would be a mistake to ignore the weight and importance of the irrational elements that frequently form the basis of a historic development.

It was said here that we must adopt a statesmanlike approach, not like the one adopted by some in the Diaspora community, to this question of direct negotiations. I was fortunate to have been born in this country and to have been educated according to the precepts of emerging Jewish independence; it is precisely from that standpoint I would like to try to explain the basic premises of our party's negative position on this issue.

Our people had a reckoning with all the nations of the world throughout the generations, but our reckoning with the German government is entirely different. This is not only because of its dimensions but because of the German people's Hitlerism: to destroy the entire Jewish people without leaving a trace or a remnant. Hitler declared war on the spirit of Judaism but knew that he would only vanquish Judaism when the last Jew was dead. We included the evil Haman in our history because he wanted to exterminate all the Jews of the Persian Empire, and here we faced mass "Hamanism."

This doctrine did not originate with Hitler. It emerged generations before him from the depths of the unique and evil core of what perhaps might be termed "the soul of the German people." The very fact that Hitler was Austrian and had to stray to Germany in order to find the chance and the tools to implement his fiendish plan proves that this is a unique phenomenon in the history of humankind. We must weigh our pronouncements at home and abroad in light of this fact.

Hitler did not declare war on the Jews. He declared that they were vermin, worms to be stamped on and squashed and that humanity must be freed of this leprosy.

We are told that we must judge, consider and determine our relations with Germany as other independent peoples and states do. Yet I ask myself, and I ask you, had Germany's war against the Allies been directed towards the extermination

---

33   Deuteronomy, 23:18.

of the British or the American people and the annulment of Britain or America, would they have acted towards Germany in the way they have? I doubt it very much. Perhaps it is strange that it was the English who coined the phrase "The only good German is a dead one" while today, for some reason, they seek Germany's friendship. Surely this is their own business, but even so, they have never faced the danger of extermination, and had Hitler triumphed there would still be an England, an English people, enslaved but alive.

We must determine our attitude to this problem in light of this fact, perhaps the most crucial. Mass extermination was part of the codex of war in bygone times, but not in the 20th century. There are those who seek to influence us to determine our position in light of the need to strengthen the liberal elements in Germany. Let us leave that to powers greater than us.

The question we face, in a nutshell, is what is the meaning of contact, what is the essence of negotiations when two peoples are in a state of war – and the Jewish people are in a state of war with the German people. It declared so, and so did we. In a state of war there can only be contact in the event of negotiating a ceasefire; there can be no other contact. Our goal is perhaps not conciliation, perhaps not drawing up a peace treaty, perhaps not atonement. It is attaining a ceasefire between the German people and the State of Israel. The question is, has the time come for a ceasefire with Germany? After being vanquished, it surrendered unconditionally and without any terms. What terms and conditions should we consider?

We are told that Adenauer's statement is the moral basis for opening negotiations. We are told that we cannot permit them to kill and then take possession. What disproportion there is between the killing, the plundering and what we are being offered! It was the Germans who coined the phrase "to go to Canossa" when a German emperor stood in the courtyard of the Pope for three days until he was forgiven. Is this how we perceive Germany's plea for the forgiveness of the Jewish people? Is it in this way, almost as in a commercial transaction, that Germany should be forgiven by the Jewish people?

Perhaps it is possible to receive compensation without negotiations; perhaps there is a possibility of a settlement on the basis of appropriate moral compensation. But to approach the problem of financial compensation on the basis of such a plea for forgiveness is far worse, in my opinion, than had they offered the money without asking for conciliation. I am even prepared to say that this is no less insulting than Hitler's contemptuous attitude towards the Jewish people.

We are told that if we decide not to open negotiations – those were the words of MK Lavon – then Germany has already achieved its objective. In my opinion the opposite is true. Germany will achieve its objective the moment we decide to negotiate with it. We will have to sit together and haggle. This will bring about a humiliating and totally inappropriate situation in view of the calamity that befell our people.

Had this entire issue of reparations any relevance to the very existence of our people, of our state, it would perhaps be worthy of consideration. But is it of such relevance today? Is the existence of our people dependent upon it? In my opinion the whole matter is simply one of convenience for this government

There is a rather illuminating phrase in the government's announcement, in which immediately after emphasizing the issue of reparations, it warns the powers against arming Germany not only out of concern for the future of the entire world but especially for the future of the Jewish people. Indeed, there are real grounds for fearing that people among whom Hitler had successfully sown the seeds of anti-Semitism would again do what he did when ever a moment of opportunity arises. I am very much afraid that in view of the murder and plunder on one hand and the possibility of settling accounts so easily on the other, others would be prepared to repeat these deeds.

I am prepared to say that our situation, as grave as it might be – and perhaps the government thinks it graver than we are think – is not so grave as to make it worthwhile to do something far more dangerous than the benefit that might accrue. Neither can we ignore the fact that the majority in this House in favor of negotiations will not be overwhelming, if a majority emerges at all. Even though it might, with time, become accustomed to the idea, public opinion in this country and the Jewish world is extremely agitated. The question is whether today, in view of such a majority, it is permissible to bring about such an upheaval in our lives.

Let us not deride our national honor. Under present circumstances and present conditions, in light of the developments of recent years, the honor of the Jewish people and the State of Israel is at stake. Opening negotiations with Germany denotes dishonor. Our conclusion is thus very clear: not this way, not today, perhaps never – but certainly not today!

MK Zalman Aran (*Mapai*)**:** Members of the Knesset, the "brotherly argument" we witnessed yesterday evening reminded me of a conversation I had in 1937 when the debate regarding partition of Palestine took place within the Zionist movement and the Yishuv.[34] At the time, a leading American Reform rabbi visited the country; I maintained close contact with him during his stay for the purpose of explaining the various problems of the Yishuv to him. Among other things, I gave him my reasons for advocating partition, to which he responded with a penetrating question, reaching far down to the roots of Jewish history: he asked me whether I believed that after the establishment of the State of Israel, it would

---

34　In its conclusions, published in July 1937, the British Royal Commission of Inquiry for Palestine, headed by Lord Peel, nominated in October 1936 after the outbreak of the Arab revolt, recommended the partition of the country into Jewish and Arab States.

prove to be a durable entity which would not be destroyed by internecine quarrels. I answered that I believed in the durability of our future state in spite of its internal social, ideological and ethnic differences. Surrounded by hostile countries, the citizens' instinct for defending themselves, as well as the inherent ties between the Jewish state and Diaspora Jews, would see to that. It would be evading a very bitter truth if I do not admit now that what happened yesterday has thrown a heavy, grave shadow of doubt on our state's future.

Let us view these matters with eyes wide open. Yesterday's attack on the Knesset was planned, organized and executed by the Herut Party and was accompanied from this podium with the threat of revolt by Herut's leader. Revolt is terrorism and terrorism is murder. On the other hand, the threats voiced by the leaders of the left from this podium, and in public meetings outside the Knesset – threats of revolt should the Knesset decide against their view, and the fact that both Herut and the left utter their threats based upon totalitarian ideologies opposed to the principles of parliamentary democracy – the state cannot take lying down for they undermine its body and soul.

Having said that, I have not yet exhausted the subject. It seems that what happened here yesterday has evoked age-old Jewish chords of fratricide echoing the time of the destruction of the Second Temple, a special Jewish trait the bloody footprints of which are found in many a chapter of the Bible.

I am not authorized to speak in the name of the state, but I can say this with full responsibility: members of the Knesset, you had better know that tremendous forces in our population, forces that built the state and are still building it, will defend the state and its freedoms in any way called for. You had better know this and think about it in advance. (*MK Menachem Begin (Herut): In any way?*) Yes. Remember: defense in any way that will protect the state (*MK Menachem Begin: We have noted it.*)

Let me turn now to the subject under discussion. Gentlemen, we are talking about the Knesset authorizing state institutions to obtain reparations from Germany for the plundered Jewish property still in their hands. That is what we are discussing. And so, my dear Rabbi Nurock, do not burden my Jewish soul with this evening's chastisement with which you tormented all those disagreeing with you about reparations from Germany. Neither forgiveness nor vengeance have been suggested or even mentioned by the government. That a day will come when the Jewish people say it forgives the citizens of East and West Germany alike for murdering millions of Jews is beyond my powers of imagination. There shall be neither forgiveness nor consolation. Nothing in the world can console the people that had one-third of its sons and daughters exterminated. No forgiveness, no consolation, no vengeance. An appropriate vengeance – the magnitude of which would be proportional to the crime perpetrated against our people by the Germans – is beyond our power. The realization of this truth needs no shocking descriptions of what was done to us. Those descriptions do not sharpen the sense of the catastrophe now, just as they did not during the years of the slaughter. Today, as then, we do not know how to express those horrors in words. There was only awkward stammering, both individual and public.

What the Knesset is discussing is our duty – and I stress the word "duty" – to restore part of the plunder and invest it in building up the country and in absorbing new immigrants. It is about negotiations with the defeated Germany. Had it not been defeated, no negotiations could have ever been conducted between us and representatives of the German people. Presently there is a possibility of negotiations because Germany was defeated, though not by us, defeated all the same. And what we want is to obtain at least part of the plundered property in the way other states restored their plundered property. The governments of certain states received reparations from Germany for plundered Jewish property as well as from their citizens who collaborated with Hitler both in the murder of Jews and the plunder of their property. Similarly, we too are claiming part of the property of the looted Jewish people, as reparations.

The serious debate is not with the commercial arena: those who reject negotiations on reparations lest the goods we obtain undermine our country's economy. If that were the only obstacle, surely our experts would determine what needs to be determined and prevent what should be prevented. In any event, if the problem were purely commercial, I have yet to hear of a person or a people whose property was plundered that would refuse to get it back lest it undermine their economy. Only a twisted mind could invent such a theory. We were told at the Foreign Affairs and Defense Committee that the Western Allies waived most of the compensation due to them from West Germany. But they made that decision for political reasons, not because the compensation would undermine their economies.

We have serious disagreement with the "coalition" of the opponents of negotiations who argue with us in the name of Israel's honor. I would like to ask them all, whatever their faction may be: for four years Jews – individuals and institutions alike – have been conducting direct negotiations on compensation with the occupation authorities and the West German authorities. They have received compensation and they still do. Among those conducting negotiations is an organization called the Jewish Restitution Successor Organization. The Jewish Agency executive is also represented on this body, and Mapam is permanently represented on the Jewish Agency executive. Why have you kept silent these four years and not cried out in the name of Israel's honor?

I ask Mr. Sapir, who argues against negotiations and reparations also on behalf of the distraught Diaspora Jewry: why do you silently evade the fact that only a few months ago, a world conference of 20 Jewish organizations, some of them global and others national, decided unanimously to support the State of Israel's claim for reparations?

I shall not argue much with those Knesset members who evade the decision and hide behind the contention that although they are in favor of receiving reparations, it is only on condition that it not be obtained directly by the State of Israel but by other bodies. They do so fully aware that such an attempt was made by the government of Israel and failed. They know that the government of Israel approached the four powers with a claim for reparations, but they, contrary to MK Yaakov Chazan's theory, refused to help us, paying no any attention to his hypothesis that with the receipt of reparations from Germany by the State of Israel, the German army would automatically become part of the European army.

I have but a minor argument with our Communists. The subject under discussion is very tragic, and while debating it, I appeal to the CP Knesset members: do not become ludicrous. For it is ridiculous that those who actively boycotted the war with Hitler as long as he did not invade the Soviet Union, those who as anti-Zionist were allied during the Arab Revolt in the 30s with one of Hitler's allies – the Mufti of Jerusalem, Amin al-Hosseini – are now defending "the honor of Israel." In fact, you are desecrating the honor of Israel.

I would also like to say a few words to the members of Mapam: I deny your moral right to speak in the name of Jewish honor in this debate. I emphasize, in this debate. The slaughter of six million Jews was carried out by one Germany and one German people. One third of that people now resides in East Germany. That one third of the German people must be held responsible for at least one third of the six million slaughtered Jews. As you well know, you recently sent a delegation to the capital of that one third, to East Berlin,[35] and there your representative spoke from the podium about Germany and to Germany regarding the slaughter of the Jewish people. Did your representative demand reparations from the government of East Germany on that occasion? Heaven forbid! On the contrary, he brought "reparations" to them. He brought forgiveness and atonement to the 20 million East Germans for the slaughter they perpetrated against millions of Jews, and he did so because the purifying water of the Communist regime was sprinkled on East Germany out of the bayonets of the Soviet army.

Thus spoke your representative Mordechai Oren in his speech in East Berlin, and I quote him from your *Al-Hamishmar* daily newspaper of November 20, 1951:

> None of us will ever forget what fascism did to us and to other people. We believe that there is only one way of taking revenge for Hitler's crimes – it is the way you, the German working class on this side of the River Elbe, have been taking; it is the total demolition of the elements of reaction and fascism and the building of a new Germany, democratic and dedicated to peace, free of any reactionary forces, racism and fascism.

And here is my question: what was that speech if not a statement of forgiveness and atonement for 20 million murderers? What defense of the "honor of Israel"

---

35 On 15.11.1951 a Mapam delegation participated in the communist-dominated World Confederation of Trade Unions council meeting in East Berlin.

was there? Let me remind you of a phrase coined by Karl Marx when he was 20-years-old: "Disgrace means groveling, even when practiced for the sake of freedom." I would advise you to seriously consider this.

I would also like to say a few words to the General Zionist members of the Knesset: Gentlemen, I would like to tell you, and not only you, what I think of your "unified" stance of rejecting negotiations in the name of "the honor of Israel." I have no doubt that there is a nucleus in your ranks that opposes negotiations with Germany for the reasons outlined from this podium by MK Rimalt. However, when I read the leading article in your *Haboker* daily newspaper of January 6 devoted to the reparations affair, and found that out of its 191 lines only three are devoted to Jewish morality; the rest deals with commercial considerations on which opposition to negotiations is based. Therefore, it is unavoidable that I should not think, or even suspect, how is it that those opposed to reparations for reasons of Jewish morality are so preoccupied with commercial considerations.

And when I read in another leading article in the same *Haboker* that the government seeks reparations "... because it does not want to reform the failing economic system," it is unavoidable that I should not think or even suspect that your opposition – in any event, the opposition of some of you to negotiations on reparations – stems from your concern lest the negotiations succeed. Were the state to survive economically, it would thus frustrate your efforts to topple the economic regime to which you are hostile. I think that there are those among you who, in their hearts, are in favor of these negotiations for the same reasons as we are, but it is easier for them to have the "dirty work" done for them by Mapai members. If we put together all your members who openly say they are in favor of negotiating for reparations – even though they have committed themselves to voting against – then the weight of "the honor of Israel" becomes greatly reduced and totally disproportionate to the weight of the 22 hands you will raise against the reparations negotiations.

I am not surprised that Herut is clinging to reparations and "the honor of Israel." Apart from their desire to reenter the public stage, apart from their hatred of Mapai, the government, democracy, and their lust for power – apart from all these there is another fundamental issue: Herut Knesset members, you are prisoners of rhetoric, but from the standpoint of history's judgment, from the standpoint of Israeli reality, rhetoric can also come from the barrel of a gun. In the name of your hollow rhetoric you opposed the activity of the Jewish National Fund and the Keren Hayesod [United Israel Appeal] which you defined as "scrounging"; you opposed the Zionist fund drives in America and the American government's grants that you defined as "begging"; you opposed the 1933 transfer that you termed "betrayal." You have opposed and derided every redemptive and constructive act. You have never comprehended the value of the physical basis of the rebirth of this people and how that basis gets built by growth.

Members of the Knesset: with all due respect to Jewish martyrdom, I think that in the defense of Israel's honor, the last three generations of our people are measured against the dozens that preceded them. All the following factors embody the honor of Israel: the immigration to this country; the transition to physical labor; the creation of resources for immigrant absorption; the raising of national capital; the founding of agricultural settlements; the revival of the Hebrew language and the rebirth of Hebrew education; the political struggle; the establishment of the Haganah; the volunteering to the British army that fought against Hitler and the founding of the Jewish Brigade; the armed struggle against the British Government; the illegal immigration; the rebirth of the Jewish state; and the fulfillment of the vision of the ingathering of the exiles.

One thing only might desecrate the honor of Israel, now and for generations to come. It is the collapse of the State of Israel. What then is our generation's task regarding this honor if not the strengthening of our state? In view of this task – only in view of this task – we will decide on the issue facing us.

MK Israel Bar-Yehuda (*Mapam*): Members of the Knesset, the right way of seeking the solution to certain fateful historic issues is through stocktaking of heart and mind alike. It is difficult, indeed impossible, to differentiate between these two. Thus, for instance, when our people in the Warsaw Ghetto were on the verge of their uprising, it was both heart and mind that guided their decision, and this is what happened in numerous fateful issues at decisive junctures in our people's history, as well as in the history of other people. The dilemma facing us also calls for the same approach: the stocktaking of heart and mind alike, for one cannot be separated from the other.

What are we are actually discussing? The very same forces that are presently influencing the government of Israel to enter into direct negotiations with neo-Nazi Germany did everything possible at the time to conceal the truth from the world, and from us. The dilemma facing us is both moral and political. These two aspects cannot be separated just as they cannot be separated when dealing with any other decisive issue. True, we were not always of the same mind with those of you presently opposing this step of yours. On dozens of basic issues in the life of our state and people, we were and still are divided, just as you in the coalition sometimes are. I do not accept Rabbi Nurock striving to impose religion on the life of our society and state. I do not accept the views of MK Mikunis who is oblivious to the Zionist solution to the problem of our people's survival. And I most definitely do not accept Begin's views.

I know one thing. I know that that there are certain fundamental issues such as the survival or extermination of the Jewish people, such as the prospect of another world war that would start with extermination of Jews. Rabbi Nurok, too, begins to understand when faced with these issues – despite his siding with the Western powers, with America's position – who the forces are that are acting behind the scenes in preparation of this war and where they are leading the State of Israel. I shall fight together with him against these forces. I will cooperate with any honest Jew who understands this simple truth.

I would like to state clearly: we have full rights to demand from all of Germany – West and East – the restitution of what was plundered from the Jewish people. Our party has always said this. We said it and demanded it, and therefore we did not object when the State of Israel demanded from the victorious powers that restitution of the plunder should be imposed on Germany. But those powers, arguing so much with us and "appeasing" the Arabs in our region, can they not mediate for reparations in Germany? No, for that is not in their interest. Their interest is in sitting down with representatives of neo-Nazi Germany to discuss reparations in our name, in the name of the State of Israel, thus granting them a moral and political seal of approval. They forced this situation.

I do not accept the Nazi racial doctrine. I know that there were tens of thousands of Germans who were imprisoned for opposing Nazism. I know that there were a few Germans – horribly few – who actually helped our rebels in the Warsaw Ghetto. But I also know that during the Nazi era, the vast majority of the German people actively or passively participated – many of them actively – in the extermination of the Jewish people and the plunder of its property. I draw a distinction between the East German government, actively engaged in denazification and trying to reeducate the people, though I do not believe that such a Sisyphean task can be accomplished in four years, and the West German government that is engaged in the opposite, the revival of Nazism. This government is abetting and covering up for all those who only yesterday openly conducted the extermination. Under its aegis, the former soldiers of Rommel's Afrika Korps can openly convene with the government's representatives. In 1941 these same men were on the verge of exterminating us too – the Jews of Palestine – for back then the British were also prepared to abandon us out of their own considerations.

I cannot and will not forgive until this denazification and reeducation process is completed in East Germany as well. And I am prepared to fight against those powers and their supporters that are reviving Nazism, for without this support they cannot ignite a world war. That is why they wish to grant Germany a "moral seal of approval". That is the only issue at hand created by the project for reparations.

Don't tell me that you are talking about the sums currently required for our own rehabilitation here. Don't you know that after WW I bigger forces than the State of Israel demanded reparations from Germany, and that Germany paid out less than 5 percent, that they stopped paying and even started receiving no lesser sums in loans and investments? Don't you know that the Thyssen and the Krupp tycoons have become wealthy again in present day Germany? But the Adenauer government lives mainly at the Americans' expense, so when the Americans told you, and they told you clearly "Not at our expense," this meant that Adenauer was saying "No money!"

Don't you know that although four years ago when a powerful state, the most powerful state in the Western world – America – agreed to give us a loan of $100 million in materials, we are still unable to obtain materials on this account? For they are preparing for war. They need those materials not for building, and certainly not for the building of the Jewish people in its own state. They are needed for preparing for war. And is the situation in Germany any different? Do you think that after agreeing on whatever sum you will actually receive a large part of it? Are any of you, the people who sit in the various economic ministries in the State of Israel, and with all the economic blunders you have been making, thinking about this seriously? Do you want to persuade us that you believe it?

But that is not the issue. There is, in fact, only one issue, and those exerting "quiet pressure", that is, secret pressure on you are doing so for another reason. (*Foreign Minister Moshe Sharett: They are pressing us to ask for reparations?*) Not to ask for reparations but to sit together with these Germans as a people worthy of contact. (*Foreign Minister Moshe Sharett: Do you believe such falsehoods?*); (*Yitzhak Ben Aharon (Mapam): It was affirmed in an official statement given to you in Washington that an agreement on reparations will only be permitted through direct negotiations.*); (*Foreign Minister Moshe Sharett: They are pressuring us? Is that pressure?*) That is the entire essence of the matter and that, in addition to what has been said here about shame in the presence of our martyrs, is what is so tragic and terrible about it, for it means the preparation of a death threat to new victims; it means the danger of more millions who will be murdered.

Are six million not enough? A new world war in any form whatsoever will first hit the millions of Jews in Europe and perhaps not only there. Whoever does not understand these basic problems – securing the existence of our people – is unworthy of leading it. The danger lurking for our people is, in addition to the six million we cannot bring back, that millions more will be exterminated when not only fate or a large external force will overcome us, but that we, too, will have a hand in it! Opposition to this in every way is a must from all these benches, from Rabbi Nurock to the most left-leaning member here – religious and non-religious. It must be exerted by all who are aware that a new world war will be a Holocaust for all mankind, a Holocaust of no smaller magnitude than the one experienced by the Jewish people in the last war, and for the Jewish people it means a threat of extermination, heaven forbid!

Who does not understand that? Who does not know that the awareness of this danger must be the principal motive governing every action by both individuals and public servants in the sphere of foreign relations; increasing our power here must also be a top priority. Why am I crying out time and time again that we are short of time, that we need more millions of people, and faster, that we must be more independent, more deep-rooted in the soil, more deep-rooted in labor, stronger in security? Let there be less use of the whip among us, more cooperation, even when we are divided ideologically. Otherwise we will not achieve, heaven forbid, the basic conditions guaranteeing our survival in this country because there is no time, because such terrible dangers are threatening us, but you are incapable of seeing the dangers and understanding them.

To this I must add something else: our Knesset faction finds itself in a comfortable position – on the issue of direct negotiations we have no need to impose factional discipline because we are all of the same opinion. However, we too did not ask the voters in the general elections in September 1951 for their opinion on direct negotiations. We propose to resolve this dilemma now, in a different way, through a referendum, and it seems to us that not only our own voters would cast their vote against but also some of yours. You too did not ask your voters in the last general elections for their opinion on this issue. Why don't you, democrats as you purport to be, ask them? Why not ask the people, your voters, our voters, at least in this matter which is threatening us with a schism, with creating a terrible abyss that is splitting us? Perhaps the people side with you? Why not ask them? For it is no secret that the same arguments MK Aran directed towards the General Zionists an MK of that party could direct towards your party. Is it a secret? Why is it that you prefer putting such a decisive issue to a vote of confidence? Why not ask the people? Why don't we take a unanimous decision here today – I believe that everyone in this House will vote for it – to approach the four powers that still officially control both Germanies, and demand that the powers that defeated Germany restore that part of the property taken from the Jews and which can be returned, as it is needed for their rehabilitation?

Let us go to the people. What is there to be afraid of? If I am not mistaken, this is the first instance in the history of the Knesset that we are asking for a referendum. You are all staunch supporters of democracy – why is this in question? Let us go to the people, each of us with his rationale, not with clubs, not with bombs, but with words, and ask them: why are you afraid? You, who claim to have saved the people, to have founded the state, to have brought in waves of mass immigration – what haven't you done? – go to the people on this matter too!

The issue continues to be extremely serious. Tomorrow its resolution might tilt the scales of possibly granting assistance for preparing the extermination of Jews. Therefore this question cannot be decided following a regular debate and a regular vote. There must be a debate encompassing the entire people. The people should be asked directly for its opinion.

Minister of Transport David Zvi Pinkas: Mr. Speaker, Members of the Knesset, it is painful indeed that we have to discuss this difficult, deep and terrifying issue as we remember last evening's events inside the House and outside it as well. What happened yesterday was an attempt to transfer the prerogative of decision making from the realm of the people's elected representatives to the incited mob summoned to put siege on this House. I deeply regret that this attempt was carried out by a party which speaks highly of national values but evidently thinks – at least it thought so yesterday – that these values would be supported by inciting masses of people to surround our House of Representatives. What was the purpose of the Herut leader MK Begin's summons to the masses to Jerusalem if not to remove from the Knesset its freedom to proclaim its position and take decisions according to its conscience? If these are the national values that Herut is trying to inculcate into our youth, it should be deplored.

A referendum on this question is called for. There are democracies that have long been accustomed to conducting referendums. In every Swiss village the inhabitants decide to nominate one priest or another, one doctor or another, one teacher or another, by a referendum, and even more important issues are decided by this method, too. In view of our past tradition of democratically electing representative bodies such as the Zionist Congresses, our people and our state are not used to this method. We hold democratic elections for our executive bodies. The elections to the Knesset were held only four months ago. Do you think that today we will come by true results by holding a referendum without experience in this voting method? Do you think that if we put this question before the people today we will achieve the true answer dwelling in the people's hearts? I am quite astonished by the proposal for a referendum suggested by both MK Begin and MK Bar-Yehuda. What will you say if the people decide differently from what you said here yesterday? It was from MK Bar-Yehuda's benches that we heard the cry, "We will not obey!,"[36] and from the benches of MK Begin's faction we heard "We will not permit it and it will not be carried out!" What then will you do – those of you who are not going to obey and those who will not permit – if the people's choice turns out to be against you?

A great deal has been said here to the effect that on this issue the heart, not the mind, should have the upper hand. Almost all or the majority of the opponents based their attitude on emotions. I understand them. It seems to me that on this question we all have one feeling. No wonder that when ever the words "Germany" or "the German people" are expressed, the terrible recollection of the extermination of one-third of our people during the Hitler era immediately engulfs each one of us. However, I disagree with those who claim that the issue of direct negotiations

---

36 These words were uttered by MK Yaakov Riftin (Mapam) in a Knesset debate on November 4, 1951, in response to a political report by the Foreign Minister Moshe Sharett. He said, after stating that the State of Israel would not participate in the Middle East Defense Pact initiated by the USA that, at the same time, "the vital interests of the State of Israel oblige it to maintain close contact, first and foremost, with those countries in which the Jewish communities are enjoying complete freedom to support it." MK Riftin contended that the government's foreign policy is serving "American anti-Soviet policy" and declared "We are appealing from this podium to officers and soldiers, to workers and men of letters: we will not obey this reactionary and anti-patriotic policy!"

is connected with an assessment of present day Germany, its morals, its social or political position. I do not think there is any difference if we accept the money from Socialist, Communist or Capitalist Germany. There is no difference. I do not think that the fact that Hitler's Germany is currently divided into East and West should be of any significance to us. I do not ask those members who – unlike Rabbi Nurock, for whom all Germans are unfit for contact – argue that it is only with Germans from the West that we should not meet in order to determine what is due to us. I would like to know what is our response to the fact that the power controlling East Germany, the Soviet Union, has not responded at all to the claim we submitted to it?

I do not believe in today's world being better than before. We are living in an unfortunate period of a morally destroyed world, and the worst of all the people we have seen in history is the German. I do not believe that we will see any good coming from them, but I still believe that we should claim what is due to us.

Several speakers have spoken here rather emotionally and asked, what did the millions who died command us to do? We have no written will and testament, but each of us strives to search his heart for an answer: what were those being led to the slaughter thinking in their final moments? I, too, have tried to hear the whispers of the souls of our brethren who are no longer with us.

Would they have wanted us to leave to the Germans the plundered Jewish property after being murdered, and allow them, with their well-known thoroughness ten years later to turn the $1.5 billion into $15 billion? Would those souls have wanted their property to remain in the hands of those Germans? Wouldn't they have wanted a monument erected in their memory, using what remains of their property and can still be returned, and to have it invested in that eternal monument – the growth of a flourishing State of Israel? Is it better that their property remains in the hands of Fritz and Hans who will benefit from it so that they can again pounce on the world? Would they not have wanted us to invest this money in making the State of Israel blossom?

MK Rimalt asked us what we will say to our children. I have heard this question, which he was asked by his son, not from young children but from elderly politicians, and I hope that the question you asked in your son's name was purely allegorical. We shall tell our children that there was an accursed time of evil, killing, plunder and destruction, that there was an arch-criminal unworthy of being called human – Hitler – who led his people and exterminated one-third of the Jewish people. We did our utmost to fight him by taking part in the war at the side of the Allies. The German people plundered Jewish property. But God showed His grace to the Jewish people and enabled it to establish its own country, the State of Israel. True, even with that grace and that miracle, we were unable to raise the dead but were able invest the remains of their property in building up this country. That is what we will tell our children and future generations, and that is the will and testament of those who were led to the gas chambers.

In my opinion, there is no more appropriate remembrance of the destroyed Jewish communities than to bring what little remains – the Jewish public property and the property that became public as it had no heirs – to the State of Israel for its strengthening. That is the will and testament we must uphold. This is not a question of money. Whether or not we need this money right now is unimportant to me. Even if we did not need it, I would not leave a single dollar in the hands of the murderers. Of course, it would have been better had the great powers acceded to our request. It would have been easier had they compelled Germany to pay us. But they did not do so, neither the Western nor the Eastern powers. And can we permit ourselves to relinquish the inheritance of the Holocaust survivors because the great powers are not prepared to act as our emissaries? If a wolf were to devour a child, leaving only its bloodstained shirt, would the child's mother not take the shirt from the wolf's mouth so that the memory of her child would remain with her? We must take that shirt. We must save the Jewish property and invest it in the State of Israel, even if it were not needed (*MK Menachem Begin (Herut): You do not negotiate with wolves!*) In March, with the Knesset's concurrence, the government submitted the reparations claim. There was no opposition. Mr. Begin even argued that we claimed too little. Perhaps that is arguable. At this moment it is unimportant to me if Germany does not pay. Even if we suppose that, we must claim the Jewish property. (*MK Menachem Begin (Herut): You are making an agreement with Germany, you are trading with Germany!*) Perhaps you want such an agreement. What I want is the Jewish money.

In March we brought this claim to the Knesset and not one person opposed it. Something happened, and some of the Germans agreed to pay us on the basis of our claim. I am not saying that the German people have changed and become better people. But am I forbidden to know what I can obtain from the respondent when the respondent repeatedly says that it is prepared to pay me on the basis of my claim? Has the money become disqualified because of this?

We have wandered from the path of reality which we are all bound to take. Strangely, in matters of faith you are so rational, and in practical matters touching upon building up the country, the money of the Jewish people, all of a sudden you become irrational. The Knesset will be doing its duty if it authorizes the competent bodies to ensure that the remains of Jewish property still in Germany are invested in the State of Israel.

MK Yizhar Harari (*Progressive Party*): Members of the Knesset, why am I opposed to reparations? Since the establishment of the state our Foreign Ministry's official policy has been to boycott Germany, and to this day it has had no contact with it through our ambassadors – not in Paris, Washington, London, Ankara, or Buenos Aires. We have been a real nuisance for Germany worldwide. Our boycott of Germany's representatives is accepted by the world at large and has never been challenged. This policy of ours stemmed from natural emotions, healthy emotions, a sense of national pride. And what has happened that all of a sudden we are talking about negotiations? When we were not talking about property or money, nobody even thought of changing this policy, nobody proposed coming into contact with Germany.

And why should they pay us reparations? Because we are a nuisance. True, being a nuisance is not disruptive enough to the degree of preventing Germany from being restored into the community of nations, but it is sufficiently disruptive to be worth Germany's while, the wealthy Germany, the wealthiest of the European nations at the moment, to give something in exchange for getting rid of this nuisance.

If up till now the foreign minister could speak out proudly against Germany with a feeling of solid ground beneath his feet, thus arousing deep echoes in the hearts of Germany's opponents, he did so with a feeling of complete serenity wheras Germany could find no answer to his words. I am afraid that once reparations are paid, Nazi Germany would find an opening, evenif only a narrow one, for such a response, and I am not willing to grant it that opening, thereby weakening the world's opposition towards reparations. I am not willing to assist it in this way; I want us to keep on being a nuisance. I am not willing to exchange this position for any sum.

We are told that we will obtain reparations but not forgive. The question is, when will we not forgive? When we enter the negotiating room or when we leave it? Whom do we tell every time that we have not forgiven? How will this non-forgiveness be expressed? Will we not forgive – when we are searching for markets for goods we do not need? And to whom else will we say that we will not forgive? To the German experts who will come here to assemble the machinery we have obtained, or when ships sail between here and Germany? They may be our ships, but they might also be German ones. How will our anger and bitterness be expressed? By repeating to ourselves every now and again that we shall not forgive while goods and contact flow between us and the Germans?

If the opponents of reparations are occasionally dubbed Don Quixotes – and I have been included amongst them – then my view is that if there are Don Quixotes here, they are those who think that we can obtain millions from Germany, that we can bring in goods, while saying at the same time: "We will not forgive." If we are to forgive Germany, if the time has come to do so at all, let us do so without reparations, without money. Why connect it to money? And if the time has not come yet, we should not forgive even for reparations. Let us remember what happened for generations to come.

We will conduct negotiations. Let no one think for a minute that I do not understand that those who favor negotiations are doing so out of feelings no less pure and patriotic than mine. But we all agree that we are not prepared to negotiate for a paltry sum. We all agree that we will only be prepared to discuss a large sum that will strengthen us economically, that will reinforce our national enterprise. But at what sum will we cease negotiations? What is the sum below which our honor will not permit us to sit and negotiate with them? And how will we look after ceasing negotiations because we have not reached agreement on the sum? Will we bury our faces in the ground? Will we continue having nothing to do with them because of a difference of some sum or because the kind of goods offered are unsuitable?

We all know we are talking about goods – there is no other alternative. What goods will we receive? We need materials that will strengthen our economy like water pipes to make the Negev Desert bloom, industrial machinery, and so forth. But to receive these items, the Germans must be prepared to offer them to us. What will we do if the percentage of "building and construction" goods is very small, and the rest will consist of luxury goods which will inundate our homes and families with all that German "munificence" that has no relevance to strengthening our country? Will we then say that we do not want what they are offering?

The verse, "Hast thou killed and also taken possession?" was quoted time and time again for justifying that we must accept anything. Very well then, will we put a refrigerator and a radio in every home and in this way enjoy the benefits of the reparations that will flood the country?

And what effect will Germany's bargaining power have on our economy? They will promise us pipes, and then it will turn out that they are not prepared to supply all the necessary sizes. They will give us half-factories and then say, "Do you want them to be completed? Then stop saying that you do not forgive us." They will say: "Your consul so-and-so behaved discourteously towards our consul, and yet another one behaved rudely at such-and-such a conference. If you want us to continue reparations, put a stop to it." Will we then reply, "Hast thou murdered and also taken possession?" No. We will soften our attitude here and there, bow our heads, and continue to obtain "our property." What dependency, what enslavement that will be to the German economy and Germany! Do we need all that? Is such an experience necessary?

I do not know if the supporters have also taken other considerations into account. Will the expected fund-raising drives abroad continue to provide what they are providing at present? And what will happen to the Israel Bonds enterprise and to American aid? Will the Americans not say, "If Israel is receiving so much from Germany, we can now divert larger sums to the Arab states?" Will the outcome not be worth the effort, thus only replacing the source of the money? Are we sure that Germany would not violate the agreement we will sign with it? Are you prepared to accept further insult, an additional failure? When in the course of a few years or months we face the fact that Germany will inform us that it is sorry: it signed an agreement for $1 million or $1 billion but does not want to give us any more – while in the meantime we are no longer a nuisance – what should we do then?

I am not prepared to take any further insults from Germany. I do not know if anybody is mentally prepared for that. I am not only against entering negotiations; I do not want this property!

Are we going to remain helpless? Can the State of Israel truly not be built up without the help of Germany, without Germany boasting of the fact that it aided us, that it put us back onto our feet? Is this what we have stooped to?

Minister of Labor Golda Meir: Mr. Speaker, Members of the Knesset, I see it as my duty to begin with one word of appreciation for those few hundred men in police uniforms, loyal and devoted to the State of Israel, who formed a wall around this House and defended it and the honor of the state. Let their proud and splendid act serve as a warning to anyone who thinks of raising a hand against the sovereignty of the state.

I have no intention of debating with the faction responsible for yesterday's scandalous and shameful event. We will know how to defend ourselves against outside foes, and if necessary – although let's hope this will never be – against elements from within. The power to do that is at our disposal.

I do not intend to debate too long with the members of Mapam as well, for it seems to me that, as in other debates, we regrettably do not share common ground. While my colleagues and I have one single viewpoint, the Jewish viewpoint, I cannot argue with people who adhere to different positions. I am completely unaffected by MK Bar-Yehuda saying that he privately opposed being represented by his party in East Berlin. The bare fact is that he was represented there, and we heard nothing in public about his opposition. I had the honor of leading a delegation to the International Socialist Conference in Zurich in 1947, and the German Social Democratic Party was prevented from joining the Socialist International only because the Israeli delegation would not agree to abstain, but voted against.

I have only one rule regarding the German people: in my view, every German, in East and West alike, is guilty. There are perhaps a select few who did not sin, but I am still not yet prepared to look for them, and I am still not prepared to attest to the innocence of a single one of them, be he in the East or the West. For me, there is only the Jewish angle, and it tells me that each of us must ask himself: why did we pay such a terrible price, why was such a huge part of the terrible cruelty that befell the world directed at us, the Jewish people? There is only one answer: we were weak, we did not have independence, we did not have a state. We asked various nations, from East and West, to protect us, but that protection did not come from anywhere in the entire world. Some of the Jewish people were living in this country at the time when we did not yet have an independent state, but it was only here that Jews were recruited as Jews for the war against Hitler. We did what we could according to our power, and it was not much.

I would very much like to avoid overusing the names of those who are no longer with us. But I cannot but ask myself: what conclusion did the great calamity that befell us warn us to reach? First and foremost, we must be strong – all the rest stems from that. We must be strong not only because by that very fact we are honoring the memory of those who were murdered, but also in order to prevent a repeat of that calamity. I believe that this was the last testament of our martyrs. We were slaughtered and burnt because we were weak, and only if we are truly strong can we prevent that from happening again. This must be the first commandment for every Jew who is sincerely dedicated to the State of Israel, who believes in its future, and who does not want to exploit the memory of those no longer with us only for the sake of this debate.

Had we been an independent state during WW II, and had our army fought against Hitler together with the other Allied armies, and had our army, together with the armies of the West and East, entered Berlin, then we would have done what all those other states did. Every country took what was due to it from that accursed place. We did not do so because Jewish combatants fought in the various units of the Allied armies. I therefore say, reparations are our due, it is not beholden to the generosity of Mr. Adenauer or anyone else. It is our due.

I know that there is no comparison between the disasters that have befallen us in different periods of our tragic history and the Holocaust brought down upon us by Hitler and the Nazis. There is no comparison, and yet after one pogrom or another in one country or another – and there are very few countries in which pogroms against Jews were never instigated – why has it never occurred to us, or to the perpetrators, to restore at least some of the plundered property to us? Why? Because we were not an independent state, we were not a nation among nations, so who was bound to take us into account? At best we could obtain an expression of pity from some neutral country. For decades, we invested all our energy and talents into such efforts, moving around the great world looking for a good gentile who would say, "It's such a pity, my heart is bleeds for you." Now is the first time we are able to talk with those who murdered and slaughtered us but as an independent people presenting its claim.

Somebody here asked, how can we sit down together with them? We will sit with them as a victorious people with a defeated one. Our first fundamental victory is manifested in staying alive. It was Hitler's intention that not even one single Jew would remain alive. He certainly did not intend that after all that extermination there would still be Jews in the world, not only Jewish individuals dependent on the good grace of the good and bad nations amongst whom they live, but Jews as a people, as a people having an independent state, a people that is the master of its own fate, a people building up its power to prevent any future catastrophes of this kind. That certainly was not Hitler's intention, and hence we are victorious. Now, after that calamity, we are an independent people growing ever stronger. We are a state that within its first years, in the first days of its existence, demonstrated its growing strength by rescuing masses of Jews and bringing them to Israel, thus ensuring that such catastrophes will never befall them again.

I wish to appeal to the members of the Knesset who, truly and from a sore heart, have spoken about these events: please bear in mind that there are Jewish children who survived but are still in danger, there are elderly Jews who survived and are still in danger. Are they not precious to us because they are alive? Is there one person in this House who can stand up and confidently state that he knows of one single corner in the world outside Israel where Jews live in safety? Those Jews, the children, the men and women who survived, do they not impel us to act? Do they not oblige us to rescue them quickly?

The lives of those Jews can be saved in one way only – in this country. We must strengthen ourselves in every possible way to rescue them quickly in order to ensure their safety and well-being. There is no injunction more sacred, no precept more Jewish, no command more patriotic, no principle that bestows more pride than this one. We are going to claim our due, and the responsible people sitting in the cabinet, the people who are determining the policies of the government of Israel, have demonstrated then and now – even before we became an independent nation – that they know how to speak with the gentiles with pride, with Jewish pride. I have no doubt that we will know how to meet with our sworn enemies in a way that will add strength and honor to the Jewish people and not, heaven forbid, the opposite. (*MK Menachem Begin: Sitting with Germans will add honor?*) We will demand the Jewish property in their hands. It is our due, and is also needed to strengthen and rescue living Jews. We shall demand this, backed by all the Jewish and Israeli forces available, with all the pride and dignity at our command.

Clearly, all kinds of accusations can be tacked onto this demand: that it is forgiveness, that it is leading to mutual friendship with West Germany, but there is neither sense nor logic in this. There is absolutely no necessity for forgiveness or friendship and there will be none. None of the proponents even dares to think of a possibility of the negotiations producing such results. We will meet with the representatives of Germany, not for the sake of peace, not for the sake of friendship, forgiveness or forgetting. The Jewish people can never forget. There can be no Jew who will forget.

In this House there are those who say, "Reparations – yes, but not through direct negotiations; we shall ask others to do it for us." But this is what we have requested, and some potential go-betweens we approached replied that they were not prepared to do so. One great power, a power whose shops in its capital city display and sell vast quantities of German merchandise, did not respond at all. It is unclear to me whether these were made in East or West Germany. I do not imagine that Moscow will view the receipt of any merchandise that it can obtain from West Germany as beneath its dignity. On the contrary – and quite rightly – it views the use of these goods as its obligation, for Hitler caused a great deal of destruction in the Soviet Union. And I ask myself – and there are certain Knesset members present here who should ask themselves more than I – what has happened here? Why is it that the Soviet Union has not deemed it necessary to even respond to us? Why has it not deemed it necessary to tell us "Go to East Germany and negotiate with them?" It knows that East Germany will not lift a finger without its consent. That door is closed for the present. Shall we accept that? No! We will claim our due from East Germany as well, for they too hold plundered Jewish property, and it is ours. We will claim from them exactly the same as we are claiming from West Germany.

I understand that there are those who cannot reach this conclusion out of genuine pain, but surely there is a wide gulf between that and the weird philosophy that rules out pure common sense, and the philosophy that there is a *sine qua non* stating that there must be a tragic contradiction between heart and mind. Not necessarily. True, sometimes a gap like this occurs, and that is very unfortunate, but it does not always have to be. In the present case, both the Jewish heart and common sense declare we should tell those that murdered and plundered that in this world, wherein no one is prepared to assist in seeing justice done, happy are we that no longer depend on the favors of others. Happy are we that we no longer need to scurry through the corridors of other countries and nations and various meetings in order find out protectors willing do something for us.

As a free and independent country that has taken this mission upon itself, it is incumbent upon us to ensure the life, security, and honor of the Jewish people. As proud representatives of the people, we shall proceed in a dignified manner and claim our due from the murderers so that we can strengthen ourselves, so that we may live.

Speaker Hannah Lamdan (*Mapam*): This session will be continued at 9:30 a.m. tomorrow.

Third Knesset Session 40, 9.1.1952

Speaker Benjamin Mintz (*Poalei Agudat Yisrael*): I hereby declare Session 40 open. We shall continue the debate on the government's statement on reparations from Germany. MK Haim Boger has the floor.

MK Haim Boger (*General Zionists*): Mr. Speaker, Members of the Knesset, permit me now to speak about this painful issue from the perspective of a veteran teacher associated with Jewish education in this country for 50 years,[37] and also

---

37 MK Haim Boger was one of the founders, directors and teachers of the legendary Herzliya Gymnasium, established in 1905 in Jaffa.

as someone who is well-known for his involvement in the formation of Freedom Fighters of Israel.[38]

I have listened attentively to the prime minister's statement about the government's approach to the four great powers with a demand to impose upon Germany the payment of $1.5 billion out of the $6 billion at which the plunder was estimated. We heard, too, that the Soviet Union did not respond and that the other three powers replied that they were unable to demand further compensation from the Germans; other nations will not receive compensation. It was under the pressure of Jewish public opinion alone that the Bonn chancellor agreed to discuss reparations with Israel.

The question is, how will the claim for these reparations from the Germans and the discussions with the Bonn government – extending our hand to the murderers of our people – affect the overall outlook of Jewish youth in the State of Israel and in the Diaspora?

In a session of the first Knesset on January 10, 1951, MK Meir Argov said as follows on the matter of German rearmament:

> Mr. Speaker, Members of the Knesset. In accordance with the Knesset decision, the Foreign Affairs and Defense Committee deliberated on the question of Germany's rearmament, and decided as follows: the first Knesset of the State of Israel expresses the concern of the Jewish people regarding the reacceptance of the German nation into the community of nations, that same Germany that cold-bloodedly exterminated six million of our people in a calculated plan and with fiendish brutality, without remorse and with no change in the German people's disposition shown to this very day. The Knesset vigorously protests the rearmament of East and West Germany, and in particular the current overt drift toward establishing special German military units. The Knesset appeals to all the nations of the world, and first and foremost to those nations that were victims of Germany's crimes in this generation, upholding their obligations to humanity and the Jewish people, to implement complete demobilization of Germany, punish the war criminals, and desist from supplying arms and other deadly weapons to the German nation, West and East alike. It is our profound belief that these arms are likely to threaten world peace in the future as they did in the past. The Knesset decides to convey this appeal to the United Nations Organization and to the parliaments of the nations of the world.

In explaining the committee's decision, MK Argov continued,

> At Lake Success, before 60 of the world's nations, from that great and lofty international podium, at a time when flattery was showered on West and East Germany together with vast quantities of arms, the Israeli foreign minister's voice was the lone voice – the only

---

38   Freedom Fighters of Israel (FFI, generally known as "The Stern Gang") was a small clandestine military organization which seceded from the Irgun in 1940 when its founder and first commander, Abraham Stern, opposed the Irgun's decision to cease carrying out terrorist operations against the British during WW II. The FFI's mode of operations was mainly assassinating British personnel. Its operatives assassinated Lord Moyne, British Minister of State in the Middle East, in November 1944 in Cairo, and the UN mediator Count Folke Bernadotte in September 1948 in Jerusalem.

one in the world – raised against the rearmament of Germany, against its acceptance into the community of nations. He said this to the entire world in lucid words, fraught with emotions that derived from the spilt blood of a slaughtered people.[39]

After what was said, if we do not demand international guarantees that these nations cease arming Germany and prevent it from sending officers to the Arab states, should we still go to Bonn and ask for reparations? I do not wish to dwell on the question, "What will the gentiles say?" They will always find something wrong with any step we take. They will always say that we are prepared to sell anything for money. Before executing the Ten Martyrs,[40] the Romans reminded them of the sale of Joseph to the Ishmaelites for money. The Christians accuse us of the betrayal of Jesus by Judas Iscariot for 30 pieces of silver. Should we receive their reparations, the Germans will be the first to say that Jews are prepared to sell the memory of their victims for the chance of obtaining reparations. We do not have to depend on what the Germans say, but their insinuations also affect our people. Now I will ask myself and you one very basic question: what will the surviving Jews say when a drop of blood still lingers in their hearts, burning for revenge, as in ours? What will they say and what will they feel when we receive money from the murderers. What will they feel when the representatives of the State of Israel return a handshake after that hand was washed in soap made from the pure body fat of a Jewish child? If the State of Israel is run only by the mind, and not the heart, there will be no State of Israel.

For generations, Diaspora Jewry's survival was based on submission. That mentality of submission, the bowed head, the bent back, must be a memento mori for us, for the State of Israel. Heaven help us if raise our children that way. The State of Israel has not taken that path. We will not teach our youth to bow their heads. The Jewish Brigade, to which Moshe Sharett[41] devoted all his energy, was established by the Jewish population of Palestine; it was their war against the Germans, a war of rescue and vengeance. The vengeance was for the blood of our brethren, spilled by the murderers employing a scientifically planned method, with satanic lust, out of a clear desire to expunge the memory of the Jews from the world. The very fact of our existence, the existence of the State of Israel, is the embodiment of our vengeance against the murderers.

Our war of vengeance against the German Amalekites is still in its infancy. Their plot to exterminate us has not stopped. The Germans did not exterminate the Jews in battle or with an atomic bomb. They invented special scientific methods to annihilate us. The university departments of Immanuel Kant at

39   See *Divrei HaKnesset,* vol. 8, pp. 743-747.
40   According to Jewish tradition, ten Jewish sages, headed by Rabbi Akiva, were tortured to death by the Romans after they crushed the Bar-Kokhba revolt in Judea in 135.
41   Moshe Sharett, Head of the Political Department of the Jewish Agency at that time.

Königsberg and of Herman Cohen[42] and Herman Zvi Shapira[43] at Heidelberg were turned into scientific laboratories for the extermination of our people. This method was broadcast by German radio; it had a marked effect on the people who heard about it, and was assimilated by far more hearts and minds than the Jewish Jesus of Nazareth's doctrine of love.

Our commandment is "Remember what Amalek did unto thee." Do not forget! That is the order of the day; an alert against the enemy that rises up to destroy us. And for those contemplating sitting quietly by in this time of tribulation, the Prophet will utter the curse: "Cursed be he that doeth the word of the Lord deceitfully, and cursed be he that keepeth his sword back from blood."[44]

The autonomous education system of the Yishuv inculcated in our youth the awareness that its objective, its purpose in life, is to redeem the people and the homeland, to establish the State of Israel and to defend it with their blood, not to surrender. That was the only way of preserving their human awareness and uncompromising devotion to their people and homeland. Any deviation from that, any head-bowing to those who hate us is like poison gas in the hearts of our children. Jewish youth must know that, today and henceforth, the State of Israel will exact vengeance from those who hate the Jewish people, not reparations and peace. "There is no peace, saith the Lord, unto the wicked."[45]

Demand, not request! Payment of reparations by Germany for the plundering and looting should be demanded only by vengeance with swords in our hands, with paratroopers blowing up Berlin, Frankfurt and Bonn, and razing them to the ground. Only then will the thought, the hope, that one day they will expunge the name of Israel from the surface of earth, be uprooted from that nation of murderers and from others like it.

That is the only way. It is still far off, but it will come if we maintain the strength of our Jewish youth and not sully their hearts with lust for money. It is the only way. We must prepare our youth accordingly and arm our nation's forces for this holy purpose: for future generations to exact vengeance from the murderers of our people. Any deviation from this path, any weakening of our goal, undermines our forces today, and endangers our existence in the future. Wise men, be careful with your words and even more so with your deeds, for our lives depend on them.

From this podium I call upon you, Ben Gurion: back down, do not introduce this poison of head-bowing into the minds of our youth. Do not divide us at this

---

42 Herman Cohen (1842-1918), a philosopher and founder of the Marburg School of neo-Kantianism.
43 Herman Zvi (Hirsch) Shapira, a Zionist leader, an ordained rabbi and a professor of mathematics at Heidelberg University. At the first Zionist Congress in 1897, he proposed the establishment of the Jewish National Fund and a Hebrew University in Palestine.
44 Jeremiah, 48:10.
45 Isaiah, 48:22.

time of trouble when we must be united. As long as we have no assurance that our enemies will not be armed, we must not go and extend our hands to them.

Back down, Ben Gurion! With a 5 percent majority, you might defeat, but not convince. This is not a clear-cut matter, neither to you nor us. This painful question must be postponed. With a torn and burning heart I say, let us not place 55 percent against 45 percent on the scales today, thereby reaching a decision, and then implementing it by such a vague and undecided vote. Back down, Ben Gurion!

MK Esther Vilenska (*I.P.C.*)**:** Members of the Knesset, Negotiations with the neo-Nazi Bonn government have been dictated to the Ben Gurion government by the Truman Administration. These proposed negotiations are not a financial transaction but a political act of Israeli and international significance alike. It is a political step that directly and indirectly aids the preparations for war by the rulers of Washington and London.

The revival of Nazism is one of the decisive factors threatening world peace. Without a Nazi army, the Anglo-American warmongers will be unable to initiate a new world war. However, the revival of Nazism's military power is vehemently opposed by the European nations. In face of this opposition, the Truman Administration needs Israeli recognition of Bonn's rulers in order to provide a political and moral seal of approval, Jewish and Israeli, for the revival of Nazism as well as for seating the Adenauer government together with the governments of Europe.

The leaders of Mapai maintain deceptively that "it is nonsensical to assume that reparations will bring about the return of Germany into the community of nations. How can we influence that?" they ask. Our reply is that any nation can tip the scales by struggle. We have seen, for instance, how the opposition of the Egyptian people to British rule has, for the time being, thwarted implementation of the Middle Eastern bloc defense plan.

We accuse you, members of the cabinet, of taking a political step with its principal objective being the aiding the revival of Nazism. We accuse you, members of the government, of taking a political step that is helping to start WW III. The very fact of the negotiations and their timing was dictated to the Ben Gurion government by the Truman Administration. The American government is exerting pressure on Israel so that it will recognize Bonn in January.

Why the hurry to exert pressure on Israel? Why are you, members of the government, so anxious to meet Washington's demands? The reason is that in the middle of February the aggressive Atlantic bloc council will convene, and then the American administration is plotting an attempt to break the opposition to the revival of Nazi Germany by the European nations. We oppose negotiations with Adenauer because their aim abets potential Nazi participation, that most murderous and aggressive factor within the anti-Soviet Atlantic Alliance.

The talk about reparations is a smokescreen. We ask, why has the government of Israel kept silent on this issue for three years? Why has it remembered it only now? The talk about reparations is intended to camouflage the true aim of the negotiations which is the government of Israel's official support of West Germany's military preparations for *revanche* and renewed aggression.

The leaders of Mapai are playing the innocents: they dare to speak of Adenauer's government as Christian Democratic. No, ladies and gentlemen, at the head of the West German government are neither democrats nor Christians; the army, the police and the senior posts of the West German government are manned by veteran Nazis with bloodstained pasts. Anti-Semitic organizations are openly active and anti-Semitic newspapers are openly publishing their racial incitement. The Adenauer government is strengthening fascism's military power to spearhead the third world war.

Even before you have received reparations, you, the members of the cabinet, are inciting against the East German government on the pretext that it did not respond to the reparations claims. We reemphasize that East Germany is led by people who rotted in Hitler's jails and concentration camps for years. East Germany has declared anti-Semitism a criminal offense and is constantly uprooting fascism. We remind those who ask why the Soviet Union did not respond on the matter of reparations: the policy of uprooting Nazism and fascism is being implemented by the Soviet authorities. It is one of the most important atonements for the Jewish people and the State of Israel.

The Knesset must raise its voice in favor of denazification of Germany and full punishment for the Nazi criminals. Concrete compensation may be possible not by recognizing Hitler's successors, but only if the four occupying powers compel Germany to pay it on the basis of the Potsdam Accords they signed at the end of WW II.

When we speak of the need to fight for peace, certain Mapai speakers reply "It is the Cominform." When we speak of the need to prevent fascism from further harming victims, they reply "It is in the Soviet Union's interest." You cannot free yourselves, even for a moment, of the anti-Communism nightmare that was and is the banner of the enemies of peace and of Israel. It is beyond doubt that all the victims of fascism, the tens of millions of dead, the millions of orphaned and bereaved, wanted but one thing: to prevent a new world war.

By recognizing the Adenauer government, you members of the government seek to erase the calamity that befell the Jewish people. Such is our accusation. The Jewish people will not forget the six million Jewish victims and the tens of millions of victims of other nations, and will fight against the plans for carrying out a new Holocaust.

The leaders of Mapai argue against Rabbi Nurock joining the left-wing parties in their opposition to negotiations with the neo-Nazi Bonn government. We reply that you, members of the government, are leading us towards the most impure combination in our history: you are guiding the Chief of the Israeli General

Staff to join the Nazi General Guderian in the Atlantic headquarters and its Middle Eastern branch. The Ben Gurion government does not have authorization to conduct negotiations with Hitler's successors. Within Mapai itself there are many thousands who oppose these negotiations and who understand the political dangers they are fraught with. On the issue of peace you, members of the cabinet, do not even represent the members of your own party. We are convinced that a decisive majority of the people, including large numbers of coalition party members, opposes recognition of the neo-Nazi Bonn government. The decisive majority of the people, in spite of political and partisan differences, are united in opposition to preparations for war, united in its aspiration towards peace. On this question, which is linked to preparations for a new war, the present majority in the Knesset does not express the views of the majority of the people. We demand that the Bonn government not be recognized. If the Ben Gurion government dare to conduct negotiations with Hitler's successors, if the government give an Israeli seal of approval to the revival of Nazism, it will do so of its own accord and with the agreement of the American State Department but not in accordance with the will of the Jewish people. The Jewish people will not remain in the same camp with the German fascists or with fascists from any other nation and will oppose preparations for war against the USSR, the bastion of peace.

We shall continue to enlist the people against Ben Gurion's proposal to collaborate with the Nazis. The Israeli Communist Party is convinced that by a massive political struggle, the Jewish people will thwart the government's policy of positioning the State of Israel in the same camp with the fascists and their warmongering American masters.

MK Moshe Aram (*Mapam*)**:** Members of the Knesset, so, members of the cabinet, Knesset members of the coalition parties, you have succeeded in disconcerting the country's population to the depths of its soul. You have succeeded in widening the gap between public opinion of all circles, even those of the coalition and the government with its cold "rational" calculations. You have deepened the division in the Labor movement. You have aroused the masses in the Diaspora, regardless of partisan and political views, that are calling "There will be no contact with Amalek." You have even attempted to coerce the conscience of your coalition partners and compel them into voting your way. Why have you done this to us, to all of us, and to yourselves?

Now you are asking for approval for an unforgivable act if indeed it is not prevented, if we cannot avert the shame and calamity and save the honor of all of us, and your honor as well. Your answer: "Contact with the murderers is indeed loathsome and faulty, but we must take the plunder from their hands and we have no choice but to sit with the Bonn government after we approached the four powers and our claim was rejected." This combination of the duty to restore the money and the necessity, as it were, to negotiate with the Bonn government, is basically false because even if you manage to save part of the plunder in this way, the smallest part of it even according to you, then what you are about to give in return – are likely to give, will be forced to give – is of immeasurably more significance for the fate and future of the state. You hope to obtain property, but you will be solicited for our soul and will have to give it. You will have to. You are claiming money from the Bonn government, and you will commit us to giving blood, real blood, the blood of our sons and daughters. Without your agreement, the murderers will take all the blood of our people on a catastrophic day.

Is that your intention? Of course not. But your intentions will not determine your policy, but rather the policy will give birth and approval to the intentions. In July 1949, Robert Schuman[46] rose in the French National Assembly and announced: "We do not have a peace treaty with Germany. It does not and must not have an army. Germany in the Atlantic Alliance? Never!" and in August 1949 Jules Moch[47] stood on a platform in the city of Sète and declared: "Were we to bring Germany into the Council of Europe, we would be providing it with the possibility of rearming in order to destroy us. We would be simply crazy." Nevertheless, later they were indeed proved crazy: Germany is being brought in, Germany is rearming.

And assuming that their intentions were good – and you do not doubt their good intentions – nevertheless the logic of a war policy comes into play and determines the intentions. Is it conceivable that we allow you to become Schumans and Mochs in order to bury us all under the burden of shame and disgrace, under the burden of collaboration with a fascist-Nazi government?

MK Lavon says that the European army, with the German army taking part, will be established whether we like it or not, and if it is indeed about to be established, then whatever we do will make no difference. This is a spurious and fatal assumption. I hope this army will not be established even without our opposition. The nations will not allow it, the opponents of war will not allow it, the peace and freedom movements will not allow it, the fear of the Soviet Union and its army will not allow it. But precisely because the chances are slim, the temptation to risk an adventure has heightened. Those seeking to appease the Nazis need to remove what their people consider moral and political obstacles. A Jewish seal of approval, a Jewish "reconciliation" with the Nazis – and contacts with the Bonn government are "reconciliation" – is a tremendous contribution to preparing hearts and minds towards a preventive war against the Soviet Union. Indeed, the Devil himself could not conceive such revenge against us: the nation

---

46   Robert Schuman (1886-1963), a French statesman who was prime minister from 1947-1948 and foreign minister from 1948-1952. In 1950 he proposed the plan for the European Coal and Steel Community that came to fruition in 1952 and formed the basis of the European Common Market.

47   Jules Moch (1893-1985), a Jewish-French socialist statesman. He served in French governments from 1945 as deputy prime minister from 1947-1950 and minister of defense from 1950-1951. He was awarded the Croix de Guerre in both world wars.

of the slaughtered and burned will assist in providing the Nazis with a seal of approval through the State of Israel.

True, we are but a weak link in the chain of international politics, but it has already been shown time and time again that a chain breaks at its weakest point, at its weakest link. This universal truth was proved correct in the October Revolution of 1917. The revolution occurred in Czarist Russia because it was the Russian bourgeoisie which was the weakest link in the capitalist world. This rule was proved correct in our own struggle for independence. It was we, the weakest link in the national liberation movements, who began the struggle against foreign rule in the Middle East, and we triumphed. This rule is also valid with regard to the unceasing attempt to introduce Nazi West Germany into the community of nations with great pomp and circumstance. Whether or not we succeed in our role as an obstacle, wholly or partially, our entire essence, our very existence cries out for us to carry on preserving the chain for the sake of ourselves and for the sake of mankind, so as to obliterate filth and contamination. The blood of our brethren is calling out to us from the ground: do everything to stop this, do everything so that no trace remains of Nazism and fascism.

This mandate, MK Lavon, was given to you and me; it is written in the fiery scroll of the crematoria. And you, knowingly or unknowingly – I would like to think unknowingly – are placing the nation and the state in a position of serving the opposite policy: leniency, aiding, expediting authorization for a plot that tomorrow will consume us and the entire world with its unclean flames. And if now, at the last minute, we are trying to help you avert failure, you throw at us that "You are prepared to give up the plunder because of foreign considerations. Even today you are prepared to forgive and waive East Germany's part in the plunder." There is no distortion and slander greater than that. We will support every effort to restore the plunder on condition that we do not pay for it with our own lives and the ashes of our dead, with our own honor and the honor of those who willed us life as well as the duty to fight to the end against the revival of fascism and Nazism. We will encourage and support any claim that East Germany should restore what is due to us. Precisely because we admire its efforts to establish a different regime, precisely because in East Germany they are uprooting fascism, and will do so for a long time to come, precisely because Nazis and fascists must keep silent there, conceal their past or condemn it as a sin or crime, while in West Germany they laud them and they rise anew – precisely because of that we shall be more meticulous with East Germany. We will not hesitate to claim from the Soviet Union, which has amicable relations with it, and demand that East Germany set an example in its attitude towards the Jews by meeting the claim of the State of Israel. This can be achieved by restitution of the plunder and by inculcating in the German people the knowledge that it will not have redemption until it bears full responsibility and atones for its crimes against us. It is not a gift that we will receive from East Germany. We are claiming from them demands, and they are fulfilling our demands: the disarmament of Germany, the uprooting of fascism and the cessation of providing German *landsknechte* [mercenaries] for a world conflagration.

But you are proposing a meeting with West Germany which means that we will forgive its crimes and endorse it as an ally. We shall certainly not release it from its obligation to restore the plunder. But if there is no possibility of us treating it as the Western occupying powers did, we shall hold them responsible, and we shall claim from them, for it is they who are fattening West Germany, who are pouring capital and power into it. Even though we have not gained satisfaction so far, we shall claim and claim again, arouse public opinion against them, enlist the best and most honest among them, and sooner or later we shall receive our due. But contact with West Germany for bringing down the axe on our necks, on the necks of the entire world – never!

I am not saying that you have sold our body, the body of the State of Israel. The state and its independence will never be auctioned; such a plot could never succeed. But by your policy you are placing yourselves in the camp that is reviving and fostering the Nazi storm troopers; you are gravitating towards it. There is also a law of gravity that applies in political life, and you cannot avoid it whether you like it or not. Negotiations with the Bonn government are one of the decisive threads in this noose. I am not saying that you purposely want to sell our soul or spiritual independence. But anyone coming into contact with filth, and compromising with it, receives filth in return and becomes a partner to it. Negotiations with the Bonn government, with the successor and perpetrator of the root of all evil, set in motion a dizzying slide into the camp of defilement. Are you so dazzled that you cannot see the yawning abyss into which you are so eagerly pushing this country?

We need money, a lot of money. There has never been a country that has taken such a task upon itself: ingathering of exiles, merging different ethnic groups into one people, housing them, settling them, sustaining them with dignity and inculcating them with a high cultural standard, and all this in a country that is still in the throes of development, of rapid population growth, of prospecting for mineral resources and their exploitation for the benefit of the nation. Yes, this necessitates tremendous financial resources, but not money that will legitimize Nazi bastards, not money that stinks and pollutes the state and its people. This money cannot bring about our redemption. This "rational" attitude will poison the essence of the state, that "irrationality" without which the rug will be pulled out from under our feet. I am not even talking about the very illusion that Adenauer's Germany will behave differently towards us than did Germany towards its important creditors after WW I. Even the crumbs of the plunder it will promise will serve as political blackmail, and then the Prophet's bitter and gloomy words – "Ye have sold yourselves for nought" – will come true.[48]

48   Isaiah, 52:3.

Finally you argue for pure democracy, for the freedom of conscience and decision. Go ahead then, put this issue before the whole population, put it to the test of all the citizens of Israel: announce a referendum. The people will sit in judgment and decide. And when it decides, its decision will be honored. Transfer the responsibility from yourselves to all of us, transfer it from the members of the Knesset to the people. Let us decide with dignity and not be defeated in shame.

MK Simha Babah (*General Zionists*): MK Rimalt said here that there is something which is above, not against, rationality. We built our country in the light of this teaching. Was all our enterprise of settling the country a rational one? Was our victory in the War of Independence a rational phenomenon?

You are arguing against irrational thinking. Well, I am not taking rational thinking lightly. Indeed, a cold-blooded accounting shows that if, thanks to reparations, we will be able to take immigrants out from their tents in winter, if we will be able to transfer them from sweltering huts to houses in summer, this would be of great importance. However, the accounting does not end here.

One should be aware of the dangerous and poisonous weapon we are handing over to the world's nations by accepting reparations. For our enemies and quasi-friends would judge us not according to our positive traits. They will say, "These people have sold themselves!" I say that it would be a rational response on their part if they said: "See, here is a poor state, absorbing immigrants and experiencing serious economic difficulties, but nevertheless when the issue reaches down to the root of the nation's soul, they refuse these reparations!"

The same goes for American and European Jews. They will understand us: here is a people suffering from financial deficits, but when they are offered reparations, they refuse them. What an enormous moral impact this will wield! And I ask you, who if not the Knesset, who if not the State of Israel will safeguard our nation's honor? Is there any other body fit for the task? I think that even the people of the Middle East, expecting and hoping to see our state crumbling, would respect us for such a refusal.

As to the Germans' impressions, I must state that I belong to those who believe there are eternal moral values which do not disappear even during the present nuclear era, when the entire world might explode. I do believe in a better future. As a Jew, as a human being, I wish and am duty-bound to believe that humanity will return to the blessed tradition of true liberalism. I believe that Germany's children, if correctly taught to imbibe cultural values, if bestial attitudes are uprooted from their minds and souls, will change. Hate is not eternal. Mutual conciliation would be needed. My mother, may she rest in peace, used to say, "Talking makes agreeing." But this does not mean forgiving. This does not mean not avenging or revenge in the Biblical sense. There can be another kind of revenge if for an entire generation a representative of the Jewish people arises and declares at every international forum attended by Germans: "These are the murderers of our people!"

I am appealing to those Knesset members who are liable to betray their own souls by voting against their conscience: there are moments in the life of a nation when the Angel of History is hovering above it. Woe to that nation that is incapable of opening the door and welcoming that angel!

I appeal to the prime minister, who is blessed with deep historical awareness, who was privileged to have had the people's angel whisper in his ear not to be rational when confronted by the dilemma of establishing the State of Israel. At this moment it is incumbent on you to prove that true force is not based on physical might alone. The strong must know when to be weak.

And I appeal to the Knesset members: Let none of us betray his soul. Facing this tragic conflict which is dividing us, I pray that at this momentous hour that the Knesset members will prove that "the strength of Israel will not lie nor repent."[49]

MK Meir Argov (*Mapai*): Members of the Knesset, I am one of the bereaved. My whole family was destroyed. With my own eyes I saw the burnt, the asphyxiated, the slaughtered at the end of WW II. And that was not the first time. In the course of my life I have seen the slaughter of Ukrainian Jewry, their bodies strewn like dung in the fields for lack of someone to bury them.[50] As fate would have it, during the pogroms and the slaughter, I was a member of an unarmed Jewish self-defense group when our whole Ukrainian town was crying out and there was no rescue. Years later I was privileged to be among the Jewish Brigade fighters in WW II, one of the 30,000 Jews who volunteered for the British army and fought under a Jewish flag against the murderers' troops. I was among the first to arrive at the end of the war at the sites of the slaughter and helped to transport the survivors to a safe haven in the brigade's vehicles. In those terrible days, when I came to the Bergen-Belsen concentration camp with my comrades in arms, we saw a horrifying scene: 20,000 Jews had died three days after the camp was liberated by the Allies, and the graves of those 20,000 Jews were marked in a foreign language with only the names of their country of origin, as if not Jews had been murdered, as if not Jews were buried in those graves, but citizens of Hungary, Poland, Czechoslovakia and all the other Jewish Diasporas. Only we, the Jewish soldiers of the Jewish Fighting Brigade, were able to discern that those were the graves of the 20,000 Jews.

What does this symbolize? When the Allies that had taken part in WW II submitted their claims for reparations from Germany for the damage caused them, the Hungarians, Poles, Czechs and Russians claimed for themselves, in the

---

49   Samuel I, 15:29.
50   During the Civil War which raged following the Bolshevik Revolution in Czarist Russia, 1919-1920, some 100,000 Jews were murdered in anti-Semitic pogroms in the Ukraine.

name of their slaughtered Jewish citizens, their plundered property. And included in the vast sums that the governments of the Soviet Union, France, England, Poland, Hungary, Czechoslovakia, and the other destroyed countries received from the Germans – sums that amounted to many billions – a large portion comprised the plundered Jewish property. They claimed these reparations from the murderers in the name of their Jewish citizens and took them for themselves and their countries. The Jews did not have a collective claimant; there was no state to submit a claim in their name.

I ask a very simple question: after the establishment of the State of Israel, why are we not allowed to decipher the names on those graves and claim part of the plundered property on behalf of those slaughtered Jews? Why is the Jewish property that the Germans restored to the Allied armies, to the Russian, Polish, Hungarian and French governments kosher, allowed to be touched? Why it is kosher for rebuilding the homes of the Jews of Ukraine who are no longer there, kosher for rebuilding democratic Poland with the property of Jews who are no longer there, kosher for rebuilding the ruins of Czechoslovakia in the name of some of its Jews who are no longer there, and why is it non-kosher and unclean when it is claimed by the State of Israel? Where have you drawn this morality from, where did you learn it? Why is it forbidden to demand that the murderers restore part of the property to us? (*MK Menachem Begin (Herut): It is forbidden to sign an agreement with the murderers.*) My question is simple. Had the war gone differently and the Russian armies had conquered all of Germany, and that could easily have happened as it did in Hungary and Poland, then the German people would have been one. It would have been entirely under the aegis of Russia, and a "pure" government would have been formed of people who had been imprisoned, a government of Socialists or Communists, of freedom fighters, and the German people would have been one country under one government. Did that people – the entire German people – murder Jews or not? Are they responsible for that murder or not? If they murdered, why should they not pay? They must pay us, at least that part which can be obtained.

The Russians took the machinery, the property, compensation, reparations, everything they possibly could from East Germany. And the question is, what will we get? That which is permissible for everyone else – getting part of the plundered property – is forbidden to us? Were it possible for a Jewish army to enter Berlin and take all the treasures without negotiations, I would have chosen that option. But we cannot do that. Even the men of the Jewish Brigade were given only twenty-four hours on German soil because they began committing acts of vengeance, and so they were immediately moved out of Germany.

Of that vast property estimated at $6 billion – it is probably impossible to estimate it exactly – we are presently claiming only $1.5 billion. Why should we waive it? I have heard from the various speakers here, particularly from Mapam and the communists, the following argument: in the West, especially in the United

States, they are not asleep. They incessantly encourage the government of Israel to claim reparations, and the government of Israel receives daily instructions from the State Department to claim reparations from Germany, for if not, they will be unable to co-opt Germany. You have fallen victim to Hitler's tale of "mysterious Jewish power." Hitler disseminated the tale that the Jews manipulate all the world's new governments, that nothing can be accomplished without the Jews. In the speeches of incitement he made during the war, he always spoke of "the international Jewish armies." You, too, have fallen victim to this myth with the difference that you claim that without us, the State Department cannot waive compensation from Germany to the USA, that without us it cannot rearm Germany. Moreover, without our seal of approval they would not have invited Adenauer to London and the Schuman Plan would not have been implemented; without the Israel Defense Forces a world war is out of the question. That is your refrain. Gentlemen, this is more than naiveté!

In our defiled world, anything is possible. When it was necessary to send greetings to Hitler on his birthday, it was done in spite of his order that Jews wear the yellow patch.[51] In our profane world, greeting and extermination are possible simultaneously. But why are you permitting yourselves to fall prey to the myth of "global Jewish power"?

The opposite is true. We appealed to the powers again and again: three years before the establishment of the state, the Jewish Agency made such an appeal, [52] followed later by the state and its government's demand addressed to the four powers for collective compensation in the name of the heirs; their claims were rejected or were met to a minuscule degree. We were given $25 million, perhaps even less. Were the Soviet Union different from the others in this regard, it should have said, "Gentlemen, we understand you; we will impose a contribution upon East Germany to be paid to you through us." But what did the Soviet Union do? It made no response at all to Israel's approach. (*MK Shmuel Mikunis (I.C.P.): It destroyed Nazism.*) Not for your sake.

The other three powers said, "True, it is your due, but you should talk to the Germans yourselves. We do not want to be your intermediaries. At best we will not get in your way. But we do not want to do the job for you." That is a very simple answer. I ask you, had the Soviet Union answered in exactly the same way, would that have been kosher? Would that have been acceptable? Moral? Permissible? With this Jewish money to be returned to us, we will settle no less than 600,000 souls, and the country that inherited that money must pay it. Hitler and his successors, good and bad alike, will pay for the plunder. Is it permissible or forbidden to demand our money? Is the money ours or the Germans'? That plundered property is ours, it

---

51   Stalin sent greetings to Hitler on his 50th birthday in 1939.
52   In the letter from President of the Zionist Executive Chaim Weizmann to British Foreign Minister Ernest Bevin, 20.9.1945 (Chaim Weizmann, Letters and Papers, Transaction Books/Rutgers Israel Universities Press, Jerusalem 1979, vol. 22, pp.51-54).

is our due. It is only part of the plunder. All the occupying armies took machinery "Made in Germany," raw materials "Made in Germany," natural resources "Made in Germany," and had no shame. So do not threaten us with "Made in Germany." Those words cannot be used as a threat. Just as others obtained machinery, we, too, shall come by machinery, pipes, steel, copper, gold.

And I ask you, the "proprietors" of history and of the Jewish people's new conscience: who gave you permission to relinquish the possibility of settling 600,000 human beings in Israel? All their property was taken in the East and in countries of Islam: literally everything was taken from them, and they are coming to us naked, poor, sick, without a penny in their pockets, abandoned here to winter floods and storms as well as to your outrageous incitement blaming us for their suffering. Who authorized you to prevent us from bringing, settling and absorbing these 600,000 souls financed by restitution of property plundered from the Jews, by this Jewish money, by the ships, locomotives, raw materials and pipes that we should be getting?

You have concocted a theory of "forbidden contact," "forbidden talks." I, your humble servant, assume the right to say that I have given this matter deep consideration no less serious than that of MK Rokach, and I take it upon myself to sit at the same table with the murderer and to say, "Restore the plunder!" Is this a betrayal of national honor? Why is it forbidden? Are the Soviets not speaking with them?

We are living in the realistic world, and the realistic world says that if I am not able to wreak vengeance – and I am not able to – it is not a question of desire or of a debatable decision. Nevertheless, I should obtain at least part of the plundered property.

I have already spoken about the "seal of approval" we are accused of granting: that is nothing but a myth. Germany is already kosher for this world, with equal status. Neither East nor West will ask us for their consent, just as no one asks our opinion on whether to unite Germany or to withdraw the occupying armies from it.

The government of Israel has stated in its note to the Soviet Union – and that note was brought to the knowledge of the Foreign Affairs and Defense Committee: "The Government of Israel and the State of Israel will never be a partner to an attack against others!" Can anyone here assure me that we will not be attacked?

We shall be judged by Jewish history, Jewish morality and Jewish conscience for claiming part of the plundered property. Our goal is to invest this money in the sacred tasks of building and the mass absorption of immigrants into the homeland, for we have been elected by the people for the purpose of implementing these national missions.

MK Abraham Berman (*Mapam*): Members of the Knesset, I would like to say a few words on this painful subject. I was in the Warsaw Ghetto, a member of the fighting underground. I did not learn about murderous German fascism from newspapers or stories. I saw Hitler's hell, the murder itself, with my own eyes.

I know what my comrades said and felt – the hundreds and thousands of ghetto fighters who proudly fought in the face of death.

I have the right to say from this podium, in my own name and in the name of the members of the underground *no*, not for this did the ghetto fighters raise the banner of uprising, so that a few years after that uprising the representatives of the Jewish people would sit down together with those who drowned the ghetto in blood and sent it up in flames. This is not a matter of sentiment. Aiding and abetting a regime like that, sitting at the same table with people who are reviving the Hitler nightmare, the SS organizations, the Nazi Wermacht, is madness, total anti-Jewish, anti-national madness. At the last minute we call upon you, members of the Knesset: Do not commit this sin, this crime! No arguments whatsoever can justify this travesty.

To my great regret the debate I have been hearing in the Knesset is not new to me. I heard the same tones and reasoning in the Warsaw Ghetto. There was a serious internal struggle there between the fighting underground and those who defended realpolitik, heaven help us from conciliation with the Nazis, from negotiations with them. And there were quite a few, not only in the Judenrats, who said, "We must think of the purpose, of the benefits of a revolt, of what would happen to Jewish property, and not fight the Nazis too vehemently." We fought those gentlemen with all our power and emotions. We viewed it not only as betrayal of the people's honor. We understood that this stance was not realpolitik but the opposite of a realistic national policy. We viewed it as a dangerous illusion that only weakened the people at that tragic time. We then decided that there could be only one kind of relationship between the Jewish people and German fascism: a fight to the death.

Now that we have a historical perspective, we all know where the fatal stance of these compromisers can lead: only to shame and disgrace, to betrayal and national disgrace. They did not save the people's honor; the Jewish fighting underground with the Warsaw pioneer youth movements and labor movement did.

Do not forget this tragic lesson, this warning! Do not lead our people and state into disgrace! You have no right to do this. No Jewish organization in the world has this right. I have here before me a list of the organizations that took part in that conference in New York which was asked to give its seal of approval to the shameful negotiations. Who were the representatives of the people there? The American Jewish Committee, an organization of the assimilated Jewish plutocrats of America; the Anglo-Jewish Association from England, an association of assimilated anti-nationalist Jews; other organizations of this kind. (*Foreign Minister Moshe Sharett: What about the World Jewish Congress of which you yourself are a member and the Jewish Agency of which you are a member as well?*) Do these assimilationist organizations represent the Jewish people? It is ludicrous.

From this podium we call upon the Jewish people throughout the world, upon Jewish youth: do not desecrate the Jewish flag, do not agree to this disgrace. I call upon the tens of thousands of new immigrants, our brethren from Poland, Romania and all the other countries that experienced the Nazi hell, the concentration camp inmates, the survivors of the extermination: let us fight with all our might against any collaboration, against any shameful agreement with the murderers of our brethren.

No artificial, formal majority in the Knesset, formed through pressure and coercion, will work. That majority – if there will be one – will be a distortion of the will of the people. The true majority of the Jewish people will oppose any negotiations with Hitler's successors. The people of Treblinka, Maidanek, Auschwitz, the ghetto fighters, will never accept any negotiation, any such false decisions. It will fight against this travesty.

MK Herzl Berger (*Mapai*): Some of the speakers in this debate have made their work easy: they have attempted to argue with us on matters on which all of us are united in debating with the entire world. Others have made their work even easier: they have argued not against issues that have risen in this debate, but against issues it is easy to argue against, and for that reason alone they introduced them into the debate.

I do not think it beneficial to the debate when attempts are made to invoke the memory of the dead that are so dear to all of us. Neither do I think that MK Rimalt was right when he stated that the path of the Jewish people that guaranteed its survival throughout its history was a path running counter to rationality. In our people's history there were irrational actions that proved beneficial. There were also irrational actions that did not.

I shall try not to speak on issues raised in this debate but on issues that are at its core, and I will explain why I am convinced that the path proposed by the government is the right one. When we experienced what we did in the Hitler era, various conclusions could have been reached. We could have reached a very proud conclusion and said there is no room in this world for both the Germans and us, and if it is impossible to destroy the entire German people, then we should depart this world. We did not say that. That was not the response of the Jewish people; it was not the response that could be derived from all of Jewish history. As far as I know, there is only one big political organization in the State of Israel with wide international contacts, and it refused to participate in an international conference that was very important to it because that conference took place on German soil. It was a meeting at which it was decided to reestablish the Socialist International, and the only organization that did not attend was Mapai. The representatives of Mapai did not put up a fight; they simply did not participate.

We could say: we will not accept compensation, reparations, restitution of the property from that people. We want nothing from them. There was one Jew who said this to the survivors in Germany – this man was the Yiddish poet Halpern Leivik. But what was the survivors' response? From the day the war ended till the present, each one of the Jews who was entitled to individual compensation has petitioned the German court in accordance with a new German law enacted after the fall of the Hitler regime. However, this can only be done in West Germany, because these laws only exist there, and the petitioners received what was due to them our without our hindrance. On the contrary, they were supported by all the Jewish organizations in the world including the Jewish Agency, that same Jewish Agency which includes representatives of parties in this House, with the exception of the Communist Party and the three Arab parties; even Herut was represented until recently in the Jewish Agency

All these organizations are conducting negotiations in Germany. While it was still possible, they only negotiated with the institutions of the occupying powers. When the latter began transferring these matters to the various states comprising West Germany, they negotiated with the local governments, and later they also started negotiating with the West German Federal government.

WW II was characterized by genocide and plunder, but the ultimate meaning of this proposal by opponents of negotiations is this: that the best way for the murderers and plunderers to keep the plunder in their hands is to ensure that no heirs survive, that nobody remains who can later claim restitution. Our position is totally different. We say a new precedent should be set in this regard too. Thus the government of Israel submitted in its note to the four occupying powers an unprecedented claim: that the murderers should know that even if you murder those who have been plundered, the victims' property would eventually be reclaimed. The claim will be submitted by the same people you sought to murder, and it will be a collective penalty. This will ensure the existence of that people in the only way that human beings can ensure the existence of a people – by securing its independence, by increasing its power and by guaranteeing its defense needs should attempts at extermination recur. In contrast, some members of this House say "No!" some for lofty emotional reasons and some out of very cold calculation.

They suggest that we avoid setting this precedent regarding the German people, and not only the German people, because Hitlerism is a global danger. They suggest we say to the murdering people, "If you murder successfully and no potential victim survives, the plunder will remain in your hands."

There is a third point of view. MK Chazan, like many of his colleagues, frequently floats from idealizing the East to idealizing the West. MK Chazan is convinced that when the Western powers need to integrate the West German army into the ranks of the North Atlantic army being established, they will not dare do so until they get approval from MK Yaakov Chazan and MK Herzl Berger; this step will not be taken without their agreement… Well, they are doing it anyway, with or without our agreement on reparations negotiations. At the same time it is evident that our leftists are not perturbed at all by the inclusion of East Germany into the Soviet bloc.

The government of Israel and the conference of the major Jewish organizations announced the following after Adenauer's statement: the German chancellor's words will be judged by his deeds. How can his words be put to the test if not by direct negotiations? Does any alternative exist? Why are you, some of you for pure national and moral reasons, granting this indulgence to someone you certainly do not want to give it to? This is the core of the debate.

I would like to make one more comment on the attempts to frighten us against deciding the issue of direct negotiations by a small majority, a majority of a few percent which will perhaps tip the scales in favor of this proposal. We have extensive experience in taking important decisions by a small majority. With what majority did my party's colleagues pass the decision for a Jewish state in 1942, voting against all leftists at the executive of the Histadrut? Was that majority any bigger? Did the leftists not say then that it was only a "formal majority," that the executive is "not representative," and that the matter should be brought before the public? Are you, Knesset members of the left, not happy today that we did not consider your arguments then? Do not intimidate us. We held elections only four months ago, this question of reparations was debated in the first Knesset, and now this Knesset is entitled to make a decision on it. It must make a decision in accordance with the fundamental interests of the Jewish people and the State of Israel.

MK Yaakov Riftin (*Mapam*)**:** I think that the majority in this House is pessimistic regarding the concrete results of these negotiations, if they ever take place. It is clear to us all that if, during negotiations, the negotiators encounter problems of individual compensation, or of goods suitable for our country, or of marketing, or a refusal by the German government to continue paying future installments of compensation, and so on – the State Department will not intervene in Israel's favor. First of all, the Americans might think that this money will ultimately have to come out of their own pockets. Second, the State Department will not want to risk its prestige in neo-Nazi Germany.

I also think that the majority in this House is of one mind that the German people must not be freed of responsibility for the slaughter. We heard the first statement on this subject from Mr. Wilhelm Pieck, the President of the German Democratic Republic, on his election. He said: "We acknowledge the responsibility of the German people for its tolerance and support of the barbaric Hitlerist regime."

I also think a majority in this House rejects a racist attitude towards the Germans. I, too, hope that neo-Nazism will never rule in Bonn, the city where Beethoven lived and wrote his music, and where Karl Marx studied.

However, while the majority in this House is united in its painful remembrance of the Holocaust and its victims, we are tragically divided in regard to the lessons to be learned from the Holocaust. To my mind, the lesson of the Holocaust is a double one. The first is surely the historic importance of immigration to and the building up of the State of Israel. Our party's members and followers proved their understanding of this lesson by shedding their blood at the front of the War of Independence.

But there is a second, no less grave lesson, and the Knesset cannot ignore it. The decisive question facing us is whether a danger of extermination is looming over us from Bonn. In other words, will the negotiations to be conducted by Israel distance the danger of this new Holocaust or bring it somewhat closer?

Members of the Knesset, a Nazi underground may possibly exist in East Germany, but if so, it is funded by the State Department's funds, like all clandestine organizations of this kind. But it is foolish not to see that Nazism is the deadly enemy not only of the Jewish people but also of communism, of the Soviet Union. It stood at the gates of Moscow. (*Foreign Minister Moshe Sharett: Did it not occupy Paris?*) Mr. Sharett, the fact that the main effort of Hitlerism was directed at the destruction of the workers' movement, of communism, of the Soviet Union, and at the destruction of the Jewish people as the ally of the forces of freedom in the world has possibly evaded you.

The day the Soviet Army's flag was raised over Berlin was the day on which Hitlerism was defeated in Europe. But the flag that was raised over the Reichstag was not raised only for one day, and a tremendous effort to take it down is being made by your various allies. And if the representatives of the 90 million workers convened in Hitler's unclean Berlin, then they have come to defend that flag. And if our party's representatives raised it with them, then you should know it is the anti-fascist flag, the anti-fascist battle flag. It is the flag of vengeance, of retribution, of hope.

But what is the situation in West Germany? Members of the Knesset, do you not know that the establishment of the German army is almost automatically connected with the date of the declaration of a new world war, with the danger it poses to all mankind and to our people? Do you not know that the Germany of Bonn is the Atlantis of the Atlantic Pact, and that Satan's divers plunge into its depths to bring up Hitler's sword which they need for a new world war? Do you not know that almost one million soldiers in Hitlerist Nazi Germany and their commanders have already polished their jackboots in order to march to a world war? Do you not know that that this Nazi offensive has reached the Middle East, that it has penetrated into Turkey, your partner in the negotiations on entering the Middle East Command? Do you not know that here in this city, this year, from the walls of the Old City of Jerusalem, our capital was observed by senior Nazi officers? Do you not know that the negotiations taking place regarding a new war are at the core of the question of Germany? If you ignore all that, then you are betraying the people who were murdered, and that murder might be committed again.

True, it is not you who are handing the cocked and loaded gun to the madman, to the Nazi murderer. That is being done by Churchill and Truman. They are presently readying the gun. But any slight pressure on its trigger can discharge it. Is there refuge from the shot? Do you not think that this very debate in the Knesset is a day of celebration for the neo-Nazis? Do you not think that even now, as you place a decision before the people, that it is a day of celebration for neo-Nazi Germany? Do you not know that this is aiding the guardians of German militarism?

You are widening the division among the people. It was noted here that I said – "We will not obey!" I would like to reiterate and say that not only are there decisions that we will not obey, but we even have no need to be ordered not to do them, for we have sworn to defend the homeland and protect the freedom of democracy. But we have also sworn to fight against an alliance with imperialist aggression, to fight against a war with the Soviet Union. We have sworn this and we will keep our oath. We are sworn to oppose this fatal step that places upon the Jewish people and the State of Israel the common historic responsibility of defending the foreign minister's "open world" with Nazi help.

MK Yona Kesse (*Mapai*): Mr. Speaker, Members of the Knesset, We are all troubled by grave concerns at this time, and on listening to the debate on reparations we should be troubled by further concerns: what is the Israeli people's moral and political image, and how do we appear before the Jewish people in the Diaspora and the nations of the world in view of this current debate which is fraught with decisive implications for our nation's future? It has been generally acknowledged that Diaspora Jewry learnt values and awareness of national responsibility from the Yishuv. Lo and behold, a change has taken place in relations between us and the Diaspora, and not in our favor. Some weeks ago there was a well-attended Jewish conference in the United States to discuss the issue of reparations from Germany. That conference represented all of world Jewry, with the exception of Jewish communities on the other side of the Iron Curtain who were unable to attend. Two things were decided there: (a) we must and are entitled to claim reparations; and (b) the claim for and obtaining reparations do not mean forgiveness for the German people.

But now, discussing this question following that conference, we have exposed ourselves in all our national and moral shame. In this House there has been an appalling, well-organized demonstration of our lack of historical responsibility towards our great national goal. The events outside this House that accompanied the debate inside it added further shame and disgrace. The front pages of all foreign newspapers yesterday carried descriptions for all to read of the shameful events around the Knesset building. Patriotic rhetoric does not frighten us. Regarding MK Begin's kind of patriotism, it was said that patriotism is the last refuge of the scoundrel. I condemn the bogus patriotism that grieves for dead Jews but is prepared to murder living ones. In his speech, MK Begin boasted that at the time of the *Altalena* affair, he ordered his men not to return fire, implying that he might now be prepared to order them to open fire on those whose view differs from that of his party on the question of reparations from Germany. Well, in the *Altalena* days we treated you in accordance with the gravity of the crime; if one shot is heard in the State of Israel, if there is one terrorist attack, the forces behind the state and this government will cut off the hand holding the gun. Terrorism will not rule in this country for even one day. We will safeguard freedom and liberty in this country. We will take action against any attempt to terrorize the elected representatives of the people. I advise MK Begin to use his imagination, and look ahead to exactly what our response will be to the first attack against the sanctity of the foundations of our state.

I would like to say the following to our Communist MKs: several weeks ago I read an article in your daily, *The People's Voice*, explaining why East Germany would not pay compensation to Israel for its share in the crimes of the German people. It said that since the State of Israel was part of the "'warmongers' bloc;" it would thus use the compensation to increase its aggressive power against the Soviet Union, no more and no less! By using such ugly lies, the Israeli Communists are purporting to prove their patriotic concern for the State of Israel. It is beyond our dignity to deny these lies and falsehoods. Every Jew in this country and the Diaspora knows what these reparations will be used for.

We have been denigrated by the opposition speakers in this debate for our pursuit of money. I would like to take this opportunity of saying that there is nothing more despicable than this mockery by those claiming to teach us moral values. What is money if not building, industry, increasing our strength? You cannot accuse us of avariciousness. We seek to accelerate the building of this country, and we want to fulfill the great task of the ingathering of the exiles.

And a few words to Mapam's MKs who say that they though generally do not oppose reparations, they only oppose direct negotiations with the Bonn government since negotiations mean taking another step towards Israel's integration into the Western Bloc. I would like to ask, what is the point of your membership in the Foreign Affairs and Defense Committee? In that committee you heard from the foreign minister about the government's policy regarding this whole affair of the Middle East Command. I shall not list the details here. You know them as well as I do, and the information you have received contradicts your repeated accusations that we are trying to become part of that body. Who gave you the moral right to incessantly disseminate this filthy lie that the government of Israel wants to become part of the 'warmongers'? You know it is not true, but nevertheless you continue weaving a web of lies because you need something to use for inciting against the government and against Mapai. You know full well that the Western powers did not help us to obtain reparations. What is this drivel, that under "pressure by the powers" we are entering direct negotiations with Germany? There is not even a grain of truth in your assertions that reparations negotiations with Germany are a part of "the West's defense plan." This nonsense is refuted because the German Social Democrat Party, which disagrees with Adenauer on his position on relations with the West, staunchly supports him on the question of entering negotiations on reparations with us. Who are you fooling with these false slanders?

I would like to say to MK Berman who has spoken here in the name of the Jewish partisans in war-time Poland: on Saturday evening there was a meeting of the veteran partisans in Tel Aviv at which they protested against negotiations with Germany. MK Berman, I am sure that when you were fighting in the ruined Warsaw Ghetto, you could not have imagined that two members of your party would travel to Berlin, the capital of Nazism, and defame the State of Israel at a Communist convention with scurrilous slanders: that "it is forming an alliance with the warmongers against the Soviet Union." How is it that you, the surviving partisans, did not organize protest rallies against MK Hanan Rubin and Mordechai Oren who went to Berlin as Mapam's delegates? Why did you not protest, why did you not cry out against this act? Are you too, a veteran partisan, distinguishing between East and West Germans? Forgive me, MK Berman, when I say that I deny your moral right to speak in the name of the partisans, and in their name demand that we not claim reparations from the Bonn government.

And a few words to those members of the Knesset whose moral feelings I fully believe to be genuine. I say that something in their Jewish emotions is flawed if they are capable of concluding that there are Jews among us, as loyal as themselves to the national values, who are prepared to forgive the German people. Even if we wanted to forgive them through a political decision, the horrible crime of the German people remains unforgivable. We are a murdered people. We were saved from total annihilation, but future generations will forever feel the pain of the murder of six million Jews in whom our national and Jewish future, talents and genius were embodied. Forgiveness is impossible. And if there is one German who demands forgiveness in return for reparations, we will tell him that the very fact that he dares to demand our forgiveness points to a dark aspect of the German psyche. There is no forgiveness. Forgiveness is out of the question. In another generation or two, perhaps, we will have different relations with the German people. Perhaps the German people will be cleansed of their crimes and purify themselves, perhaps a climate will evolve enabling different relations, but the account will never be erased. And where is your national honor, your Jewish sensitivity, when you say that claiming the plunder is forgiveness and atonement? You say this to us? You demand from us sensitivity towards our national honor? Our party was the first organization in the Yishuv to encourage youth to enlist in the British army in order to fight Hitler. Ours was the first to contact the Jewish survivors in the camps, organize them on German soil and then mobilize them in our desperate war for the establishment of the state. Do not our daily actions attest to the fact that national honor is our watchword? But, ladies and gentlemen, there is a bottomless abyss between us in understanding the true meaning of national honor. Our national honor is embodied in every project we have initiated and accomplished in this country, for national honor means the creation of strength so that we can stand firm against murderers, haters and destroyers.

Members of the Knesset, do not use the terrible term "vengeance" in vain. I dare to say from this podium that we shall not exact vengeance for the six million Jews because it is impossible to avenge the blood of even one little child, just as it is impossible to avenge the blood of six million Jews, including one million children. The very impossibility of avenging the blood of our brethren testifies to the huge, black stain bonded forever on the body and soul of the German people. Had we even sought vengeance, how could we exact it from such a big and powerful country? Should we be consumed with helpless anger and dream of vengeance while the entire world from East to West is rehabilitating the German people, fawning before it and seeking its friendship and aid? Who is listening to our firm protest against the reintroduction of Germany into the community of nations?

On several occasions the foreign minister has voiced our cry against Germany at the United Nations General Assembly and said some very clear words about our historic account with the German people. He voiced the protest of all the Jewish people in the Diaspora. His patriotic courage and sense of national honor were not found wanting when he uttered the grave accusation against the people everyone desires to be linked with today. The Germans murdered some 20 million Russians – are the Russian people destroying the German people, or are they like the Western powers, aiding in its rehabilitation?

We are the only people left that are preserving their historic accounting with the German people, and we have only one way of taking revenge: the creation and increase of strength. Our vengeance is embodied in the Zionist revolution we have brought about in the life of the Jewish people. National honor is to be found in mustering our strength, in having a sovereign State, in the ability of the Israel Defense Forces to fight back. That is true national honor. To those who recite fiery words about vengeance, wishing to agitate us emotionally, I say that they are cheapening the term of "vengeance." There are indeed times when vengeance should be exacted, but in this realm, too, a sense of historical responsibility should rule, as well as awareness of limits. And what is all this talk about lack of national honor in having direct contact? I can well imagine the meeting of our representatives with the Bonn government representatives during the reparations negotiations. What will our representatives say? "We have come to forgive your sins?" No, they will say that they have come to claim restitution of part of the plundered property and for this sacred objective they are prepared to sit with representatives of the murderers of our people.

I too am a Jew, an Israeli Jew, and I too have a sense of national honor, and I will not feel insulted when my representatives sit down at the negotiating table with representatives of the Bonn government, for sitting at that table would be one manifestation of our historic revenge. Hitler sought to exterminate our people; he sought to exterminate the Jewish population of Palestine that later established the State of Israel. Hitler wanted to overrun us and slaughter the 600,000 Jews that lived here at the time of WW II, but his plot was foiled, his regime was destroyed, Germany was conquered, and we are sitting – or will sit – in these negotiations as living representatives of the thwarted plan. Is that a national disgrace?

You are concerned lest the German conscience will be cleansed, and therefore you say that there should be no negotiations on reparations. But would not our abstention from negotiating absolve Adenauer from sin? For what would Adenauer say? He would say, "I wanted to pay reparations, I wanted to somehow atone for the sins of the German people, but the Jews rejected my offer." And in the eyes of world opinion he will come out of it with clean hands while our claim for reparations through intermediaries will have gone unheard. You, who fear that the German conscience will be cleansed, are adopting a position that will allow the Bonn government to evade the obligation of payment with ease. Moreover, I do not fear saying this: suppose we conduct negotiations and it transpires that Adenauer was lying, that he is not prepared to pay reparations? What would we do then? We should then inform world public opinion that our effort to find out whether the German people were prepared to take a different road from that of Hitler had failed. And we would inform the world that it became clear that the change of regime had not changed the character of the German people, that all the talk about willingness to pay reparations was nothing but a smokescreen and diplomatic lip service in face of international pressure. To you who are demanding that we indeed obtain reparations but only through intermediaries, I ask a question: in which case would our moral pressure on world public opinion be stronger – when it is proven that the Germans are not prepared to pay, or when it becomes universally known that we refused to enter direct negotiations?

Your entire concept is foundless both morally and politically. It is a sick concept, unworthy of the elected representatives of the Jewish people living on the soil of their homeland, for you are oblivious to new concepts and psychology that have evolved since our independence. Had we a genuine sense of national honor and of historical responsibility, we would have stood united on this issue and instead of arguing with one another. We would have said as one man to the Bonn chancellor: "We will conduct negotiations on reparations, but do not expect us to forgive; should you demand this of us it would demonstrate that the Bonn government is ignorant of what the German people perpetrated against the Jewish people." We would say as one man that the negotiations on the first billion are just the beginning of further claims.

What has befallen this people in its homeland? Why have the foundations of our national, Zionist and human wisdom been undermined? Have inter-party struggles, oppositional drives and narrow partisan considerations overcome us to the point that we are unable to present a united front on such a fateful issue?

Members of the Knesset, would it be far-fetched if I express a sincere wish that we appear before the world and the German people as a people and a state who stand firm, that we show that we are capable of fighting for our national honor and for the achievement of positive results from these proposed negotiations, results that will increase the productive power of our country and enhance its capacity to absorb mass immigration.

MK Israel Rokach (*General Zionists*)**:** Members of the Knesset, our people's spirit of unity is cherished by almost all factions of the House, for this is our most precious asset, now even more than at the establishment of the state. I am now extremely fearful and worried that this thread of unity may break.

I am of the opinion that money is not the decisive factor in the life of the individual or that of the nation. In the course of my lifetime I have seen quite a few people who inherited many millions yet ended up being buried in shrouds that were not theirs. I have seen many whose money did not protect them from persecution and death. I cannot build my life and faith on money or its equivalent. (*Foreign Minister Moshe Sharett: Did the building of Tel Aviv not cost money?*[53] *Did the settlement of Jews not cost money?*) That was not done with reparations money. It was done by labor and sweat, and by Jewish talent and Jewish effort.

I therefore cannot view this issue from a monetary perspective, as did quite a few speakers in the last two days of the debate. I believe in national spirit that should beat in the hearts of our young people and the great desire to continue building and to take part in the responsibility and commitment to the state. These elements will bring about a partnership that will complete the building of the state.

I was born and raised in this country and have never experienced life in the Diaspora. Nevertheless, I feel deep and painful ties with my fellow brethren who were murdered so brutally. Therefore, it is beyond my comprehension that our state is considering sending its representatives, our leaders, to sit at the same table, in the same building, with the murderers of our people and to sign an agreement, even if it were for all the money in the world. This money will not make our life easier, it will not develop this country and it will not save us.

I ask from the depth of my heart and soul: would it not be unforgivable if we sit with our enemy for discussions, even if we tell them that we cannot forgive? Saying this will not cancel out the fact which would gain worldwide publicity: that the Jews are going to compromise and put an end to this affair with the Germans. Only seven years have passed since the Holocaust, and what are seven years in the life of a people? It is not much even in the life of an individual. Only seven years, and can we already be considering negotiations with the Germans,

---

53   MK Israel Rokach was mayor of Tel Aviv from 1936 to 1953.

sitting together with them, even with those who did not plunder and murder but also did not raise their voices against horrifying murder?

That accursed Germany declares that now it can settle the historic account by paying money, but later, when we announce that they do not want to give us a specific sum, will we come out of it honorably if they do not pay us what is due?

And you, members of Mapai, can you not grasp that this matter of direct negotiations runs counter to the common feeling we all experienced throughout the years of the Holocaust? You are talking about 600,000 immigrants. Have we not absorbed that number already? Have we stopped absorbing immigration? Have Tel Aviv and Netanya not absorbed tens of thousands? After the War of Independence, Jaffa was a pile of rubble, without a school, a kindergarten, nothing. Today there are 60,000 immigrants settled there, and this was done by the efforts of the veteran population. Today, those immigrants are living and working with dignity and will not receive German money to be rehabilitated. They will not want it. I have no doubt that they will reject it.

I appeal to you to abandon this path. We must save the spirit that is so vital for building up this country. We need spirit and morality far more than money, which I normally do not belittle but not under these circumstances.

I appeal to you not to shatter the moral foundations upon which – and only upon which – our work here has been laid, as well as our relations with the Diaspora. Their feelings are more important to us than anything else. I am certain, and I say this in good faith, that signing an agreement with Germany will fill our people in the Diaspora with despair, and our citizens even more so. I believe in redemption by the sweat of our brow.

Speaker Ze'ev Sheffer: The foreign minister has the floor.

Foreign Minister Moshe Sharett: Mr. Speaker, Members of the Knesset, in this protracted and tense debate, a few of my colleagues from the cabinet, my party and the coalition parties have taken a most active and valuable part, and I see neither need nor obligation to repeat what they have said and to address the same aspects of the issue, for they have left no room for additions. In any event, I do not intend to dwell on those words spoken and acts committed both outside the Knesset and from this podium, which in my view are nothing but death throes, very ugly death throes that are also poisonous to all those around. They attest to the ebbing of a party and the decline of someone with pretensions of leadership. I will say only this: that leader's ambition is that he would be able to stop the death throes and breathe new life into his diminishing party by shedding blood anew, but this will never happen. On this I have nothing to add to the agreed, clear and incisive public response given by the prime minister to the challenge against the authority of this House and the democratic institutions of Israel.[54]

Members of the Knesset, although this debate is in its third day – and is only now coming to an end – I permit myself to take up some more of your time in order to clarify several basic concepts and some central facts, concepts and facts that are bound up in the issue before us. I speak on this issue from this podium after an interval of nine months. On March 13, 1951 I read to you the full text of the note submitted by the government to the four occupying powers, with the claim for reparations from Germany. I think I would not be mistaken if I said that in later debates regarding the issue of reparations, there was a very high degree of agreement that the claim for reparations was just and right. There was disagreement over the timing, over the possibiliy that we had missed the boat. There was almost no argument on the question of whether these reparations are our due or whether we were, or are, duty-bound to claim them. Indeed, MK Yizhar Harari reminded us that he had already predicted then that the reparations claim would force us into contact with the other side – and I shall say at the outset that I completely agree with him on that – while at the same time, his exemplary clear line of reasoning led him to oppose claiming reparations already at that time, and on that I disagree with him completely. I think he was alone in expressing that prediction; in any event, he was in a very small minority in the Knesset. The main argument of the criticism heard then was "you have missed the boat."

MK Mordechai Nurock is totally opposed to the steps we are proposing, which are the only effective steps to obtain fulfillment of the claim. He is doing so out of profound moral motives, but he does not stop there. I do not only respect; I stand in awe of the spiritual motives of my esteemed colleague Rabbi Nurock. But he has also entered the sphere of an apparently business-like political debate. He spoke not only as a man of high moral values. He spoke also as a man of cold logic. However, once we enter the sphere of logic, it becomes incumbent to point out any logical fault and contradiction in his line of thinking. On the one hand, he argued that we must reject, that we must avoid all contact and relations with Germany. On the other hand, he repeated the argument of "missing the boat" and asked why did we not submit our claim to the Western powers' conference in Brussels? Had he said, "I vehemently oppose it, I cannot bear the thought of it," I would have kept silent, for I would have had no argument with him. But if he is descending from the moral high ground to the slippery slope of debating stratagems and methods and *modi operandi*, then I am prepared to come over to him, to brake this descent and to set his feet back on the firm ground of reality.

I leave out the question what we could have achieved had we had a state of our own when the issue of compensation from Germany was concluded by

54   Prime Minister David Ben Gurion's response to the Herut anti-reparations aggressive demonstration and its assaults on the Knesset building was broadcast on state radio on January 8, 1952.

the Allies, whether in theory or in practice. Nor will I dwell on the question of whether we were at all free to devote our attention to the issue of reparations – inasmuch as opportunities were opened for presenting a relevant claim – when we were engaged to the utmost with vital problems of survival during the first years after the War of Independence in 1948-1949. In any event, the fact is that nobody in the Knesset or in the Provisional State Council[55] seriously demanded this from us; perhaps a lone voice was heard on one occasion, the voice of MK Zerah Warhaftig.[56] But I shall not touch upon these questions. Instead, I would like to examine the issue this way: let us assume that we had acted in time as these members suggest, that we had presented our claim then – had the State of Israel been established a year or two earlier – or immediately with its establishment, or, if you will, had this claim been submitted before the Yalta and Potsdam Accords,[57] or on the eve of the Brussels Conference[58] which was the last opportune date according to Rabbi Nurock – what would have happened then?

I will try to describe the chain of events which would have resulted had we submitted such a claim on those occasions, assuming that its justness, logic and legitimacy were accepted by the powers that determined the terms of Germany's surrender on the eve of its capitulation and after it.

The outcome would have been as follows: first, we would then have become a member of a certain group of states that appealed to the powers occupying Germany. We could not have become both a member of that group and at the same time, kept ourselves aloof; we could not have been both legitimately accepted into that group and filed our claim while demanding equal status with other claimants and standing behind someone's back, saying, "Yes, we are submitting a claim, but you will obtain the money for us, you will conduct the negotiations on payment arrangements on our behalf – whether payment is to be in currency, machinery or goods, how much currency, how much machinery and what quantity of goods; and if it is to be in machinery and goods, what machinery exactly and what goods? You will do all that for us and we will stand aside. Our hands will not be sullied by this unclean contact. You will be sullied, we will not." Do you think that such a proposal would have been accepted by anybody?

We have been reminded here of the exemplary cases of Egypt, Pakistan and others who did not fight or shed their blood in WW II but succeeded in placing themselves in the position of claimants. To my interjection, "How much did they get?", MK Rabbi Nurock replied that what they received is unimportant. What is important is the principle. I understand that position. However, did Egypt and Pakistan join that group while oppoing direct contact and negotiations with a

---

55 The temporary legislative body of the State of Israel. It functioned till the convening of the first Knesset in February 1949.
56 At a Knesset meeting in December 1949 (See *Divrei HaKnesset,* vol. 3, pp. 228-237).
57 In February 1945 and July 1945 consecutively.
58 In March 1948.

Nazi, neo-Nazi or anti-Nazi regime? Second, we would then have been obliged to accept the basis on which the Allies' claims were submitted. What was that basis? It was to cover war damages. Moreover, we would have had to accept another, very central principle pertaining to the methods of collecting those payments: it was decided that payments would be collected solely by expropriating existing means of production, not by taxing current German revenue and production.

What would have happened then to our claim? Not only would we have had to compete with other claimants; not only would we have obtained crumbs, we would never have been able to submit a claim for $1.5 billion in the framework of those negotiations and the existing financial arrangement. We would have completely blurred our unique position on this issue and the special character of our claim. For what are we claiming from Germany today? Are we claiming war damages? True, we, too, suffered war damages: homes in Tel Aviv and Haifa were bombed[59] and people were killed, leaving widows and orphans; a troopship carrying Jewish soldiers sank on the way to Malta, with 200 dead, leaving behind bereaved parents and orphans;[60] our soldiers serving in the British Army all around the Middle East were killed during the war, and financial support for their families falls largely on the state. We also suffered commercial war damage. Is that our account with Hitler? Is that our account with the German people, with any German authority, regarding property plundered? The plunder of this property began years before the war and would have doubtless continued even if the war had not broken out.

Let us assume for a moment that WW II had not broken out. Let us assume that there had been a revolution in Germany before the outbreak of that war, and that Hitler's regime had been toppled and replaced. Would we not have viewed that new regime, whether Nazi or anti-Nazi, as the successor of the regime of blood and destruction and plunder? Would we have relinquished our right to claim restitution of the plunder? And even if individual Jews had waived their right, would the Jewish people have done so? Had the State of Israel been established under those conditions, as a state that absorbed hundreds of thousands of victims and survivors, would it have ignored that plunder?

This has nothing to do with the WW II or with its damages. It is a unique, exclusive accounting, an absolutely separate account with Germany concerning the plunder of Jewish property, for there can be no accounting of bloodshed and loss of life. There is only remembrance for all time.

And lastly, those crumbs, those leftovers we would have received as the outcome of a claim forwarded within the framework of an overall arrangement, that same paltry sum we would have had to accept to close the account, a

---

59   By Italian bombers flying out of Rhodes.
60   The British troopship *Erinpura*, en route from Alexandria to Malta, was sunk by German aircraft on 1.5.1943. The vessel was carrying Jewish soldiers of Transport Company No. 462 who were to take part in the invasion of Sicily. 148 out of the unit's 344 men perished.

complete settlement of our claim. Do you know what was the sum of the Western powers' assessment of the war damages? $53 billion. Do you know how much they received? $500 million, less than one percent, and they decided to take no more. We have heard here the good news that the Soviet Union is still receiving payments, but the Westerners decided – and they surely had their reasons – to stop collecting them. Had we joined that group of Western claimants, would they have made ours an exceptional case? Would they have cancelled their own claims and continued collecting payments for the Jewish people through their Occupation Army and by force of being the occupying powers, after they had taken a decision that collection of payments should stop and be waived? Who among us could be a party to such considerations?

On the face of it, the three Western powers have not waived completely. In their response to our note, dated July 5, 1951, submitted four months later, from which the prime minister quoted several important paragraphs, an attempt was made to contend that we had actually received compensation when the account between us and Britain as a former mandatory government was closed. They credited the State of Israel with £300,000 as its share of the compensation which was due to the territory of the Palestine British Mandate for war damages. Lo and behold, we received compensation! However, at the same time we were told: "Please do not think that our account with Germany has been completely settled; it will not be closed until the final peace arrangement is formulated, but we cannot determine the date of this final arrangement", which actually meant that this was a matter for the distant future and who knows when that day will come. And then they added: "On the other hand, as of today, we have undertaken not to make further demands, and so we are unable to accept your claim."

What was our response to this note? We contended that our claim is unique. It cannot be squeezed in the procrustean bed you have made for yourselves; it belongs to a different category and must be discussed within different parameters. On the one hand we are not raising at all the question of war damages in this context, but on the other hand we can never agree to its postponement until the final peace arrangement, which no-one knows when it will come about, and who knows if the account will be settled then, for this is a most pressing and urgent matter. This was the argument between us and the Western powers. It stemmed out of our claim not to be included with all the other claimants but to be recognized as a special, separate case.

To this day we do not know what the USSR thinks about this issue. It has not revealed its opinion to us. In fact, we do not know if it has an opinion. We have written to it just as we wrote to the others. We were patient with it just as we were patient with the others at first. Then, with all due respect, after months went by with no response, we sent a reminder in a written note. As more months went by we reminded it again in writing, and at the same time we reminded it several times verbally. We have still not received a response.

But there is another aspect to this question of compensation; it concerns not those who wish to pronounce historic claims and vague principles, but those who are genuinely interested in the fulfillment of the claim, in restoring the plunder, and that is a very important consideration. Here the question is what would have happened had we submitted our claim three or four years ago, or even two-and- a-half years ago? Against what actual background would that claim have been submitted? It would have been submitted against the background of a bleeding German people, of a destroyed country, of a ruined economy, of nonexistent industrial production. It was against that background that the Allies determined the principle of Germany's payment from its existing means of production and not from current industrial production. However, against what background was our claim submitted in the spring of 1951? It was submitted against the background of the surprising, astonishing, even frightening recovery of the German economy, of tremendous growth and a dizzying rate of production. The following are the words of the German Minister of Economics Ludwig Ehrhardt in a public announcement he made in October, less than three months ago: "The German economy has never progressed in any period as it has under the Bonn government, and no other national economy in Europe has made such progress in this period of time." He also provided figures: "If we take the production of 1936, that is, the production of that part of Germany presently constituting the Western republic, as 100, then the production for 1949 would be 58, and that of 1951 would be 127."

We know full well that this tremendous growth in production is also manifested in export growth. West Germany's export surplus over imports in the first ten months of 1951 stands on a monthly average of $35 million.

MK Yizhar Harari was right on one vital point, and that is the inevitability of direct contact with the Bonn government at some stage if we really mean business and not only declarations. Just as by claiming compensation we cannot avoid accepting goods, and that does not mean accepting everything in the form of goods since we might be able to obtain something in the form of currency. But we cannot avoid receiving part of the compensation in goods, perhaps the greater part, so in the course of the payment, direct contact is unavoidable at some point if we truly want it to be paid and if we truly wish to accept compensation.

Let us assume that the Western powers had responded differently, and that, happily, the Soviet Union, too, had given us that same response: "We are prepared to exert pressure on Germany and impose this arrangement upon it." Honorable Rabbi Nurock would then delude himself into thinking that, successful as we were, all our labor would have been done by others, down to the smallest detail. But could we really have relied on agents to conduct these negotiations efficiently on our behalf, to decide on the quantity of goods, which goods, what yes and what no, how much currency, and so forth? Had we gone into this seriously, as a state should, not only by preparing decisions for publication, not only by declarations and newspaper articles, but with serious intentions of achieving implementation, do you really imagine, my dear and esteemed friend, that you could have avoided direct contact and compelled others to do your work? And after those others had done something at first, and left it to you to go in and complete the deal, would you have retreated at that point, would you have demanded that the government cave in? Would a mayor like MK Israel Rokach have caved in?

I would like to ask my honorable colleagues, the General Zionists' members of the Knesset, how is that you, practical and business-minded people like yourselves, did not realize then, when we submitted this claim, that one of two things would happen: either nothing would come of it, for we did not embark on this course of action as contractors of success, or that perhaps something would indeed come of it? Did you not understand that in this case direct contact could not possibly be avoided? And if you did understand, where was your voice then, why did you remain silent? Can it be that you hoped that in the meantime you would become our partners in the government coalition?

This is not only a practical question. Indeed, you are not posing it as such. You are basing it on moral principles. Gentlemen, what kind of morality is it that permits us to ask others to obtain compensation for us while we are forbidden to lift a finger to do so? What definition could this morality be given? Is it your opinion that indirect approach is permissible while a direct one is not? No, the real question is whether the matter *per se* is permitted or forbidden. If it is permitted, then it is permitted for us; if it is forbidden, then it is forbidden for others, too! What justification is there in troubling others if you are not prepared to take the trouble yourself?

It is one thing to demand help – to enlist pressure – when you, too, are prepared to carry out your share. It is a different thing altogether to impose all the trouble on others, to keep your hands clean and escape into the mists of supreme moral purity.

Honorable members of the Knesset, it is about time you realized that both the practical and moral questions have been resolved, and resolved by a clear decision in favor of direct contact in order to obtain what remains of plundered Jewish property. Several Knesset members have already touched upon this aspect. Still, I would like to take up some of your time to present a clearer, more comprehensive and more precise picture of the issue.

It is a matter of record that right from the beginning of the occupation – from the beginning of eradicating the Hitler regime until the last of our surviving brethren emerged from hiding and was liberated from the death camps – systematic and wide-ranging steps were taken to obtain compensation and to restore the plundered property. The first issue was that of individuals' property, property that has been preserved whose owner has survived and is claiming. But it was not all that simple to expect that every survivor would take this step on his own initiative, all by himself, for thus much individual property might have been abandoned. There was a problem here, calling for a solution by representatives of our people to take responsibility to restore this kind of property. The central Jewish institutions felt that leaving the property of so many Jews to individual initiative was out of the question, and they took action on the basis of this premise. This necessitated legislation on restitution of the plundered property, and once legislation was passed, it depended on procedure and on the process of implementation.

True, at the start of this process the various Jewish institutions' claims met with greater success than ours did. At first, they too approached the occupation authorities, West and East alike. Only the West responded, not the East, and in the West, too, there were varying degrees of response. The first to respond was the American Occupation Authority; it was followed by the British and French, but the latter two did not equal the efforts of the former in all points. I would not say that the American authorities did everything they could, but under the circumstances they did quite a lot, and in any event, more than the others.

And so at first there were negotiations with the occupation authorities, and they – by virtue of the authority they vested in themselves – issued an instruction to the German authorities to attend to the Jewish institutions' claims, and from then, two processes began. One was that while making use of these laws and instructions pertaining to property restitution, the Jewish institutions' representatives were unable to avoid direct contact with the German authorities, both in what the Germans call *Länder* and with the Bonn central government. Second, a process began of transferring the authority of the occupying powers to the German authorities. At that point the Jewish institutions faced two alternatives: either to waive all individual claims in view of the transfer of authority to the German government to avoid "crossing that line" or to continue submitting these claims, which meant entering into direct negotiations with the German authorities.

What were the basic principles of the restitution legislation? In his opening remarks, the prime minister drew a general distinction between property that has heirs, and property that does not. I permit myself to introduce a more precise addition to that distinction: so far this entire legislation has covered only one type of property – that which was identifiable. That type is a minuscule part of the Jewish property plundered by the Germans throughout Europe, though that minuscule part adds up to very large sums since the overall worth of Jewish property is staggering. There are several categories of identifiable property: it can be property whose owner is alive, in which case it is relatively easy to restore it to him. It might be property whose owner is no longer alive, but whose heir can prove his status with documentation, and then, too, the property must be restored to the heir. It might be an heir-less property, and then the legislation obliges restitution to an authorized Jewish institution. It might also be a property with unclear status regarding heirs: such property is called "presently unclaimed property," for it is uncertain that an heir will not be found. In such cases, the law obliges handing it over meanwhile to the claiming insitution, while imposing upon it the responsibility of meeting the heir's claim if and when submitted. Lastly, there is identifiable abandoned property, and it is clear that it does not, and will not, have heirs. For instance, the property of a certain community that has ceased to exist and was completely annihilated. In such cases, too, the law obliges restoring it to the authorized Jewish institution. That is the picture of the legislation in the American Zone. The picture in the British and French Zones is less complete and action has been taken to complete it.

What is the "authorized institution"? Members of the Knesset should be aware of the existence of an organization called the Jewish Restitution Successor Organization – JRSO – comprising several Jewish organizations and institutions. In the American zone of occupation, this organization comprises the Joint Distribution Committee, the Jewish Agency, the World Jewish Congress, World Agudat Yisrael, the American Jewish Committee, the American Jewish Conference – a body that was mainly Zionist – the British Board of Deputies and several committees representing the claimants themselves. In the British Zone of Occupation, too, an institution authorized to act as heirs has been set up. It too comprises the Jewish Agency, the Joint Distribution Committee, the Central Jewish Fund – the biggest aid organization in Britain that has dealt over the years with refugees from Germany – World Agudat Yisrael, the World Jewish Congress and other Jewish organizations. The first institution has an executive council in New York while the second has one in London. If my information is correct, negotiations are presently being conducted to complete this setup with the establishment of a similar institution in the French region and the formation of an executive council in Paris. In both the American and British institutions there is equal representation of the Jewish Agency and the Joint Distribution Committee. It has been active on German soil for two and half years. It acts in constant contact with the occupation authorities, but not only with them, and conducts direct negotiations with the West German authorities and with the federal center in Bonn and in the *Länder*.

MK Nurock, this institution is functioning on your behalf! It is doing so on behalf of the Mizrachi Party that is a member of the World Zionist Organization. Members of the Knesset from Agudat Yisrael, this institution is working on your behalf! World Agudat Yisrael, of which you are members, takes part in part in this institution's activity. Members of the Knesset from Mapam, you sit in the Jewish Agency and take part in deliberating this institution's activities in its Executive! When did you raise the question of direct contact? When did you complain about this misdeed? At which meeting of the Executive? I do not read the minutes of the Executive, since I do not belong to that body. But when did you raise it at the meetings of the Zionist Executive, to which I was invited? When did you raise the issue at the Zionist Congress? Why did you not warn there against this terrible misdeed? Are the Mapam members of the Jewish Agency's Executive so delicate and sensitive that they would not raise a difficult and perturbing issue? I know them better. Did they not know about it? They sit in the Jewish Agency's Executive in Jerusalem, They sit in the Jewish Agency's Executive in New York. Could they not have known? Did the Agudat Yisrael members of the Knesset not know about it?

I do not reject this direct contact. Blessed be all those engaged in that work! They have been performing a sacred task: the rescue of individuals' property and the rescue of property for Jewish institutions. More strength to them for what they have done so far, and for what they will do from now on.

I would like to reiterate that all this has been done only in West Germany. There is no trace of such arrangements in the East. A Jew unlucky enough to have been plundered in Düsseldorf, Hessen or anywhere else in West Germany now has a real chance of having it restored, if his property still exists and is identifiable. This legislation also applies to West Berlin. But a Jew who was unfortunate enough to have been plundered in East Berlin, or who lost his parents after coming here as a pioneer, has no one to turn to, and there is no organization that can help him.

True, in this way East Germany has freed us of the malignancy of direct contact since it has shut its ears to every claim by Jewish individuals, institutions or organizations. I say "us" in general terms. I have not yet come to the matter of the State of Israel, but as Jews, as members of the Zionist Organization, Agudat Yisrael or the World Jewish Congress – in which, by the way, you all participate, and the Mapam members who participated in its conferences are fully conversant with its activities.

I would like to devote a few words to another aspect of property restitution, one touching upon Tel Aviv and Netanya, mentioned here by MK Rokach: what happens to property that has been restored? What does restoring a Jew's house mean? There are cases in which the owner remained in Germany and went back to his house or apartment and resides there. To our shame, there are cases of Jews who went back to Germany and settled there, having found refuge in other countries during the years of persecution and hardship. But those who have settled here with us and have no thoughts or intentions of going back, can they waive this property? Why should they? Had immigration from Germany to Palestine been possible in the years before WW II, they could have brought their assets here and invested it in building this country. Now that they can, should they waive this option?

So what will a person do if he owns a house, or a factory which has remained intact? In almost all cases he sells what he owns, and then what should he do with those marks he receives for that property? What will those who receive individual compensation for physical injury or imprisonment in a Nazi concentration camp, or as pensions and so forth, do with those marks?

Clearly, in 99 cases out of 100, each one of them will do one thing: the owner of a usable factory or of a house will liquidate his assets and receive money. Yes, money, that asset that has suddenly been called by so many derisory and contemptible names here. With that money he will buy machinery, goods or raw materials. For whom will he purchase these goods if he is not an industrialist? He will purchase machinery or goods or raw materials in order to sell them on his arrival here.

And here I get to the point about Netanya. Early in 1950 I was honored with a very courteous invitation from a respected member of the General Zionist Party, a man mighty in deeds, a man credited with the establishment of a city, Mayor Oved Ben-Ami of Netanya. He invited me to visit his city, and among other things he showed me a new industrial zone. The zone is now fully built, but then it was still in its infancy. And even then, among the piles of cement and bricks beside the tents and huts where new immigrants lived, I could see the entire area was full of machines and stocks of raw materials; all this had been brought from Germany by the people who had been allocated plots to build industrial plants. I saw a spanking-new machine bearing the legend "Stuttgart 1949," an item which clearly had not belonged to that immigrant before the war. "Stuttgart 1949"! Were those machines invested in the building and development of our country or not? Did they come from compensation payments for plundered property or not? Was it permitted or forbidden?

I also know of a factory, small but valuable, in the Tel Aviv area, comprising only of German machines. A Jew who obtained some money from the restitution of his property invested it in a factory for the manufacture of tiles, and a well-known member of the General Zionists Party bought the factory from him; it is now in full production, and making its contribution to building this country. Did it come through compensations or not? Was it permitted or forbidden?

What about kibbutz members whose fate decreed that their parents and relatives would perish in Germany but whose property was preserved? Some of those kibbutz members were fortunate that their parents' property was in West Germany, not the East; should they go to West Germany to realize it, or waive it? Evidently, not only are they going to Germany on their own initiative, but their kibbutzim are sending them there, where they are of course assisted by the JRSO and its branches – how else could they achieve their aim? – and then they return home with tractors and cement mixers and prefabricated buildings, all of which are economic assets helping the ingathering of the exiles and the economic strengthening of those kibbutzim.

Do only members of Mapai go to West Germany, while members of Mapam wait until they are allowed to go to East Germany and claim compensation there?

No. Members of both parties are traveling to West Germany, and both are waiting for the day when they will be able to enter East Germany with the same objective. True, at the moment they can only wait, for that country is governed by the iron law of the closed world.

But a most serious question arises: will our account with Germany be settled by all this? Will the compensation I have just enumerated fully satisfy us? What of property claims that cannot be submitted to a *Länder* authority but only to the central government? The Nazis imposed a tax called *Reichsfluchtsteuer* – a tax on those fleeing the country – and a tax called *Juden abgeben* – Jewish property tax. I will not go into the details of these terms; Knesset members can check them later, but all these payments were collected by the Reich, and we view the Bonn government as the Reich's successor in West Germany. Should we waive this? Should we waive other claims that can be submitted solely to the central government?

And what of unidentifiable property? What of businesses that were destroyed? What of all the assets that went down the drain, property that was destroyed, that vanished, that was plundered and is no more? What of all this plunder, and what of the uprooting of people and making them scatter like dust over the whole world? What of the huge amount of property that disappeared – should we waive all this?

Members of the Knesset, where do we draw the line? Why can existing property be redeemed, while we are forbidden to claim compensation for property that no longer exists? Why can we bring machinery to Israel if there is an heir, whereas if there is no heir, it is forbidden for an institution to obtain compensation?

Where do we draw the line? Up to what point is something permissible, and from what point does it begin to be forbidden? Up to where does it still fall into line with the precepts of the Torah, MK Rimalt? I paid great attention to your words and admired your eloquence, but as I said, in matters of policy, of the good of the nation, logic is mercilessly in command. Up to what point do the precepts of the Torah apply to obliging compensation payment for plunder, and from what point does it begin to run counter to that precept? Who knows how much of this vast amount of property which, but for the slaughter, would have flowed into this country to make its deserts bloom and pay for the ingathering of the exiles; this property which has been destroyed, plundered, vanished? If it is still possible to restore part of it, is that forbidden? Is it not our duty to take it and bring it here? Just as we do not lock our door – not only do we not lock our door, we open wide our gates to every Jew who comes to us with only the shirt on his back after all his property has been plundered from him – thus we must open wide our gates and with our own hands bring in that property whose owners did not live to bring it in themselves for they were murdered. We should discuss this question without floating up into the higher world of abstract morality, and if possible without exploiting the profound feelings of masses of Jews by demagogy, as not everyone is familiar with the complexities of this issue.

Clearly, we can view this whole problem through a narrow prism and approach it from a political-scholastic standpoint; that standpoint determines that everything in our world is dominated by the East-West conflict, and examines each matter in light of its benefit to the Soviet Union. I listened to MK Yaakov Chazan. I have been listening to him for many years now, and I always draw a distinction between the content and quality of his words; on the one hand, in most cases I have not agreed with his hypotheses and conclusions in political debates of years gone by; on the other hand, he demonstrates his sincere belief, his moral integrity and power of persuasion. His speech on this occasion, to which I listened carefully, was totally different from his former ones. I saw a new Chazan before me. Once, after having heard his colleague MK Yaakov Riftin's speech, I had the same feeling, and I told him so. Now I say to MK Chazan, you too have been afflicted by an intellectual nosedive, just as all your colleagues have and will be. It is an unavoidable process. We are witnessing here that same paucity of thought and deterioration of articulation that is so characteristic of the world communism camp that you seek so strongly to join. In your soul, mentally – not yet physically, although through no fault of your own – you already belong to that camp. Joining them cannot but destroy all independent thinking and original self-expression. Acceptance of the political discipline of that party mandates subjection to its line of thought and style of expression. It first and foremost unavoidably leads to total relinquishment of the control of one's individual self; it obliges adopting a rigid, hollow and simplistic routine.

MKs Yaakov Chazan and Israel Bar-Yehuda, and later MK Yaakov Riftin and others, claimed there was an inner connection between obtaining reparations and entering the Middle East Command, between negotiations with Germany and obeying the State Department. Suppose we did not obtain reparations, suppose we did not claim reparations. Would it have delayed in any way what is taking place in the world today? What does "State Department pressure" mean? Did this body prompt us to submit the claim? I would like you to read the American response to our note, for in truth we only imposed a demand that no one thought we would impose. The Americans tried to rationalize their negative response with various excuses. When we exerted further pressure, they told us "Why come to us? What's the idea of your directing complaints against us? Go to the Germans!" And that is called "pressure"? Was this their initiative? Did they need it to bring Germany into their sphere of influence? Would they not have done so without our submitting a claim for reparations?

Much has been said here in the name of the dead. I would like to say that with regard to the dead, we are all equal. This is not a question of who lost a dear one and who did not. First of all, among those who lost relatives or were orphaned, there are those in favor of direct negotiations and those against. Second, the question of what the dead said is absurd. Still, I myself believe that had we asked the dead if the day would come when we could restore a part of the property –

should we or should we not? – they would have said "Take it, and be blessed!" I
have spoken with numerous survivors, ordinary citizens of this country, and they
replied "What a question!" There were amongst them people who themselves
had lost property, people who lost their brothers and sisters in Treblinka and
Auschwitz, and they said, "If you can obtain it, there is no question!" I spoke on
this issue at a public meeting in Beit Dagan before a large audience of ordinary
people. I explained the matter. No one opened his mouth. No one uttered a
word of protest. They listened attentively. I reject conducting a referendum as a
method of resolving complex political problems, but I believe that a referendum
on this problem would show that the majority would be in favor of accepting
reparations, if at all possible. I believe in the common sense and healthy logic of
the majority of the people in Israel, as well as in the Diaspora.

MK Berman spoke about the New York conference and tried to prove that
it was attended entirely by plutocrats and assimilated Jews on account of the
participation of the American Jewish Committee. But was the World Jewish
Congress present there or not? The American Jewish Congress, the English Jewish
Congress, the Canadian Jewish Congress – were they there or were they not? Is the
World Jewish Congress too a "plutocratic organization"? If so, why do you yourself
participate in it? Is it an "assimilationist" organization? Why do you sit on its
Executive and attend its conferences? Was the World Zionist Organization present
there or not? Why are you a member of its Executive to this day? Whatever you
might say about it, Agudat Yisrael is neither a "plutocratic" nor an "assimilationist"
organization. The representatives of the Argentinean communities' organization,
the D.I.A.A., is it too a "plutocratic" or "assimilationist" organization? Your party
colleagues sit there – why don't you leave? And there were other organizations
attending the New York conference, some 20 of them, including three world
organizations and the rest national – are they all "assimilationist"?

As we all know, the executive committee of this conference decided in its
meeting in New York on November 16, 1951 that direct contact must be made
with Germany to clarify the prospects of reparations. This committee is presently
awaiting the Knesset decision on the decisive negotiations. In principle it decided
positively, but for understandable reasons it postponed its formal decision until
the Knesset made its decision; it does not want to act alone, but hand-in-hand
with the government of Israel. If we go into this matter together, the conference
will probably succeed in claiming sums due from the Bonn central government
in the names of the many individuals entitled to reparations; to this day there
have never been negotiations of this kind, and we, the State of Israel, have the
chance of obtaining the reparations we are claiming.

We were told, "Nothing will come of it!" "You will get pennies." I would
like to ask if that is truly the question – how much we will get – then why all the
uproar around the moral issue? If, from a moral standpoint, the state should not
conduct direct negotiations, taking all possible measures to obtain restitution for

the plundered property, then the matter has nothing to do with the amount we will get. Supposing I could prove that we could get more, would that be permissible?

I am not prophesying. There is no room for prophecies here or for taking anything for granted. I know just one thing, and it is this: how many times have we embarked on endeavors and were told they would not come about? We were told, "You are deluding the people!" "It is impossible!" Debating against us, our critics also based their contentions on historical precedents and proofs; they advanced clear considerations and arguments, but time after time these were proved wrong. From where do you, members of the Mapam Party, draw this stubborn reluctance to learning from past mistakes, to ignoring lessons of past disappointments such as the one you experienced when your historic prophecy "A Jewish state will not be established in our time" was proven wrong? Why do you not learn from experience? True, this matter of reparations is unprecedented. But our entire Zionist endeavor has been unprecedented. The establishment of the State of Israel has no precedent. Germany's positive response to our claim for reparations, on paper for the time being, is also unprecedented. Why shouldn't this unprecedentness, so to speak, apply in the implementation phase as well?

We are being intimidated: "German machinery is upon you, O Israel!" As if building and developing the country is possible at all without vast imports of raw materials and equipment. And another threat: "You will be German agents in the world market!" Suppose we had a trade agreement with Country A according to which we want to purchase goods and raw materials for a specific sum, but since we were unable to pay in dollars, we offered our own goods which Country A was prepared to purchase for a specific sum. But we are left with a deficit, so what is wrong if, in the meantime, we received goods from Country B, Germany, say, and offered them to Country A to cover the deficit? Which country would not do such a thing?

I would like to ask something else: assuming we obtain reparations, will those opposing the entire matter, or just direct negotiations, waive their share? Members of the General Zionist Party, say, owners of citrus groves and factories, mayors and company directors, will you waive your share of this sacred booty that is the people's due, that every citizen and every factory would be entitled to enjoy in accordance with the law enacted for this purpose? And you, members of Mapam, will you waive it and close your kibbutzim and your various enterprises – in industry, agriculture, transport – and refuse these goods, these raw materials and installations?

And again, why should what is permitted to an individual be forbidden to Jews in general? And conversely, why should what is forbidden to Jews in general be permissible to an individual? Some say, "The state is something different. It cannot be involved with Germany." But why was the state established? Was it established in order to collect or not to collect what is due to it? Was it established in order to waive what is due to it or not to waive it? Was it established in order to claim sacred debts due to the Jewish people or to free the debtors from that responsibility? Is there one state in the world that will waive what it is owed? It will waive it if it suits it to do so, when it gains something else in return. But to waive what is due for no reason, out of moral fastidiousness! When was there such a state in the world?

We have already gone through the same debate before, in the early 1930s. Had it not been for the property transfer from Nazi Germany, is it not now clear to all that today we would have been far fewer in number, smaller in area, weaker economically and militarily; that we would have faced WW II and the War of Independence differently? Any addition in numbers and wealth increases national strength, and any such increase might be decisive in tilting the scales on the battlefield. Who knows if we would be sitting here had it not been for the Transfer of the 30s? We are now preparing ourselves for future challenges. Can we afford to waive what is due to us, that which we so desperately need for building up our state?

What is all this talk about a connection between direct negotiations and a world war? Indeed, if there is a connection, it is only this: receiving reparations or not has nothing to do with bringing a world war closer or distancing it, with its prevention or non-prevention – I personally am one of those who believe that a third world war can and will be prevented, but I do not seek to impose my opinion on others. However, if such a war does erupt, if we attain a majority against entering into negotiations, and we have no choice but to endure it, who knows what kind of catastrophe could then befall us? It could well be that the reparations we might have received would be decisive in making us powerful enough to withstand such an eventuality.

Only a fool is capable of believing that waiving reparations will prevent a world war. But our non-waiving could have a decisive impact on our state's future strength.

Those opposing reparations seem to be living in a world in which our state has not yet been established. What has everything said here in favor of rejection to do with the existence of the state? How does this rejection derive from the existence of the state? In other words, is there any argument or contention advanced here by the opponents that could not be advanced had the State of Israel not been established? Clinging to Jewish moral principles, declaring boycotts, forbidding contacts, keeping silent, unforgiving, and so forth – were not these forms of behavior a constant phenomenon in our people's lives throughout the generations, used after every slaughter, every disaster? In what way are you, honorable members of the Knesset, now seated in this hall symbolizing our sovereign state, different from others like you who sat in another body such as a community council in the Diaspora with no state, no Knesset, no parliament, no government, none of the responsibilities imposed by being an independent nation? In view of the existence of our state, what conclusion do you reach regarding the issue at hand? For there is not one single problem in our national life that can be addressed without taking into account the existence of the state. There can be no serious discussion of any decisive question that cannot but begin from this point of departure.

All these ideas of maintaining an everlasting boycott, which means no contact whatsoever – even if it causes tremendous losses, even if it undermines the functioning of the state and endangers its future – are borrowed from past modes of our people's life, modes that have gone, never to return. There is a chasm, my opposing colleagues, between the reality of your present life and your overall comprehension. Your comprehension is lagging behind reality! You are still prisoners of bygone concepts. The reality of a dispersed people whose existence could constantly be threatened, of a people with no control over a territory of its own, unable to become integrated into the international family of nations – such a reality informs opposition to direct negotiations.

When I recently attended the U.N. General Assembly in Paris, I met a delegation from the Auschwitz Survivors Committee, two men and a woman. They spoke emotionally against the intention of the Government of Israel to enter into negotiations with Germany on reparations. I promised them that I would convey what they said to the Knesset, and I hereby keep that promise. They are worthy of this. They were pained Jews, anguished, embers saved from the fire. I regarded their feelings as sacred and respect their views. Loyal to my promise, I will convey what they asked me to pass on. They argued in the name of the desecration of the victims, desecration of their suffering. They said it is out of question to extend a hand to Germany; they demanded an everlasting boycott! For them the State of Israel did not exist. As far as they were concerned, it existed only negatively; it only existed as a body to pressure to abstain from negotiations. The problems arising from Israel's reality, problems pertaining to its development, its attitude towards the Holocaust, to what degree it inherited the Holocaust's victims and to what degree it serves as a guarantee against a future Holocaust – all this was utterly beyond their field of vision.

I saw before me people living their terrible suffering, exclusively enmeshed within it. I did not judge them, heaven forbid. I stood before them filled with compassion and respect. Following the dictum I did not judge them: "Judge not thy brother until you have stood in his place,"[61] and who knows, perhaps I would have felt and acted in the same way had I been in their place. However, I have met other Holocaust survivors, particularly in this country, who were in Auschwitz and other horrible places, who felt differently because they had become part of the fabric of our life here. They did not think only of the death they had evaded and their friends who had not. They thought about their future lives; they looked forward to opening a new constructicve chapter in their lives. They understood the uncontestable justification of the reparations claim. I said to the delegation, "You are living in the past. A state cannot live solely in the past. The state looks forward, to

---

61   *Ethics of the Fathers* (Aboth), 2:44.

the future. A dispersed, powerless people can, and perhaps must, live only on past memories, nursing a messianic hope for eventual salvation. A state must take stock of every shift in the ballance of power around it in the world at large."

I was dumbfounded by the words from this podium of my old teacher, Dr. Boger.[62] What he said here for all our people to hear, he can no doubt say to his students. Instead of preparing them for fulfilling difficult concrete tasks, instead of directing them to put themselves in the front line of our generation – the building, reinforcing and defending this refuge of our people – he plant in their hearts some kind of dream of Jewish paratroopers raining fire and brimstone on Berlin saying: "Don't worry if it doesn't happen immediately – its time will come." I would like to caution you, my dear teacher, Haim Boger, from getting immersed in such futile and destructive musing, as well as from stuffing such ideas in the heads of the young people in your educational care. Do not confuse their minds. Instead, furnish them with a clear vision of the needs of the state and make them aware of the actual limits of their power.

A sovereign people, a people controlling territory, a people bound to be alert to every movement in the balance of power around it and in the world at large, cannot, under any circumstances, waive any available addition to its power in order to ensure its future. It knows what money is – it is building, it is a plow, it is a tractor, it is an artillery piece – and the money we are claiming in this case is Jewish money. It knows that every single moment is precious in its life. It will do what it has to do in time, missing no opportunities to strengthen itself, as these might well determine its future.

In concluding my remarks by saying that all the preaching about non-forgiveness and non-atonement and about the dangers of neo-Nazism has been directed to the wrong address. It is not this government that needs it. At the United Nations, on its own initiative and without encouragement from the Knesset opposition, this government raised the banner of war on the Nazi heritage, against its being left alive in both East and West Germany. Five speeches by representatives of Israel on this subject were heard in the General Assembly presently in session in Paris. True, the distance in approach between us and the Eastern bloc on this question is vast, and yet we voted with them, with the East, because our conclusions were identical. The Western delegations argued that the draft resolution presented before the General Assembly calling for a commission of inquiry to determine if the German people were capable of conducting general elections was insulting to the Germans. They are a civilized and admirable people, and this besmirched their honor. We said that the question is what role are the German people expected to fulfill in the course of future human history in light of their past. We were not taking a racist line, and are against wholesale condemnation of the entire German people. However, the fact is that time and time again they have produced great evil, shaking the

62   Moshe Sharett was Dr. Haim Boger's pupil at the "Herzliya" gymnasium in Tel Aviv, graduating in 1913.

continent of Europe and causing bloody world wars. They have murdered peoples and plundered their property. What guarantee exists to ensure that the German government will not behave in a similar fashion in the future? We contended that the German problem must concern all who are striving toward future world peace. The government of Israel has no intention of deviating from that position. The negotiations it will conduct will be negotiations on reparations, on restitution of the plunder. There is no question of diplomatic recognition or establishing relations. The effort of restituting the plundered property might possibly involve unavoidable contact. The State of Israel stands now before the German people, before the German government, before every German representative, and precisely in doing so, it proves the historic failure of Nazism because Nazism sought to bring us down on our knees; but now we are seated among the members of the United Nations, while the successors of Nazism only knock on its door. Nazism sought to exterminate us, but – as was declared at the General Assembly – we fought and we are alive. Today we are an independent state. What kind of a submission would it be on our part when the heirs of the Nazi regime sit down in a neutral capital to conduct negotiations with representatives of an independent Jewish state, whose very appearance embodies the total defeat of the Nazi plot?

I would like to conclude with the following statement on behalf of the government: the government believes that the Knesset should adopt its view to transfer the decision to the Knesset Foreign Affairs and Defense Committee to advance and complete the reparations claim.

Further, the government stands firm in its view that the responsibility for the extermination of the Jewish people in Europe rests on the entire German nation. Second, the government sees no convincing signs that the hatred of Jews has been eradicated from the German people, in East and West alike, even after the war. Third, we do not view reparations as the total rectification of what occurred; the reparations claim is but a claim for the restitution of part of the property plundered from Jews. Meeting this claim cannot erase the horrendous crimes perpetrated by the Nazis and the remaining traces of these crimes among the German people.

Speaker Ze'ev Sheffer: There is a series of resolutions, and I think it best if I allow the proposers to read them. MK Govrin will please read his resolution.

MK Akiva Govrin (*Mapai*): On behalf of the coalition parties and three members of the Progressive Party, I hereby propose the following resolution: the Knesset, after hearing the government statement on the claim for reparations from Germany for the plundered Jewish property, authorizes the Foreign Affairs and Defense Committee to determine final action to be taken in accordance with circumstances and conditions.

MK Yosef Sapir (*General Zionists*): Members of the Knesset, the General Zionists draft resolution proposes that the Knesset rejects the proposal for negotiations between the government of Israel and Germany on the matter of reparations.

MK Hana Rubin (*Mapam*): The Mapam faction proposes that the Knesset reject the proposal for negotiations between the government of Israel and Germany on the matter of reparations.

MK Esther Raziel-Naor (*Herut*): The resolution of the Herut Party proposes that the Knesset reject the proposal for negotiations between the government of Israel and Germany on the matter of reparations.

MK Shmuel Mikunis (*I.C.P.*): The draft resolution of the Communist Party proposes that the Knesset reject the proposal for negotiations between the government of Israel and Germany on the matter of reparations.

MK Mordechai Nurock (*Hamizrachi*): I am honored to propose the following in my own name: The Knesset expresses its opposition to any direct contact with Germany.

Speaker Ze'ev Sheffer: I put MK Govrin's draft resolution to a vote as Resolution A, and the draft resolution of the opposers as Resolution B. Each member who votes for one resolution will, of course, be voting against the other.

Secretary of the Knesset Moshe Rossetti reads the name of each member of the Knesset, and each of them votes individually from his or her seat.

Speaker Ze'ev Sheffer: The results of the voting are: Of the 120 members of the Knesset, four were absent and five abstained.
In favor of Resolution A: 61 votes.
In favor of Resolution B: 50 votes.
Resolution A is passed.
This meeting is closed.

[19] The Violent Herut Demonstration

Telegram from Moshe Sharett to Israeli Legations, 8.1.1952

Tension concerning the reparations issue has emerged in Israel in recent days as a result of propaganda by Herut and Mapam, assisted by the General Zionists. Herut and Mapam have organized street rallies. Begin announced that Herut will thwart the negotiations "plot" and called for mass action. Prior to the Knesset debate, Herut mobilized its members in Jerusalem and called-up hundreds from other cities for a demonstration against the Knesset. As the debate began, Herut followers gathered in Zion Square, Begin incited against the government and called upon the demonstrators to march on the Knesset. At the opening of the session, the prime minister reviewed the chain of events regarding reparations, and announced that the Bonn chancellor had proposed negotiations in writing and undertaken to accept our claim with the March 1951 note as the basis. He concluded with a statement that the government would do everything to secure that claim. His speech was heard in a silence that continued through the speeches by Rimalt (*General Zionists*) and Chazan (*Mapam*). In the middle of the speech by Raphael (*Hapoel Hamizrachi*), who was in favor, the Herut demonstration reached the Knesset area from Zion Square equipped with sticks, stones and tear gas. The demonstrators also threw stones from rooftops. The police stood by, ready with barbed wire, and used their batons and tear gas. A specific order not to open fire was given and was strictly observed. Some 100 policemen were injured in the fracas, some critically. Stones were thrown at the Knesset windows, splinters of glass showered the interior of the House, and tear gas drifted inside.

The session continued. When the army was brought in, and it also did not open fire, the attackers dug in and it became quiet outside. In his speech, Begin hurled an insulting epithet at the prime minister and refused Speaker Serlin's demand to retract it. The Speaker suspended the session which resumed three hours later with Begin's apology. The conclusion of his speech was an overt call for revolt. He announced that this was his last speech in the Knesset as he was waiving his immunity, for when the *Altalena* was shelled he had said "No," but this time he would say "Yes" for there will never be negotiations and people had taken to the barricades for lesser reasons, and so on. The clear meaning of the speech was the renewal of the Irgun underground and acts of violence. The session was concluded with an extremely fiery speech by Lavon. The debate was renewed in the evening and will be concluded with a vote tonight. The challenge posed by Herut obliges the government to make a considered and vigorous response.

[20] Shall We Live in our State as a Diaspora People?

Moshe Sharett's Speech, Mapai Activists' Meeting, Tel Aviv 10.1.1952

The main guidelines of our party are made up of two intertwined threads: the concern for the existence of the State of Israel and the concern for the existence of the Jewish people. The existence and strengthening of the State of Israel is the essence of the first thread, and here is where our position on the reparations issue comes to the fore.

I believe that if there were one issue over which we unfurled the banner of our moral independence, and raised it high, it was that of our relations with Germany. We said that we would not flinch from any hardship, from any burden and from any inconvenience and distress caused by our pressuring the Western powers for our reparations claim. True, in many ways we are quite dependent on them, on their friendship and aid, but nevertheless we shall not flinch while striving to settle our historic account with Germany.

But what is that historic account? It is not one of vengeance. Vengeance is generally a personal impulse. It cannot be the impulse of a people. A nation goes to war to defeat its enemy, hoping to succeed, but prepared that it might fail. It does not go to war to seek vengeance. In any event, taking vengeance against Germany is impossible. To talk of vengeance is ridiculous. I was amazed to hear an elderly veteran teacher speaking from the Knesset podium about telling his students that the day would come when Israeli paratroopers would be dropped on Berlin and raze it to the ground. I was ashamed to hear such nonsense.

The historic Jewish response to Hitler has been the establishment of the State of Israel. The response of the Jewish people to the German people today is the emergence of the State of Israel as a dynamically growing independent state, accepted as a legitimate member of the community of nations. The Germans are still standing in the corridor, knocking on the door of the United Nations, and we, from inside, will do everything to prevent their entry. It may well be that we will not succeed, but they will gain entrance not without our efforts to hinder their bid.

But there is another account with Germany – the world's account. There is the question of the historical role played by Germany in the history of the modern era. The conclusive fact is that the German people were partners in the rampage of internal destructive forces that seized it, and, by enlisting it to their cause, attempted to dominate all of Germany and the whole world in the recent world war. The world witnessed the phenomenon of Prussian militarism, the phenomenon of racism, of Nazism, of German fascism. It witnessed the phenomenon of the enslavement of German assets – with its tremendous production resources – to these destructive ends in order to impose German domination on the world. We have learned this from bitter experience, perhaps more than any other people.

However, even if awareness of the German people's past crimes is universal, at present it is impossible to find an attentive ear to a demand for Germany's harsh punishment. The question is: will Germany's future behavior be different, and is the world protected against renewal of the terror and catastrophe Germany caused in the past? We contend that it is not. We are ready for others to prove us wrong, but so far they have not. Meanwhile, our warnings fall on the deaf ears of the Western powers; they are treated as bothersome, perturbing and unpleasant. Germany is now needed by the Western powers for a certain purpose, and they are attempting to make it kosher, to cleanse it from all its past sins and to bring it into their circle as quickly as possible. Evidently, they are doing this with a very heavy heart, out of the "lesser of two evils" approach, in spite of themselves. They are attempting to calm the gnawing at their conscience, and we are in their way. At the last UN Assembly, on five occasions we spoke out before 80 nations on this issue, including Germany, without flinching or obscuring the facts, while emphasizing our concern for the future of world peace.

There is another problem bothering many of us, and that is whether receiving reparations involves changing our attitude towards Germany. Here I say, first of all there is no forgiveness for what was plundered. Were European Jews alive and still incarcerated, would we forgive and cease demanding their release? They perished, and there is the question of the plundered property. The dead cannot be freed, but we must free the plundered property. Had the victims survived, they would certainly have come here with their property, as many German Jews did before the war. Jews who survived are now coming to us without any property because it was plundered.

There is also property that remained and whose owners were murdered – shall the German people inherit that property? It, too, is part of the capital of the Jewish people. I ask you, why should we relinquish it? Was there ever a country in the world that waived what was due to it? A country might make a gesture of waiving what is due to it because this serves its interests, because something can be obtained in return. But on what basis should we waive what is due to us? If an individual does not waive it, then a country certainly cannot do so.

I will now describe the process for restitution of Jewish property step by step. Please interrupt me and point out when I cross the line of morality: the arrangements we are making are moral, and once we cross that line, everything ceases to be moral.

Suppose there were a Jew living in Berlin, Frankfurt, Stuttgart, or someplace else in West Germany, and he had a house there that was taken from him. The Jew left Germany and had to pay a special tax to do so. He remained alive and is now living in Israel. Would anybody tell him to waive his property? Let every one of you imagine that the house was yours, your family built it and you were born in it. It is the fruit of your family's labor, and the plunderers took it from you. How can you waive that house if you have the possibility of getting it back?

Now, how can that Jew in Israel obtain such property? Should he write a letter to the government of some country, say, Switzerland or Portugal – not Germany – and ask for his house? He knows full well that if he does not go to Germany himself, he will get nothing, even if there is a law there on this matter. He himself must go to Germany because the house is there. Once there, he must approach the German government. When he receives the house he cannot dismantle it and ship it to Israel; he has to sell it for German marks. Those marks are worthless in Israel, and to reconvert them into an asset he is compelled to invest them in something else while in Germany. If by chance he is a kibbutz member, and knows that his kibbutz needs a tractor, then he will purchase a tractor and bring it here. If you go and visit kibbutzim, whether they belong to Mapai, Mapam, or any other party, you will see such tractors, as I have. They bear the legend, "Stuttgart 1949."

But supposing the Jewish owner died and, his son immigrated to Palestine as a child while his father perished in Nazi Europe. There is no reason for the son to waive the property he inherited, when in fact he can obtain it, and the same process begins again: he can only obtain his property by virtue of German law.

But is that law the fruit of German pangs of conscience? No. An initiative began this process. It did not come about from a people living on some remote planet. It resulted from Jewish initiative. It was initiated by Jewish national organizations led by the Jewish Agency. They approached the occupation authorities and these authorities approached the German authorities. In cases when a delay occurred, or when the law did not apply or was ignored, the Jewish organizations approached the German authorities and negotiated with them.

Suppose, now, that a house, or some other identifiable asset which has proved to be the property of Jews remained, but there are no heirs to claim it; the owner and his children are dead. In such cases, the Jewish organizations intervene and say we will not give up this property. German law determines that property that has no heirs will revert to Jewish institutions. Then, when these institutions receive the value of the property, they may – like the individual Jew I spoke of earlier – purchase steel pipes or prefabricated buildings and ship them to Israel. They claim that this is Jewish property, it is part of Jewish assets, and there is no reason not to invest it in Israel for the rehabilitation of Hitler's victims. And not only them, for we are building the State of Israel on the ruins of Hitlerism; we are building it as a bastion against future Hitlerism.

But that is not all. There is also the matter of unquantifiable damage. For our people have incurred damages that cannot be measured in property. I speak not of murder, for life cannot be measured in money; I have in mind the overall destruction of Jewish life, the damage resulting from expropriation and expulsion. And, certainly, there is no reason to waive expenses incurred by the Jewish people for the rehabilitation of the 500,000 Jewish refugees who survived. What was destroyed is unidentifiable, but it can be assessed by our country, a country that demands its due.

By what logic, according to what moral values, should the State of Israel waive all this? Let it be clear that I am speaking of payment for the plundered property, for material damage. There could never be payment for loss of life.

There are those who say that in this way, by demanding reparations and being prepared to enter direct negotiations for obtaining them, we will shake the hand of the murderer. These people speak in terms that are nonexistent in international relations. Our people face a decisive choice: do they wish to keep on living in their countries as Diaspora communities, or do they seek to live as a people belonging to a sovereign state? These two modes of life are incompatible. Those who argue against conducting direct negotiations with the German government make use of the same arguments they could have proposed had the State of Israel not come into existence.

For three days I listened attentively to the debate in the Knesset and heard arguments advanced by all the opposition parties against entering into direct contact with Germany. Not even one of those arguments had any relevance to our times, nor did any of them derive from the reality of the State of Israel's existence. For generations we were a dispersed and scattered people, our lives hung by a thread, we had no control over any territory, we were a people lacking responsibility for the maintenance of state services and assets, lacking the capability of fully understanding the far-reaching consequences dictated by sovereignty. As a stateless people we managed to hold on spiritually by prayer, by humble protest, and no more. But now we are a sovereign people, in control of our own land. We have ships that ply the seas and the seas have no frontiers. We have aircraft crossing the skies, and an accident might occur whereby an El Al aircraft might make a forced landing on German soil. The pilot would certainly not commit suicide. He would ask for help from the German authorities. A storm in the North Sea might force one of our ships to seek a safe haven in a German port and ask for assistance. Our seamen would certainly not commit suicide. I remember a case of a Polish soldier who was hospitalized in this country during WW II who, even when he was dying, refused to be injected by a Jewish soldier serving with a British unit. A state cannot exist that way.

We are living on the face of this earth, and even if we boycotted Germany a thousand times, we would never be able to erase it from the face of this same earth. A state can fight against Germany if it sees a chance of winning. It cannot commit suicide. It will resolve its problem by international means, which also include war. It will not conduct itself foolishly as a hermit, oblivious to worldly needs, but will look after its needs for survival. And, first and foremost, it must see to its immediate sustenance, and fulfill its tasks by all available means. And when it convenes and makes its calculations on paper, with one column including a minimal list of its vital needs over the next five or six years and the opposite column listing the various sources of its income – either from exports, from the aid of world Jewry, or from grants and loans from various governments and international bodies – and the sum total shows a deficit, that deficit threatens its very existence. And then it remembers that it has property, the property of its people, the flesh of its flesh, and that property is in the hands of evildoers or their successors. Then this state will go even to Satan himself to claim this property. The moment it waives that right, it ceases to be a sovereign state.

This, and in no other way, is how the reparations problem must be presented. Our Mapam colleagues' arguments against conducting direct negotiations remind me of an anecdote about those men in Russia who would warm up by the stove, and only then start dancing. A saying was coined about those who "can start dancing only from the stove." They too, speakers of Mapam, are incapable of approaching any problem unless they "start from the stove" in which case it is the point of view of Moscow regarding the danger the Western powers are posing to the Soviet Union.

Suppose that the Soviet Union were in danger, suppose the West German army were mobilized for war against it. According to the perception of Mapam's leaders, a direct line leads from our entering direct negotiations to a war waged against the Soviet Union. Pure and simple: once the State of Israel claims reparations from Germany under the pressure of the Western powers, then one or two days later a third world war that will certainly be won by Germany will break out, one which will again exterminate the Jews. And what is the simple truth? It is that nobody except for the State of Israel thought of raising the question of the restitution of plundered Jewish property. In fact, no Jewish organization dared raise it. That claim, voiced by us, was a thorn in the flesh of the Western powers, first and foremost the United States and Britain, and they sought all kinds of excuses and arguments to evade our claim. In the end they told us candidly that they would not demand it, that if we wanted it, then we must act alone. This is interpreted by the members of Mapam as "being pressured to enter into negotiations with Bonn."

The truth is that West Germany, willy-nilly, is on the verge of becoming a member of the Western camp, and in any case it is being compelled to allocate vast sums for rearmament. Some of us say that we were tardy in voicing our claim, but if there were a real danger of tardiness, it would be if our claim on Germany come after it has undertaken to spend a very large sum on rearmament. Such a danger exists. But either way, the reparations claim is only likely to hinder Germany's process of rearmament and will in no way assist it. The measure of the kosher stamp that we will provide by negotiating with Germany is negligible compared to the validation it has already been given. After all, Chancellor Adenauer has already had an audience with the King of England. To whom else must he present himself? He did not need the approval of the State of Israel to enter Buckingham Palace.

As I said, our kosher stamp is insignificant compared to the global motives currently pressing the Western powers to bring Germany into their councils. However, the question of a world war has already been raised, and the reparations issue is being presented against the backdrop of preparations for another world war. Even though it is clear that this is not the reason for the reparations claim, we all understand that in face of the danger of a world war and our need to strengthen ourselves for such a contingency, obtaining or not obtaining reparations, that is the machinery and raw materials purchased with them would make a huge difference, perhaps a decisive one.

Other opponents of obtaining reparations or of conducting direct negotiations claim that the Germans will cheat us. Before the establishment of the state, MK Moshe Sneh, then a member of the Zionist Executive on behalf of the General Zionists, telephoned me in New York from Paris to warn me that America would not vote at the UN General Assembly on November 29, 1947 in favor of establishing a Jewish state in Palestine. Lo and behold, though I did not want to disappoint him, for we were friends then, the United States still voted in favor of the establishment of State of Israel even though it was completely irrational and acted in total contradiction to Dr. Moshe Sneh's clear thinking. So how do we know we will be cheated now, and to what extent we will be cheated? If it is only by a small percentage, then perhaps we should take that into account? I, for one, reject a premature assumption that we will be deceived.

This matter of reparations has been successfully accepted in principle, in no small measure due to our existence as a sovereign state. This exerted pressure on Germany forcing it into announcing that it is prepared to pay reparations and enter into negotiations, with our claim as the basis. Should the fact of the existence of the state release us from exerting pressure on Germany? On the contrary! Therefore, we must keep on acting as vigorously and forcefully as we did during the Knesset debate. It has been a long time since I was so proud of our party as during that debate. The party adopted a very courageous, exemplary, assertive, and a 100 percent Zionist position. There was no other Zionist bearing like it during the debate.

In contrast to the positions taken by representatives of other parties – some of which were clearly characterized by a Jewish Diaspora mentality while others were insincere, full of distortions, devoid of vision, lacking feelings of collective responsibility and even advancing immoral arguments – the speakers of our party took a constructive path, an intelligent and creative though a very difficult path – a path ensuring the future of our state.

It is now incumbent on us all to inculcate the general public with these truths, and to courageously implant in it confidence in the rightness of our party's path. This will not help the party and the government that depends on it, but it will contribute greatly to educating the people towards understanding the deeper meaning of the historic passage from a stateless existence to sovereignty.

[21] We Shall Not Relinquish the Plundered Property

Moshe Sharett's Speech, Open Public Meeting, Tel Aviv[1] 12.1.1952

My friends! We must constantly remind the public that our country's existence is not self-evident, and its future will not be ensured solely by a divine spirit, although we hope that a divine spirit will permeate our efforts in building it up. The State of Israel has risen and will survive, grow and flourish only if it is supported by two pillars: the pillar of Zionism and the pillar of democracy. As a human society, the State of Israel must be democratic if it is to survive, grow and develop. As a Jewish society it must be Zionist if it desires to ensure its future. These two elements enabled us to erect the edifice that brought about the creation of the State of Israel, but the building we erected before our independence has become the foundation of a taller and more splendid one, which we continue to develop. And just as Zionism and democracy were the elements supporting our state's foundations, they must also be the ones from which the entire, completed country will be built. Defending democracy and Zionism obliges us not to only be loyal to them, to walk in their light, to resolve through them all the problems we encounter according to their premises, but also to confront the negative, destructive forces, both internal and external, threatening them.

Since the inception of the Zionist movement, from its first steps along the road towards the realization of its ideals, we have fought against those who would hinder us from both within and without. We had to surmount obstacles placed in our path by external enemy forces, but first we had to overcome internal weaknesses: the denial of our democratic and Zionist precepts from within. It is therefore incumbent upon us to continue fighting simultaneously on two fronts – the foreign front and the domestic. For even after the establishment of the state, its building is not assured and it is still incomplete. Again and again we must remove obstacles placed in our path by enemy forces. Again and again we must rise up against the hindering, treacherous and destructive forces rising from within.

---

1   The meeting was convened by Mapai under the slogan, "In Defense of the State and Democracy."

The enemies of democracy are fascism on the one hand and communism on the other. They both seek the destruction of democracy. Each of them has a different objective, but what they have in common is hatred of democracy, opposition to the process by which decisions are made by a majority vote after an open debate, and to the implementation of these decisions. Both fascism and communism endeavor to place control in the hands of a minority, in most cases an organized and armed group, over the majority. Israeli democracy is at loggerheads with internal fascism and communism.

The internal enemy of Zionism is the Diaspora spirit, the refusal to accept the basic tenets of Jewish sovereignty, an effort to live in the past instead of in the present, an attempt to impose obsolete concepts, stratagems, thought patterns and moral values on our state. These traditional concepts were perhaps justified when the existence of the people was hanging by a thread, when it had no physical but only spiritual values to rely upon. They bear no relation to the work we must do today.

In the recent stormy days, the two pillars of democracy and Zionism were put to the test. We had to prove that not only do we aspire to live a democratic life, but that we have the strength to uphold that democracy in the face of enemies from within. At the same time we faced a serious and decisive Zionist test: the test of the Zionist fulfillment embodied in the State of Israel.

How did the first test come about? A gang of Herut rioters led by a hysterical clown attempted to defame us in our own and in the world's eyes. These rioters sought to turn the Knesset into an ugly, humiliated arena, the likes of which only barely civilized and barely democratic nations have known. Each time when, in one of our neighboring countries, an outrage has erupted, shots are heard, people are murdered, rioting breaks out, our stature is elevated in our eyes as well as those of the world. This time a shameful, ugly attempt was made to humiliate us, to besmirch us, to bring us down, by demonstrating before the world that this country is like any of its neighbors (I do not wish to insult even an enemy country by naming it.) This attempt was made and we should not belittle it. But neither should we ascribe too much importance to it. Its seriousness lies not in its scope, for faced by only this group alone we could say, do not worry and do not be concerned, because they are on the way down. They are declining. They are losing public credibility. They are trying to hold on but are experiencing their death throes.

True, a dying animal should be isolated and must sometimes be put down, but this one need not frighten us overmuch. The seriousness of the danger we face is that it is not the only force attacking democracy in this nation. There are more serious forces seeking to destroy it so that they can build their antidemocratic regimes on our ruins.

When reading the daily newspaper which serves as the mouthpiece of the General Zionists, one gathers the impression that they were worried by what they define as "the utilization of the Herut attack on the Knesset by Mapai" more than by the attack itself. Their fear of Mapai's enhanced power is greater that that of the weakening of the State of Israel. They are incapable of joining Mapai for the defense of our democracy lest it should strengthen Mapai, and thus their loyalty to the principles of democracy is shackled. As a result they say to themselves: "Never mind, let the Herut boys play their game, they will not hurt us, they will hurt Mapai…"

Historic experience has demonstrated that time and time again, right-wing, plutocratic forces join forces with dark political elements – with fascism in Italy and with Nazism in Germany – for their own ends. I doubt whether our own plutocracy is powerful and far-seeing enough to the point of allying itself with the extreme right in our country, but it seems a few of its people think along these lines, even though they do not admit it. Anyway, it is clear that the Israeli right, including the General Zionists, cannot be counted upon as a force bent on defending our democracy.

Yet another anti-democratic segment dwells within Israeli society, this one located in the labor movement. It constitutes a large social group and is a strong economic force. Today it utilizes democracy: it enjoys freedom of speech, freedom of organization, freedom to criticize the government, freedom of maintaining foreign contacts, both overt and covert. It exploits all these freedoms – which do not exist in the Soviet world with which it identifies – while aspiring to impose that regime here. I have in mind the Communist Party and Mapam.

These two parties exploit all these democratic freedoms with the purpose of ultimately destroying our democracy. They say this explicitly and implicitly, and they pursue a certain path, one taken before by communist parties, and thus they do not view those who rioted inside and outside the Knesset last week too severely. The first question Mapam MKs asked both in the plenum and in the Knesset committees was, "What did the police do?" Their first concern was to check if a policeman had raised his baton a moment before it was permitted and justified. If you read the description of that shocking and ugly fracas that appeared the following day in Mapam's daily, it was like reading a report of a football match: there were simply two sides fighting each other, the police and the demonstrators. However, we are fully aware of what really happened.

There is an old Jewish saying: "Israel is unlike other nations." Living today in our sovereign state, we indeed aspire to be different, but different for the better. At the same time we also hope to be like many other nations, likewise, for the better. We do know that there is something unique in us, just as every nation and language has its unique traits. Moreover, we also say that the preaching of our ancient prophets and the indescribable sufferings of generations upon generations have surely endowed our people with singular mental and spiritual qualities which perhaps are unlike those of many nations. This is quite possible. Nevertheless, in the same way that our economic activity – producing food, buying and selling, being engaged in financial matters – is subject to the iron rules of economics, our state, too, is governed by the same processes and factors that are clearly evident in the development of other nations, and we should learn from their experience.

We have witnessed a period in which communism and fascism have been very close to one another, when these two sworn enemies forged an alliance,[2] an implicit alliance, and acted in concert. Why? Because they had a common enemy, democracy.

To what can this be compared? A man is walking along carrying his baggage and two robbers are lying separately in ambush. One says to himself, let the other one attack him first, and I will attack at the last minute and rob him, and the booty will be mine. By bringing up this parable, I have in mind a rather extreme and bleak eventuality. That such an eventuality exists in our country is clear to all who do not shut their eyes. Consequently, we should stand firm, put an end to this threat and repulse any speedily attack on our democracy.

The State of Israel will not deny freedom of speech to anyone, it will not deny anyone the freedom to criticize the government, it will not deny freedom of contact with the outside world, and it will certainly not deny the freedom of organization. It will uphold these freedoms. Should a Knesset faction declare that it will continue its struggle against a Knesset decision, it has the right to explain its views and gather public support for them. But the State of Israel will use all the power at its disposal against any attempt to actively sabotage and disrupt its executive capability; it will also ensure that its various law-enforcement branches – the army, the police, the courts – be directed towards defending democracy. And it will remain alert to any danger to democracy and always endeavor to nip evil in the bud.

Our party, Mapai, the cornerstone of Israeli democracy, calls upon all its members and all citizens who relish the democratic atmosphere of our society – people who believe that only such a society is worth creating and living in – to join hands in defending it. If, facing the threat to this precious asset of democracy, we respond with alertness, intensive public and educational activity and a clear understanding of the danger, then the curse that so horrified us in Jerusalem last Monday will turn into a blessing.

As I said before, we are facing another test, the test of Zionism in its stage of fulfillment, the stage of statehood that we have reached. The reparations issue confronted us with this problem, and I shall formulate it in simple terms: the problem is whether the Israeli people can recognize that it is no longer a persecuted and oppressed people, that it has ceased being a dispersed and exiled people, always a minority, that it has ceased being human dust blown to the four corners of the

---

2   On 23.8.1939, Ribbentrop and Molotov, foreign ministers of Nazi Germany and USSR, signed a non-aggression pact. Earlier, in the German elections on 5.3.1933, the Communists fought mainly against the Social Democrat Party, and some of them crossed the line over to the Nazis.

earth; it has become a political entity, a sovereign entity, running its own country with full responsibility for the entire range of its material assets. In other words, the problem is whether the Israeli people are really aware that since 1948, the mode of its existence has changed, and therefore its consciousness must change, too.

What has characterized all previous generations of our people? Certain Jewish moral, spiritual and social values existed: suffering was accepted; relying on internal strengths to surmount external obstacles was adhered to; prayer and protest provided a refuge. Jews, masses of Jews, for generation upon generation lived with memories of the past, with the hope of messianic salvation that might arrive sometime in the dim and distant future. They did not constitute a political factor. They were not responsible for their living conditions and were unable to express a collective desire for action and for creating a different reality. They were helpless, always potential victims. Their morality was directed towards shaping spiritual fortitude that would one day enable them to mount the scaffold with the right spirit, a strong spirit. They had no more than that. They were isolated, undefiled by contact with others, abiding the salvation that would one day come.

Zionism turned its back on this tradition. Had this tradition continued to dominate us, the Zionist movement would not have come about. Zionism took a different road, one which, first of all, assumed a different attitude towards the element of time: it rebelled against the age-old belief in the guaranteed, everlasting existence of the Jewish people. It said, first and foremost: our people's future is uncertain. The Jewish people can be exterminated. It also said something else: even if the Jewish people continue to exist forever, it should not continue to exist as before. In any event, if it is possible to live differently, then we must. And the nation took a two-lane road: one was undertaking political action, entering the political arena, making contact with external elements. Dr. Theodore Herzl went to the Czarist Minister of the Interior Vyacheslav Plehve, who was responsible for pogroms against the Jews in 1903; he saw the Ottoman Sultan; he contacted British leaders. He understood that only by entering the political arena would the road be open for introducing a change in our people's lives. The Zionists realized that a real change could not be attained only through protest and prayer, that it could not be accomplished by isolation, that we must become an active element in this world, and that if we seek to improve our situation, we could only do so through contact with others.

The second lane was the taking immediate and concrete actions such as building settlements in Palestine, such as accumulating political power, not to rely on eternity and refrain from doing today what needs to be done today. Zionism meant understanding the importance of concrete, active power as opposed to remaining satisfied with pursuing moral values. In other words, it said that the exercise of power is moral, that our morality tells us not to be weak, for if we are weak we will always be held in contempt, humiliated and slaughtered like lambs.

It held that every step we took would be morally evaluated according to one standard: will it lead to the creation of Jewish power, or will it weaken us?

Even before the establishment of the state, we experienced internal struggles resulting from vacillation between these two moral concepts. I will not elaborate here on the fact that whenever there is a debate in human society, it is also exploited negatively for various individual or factional reasons. When Herzl went to Plehve, there were Jews in Russia who said "It is humiliating. Our leader should not go to our murderer." But Herzl's statesmanship impelled him to go, so that perhaps he could attain something for the Zionist movement in Russia.

More recently, in the early 1930s, what an uproar there was in this country and the Diaspora alike around the issue of the Transfer! Some people said "Trade with Germany? No, a boycott of Germany!" Again, there was the demand for "boycott of Germany!" and the demand for "goods to Palestine!" The slogan "Boycott Germany" was derived from the Diaspora mentality, while the second slogan was a Zionist one. Hitler's discriminatory and later murderous campaign against the Jews of Germany could only happen in a world without Zionism. The slaughter of Jews in the Crusades occurred before the rise of Zionism, and the same can be said for the first pogroms in Czarist Russia. All kinds of blood libels, like the one in Damascus in 1840 and campaigns of the destruction of Jewish communities in other countries, took place before Zionism. Then Jews could have responded with a boycott. But this kind of response does not necessarily lead to concrete results. Can anyone assume that had the spirit of appeasement with Hitler prevailed in England or had America and other countries been interested in trading with Germany, that they would have been put off by a Jewish boycott? Boycott is no more than an act of satisfying wounded feelings.

However, a disturbing question arose: Jews were being expelled from Germany, their property expropriated, where could they go? And if they came to Palestine, would they come penniless and naked? But perhaps their property could be rescued – was that permissible or forbidden? And how could their property be rescued? Should we demolish their houses and bring the bricks here? Clearly, they had to realize their assets in currency, in German marks. But what happen to the German marks they will bring over here? Clearly, with those marks they should purchase some goods of value to this country, or sell these goods in another country and bring the proceeds here. There was no other choice if we sought to rescue German Jews and absorb them here. So the question boiled down to what was our aim – boycotting Hitler or rescuing German Jews?

There was an even more trenchant question deriving from the former one: what should our response be? Are we to remain as weak as we were in the face of Hitler's attacks against the Jewish people and only raise our voice in protest, or should we strive to become stronger in order to prevent such attacks in the future? Here, too, the Zionist response prevailed, and who knows, had we not brought the tens of thousands of persecuted German Jews here between 1934 and 1939, with their millions in assets and their industrial machinery following our negotiations with the Nazi regime which led to the Transfer – for there was no other way! – how then would the Yishuv have met the challenges of WW II? Would we have been as powerful and highly developed economically, industrially and culturally as we have become, thanks to the Transfer? And how would we have prevailed in the War of Independence? If not for the courage we mustered in carrying out the Transfer deal with the Nazis, if not for the immigration of the 1930s and the transferred assets that came with it, which consolidated and expanded Jewish settlement in this country and whose money built settlements, developed new production opportunities, established factories, expanded Tel Aviv and built a new Haifa – would we have had the courage to seriously declare our claim to statehood and to fight the War of Independence through to victory?

There was another debate broke out, at the beginning of WW II. We said that we should enlist in the British Army to fight Hitler, not for that purpose alone but also in order to become an active, recognized factor so that a representative of Israel, on the first occasion when he stood on the podium at the United Nations – could declare: "We are your equals because my people in Palestine also fought against Hitler!" And not only for that specific purpose, but also in order to increase the military power of the Yishuv, because we knew that the future would hold other serious battles for our country.

What was our military rationale then? It was defensive. But by defense alone we could not have survived. What did we have? Rifles, light machine guns, mortars. There was not a single artilleryman at our disposal then, not one air force pilot. We were unfamiliar with combined military operations. We said "we will enlist to the British Army in our thousands, serve in all theatres of war, join the Ordnance Corps, the Engineering Corps, the Artillery Corps, and constitute a whole infantry brigade. Nothing is more precious than that! When will we ever have had such an opportunity for weapons training and operating large army units? Who knows what awaits us in the Middle East, who knows what will happen between us and British rule? We must seize this opportunity!"

We were told then by our political rivals, who stood aside and even tried to hinder us: "You are collaborating with the British government responsible for the Struma[3] and the *Patria*[4] disasters! You, our volunteers, are going to wear British

---

3   A ship carrying 769 Jewish refugees from Rumania that reached the port of Istanbul. The Turkish authorities refused it permission to anchor in Turkish waters and sent it back to the Black Sea where it was sunk on February 2, 1942. Appeals to the British Mandate Authority in Palestine to let the refugees enter Palestine while they still anchored in Istanbul were refused. Only one passenger survived.

4   A ship anchoring in Haifa port with 1,800 illegal Jewish immigrants on board, about to be exiled by the British to the island of Mauritius. It was sabotaged by the Haganah (which miscalculated the power of the charge) on December 12, 1940 in order to prevent it sailing, and it was sunk. 216 of the immigrants perished.

uniforms and raise Britain's flag!" Once more, this was derived from a Diaspora mentality as opposed to a Zionist one. The Zionist policy was to repress the pain and join the British Army for that was the way of life, for that was the constructive way of increasing our power, because in the existing circumstances it was the only road leading to redemption. The other road meant missing the opportunity of increasing our military strength for the sake of not "defiling ourselves with the British uniform." You can go on living that way if your aim is not to become powerful and achieve national independence. You can go on living that way if the aim is only to hold on spiritually.

What actually happened? Numerous Diaspora Jews of the allied countries fought Hitler because they were conscripted by force of their country's law. They fought not as Jews but as their country's citizens. Here, in Palestine, an opportunity presented itself to form the Yishuv's volunteers, prompted by Jewish national will, to fight as Jews, which in turn opened the road to forging Jewish military power.

Let me remind you of a third internal debate: which of you does not remember when, after WW II, the battle in favor of and against partition of Palestine and the question of the future of this country was raised. How our opponents scornfully said: "Partition? You are touching upon the Holy of Holies!" There were always those who spoke in the name of the holy values of our people and accused us of ignoring them: "The integrity of this country is the Holy of Holies, and you are prepared to negotiate for a state in only part of it? To reduce its size? How dare you?" Yes, indeed, we dared! We demanded part of this country because if we adhered to the sanctity of its integrity, we would have handed ourselves and this country over to British rule, to British oppression and to Arab destruction [due to the Arab majority in non-partitioned Palestine]: we demanded an independent state in part of Palestine, we said that we wanted to exist as a people with honor, a people possessing a respected, recognized position in the world, an independent people; there is no other way to attain it but through partition, and finally, because we did demand it, we achieved the United Nation Assembly's decision to partition Palestine, and having achieved it, we fought for it.

The debate about reparations from Germany which we are witnessing nowadays is an exact repetition of the same phenomenon. Our history is repeating itself! Here my argument is not with those who are merely exploiting the sensitive issue for the purpose of attacking Mapai, the government and the state. My argument is only with those whose opposition to reparations is sincere, deriving from a pure Jewish conscience, from Jewish moral values, and to these opponents I say, with all due respect to your arguments, to your spiritual motives, I deny one thing – I deny that they are Zionists. These are not Zionist reasons, these are not Zionist considerations. Not everything Jewish is Zionist.

Our people, in Diaspora mode, have embraced and imbibed all kinds of characteristics, all kinds of ways of thinking, all kinds of attitudes. Not only did we live for centuries under Diaspora conditions, but we also acquiesced to seeing life in the Diaspora as a constant, to be changed in an indefinite future when the End of Days brought salvation. We did not think in terms of political salvation. The vision of political salvation, not a mystical, messianic one, is a very recent and new phenomenon in the history of our people. This vision of Jewish national salvation resulting from taking active, concrete political steps towards its achievement is but a few decades old, and it is only natural that consciousness lags behind. One moves over to a different stage of reality, but one is still governed by values which were ingrained in the past, and thus one does not take stock of the obligations and needs of the new situation and unawareness that inner motives have become obsolete, to the extent of endangering vital needs.

How did the reparations issue arise? What are its origins? It originated in the plundering of property by the Nazis. And take note of what we are being told by our opponents: "Had you come to Germany, together with the occupying powers and imposed a war damages levy on Germany, that would have been another matter." Or: "You were tardy; why did you not claim reparations earlier?" These are complete distortions of the most basic facts of the situation.

What is our account with Germany? Is it the sum of the damages caused to us as a fighting people during the war? Is that it? You perhaps recall the Italian bombers that flew over Tel Aviv dropping bombs, destroying buildings – that was war damage. The same applies to Haifa: it was bombed, people were killed, we buried them and they left behind widows and orphans. We fought in the various theaters of war and soldiers fell; 200 young men of ours drowned in the depths of the Mediterranean when their troopship was sunk The graves of our soldiers are strewn from Tripoli in North Africa to Basra in Iraq. These hundreds of people are considered "war damage." There was perhaps other damage: trade that was cut off between us and an enemy country, the assets of citizens of Palestine that were seized, and so on.

My dear friends, is that our claim from Germany? Is that all that happened to us? First, let it be known that if that is our claim, then to a certain extent it was honored. After we drew up the account with the mandatory government, we received £300,000, what was due for the area of the Palestine Mandate which became the State of Israel; this amount came from the overall compensation paid to England by Germany for war damages, and thus the matter was closed. In that case we were not tardy at all; we were treated justly and honestly. In fact, we were treated more leniently than was required, since the Allies decided that all the gold in Germany that had not been minted into coins, and the German cash deposits in foreign countries, such as Switzerland and Sweden would be devoted to refugee rehabilitation, and 90 percent of that gold's worth was earmarked for Jewish refugees. Do you know how much the Jewish Agency and the Joint Distribution Committee received out of that? $16 million, a larger sum than the £300,000.

Can that $16 million be compared with what happened to us, or reflect even a trace of it? There was genocide and plundering. There is no negotiation, no forgiveness, no atonement, no compensation for genocide. Some demand vengeance. I prefer not to discuss here the possibility of taking revenge for the murder of one-third of a people, but property is another matter. Suppose for a moment that the plundering of a people occurred, but that there was no war. Was that impossible? It was possible. Supposing that after Hitler had rampaged for years, expelled Jews, expropriated, plundered, that there was a revolution in Germany, and Hitler's regime was toppled and replaced; and even if it were not entirely clear whether this new regime was clean of Nazism, clearly it would have inherited all the former regime's assets. Would we then have waived the property? Suppose that the new regime had come to power while masses of Jews were still in concentration camps – and there was no war, and the regime tried to keep them in concentration camps – would we not have demanded the release of those Jews? I reiterate: there was no war, no question of occupying powers and no question of addressing a third power that would approach Germany on our behalf, because there was no war, Hitlerism was eradicated, a new regime had come to power headed by a man who did not murder Jews but kept on detaining them. Would we have not approached that new regime? Even directly? Suppose that the new leader released the detained Jews but not their property, would we not have directly demanded the release of that property? Would we not have said, "That property in your hands is theirs. Give it back?" Which third party would we have approached to act on our behalf in such a matter?

The present situation is, of course, different. Naturally, it would have been easier for us had the powers taken the plundered Jewish property from West Germany. In any event, it is important for us to enlist their support in this matter. Indeed, as a first step we asked for their help. What did they reply? They considered us as one of the combatant parties and claimed that our war damage claim had been met. The three Western powers received $500 million on account of their war damages and then stopped. It served the political interests of America, Britain and France not to take any more. Do we share those interests? Suppose that we were part of their group, would we have ignored the special nature of our relations with Germany?

Now, what was our response to the powers' contention? We said, "Your attitude is basically flawed – what we are concerned with is not a matter of war damage. It is one of plunder of a people's property that took place both before and during the war. It is utterly unrelated to the war. Did Hitler's war needs lead him to the slaughter of millions of Jews, to transporting them from one country to another and into the death camps? Had he remained alive and in power, he would have accomplished this murderous operation to the end even after the war."

They replied, "If that is the case, approach Germany yourself. Why come to us? We are the occupying powers. Our occupation was an outcome of the war. If you have another account, approach Germany directly as a sovereign state."

If there is someone here in the audience who once lived in Germany and left, leaving behind a house, he would certainly know that according to West Germany's law the house is his; he can return to Germany to receive it, and if he wishes to remain a citizen of Israel, he can sell it. And then what? Bring the marks here? No, he will buy something with them, something that will be of benefit here such as industrial machinery. This is considered permissible by the defenders of our Jewish morality.

But suppose that someone is not the Jew who left Germany but his son. He came here as a boy, but his father stayed there and was murdered by the Nazis. The German law entitles the heir to claim that property. But what about those cases in which both the father and his son were murdered but the house remains identifiable? There is a law governing such cases too – only in West Germany! – which determines that certain Jewish institutions, namely the Jewish Agency – the executive of which includes representatives of Agudat Yisrael and Mapam – and the Joint Distribution Committee are entitled to claim and receive that house. These institutions will sell it, and with the proceeds buy materials to bring here. Whom do they approach for obtaining that property? Do they have to approach the German municipal authorities, or not? And if that property is under the jurisdiction of the Bonn Federal Government, do they have to approach it, or not? And if one of the states of the Federal Republic of Germany has not enacted a relevant law, should they approach Bonn and demand legislation? And if it transpires that the law is incomplete, should they not demand from the legislative authority that it be amended? Is all this not permissible according to our guardians of Jewish moral values?

And here a question arises: if what others can obtain for you is permissible, why are you forbidden to obtain it yourself? Furthermore, if you are permitted to claim your due, are you not entitled to have others do it for you? But why not do it yourself if obtaining your property is considered moral? And if it is immoral, then again, why demand from others to do something immoral for you? Either you claim or you waive. Moreover, if it is permissible for an individual, why is it forbidden for the people? For a Jew who survived it is permissible but not so for the Jewish people to claim the property of a Jew who perished? Where is the logic here? Where is moral consistency? If the property exists – say, there is a house, or stolen paintings whose Jewish ownership is provable – steps taken to obtain it are permissible. But if vast property was stolen, plundered, dispersed, vanished, went into people's pockets, into cellars, can it not be claimed? If it is logical to infer that what an individual is morally permitted to claim is of course morally permitted to the people, it is all the more logical to say that while an individual can waive what is due him, the nation or the state cannot. Indeed, is there a country in the world that would waive its due? This is unheard of!

Let me now move on to the issue of direct contact: an individual Jew, a citizen of any country, can say to himself: "My foot will never tread on German soil, and I will never open my door to a German." That attitude is praiseworthy, and I wish such sentiments were expressed by Jews the world over. But can a state impose such limits on itself? Suppose that an Israeli ship in the North Sea finds itself in distress, and it is approached by a German vessel offering help. Would the captain say, "I would rather sink than be rescued by you"? Suppose that it can be towed into a German port. Would it waive that possibility? Suppose that an Israeli aircraft is caught in a storm and is forced to land in Germany: would its crew take their own lives rather than land there? Suppose that a German vessel finds itself in distress in the Eastern Mediterranean and broadcasts an SOS. Could we later appear before the world and say, "We heard the vessel's call but didn't want to rescue it because it was German?" Or would we close our port to them?

Occurrences such as I have just described, and the immediate decisions they call for, were never included on the agendas of Jewish rabbinical seminaries or those of various American Jewish committees, but they are of vital importance in the sphere of international relations. When such considerations occupied the minds of Diaspora Jews they were of a purely theoretical nature, as the Jews were a minority in their countries. Jews did not ask for decision-making autority since the required and pertinent steps to be taken by local authorities were decided upon everywhere by a majority of gentiles.

But now Jews are the majority in their own country, whose existence is no longer theoretical; it is a state occupying a defined piece of the earth. Such decisions cannot be evaded. Germany, too, is part of that globe; it is not situated on another planet. Its ships sail the same seas as ours. Its airplanes fly through the same skies as ours. Do Jews feel bad about it? Then let them not establish an independent state! Then they will be free to pray and protest and boycott and be slaughtered helplessly. They will also enjoy spiritual harmony. Do they want a state? Well, then they must confront these contradictions, which are only *prima facie* contradictions, for having a country, belonging to the family of independent nations, maintaining direct contacts with all other countries is not immoral. It is moral! For the foundation of morality is first and foremost guaranteeing survival. Without life there is no morality. First of all there must be life.

It has been made clear to us that it is impossible to survive if we remain eternally weak. Survival necessitates power, and power means enough people, and work, and property, and first and foremost, not waiving what is rightfully ours. Our country appeals to other countries and receives aid. It does not make do with the aid of the Jewish people in the Diaspora. It appeals to other states and requests aid. It receives aid, and it asks for more. And is this state, out of some hyper-sensitivity which has infected it, to declare that it will not claim the property due to it from Germany when the other side has invited it to negotiate? Does it strengthen its appeals for other countries' aid if it publicly declares that it is waiving its claim to its own property?

Some say that the West German acceptance of our claim is a fraud, that Germany has never fulfilled all its obligations. But, ladies and gentlemen, since when have the precedents of other peoples represented guidelines for us? Precedents should not frighten us; the very fact that a dispersed and scattered people, owing to necessity more than to an effort of will, succeeded in ingathering its exiles and in establishing a state that entered the United Nations like any other nation – is there a precedent for that?

Is the fact that this once-persecuted people stands proud on the world's stage and denounces Germany not a precedent? Lo and behold, it denounces Germany at the United Nations, the one single country that does so and speaks out there: "Don't think that I am doing this because I am motivated by an impulse for revenge. No, my revenge is embodied in the fact that I am alive. Others wanted to humiliate me? I am now an independent state! My revenge is to make the German people know that the stain with which it has besmirched itself, the stain of Jewish blood, will never be erased from the annals of history!"

But there is an account that is not ours alone, it belongs to the entire world. And it does not only pertain to the past. It pertains to the distant future: the German people has demonstrated once, twice and thrice that it is capable of becoming prey to forces of oppression, to impulses of slaughter and destruction, to warmongering, to forces that oppress other peoples, that emasculate the divine image of mankind. It has not proved immune against such barbaric forces. Are you sure that this rampage will not be repeated? When looking into the psyche of this people, are you sure that the evil spirit has been expunged within? Heaven help you if you restore this people to the community of nations and arm it before you exorcise this filth from it!

And we have said this four and five times at the UN General Assembly for the entire world to hear. And these words echo, and their first echo reverberates in Bonn and the whole German press. Is it easy to hear? Is it comfortable? At the same time we also declare, "They plundered and inherited and are not restoring – and they are able to restore it!" For what has happened in Germany in the meantime? If we take the production of 1936 as 100, that is, the production of that part of Germany presently constituting the German Federal Republic, then the production for 1949 would be 58, and that of 1951 would be 127. Bonn's trade surplus in 1951 was $35 million per month. At the present time, this is the plundering people.

At the present time, ours is the plundered people: we have not doubled our production in two years. On the contrary, owing to mass immigration, we have more than doubled our consumption in the last three or four years. We have no export surplus. Due to our situation, we have a tremendous deficit of exports over imports. We do not have vast industrial means that have remained intact or have been rebuilt. We have to import them. And these plundered people have taken upon themselves the rehabilitation of the surviving victims. Are these words easy to hear?

And this nation declares: "We will never forgive and we will never forget the victims," and then Bonn responds "At least we can get rid of this accusation. We should pay something." It might have said, "Are we accused of murdering? But we did not murder. It was the Hitler regime." But how can they say that as long as they are holding plundered Jewish property and not restoring it? This surely casts suspicion on the sincerity of their statements, as if they do not acknowledge the murder was committed by them. Do they not have a political interest in this?

In any case, precedent or no precedent, when did we enter negotiations convinced of our success? The statement "We shall not negotiate because negotiations mean forgiveness" in fact means we give up. If we do not enter into negotiations, we waive the property of the people, the possibility of the empowerment of our society.

When addressing this question, Mapam has only one point of departure: how their position will be recorded in Moscow where there is "an open book and a moving finger," and "all your deeds are inscribed in a book."[5] That is their concern. There is an account in Moscow for each of Mapam's leaders, and it is inscribed there: on a given day, comrade so-and-so wrote a certain article, and expressed a certain idea in a speech and that Mapam's faction voted this or that way on a given issue. In order to be kosher in the eyes of Moscow, they must prove that they have nothing to do with the contact of the State of Israel with Bonn; if an Israeli delegation goes to Bonn, it does so because the United States is sending it there. The fact is that America never dreamt that we would submit this claim for reparations, and that it was unpleasantly surprised when we did so. It would have been much more convenient for America to come to an agreement with Germany, but we complicated matters by our demand for reparations, and as a result we were told "Go and talk directly with them." That is what Mapam calls "Going to Bonn because America is pressuring us," and thus the matter of reparations ceases to be the desire of our people and our country to restore part of the plunder, but becomes "a plot of the Ben Gurion government to be a pawn in Truman's war against the Soviet Union."

One can draw a picture of a dog and write under it "This is a lion." One can draw a stormy sea and write under it "This is a peaceful desert." Here, the State of Israel stands firm on its claim for this property, and is first and foremost troubling Germany – and Britain, France and the United States – and also attempts to trouble the Soviet Union. But there in Moscow, the headline reads "A pawn in Truman's war against the Soviet Union…"

Chancellor Adenauer has already met in Paris with all the foreign ministers – Acheson, Eden, and Schuman – and reached an agreement with them. He was received by Churchill and the King of England. There are German legations in London and other capital cities, and Germany's diplomatic relations are constantly expanding. But in Mapam's view, the West cannot include Germany within its

5   *Ethics of the Fathers* (Aboth), 2:1.

camp unless it obtains a "seal of approval" from Israel! What the King of England really said to Adenauer was, "I received you, but not formally. I can only receive you formally after you have paid compensation to the State of Israel." That is Mapam's view for you.

Western Europe wants to be prepared for the eventuality of war, and there are statesmen there who say that this cannot be done without Germany. There are plans prepared by the Western powers for that contingency, and we know that they are about to rearm Germany, that they are going to earmark large sums for that purpose, but all this is being held back because Bonn did not pay us reparations? Would all that has been going on between the Western powers and the Federal government not have happened had this project of reparations to the State of Israel not existed? Has it all begun because on a certain day, the State of Israel submitted a note claiming reparations? What a fantasy!

My friends, that does not mean that we can remove the threat of a world war from our agenda. But when taking the possibility of the eruption of a world war into consideration, we must first of all realize that whether or not Germany plays a role in it, and whether or not this role is destructive, our influence in this context is nil. At the same time, if a world war erupted, how would the State of Israel meet it? Will it be somewhat stronger or a great deal stronger? Will it be somewhat weaker or a great deal weaker? This is a matter of vital interest to us, and whatever steps we take in preparing ourselves for such a contingency will be of great importance. We can and must ensure that if, heaven forbid, a world war broke out, we could meet it when we are much stronger.

What is the conclusion? If we can obtain reparations from Germany under these circumstances – acquiring raw materials, machinery, installations and goods, and thus enhancing our economic capacity, and strengthening our defense capability – is it not incumbent upon us to do so? I am not saying that we are seeking reparations in order to prepare for war. We seek reparations for one reason only: because they are our due and we shall not waive them. But, in view of a world war contingency, that linkage is vital.

By the way, was it only on reparations that we heard this "Nay" from Mapam? Did we hear "Aye" regarding our appeal for the American government's grant? On that, too, we heard "Nay." And did we hear "Aye" on the American Bank loan? On that, too, we heard "Nay." In fact, when did we hear an "Aye" from Mapam – an "Aye" not as an echo of one of our proposals, but expressed on their own initiative? When, since the early beginnings of those days of heroism and splendor of our War of Independence and the terrible suffering and hardships we experienced while sustaining the nascent state and implementing the ingathering of the exiles, when have they made any positive proposal to solve one of the problems facing us? They demanded that the government cover all its expenditures by siphoning all available resources out of the country, by imposing more and more taxes. Could that furnish us with the huge sums we needed in foreign currency for importing the food which was so necessary? Could our long-time citizens, together with new immigrants produce food here, by the sweat of their brow in the near future? Was that Mapam's contribution to the ingathering of exiles? Never an "Aye?" They, with their own hands, have implicitly falsified Zionism, just as they implicitly reject democracy.

We will not curtail our democracy. We will neither detain demonstrators nor gag mouths. We will not adopt a system of closing down newspapers, and we will not eject people from the Knesset. The soul of democracy is in free elections, and there will be a free press and freedom of criticism, but we will staunchly defend Zionism and democracy throughout the country.

We will open the eyes of the blind, we will educate the ignorant, we will explain these principles to our youth, we will gather an ever-increasing camp around us, we will build up the power that will withstand a future test of battle, if it is imposed on us, for we will never initiate it. We will elevate the consciousness of our people, we will strengthen the foundations we have laid and on which we will continue to build, until our mission is accomplished.

[22] Freedom of Action for the Government

Knesset Foreign Affairs and Defense Committee Meeting, 15.1.1952

Chairman Meir Argov: We now move on to a discussion on the issue of reparations.

Foreign Minister Moshe Sharett: I would like to inform the members of this committee that the government will do everything in its power – within the parliamentary and constitutional framework, of course – to prevail over any attempt at delaying its entry into negotiations on reparations. The government views this matter not as a vision to be fulfilled in the days of the Messiah, but as an urgent, concrete matter and is determined to advance it. We have decided not to mark time and not to retreat, but to advance.

On behalf of the government, I present before this committee a proposal to authorize the government, as it deems fit and in accordance with its needs, complete freedom of action in this matter. I request the committee's approval for this, if possible, its unanimous approval but if not, then a vote will be taken.

I would like to explain the background of the matter before us: the government, in accordance with the state's foreign policy interests and not only because of the complex internal situation in the Knesset, has not brought a proposal authorizing its entry into negotiations with Germany to the Knesset. The government is of the opinion that it is preferable that such a decision not be made by the Knesset, nor by its Foreign Affairs and Defense Committee, nor by any parliamentary body. It is desirable that a simple, regular cabinet decision be reached on this matter. A solemn declaration by the Israeli parliament or by any another Israeli parliamentary body will take the form of a routine implementation and will not appear to be a turning point in the position and attitude of the Jewish people. At the same time, the government views this matter as substantial and urgent. The meaning of the decision we expect to reach is not that it requires the government to enter into negotiations. Rather, it enables the cabinet to enter into direct negotiations if, after further debate, it finds direct negotiations necessary and beneficial under the terms to be decided upon in the future.

Obviously, there could be an exchange of views in the committee. But first let me state the government's proposal: "It is proposed to grant the government full authority to act as it deems fit in this matter." Furthermore, if this authority is approved, it must be clear that the government can also decide on direct negotiations.

MK Shalom Zysman (*General Zionists*): The Knesset decided to transfer the final decision regarding negotiations to this committee, and that it should be reached according to circumstances at that time. Accordingly, I think the foreign minister should now clarify the present circumstances to us.

MK Yaakov Riftin (*Mapam*): If you had wished to reach a final decision on negotiations, why didn't you present it to the Knesset for a decision? I think that the cabinet should discuss the whole matter anew, and inform us of any changes in the circumstances.

MK Haim Landau (*Herut*): If the government was of the opinion that the time was right, and direct negotiations with Germany should begin, it should have brought an appropriate proposal to the Knesset, but the Knesset decided to transfer the issue to our committee. I think that we should discuss the matter in full and reach a decision in view of any new developments. I propose that the Committee decide to call for a national referendum on direct negotiations with Germany.

MK George Flesh (*General Zionists*): The foreign minister now asks for authority for the government to act as it sees appropriate. This, in fact, bypasses the Knesset and the Foreign and Defense Committee (*Foreign Minister Moshe Sharett: This is how the government implements all matters.*) I see it as a cowardly step if the government does not bring the proposal we heard here to the Knesset. There are many issues involved awaiting clarification, and we should discuss them here first.

MK Shalom Zysman (*General Zionists*): The foreign minister should report the government's planned activity for the coming months to us. Then we can make a final decision.

Foreign Minister Moshe Sharett: Gentlemen, why try to obfuscate the issue just in order to play for time? The issue is completely clear-cut. Anyone wanting to, can see it clearly.

The government has reached the conclusion that present circumstances are conducive to direct negotiations. If this is unclear to you, or if there is anything doubtful in the detailed statement I gave at the last meeting of this committee – perhaps it was not sufficiently detailed for the satisfaction of all? – then the presentation of the matter by the government in the Knesset was also unclear to you, as well as the proposal we submitted to the Knesset. That being so, I permit myself to reiterate: the government has reached the conclusion that present circumstances are conducive to direct negotiations, and it seeks approval to conduct such negotiations. That is the meaning of the decision. The government is not committing itself to enter direct negotiations with anyone, and it is not in its interest to commit itself. It seeks authorization to follow this path, and in our view the conditions for taking such a step are ripe.

All the questions presently directed to the government, such as how negotiations should be conducted, who it will send to conduct them, whether or not they will be conducted about goods or currency, and what quantity of goods and how much currency, cannot be answered yet. And I will tell you why: because the government has not yet discussed these matters as it is not clear if it has the authority to conduct direct negotiations. The government views these negotiations with all due seriousness and as a decision that must not be implemented before it is brought before the Foreign Affairs and Defense Committee. This committee wanted a debate in the Knesset. There was a debate in the Knesset, and the matter was returned to the committee. A final decision has not yet been made; so long as a decision authorizing the government to enter into direct negotiations has not been made, it will not enter into such negotiations. That would be neither reasonable nor decent. The government, first of all, seeks this authority – was it not given such authority by this committee's decision? The first round ends with this, but that does not mean that the government will not open a second round. If it is granted the authority to act, it will embark on taking steps. It may declare that we are prepared for negotiations. It may declare that some preliminary steps might be needed, and these steps might possibly necessitate a decision regarding our readiness to conduct direct negotiations.

The government cannot enter into such preliminary clarifications before it is granted this authorization; it will not engage in self-deceit, and will not deceive others. It therefore needs to know that when it takes action, it is probable that it will enter into direct negotiations immediately, but only on condition that it is authorized to do so.

I would like to reiterate that the issue debated in the Knesset centered on whether direct negotiations with Germany were permitted or forbidden. It seems to me that the government was perfectly clear on this point: it argued that negotiations with Germany are permissible. In any event, I and other members of the cabinet who spoke from the Knesset podium made it clear that the government feels that direct negotiations with Germany are permissible. You cannot contend that the government obscured or concealed its position.

A draft resolution prohibiting direct negotiations was submitted to the Knesset and was rejected. Some years ago, a draft resolution prohibiting the Jewish Agency Executive from conducting negotiations regarding the establishment of a Jewish state in part of Palestine was submitted. It, too, was rejected. The positive decision on the issue of direct negotiations was transferred by the Knesset to the Foreign and Defense Committee. Now we are asking the committee to confirm that direct negotiations should be permitted. I said in my opening remarks, and I say again: if you accept the government's proposal, it means that the government can conduct direct negotiations, which means that they are permissible. I will reiterate: if you accept the government's proposal, it means that the government is also allowed to conduct direct negotiations; it means that direct negotiations are permissible. The government holds the view that we can enter into negotiations on the basis of Chancellor Adenauer's note on behalf of the Bonn government.

Now I would like to make some further clarifications. It is a fundamental principle that it is the government that rules. Knesset committees do not rule in place of the government. If it was said that the Foreign and Defense Committee was authorized to make a final decision. This meant that it was asked to reach a final decision on an issue which had been put before the Knesset, not that this committee was granted a standing authorization to decide on the issue at each stage, for if so, the committee would become the government, the government would resign and this committee would become Israel's government. This is, of course, unreasonable.

The government presented a matter whose time has come to the Knesset. Had it felt that it was not the right time, it would not have done so. The government waited for months after submitting the note to the powers and the debate that followed it in the Knesset. The prime minister announced that no action would be taken by the government before it was brought to the parliamentary authority. Why wasn't it brought immediately? Because the time was not yet ripe, and so the government waited for nine months. But those months have not been wasted, for every effort has been made to clarify the matter – first with the occupying powers, which has yielded certain results. Once the government realized that the time had come for implementation, it was impossible to do so without a decision, and it presented the question for a decision. Had it not come to the conclusion that the timing was right, it would not have done so. In the government's view, the time is now ripe. This view is immutable.

Steel is forged when the iron is hot, and my limited experience has taught me that, as a rule, any action not taken in time ends up somewhat flawed. If a window of opportunity opens for action, that action must be taken immediately. I do not know what the future holds for Germany, what it holds for the world and what for the Middle East. Who knows what will happen between the Western powers and Germany? To assume that all kinds of changes may take place, and that the reparations issue alone will remain untouched is utterly improbable. I think that those who are proposing that we wait a few months, though they may be sincere, are irresponsible. Matters such as this cannot be postponed; the time has come for action.

For my part, this is enough reason, and the main reason, for opposing a referendum for it means losing time. Do not assume that should a referendum be held, it would be completed in the space of a few days. It will cost us time. This is my personal opinion; I assume that should this issue of reparations be put before the government, many of its members would oppose it in principle, because a referendum and democracy are not one and the same thing. A referendum does not allow due deliberation. Were a referendum the best way, there would be no need for a parliament.

As to the contention that the German government seeks to link the reparations negotiations with the establishment of diplomatic relations with us, I hereby state that the moment the other party to the reparations negotiations attempts to raise this issue, our delegation will say that it has no authority to discuss it. Should Germany insist on such a demand, our people will suspend the negotiations. That would be a greater blow to Germany than not initiating negotiations because of this issue. I have reason to believe that they are fully aware that there can be no talk of diplomatic relations in this framework. I do not want to say that they don't hold out any hopes of establishing diplomatic relations with us. Of course they do. But they know full well that if they wish to make progress in this matter, they must not raise it now, and if they do, it will be as I say. It stands to reason that if negotiations take place, they will be held in a neutral country.

Chairman Meir Argov: I will now read the government's proposal. Based upon the authority vested in the Committee by the Knesset, and after the committee has heard the preliminary assumptions according to which the government seeks to act, which the foreign minister has stated here – that the negotiations will not take place in Germany, that diplomatic relations will not be established, and so forth – the committee has decided to authorize the government to act on the matter of reparations as it deems fit and in accordance with present needs and circumstances. Once the government has determined its plan of action for the first stage, a report will be submitted to the committee.

MK Zalman Aran: I propose that the phrase, "Including the possibility of direct negotiations" be included.

MK Eliezer Livneh: I propose that the following be included: "On the basis of the government's statement to the Knesset on the matter of our relations with Germany." That statement includes several conditions.

Chairman Meir Argov: The wording will be as follows: On the basis of the government's statement to the Knesset, and on the basis of the authority vested in the Foreign Affairs and Defense Committee by the Knesset, and after the Committee has heard the preliminary assumptions according to which the government seeks to act, the Foreign Affairs and Defense Committee has decided to authorize the government to act on the question of reparations from Germany, including the possibility of direct negotiations, in accordance with present needs and circumstances. Once the government has determined its plan of action for the first stage, a report will be submitted to the Committee.

The vote:
In favor of authorizing the government: 8 votes
Against: 6 votes
The proposal was passed.

[23] The Government is Ready to Enter Negotiations

Cabinet Meeting, 27.1.1952

Minister Moshe Sharett: Regarding the reparations issue, I am of the opinion that we should take action immediately and inform the Bonn government through a proper channel that we are ready to start negotiations. At the same time we should suggest a date, say, between February 15 and 20. We should also appoint a committee that will choose the members of our negotiating delegation.

I would like now to report on our deliberations with the New York Conference of Jewish organizations. They opt for arranging an informal meeting of an appropriate representative, perhaps Dr. Nahum Goldmann, with Chancellor Adenauer, before beginning the negotiations. In a consultation I had on this matter with several people from the Foreign and Finance Ministries, we concluded that we should not participate in such a meeting. We have at our disposal a clear and detailed document signed by Adenauer in which he accepted our claim as the basis for the negotiations. This document has granted us a firm base for starting the negotiations. If, at a later stage, a meeting with Adenauer proves necessary, it would be possible to arrange it, but if we meet with him now this would mean that we do not have complete confidence in the nature of his letter, and this may weaken our position. I informed Dr. Goldmann of this consideration.

It is necessary to begin the negotiations soon, for the London Conference of Creditors is to begin by the end of February, and it is in our clear interest that our claim will not be added to Germany's war debts. Everything possible should be done in order to bring the Germans to take upon themselves at least an initial obligation to us outside of the framework of the London Conference, before it begins.

Initially, I had thought of February 15 as an appropriate date for starting the negotiations, but Dr Goldmann suggested that we first meet with the Jewish organizations and settle matters of procedure and coordination between us. Since I will be in London from February 6, and the Finance Ministry's Director General will be there too, I propose that the cabinet authorizes both of us to meet with the Jewish organizations' representatives who will also be there. I also propose that we leave the matter of a preliminary meeting open with the Germans. If we find it convenient, we may perhaps meet, but even if we do, this should not postpone the start of negotiations.

Prime Minister David Ben Gurion: I suggest that there will not be any preliminary meetings. They will only complicate matters. In view of the London Conference meeting, we should start negotiating as early as possible.

Minister Benzion Dinur: Any unofficial negotiations will only weaken our position. We always said that we will only conduct direct negotiations.

Minister Golda Meir: There is no need to complicate matters by preliminary negotiations. Our line must be clear. In the negotiations we should arrive at only a "Yes" or "No" response. If we get what we want, then very well; if we do not, we should officially declare that they have deceived us. I do not believe that any unofficial contact will be conducive to clearing up the issue. It could only postpone reaching clear results.

Minister Yosef Burg: Contrary to the minister of labor's opinion, I think we should once again find out whether there is a concrete basis for receiving reparations. There are still some unclear issues at hand, such as the form of payments in cash or in goods and the time-span of payments. It is also important that we can inform the Israeli public that it has become clear that the Germans do mean business. I am for a preliminary meeting.

Prime Minister David Ben Gurion: I am against Dr. Goldmann's suggestion for a preliminary meeting. We need no go-between emissaries. There are three questions at hand: how much will they pay to the State of Israel and to the Jewish people; what the form will payment be; and when and over what time-span will the payments be made. Only when we know the answers will we be able to decide on the next steps.

I understand those Jews who oppose direct negotiations psychologically, but our law says that Knesset decisions are made by a majority vote. There was a majority vote in the Knesset on this issue and the matter was clinched. I need no kashrut certificate from anybody. I am kosher as far as I myself am concerned. If nothing comes out of the negotiations, I will not see it as a moral failure on our part. Are we responsible for Germany's behavior? There is no need for any secret meetings behind the scenes. We cannot rely on anybody else. Only we can find out what the chances of our initiative are since only we know what our country's needs are.

Minister Moshe Sharett: I suggest, as a way out, that we do not take a decision on the issue of a preliminary meeting at this juncture. If we do, I will vote against such a meeting. However, since it seems that Adenauer will not be leaving Bonn in the forthcoming weeks, and since nobody suggests that we go to Bonn to meet with him, no decision is necessary now. To be practical, I suggest that we declare our readiness to enter negotiations, choose a date for this purpose, start appointing our delegation's members, and clear up matters with the Jewish organizations. If, during the forthcoming weeks it turns out that a preliminary meeting is possible, we will discuss at the right time.

It was decided:
A.   The foreign minister will examine the background for a preliminary meeting with the Bonn government and will bring the matter to the government before the meeting is arranged.
B.   To appoint the prime minister and Ministers Peretz Naftali, David Pinkas, Eliezer Kaplan and Moshe Sharett as members of the committee to set up the Israeli delegation to the reparations negotiations.

[24] Meeting With a Delegation of the Jewish Organizations

Cabinet Meeting, 17.2.1952[1]

Minister Moshe Sharett: When we initiated the World Jewish Conference in New York, we could not have imagined what difficulties awaited us. Let me remind you when the idea of this conference was first raised: it was when the impact of the reparations claim was at its lowest, the reverberations caused by our reparations initiative had subsided, and it was unclear whether there would be a response from Germany. The governments of the occupying powers did not accept our claim. We sought to reinforce our initiative, to boost it, to generate a response. We thought that if international Jewish organizations from Britain and the United States convened and raised the banner, they would unite around Israel and this would have a potent impact on Germany and the powers. These organizations were fundamentally skeptical about our claim, to put it mildly. Some rejected it because they viewed its basis as flawed. It was not to their liking that the State of Israel was acting on behalf of the entire Jewish people. In any event, there was no enthusiasm about our initiative but rather a cool acknowledgment by the Jewish public.

Something happened between the initiation of the conference and its meeting. When Chancellor Adenauer delivered his speech in the Bundestag, the mood of these organizations changed radically, as they began to believe in the new reality. Adenauer said that the Germans were prepared to talk with representatives of the Jewish people and of Israel. At this stage the organizations voted wholeheartedly in favor of Israel's claim, but now their appetite was whetted, too: "What, are we merely an auxiliary?" they asked. Furthermore, Adenauer's attitude became apparent when he stated that he wanted to talk with representatives of the Jewish people and of Israel, and as a result the representatives of the Jewish people should also have their say.

---

1   Moshe Sharett had returned from a visit to Paris and London. In Paris he met with General Eisenhower and in London with British Foreign Minister Anthony Eden as well as with representatives of Jewish organizations.

When I was in London and I saw that so many Jewish representatives attended, I thought it prudent not to sit alone at the table, and so I summoned Maurice Fischer, our ambassador in Paris, and Dr. Jacob Robinson, to join me. In the meantime, the two negotiators we had appointed arrived.[2] Thus, the delegation of the State of Israel numbered five members. The delegation of the Jewish organizations was twice the size of ours: Jacob Blaustein,[3] Moses Leavitt[4] and Nahum Goldmann were there. The Joint people brought their own experts including some good people, one of them a very able man, Benjamin Ferencz.[5] We held preliminary meetings, official meetings, personal conversations, ate some meals together, and so forth. Activity was quite intense. In brief, there was the question of what they were claiming? Some of them had worked up an appetite to submit a claim parallel to that of the State of Israel. In other words, a vague collective claim for the Jewish people in the Diaspora. That was removed from the agenda, and it was decided that they would make a claim, but it would be a unified one on behalf of individuals who have no heirs.

Perhaps I should explain this further. So far, all the negotiations on the claims have been between Jewish organizations and the *Länder*. There have not yet been any negotiations with the central government. There are individual claims that can only be submitted to the central government. There is the matter of *Judenvermögensabgabe*, or compensation for personal suffering. Here, rehabilitation is imposed on the federal government, not the *Länder*. What was decided is that Jewish organizations should submit this claim to the Bonn government. In other words, the Bonn government must first enact specific legislation. Once that is done, numerous Jews the world over could submit claims. A Jew who paid his tax for getting out of Nazi Germany could now ask for it back. There are also Jews who paid that tax whose payments were recorded but who have no heirs. The regulation regarding property in the *Länder*, such as homes and bank accounts, applies here in a similar way: in cases where there are no heirs, the property is handed over to the inheriting Jewish institutions. So here, too, the institutions must inherit. Numerous claims of Jews who have no heirs are included in this category.

Then the question arose of whether or not to stipulate a sum. Some of the organizations were prepared to do so. But then another question immediately arose: if the Germans pay, we will have become committed to numerous individuals. What do we undertake for them? The organizations' experts figured this out and arrived at two sums. The organizations' claim for sums for plundered property without heirs came to $.5 billion. The total claims of individuals came to

---

2   Dr. Eliezer Felix Shinar and Giora Yoseftal.
3   Jacob Blaustein (1892-1970), head of The American Jewish Committee 1944-1949; AJC's president 1949-1954.
4   Moses A. Leavitt (1894-1965), deputy chairman of the Joint Distribution Committee. Between 1944 and 1945 he served as an advisor to the US War Refugees Board.
5   Benjamin Ferencz, director of JRSO, a special advisor to the Jewish organizations' representatives at the reparations talks.

$.5 million. They were prepared to say to Adenauer: "although you have accepted Israel's claim as the basis, $1 billion, you should know that you must earmark another $1.1 billion." Goldmann fought against this saying that it was liable to ruin the entire claim. The Germans would take fright and say, "We have decided on a certain amount, so divide it up between yourselves." In brief, the following was decided: the overall sum of the individual claims would not be specified. In the meantime they will take action in the *Länder* which will bring that process to completion with the central government. A final Jewish claim will not be formulated with an overall sum.

In fact, our negotiations are unlike theirs. Ours can immediately take a practical turn since our claim has already been accepted in principle. We must, of course, determine the precise sum, over how many years it will be paid, how much in currency and how much in goods, and we must certainly establish a system for this purpose. The Jewish organizations, on the other hand, must first clear the legal aspects with the Germans to ensure that the Germans enact the necessary legislation, and only afterwards will they be able to address the practical aspect.

There was a second question: whether to negotiate by a joint delegation or separate ones? I was in favor of separate ones in order not to blur the special character of our country and its claim. Blaustein supported me from a different viewpoint. The others were skeptical. I suggested that an observer be appointed from the Jewish delegation to our delegation, and an observer from our delegation to theirs. I further stated that I had no doubt that when both delegations reached the practical stage, they would merge. When the level of concretely discussing transfer of currency and goods is reached, there will be no point in talking about it twice.

The general question arose as to what purpose will the money we receive be devoted, and to what purpose will the money they receive be devoted? Regarding our money, an agreement was reached with the Joint Distribution Committee and the Jewish Agency that from the sum we receive, 65 percent will be allocated to the government, 20-25 percent to the Jewish Agency, and 5-10 percent to the Joint, and the Joint and Jewish Agency money will be devoted to Israel. There was a question of reaching a similar arrangement with the money the organizations will receive. I must say that both Blaustein and Leavitt, and needless to say, Nahum Goldmann and Frank Goldmann, as well, adopted the following line without any pressure: we are here to assist the State of Israel and we accept the position of the Israeli foreign minister as decisive. I sought a clear distinction between the individual and collective claims. Blaustein entered into an ideological debate with me. Frank Goldmann said, "I agree, perhaps, with Blaustein, but your view is decisive for me." Without any pressure, they declared that the lion's share of this money would be devoted to Israel. I attempted to establish hard and fast rules, but Nahum Goldmann persuaded me not to raise the issue because he thought it would cause friction between the Joint Distribution Committee and the Jewish Agency on the one hand and the organizations on the other. He added, "Let's not skin the bear before we've trapped it: if it transpires that the Jewish organizations are about to receive a significant sum, there will be time to set fixed rules." Those are the opinions that were voiced. At the conclusion of the meeting, I said that I had heard with great satisfaction the statements by Blaustein, Leavitt and the othersto the effect that the monies should be devoted to the State of Israel.

There was much debating on the question of whether or not to hold a preparatory meeting with the Germans. One of the delegates voiced an extremely rigid line saying that there should be no negotiations before clarifying how much money they would pay, over how many years, and what would the arrangements be for supplying the goods. We must go to Adenauer, present the questions and demand clear answers. I said to him: "What you are proposing means negotiations on condition that they are held with Adenauer. Adenauer might tell you, "I cannot answer your questions. I must first consult with my experts." If you enter into negotiations with Adenauer, the question is whether he will be prepared to negotiate for weeks on end, and then he would be right if he were to say, "I would like to sit down with Ben Gurion or Kaplan." That is not in the best interests of the State of Israel."

Regarding the idea of a preparatory meeting, I explained the position of the majority in the cabinet, which views it as unnecessary. Not only that, we view it as damaging. The Jewish organizations might have need of such a meeting, but the state will not be able to take part in it. There was a period of probing, of feeling out the other side. But from the moment this proposal saw the light of day, and was approved by the Knesset, the state cannot participate in unofficial probing. Everything it does must be done publicly and officially.

In the end it was decided that the Jewish organizations would attempt to test the water. There was a question of who would be appointed to do so. Here Nahum Goldmann insisted, with my support, that he should go alone, although I told him that I had no right to intervene, as it was their executive's business. The alternatives were either Goldmann or a delegation. I said that in my opinion sending a delegation would be humiliating. If Goldmann meets with Adenauer they meet as equals. If a Jewish delegation is sent it would not meet Adenauer as an equal. Practically, that would be valueless, for it would not be a talk that would have any influence, a formal discussion. From the standpoint of its political impression, it would certainly be negative. In the end, the discussion moved on to more limited alternatives, whether Goldmann alone, or Goldmann and Blaustein together, would go. As Adenauer does not speak English, Goldmann would have to translate Blaustein's text. Blaustein tried to convince me to say that he must go. He argued that the American Administration expects him to. To persuade me, he brought along a folder filled with documents proving what he has done for the Jewish people. He has a memo that he presented to Truman. He sought to prove that he had taken part in every stage of the founding of the State of Israel, and that it was he who had helped to obtain the American vote for partition of

Palestine on November 29, 1947. Of course, I did not deny it. I said: "When you went, it was on your own. You went to see McGhee[6] alone. Had Goldmann come to see me at the same time and asked, 'How can you allow Blaustein to go on his own, for he will use it to reinforce the American Jewish Committee's position?' I would have told him that you should go alone." Blaustein is afraid lest Adenauer discover that there is a Jewish Agency, and this is about the Agency's status. I assured him that this has not yet been made public. I added, "Had Goldmann demanded to go with you, I would have said, 'You cannot go. Blaustein should because he enjoys personal access to President Truman. That is what I am telling you now about meeting with Adenauer.'"

Incidentally, I discovered that the first time Goldmann became involved with the reparations was a result of an initiative by Theodor Heuss, the Bonn president. At that time, Heuss was president of the German Palestine Committee. It was Goldmann who broached the matter to him. On numerous occasions they had delivered speeches on the same Zionist platform. When the reparations issue began, Heuss said he wanted to bring Goldmann into the affair (*Prime Minister David Ben Gurion: Did they accept your proposal?*) It came to a vote in their executive, and by a majority of four to one it was decided that Goldmann should go alone. Among those who voted in favor of my proposal was Held, representing the Jewish Labor Committee. He conducts himself admirably, out of a sense of Jewish responsibility and practical understanding of the issue, totally without pomposity. Those in favor were Nahum Goldmann, Frank Goldmann, Held and Leavitt, with Blaustein casting the only dissenting vote. The meeting is to take place in London today, and in fact today we should inform the Germans of our readiness for negotiations and set a date and location. We think that it cannot take place before March 15. We were informed that the Germans are still preparing the material needed for the negotiations.

I would like now to say something we were told by inside sources in Bonn, for whose veracity I cannot be responsible. Their *Wirtschaftsministerium* [Ministry of Economy] is thinking in terms of $700 million as reparations to Israel. We were also told that the Ministry of Finance is insisting on giving us no more than $500 million. Those inside sources advised our people that they must overcome the opposition of the Ministry of Finance, and that only one man will ultimately decide. That man is Adenauer. Therefore we must meet Adenauer and influence him. He is the only one who can say, "This is not a matter for haggling, it is an important matter – we either do it or we don't, and if we do, we must do it fairly. There cannot be an issue of $200 million more or $200 million less. It must be done generously." In order not to leave the outcome to a clash between the Ministries of Economy and Finance, and in view of the fact that the

---

6   George C. McGhee, oil industrialist. From 1949 to 1951 he served as a special assistant to
     the American undersecretary of state.

Ministry of Finance does not accept the maximum we are claiming, we must put as much as possible pressure on Adenauer.

I would like to bring up another interesting fact. Attempts are already being made by German firms and corporations to offer goods, materials and machinery to Israeli firms on credit, so that payment will come from the reparations. When I asked why they are in such a hurry and why they don't wait until the deal is approved, I was told that they want to get into the market. In any event, it shows that they are confident that reparations will be paid.

[25] Facing the Delay in the Negotiations

Cabinet Meeting, 6.4.1952

Minister Moshe Sharett: The situation in Wassenaar is not so simple. Even before the negotiations began, it had become clear that Bonn is divided between two camps: one politically-oriented and one financially-oriented. The outlook of Adenauer, his chief political adviser Herbert Blankenhorn and Professor Böhm[1] about reparations is a political-moral one. They view the whole matter as obligatory, and therefore they want to conclude the matter generously and on a broad scale. In contrast, from the side of the finance people, the contention is that Germany lacks such huge resources, and that it cannot afford to take upon itself these obligations, all the more so in view of financial burdens accruing from the London Conference of Creditors.

I must confess I was worried about this all the time, particularly because of the many weeks that have passed with no action since the Knesset at long last approved our entry into negotiations. True, the delay was caused by our involvement with the Jewish Organization's conference. My fear was that if our negotiations would start at the same time as the London Conference, our position would deteriorate, and indeed this is what has happened.

When negotiations began, we broached our case with an announcement, as did the German delegation. They based their position only on Adenauer's announcement in the Bundestag – not on his letter to Goldmann – and they suddenly remembered Germany's ability to pay and referred to their agreement with the London Conference of Creditors. In view of this, we began consultations in which Goldmann participated, and decided to respond strongly. Dr. Yoseftal delivered a sharply-worded speech in which he said, "Ours is a unique case and this uniqueness is the root of the whole matter; we were given a clear undertaking

---

1   Franz Böhm (1895-1977), politician, lawyer and economist. Headed the German delegation to the reparations' negotiations in Wassenaar. He was associated with the resistance movement in Nazi Germany. In 1938 he was dismissed from his post as a university lecturer because of his opposition to discrimination against German Jews.

from the chancellor, in which he accepted our claim as the basis for negotiations, and that obligation is not conditional upon Germany's ability to pay or any agreement with the London Conference of Creditors. Furthermore, it was on the basis of that obligation that our government asked for the approval of our parliament, which it succeeded in attaining with much difficulty. Changing the negotiations' basis now is out of the question."

The Germans then asked for a break, and after an hour-and-a-half returned and announced that they would give us an answer the next day. They immediately added that even though a clash appeared to have occurred between the two delegations, they did not view it as a rift; they are confident that there is mutual understanding. Second, they are of the opinion that it would be possible to reach an agreement at this stage of the negotiations, not about the total sum but perhaps about the timetable of payments, but this depends on the London Conference. On the next day they handed our delegation a written, more flexible announcement.

It was clear that they have no interest in a breakdown of negotiations. We then began discussing the dimensions of our claim and how it would be realized, in cash or in goods. They received written documents from us in which the basis for our claim was put at $1 billion.

It was certainly appropriate that one of the chief members of our delegation, Giora Yoseftal, who serves as the director of the Jewish Agency's Department of Immigrant Absorption, and is himself German-born. In an incisive lecture, he described the plight of the camp survivors and their horrific march to the Mediterranean ports, their voyage to Israel and the difficulties entailed in their absorption; he also described the true meaning of the enormous undertaking of absorbing 500,000 war refugees who arrived empty-handed in the State of Israel after their property was plundered. He stressed the difficulty of their absorption in a country which is only now beginning its development.

When the negotiations began, the atmosphere was extremely tense and rigid. At the first meeting, there was no hand-shaking. Psychologically, the Germans were in great distress. When Gershon Avner[2] read out our opening announcement, which included a major part of our description of the Holocaust from our memorandum to the powers, only one member of the German delegation sat stony-faced – all the others lowered their faces to the ground. They were utterly dejected. In the course of time the ice began to thaw a little. When one of our delegation's members died in a tragic air crash, Professor Böhm expressed his sorrow upon hearing what happened in most touching words, to which our people responded, and so the atmosphere became less icy.

---

2   Gershon Avner (1919-1991). Joined the Israel Foreign Office in 1948. From 1949 served as head of the foreign ministry's West-European department. In 1952 was a member of Israel's delegation to the reparations' negotiations in Wassenaar. Later served as an ambassador to various countries.

After deliberating the needs of absorbing the immigrants, the Germans tried to challenge the number of 500,000 immigrants, contending that it should include only immigrants who survived the Holocaust. Our response to this contention was fierce and they waived their demand.

A difficulty arose when the subject of the sum of the reparations came up for discussion. They claimed that they are not authorized to inform us of the sum, contending that their government is not yet ready to divulge it. Meanwhile, however, the sum the German government has in mind became known to us – it is $750 million. The question is whether that sum will go to the State of Israel and in addition there will be something more for the Jewish people, or whether that is the total sum. This is still unclear.

Yesterday I tried to contact Goldmann by telephone but to no avail. Later I cabled him that he should contact Adenauer and tell him that his integrity, and our integrity in the eyes of our voters, are now being tested. His obligation was the act that triggered the whole process. It was on the basis of that act that we entered the negotiations. If he succumbs to internal German pressures, we will put the blame on him for making us enter negotiations on a false promise.

Minister Eliezer Kaplan: I propose that we act according to our intuition. There is no need for sharp rebukes. We should simply tell them "We came here in view of Adenauer's obligation. There is no point in sitting here as long as we do not hear your answer regarding the sum of the reparations according to what was promised. We are returning home. When you have something to announce, we will consider the offer."

Minister Levi Eshkol: I must admit I do not see any sense in demonstrating such anger. We are demanding $1 billion from West Germany. We are negotiating with a country: they contend that they still have to clarify several matters. Let them do so. Why should we claim that they are not willing to honor their promise? It is too early to show anger.

Minister Moshe Shapira: If we say we are continuing the negotiations, the opposition can raise the question in the Knesset; and I am afraid it might attain a majority against the government in the voting. Outwardly we need to create an impression that we see no sense in continuing negotiations under the present circumstances. Our delegation should return home.

Minister Moshe Sharett: We must avoid two extremes: one is cutting off all ties with the other side, and relieving it of any responsibility, thus letting it evade the whole matter of reparations. The other extreme is accepting whatever the other side is saying. We should not talk about a complete end of the negotiations, as if all has come to naught. On the other hand, we cannot agree to wait six or eight weeks. In order to shorten the current debate, I propose that we make the following announcement: "The government of Israel entered negotiations on the basis of a clear obligation by the other side. In the course of negotiations, the other side advanced several qualifications which were unknown to the government of Israel when it entered negotiations. Moreover, the German delegation is not prepared to declare its position; it proposes delaying negotiations for a certain period of time. At this stage and under these circumstances, we believe that the negotiations should cease. Renewal of negotiations is thus incumbent on the other side and is conditional on the proposals it is able to produce."

Minister Yitzhak Meir Levin: Why should we mention the renewal of negotiations in our announcement?

Minister Moshe Sharett: Because I want them to be renewed. I propose that we consult the Prime Minister on this matter and that a committee of three – Ministers Kaplan, Shapira and I – will draft the government's final announcement.

It was decided:
A ministerial committee will draft an announcement to be transmitted to the German delegation by the Israeli delegation to the negotiations. The committee members: Ministers Kaplan, Shapira and Sharett.

[26] The Israeli Delegation Reports

Knesset Foreign Affairs and Defense Committee Meeting, 15.4.1952

Chairman Meir Argov: I welcome the foreign minister on his return from his tour in Europe and Mr. Gershon Avner, a member of our delegation to the reparations negotiations.

Minister Moshe Sharett: I propose that we open this meeting with Mr. Avner's report on the progress of the reparation negotiations. May I stress that the proceedings of the present meeting must be kept completely secret. The report you will hear must not reach the press.

Gershon Avner: I am confident that members of this committee will be pleased to hear that the Israeli delegation functioned with dignity and pride. We maintained our distance from the members of the German delegation while they tried to make personal contacts with us, both inside and outside the meeting room. Our tone of speech was incisive, and always that of a prosecutor. We had several dramatic meetings; the opening session was the most dramatic and tense of them, with not even one superfluous word spoken.

Our third meeting too was rather dramatic, especially when the Germans raised questions about the expense of immigrant absorption, and the number of immigrants who were Nazi victims. Giora Yoseftal retorted with a short but very forceful speech which he concluded by saying, "To sum up, this debate is over. You have no right to ask more questions on this subject!" He thus put an immediate end to that debate.

We know that the Germans were surprised by our emphatic behavior. Opposite them sat a group of young men, well-versed in the subject matter, fully aware of what they hope to achieve, expressing themselves coherently and methodically. Delegates of the Jewish organizations were most appreciative of our dignified stance vis-à-vis the Germans. At the same time, we praised the earnest and dignified behavior of their delegation: all its members, Zionist and non-Zionist alike, behaved as Jews rather than as Americans. At a certain moment, when the Germans said to them, "But you are Americans; you should be loyal to America first," they responded "We came here as Jews. We are submitting Jewish claims." May I add that the members of this delegation proved very efficient and demonstrated great expertise. They functioned as a solid group, not as a collection of individuals, each representing a different organization, the result being complete and earnest cooperation with us. Their delegates willingly recognized the primacy of the Israeli delegation. This was also abundantly clear to the Germans. They said to us, "You are the striking force of the Jewish people. We are more interested in reaching an agreement with you than reaching an agreement with the Jewish organizations."

I now turn to the negotiations proper. I doubt if anyone among the supporters of direct negotiations had thought that they would be a simple matter – the Germans would come, propose a payment of $1 billion at the first or second meeting, and then discuss the process of payment. We at the Israeli delegation had a different outlook. We were aware that while Adenauer accepted our claim as the basis for the negotiations, the process itself would not be smooth, pleasant and speedy. Even at our first meeting, it became clear that the Germans wanted to link the payment to Israel with other payments that would have to be channeled to their creditors from the London Conference.

At the second meeting with the Germans in London, a hard and bitter debate ensued at the end of which we succeeded in reaching a satisfactory solution: the final sum would be agreed upon at an appropriate stage at our meetings in Wassenaar; the procedure of the payment would be determined after Bonn would have a complete picture of its debts to the London Conference of Creditors.

At the end of the first week of our talks in Wassenar, it became apparent that a grim struggle was taking place in Bonn about determining the final sum. The German finance ministers came out strongly against Adenauer and the German delegation to the reparations talks. They contended that the sum must be determined in accordance with the outcome of the London Conference of Creditors, and they succeeded in convincing Adenauer to agree with their position. The chief German negotiators at Wassenar, Professor Böhm and Dr. Kuster, both well-known anti-Nazis and fighters against anti-Semitism, then came to us and said, "We accept the principle of your claim being unique, but Germany has only one treasury, only one system of taxing, and thus it cannot pay any of its debts without taking into consideration all its other debts." We opposed this contention, which meant a differentiation between the admitted sum in principle and the concrete sum to be paid, and our opposition has created the impasse which we are now facing.

To sum up, there is a consensus among our delegation's members that reparations are certainly within our grasp, that both German politicians and financial experts agree in principle that reparations must be paid. The struggle going on in Bonn is between Adenauer and his aides, whose wish is to expedite the procedure and pay a maximal sum and the finance people, who aim at a smaller sum and a more favorable, convenient payment procedure. We are thus facing a long and hard struggle.

Foreign Minister Moshe Sharett: I would like to add a few explanatory remarks. First, when we demanded $1 billion from the Bonn government, it was not our intention to receive only that sum, and by no means a lesser one. I think this was clear, and if not, I want it to be clear now. We demanded all in all $1.5 billion based on our immigrant absorption expenditure. We thought that such a base would be well-accepted by German public opinion as well as by the world at large. We could, of course, base our claim differently, without mentioning the immigrant absorption expenditure at all, but our aim was not just to make a historic declaration vis-à-vis Germany; our aim was to achieve concrete results, and consequently we had to take world public opinion into consideration. Indeed, basing our claim as we did proved correct. Responses everywhere indicated that this argument was a strong one, or even the only possible one, since world public opinion is not over-impressed by our other arguments.

There was also another consideration in determining the sum to be claimed, a tactical one. We were aware that the financial damage caused by the Nazis to our people was much larger, but at the same time we deemed it necessary to advance a claim which had a chance of being accepted. We realized that otherwise our claim would sound immense, submitted by unrealistic people living in an imaginary world. Thus, although the damage has been estimated by the World Jewish Congress experts at $6 billion – sometime afterwards they arrived at an even greater estimate – we realized that this sum had no chance of being accepted as a basis for our claim. On the other hand, the expenditure for absorption sounded reasonable, and since one-third of the claim was left for East Germany to pay, the final sum we demanded from West Germany was reduced to $1 billion. Even so, I must admit that this sum of $1 billion was still seen by non-Germans as unbelievable, and that is the opinion of the White House and State Department circles to this very day.

When Adenauer said he was prepared to accept our claim as a basis for negotiations, we did not by any means take it as an obligation to pay that specific sum, for otherwise he would have said straight out that he accepted that sum. Saying he accepts it as a basis meant conducting negotiations. At the end of a series of probing questions, when it became apparent that the Germans were prepared to pay hundreds, not tens of millions, we said that the road to negotiations was open, and this was reinforced by Adenauer's letter in which he clearly accepted our claim as the basis for negotiations.

When the German delegation in Wassenaar announced that they were going to recommend to their government the payment of $750 million, we accepted it as a roughly appropriate response to our claim. We did not see that as a default on an obligation. If 100 is the basis for negotiations, and as a result of these negotiations 75 is offered, proportionally that is quite a high percentage and in fact quite a high sum. In view of the world's general financial situation, a German obligation to pay $750 million to the State of Israel is a tremendous achievement. It was not here that the turn-about occurred, that is not in reducing the amount from a $1 billion to $750 million, but in the complete change expressed in differentiating between the sum that the Germans acknowledge is due and the sum that they said they were prepared to actually pay according to their financial ability.

In this context I would like to say something about the London Conference. We started dealing with the reparations claim long before the conference convened, but once it was announced, I became anxious to expedite the process. I had already said in the meeting of this committee on January 15 that we should definitely not delay our action in this sphere lest we miss the opportune hour. Even then I foresaw the potential danger of both our negotiations and those of the London Conference taking place simultaneously.

Why had the negotiations not started earlier? Because of the solidarity established between us and the Jewish organizations. It took weeks till agreements were reached between us and the organizations and among the various organizations themselves. Altogether, their pace was much slower than ours, for on each step to be taken they had first to consult together and only then reach a consensus.

MK Peretz Bernstein (*General Zionists*): When the foreign minister announced that Adenauer's government accepted our claim for $1 billion as the basis for negotiations with us, I remarked that had they offered a smaller sum I would have seen it as more serious response since I was cognizant of Germany's historic stratagems when it evaded payment of compensation after WW I.

Not one of us here would say that payment of $750 million instead of $1 billion can be considered a failure. However, it seems that the technique of Schacht, that financial genius, in evading payment of compensation was learned well. Apparently there is a division of labor between the German delegation and the German financial people. They are playing the old game of "good cop, bad cop." It may well be that the delegation's members were directed to play the part of the decent ones.

The question now is, should we continue negotiating? I assume that even if they now suggest a smaller sum, they will not pay it. Perhaps they would pay one or two installments, and by then – who knows – Adenauer may go, Germany's unification could be put on the agenda, new general elections could be held, and the reparations agreement would remain on paper only.

I propose that the government does not continue negotiations.

MK Yitzhak Ben Aharon (*Mapam*): Continuation of negotiations would not only be a crime against Jewish history; it would also make us seem ridiculous before our public and the world-at-large. I would like to reiterate that our party opposed negotiations both in principle and in practice. We not only contended that we should not be in contact with Germany, which is a resumption of Nazi Germany but argued that nothing concrete would result from the negotiations. We will not get money for rehabilitation purposes.

It has become clear by now that the government entered negotiations based on misinformation. The government's assumption that our claim would be considered *sui generis* was unfounded. It has become obvious that Germany is going to combine its debt to Israel with the debts it owes to the creditors. I was informed by Mr. Avner that the Western powers first demanded the amount of $3 billion, and then went down to $2-2.5 billion. It is an unbelievable assumption that America, France and Britain would agree that Germany would pay them $2 billion while paying $1 billion – one-third of the total amount – to the State of Israel. I contend that what Israel will receive would be just a small fraction, and that this small sum would be paid over 10-15 years. It means that the sum we would in fact receive would be negligible.

In view of all this, there is no sense in going back to Wassenaar. The minimum that can be asked now is that the government rescue us from the shame of begging. It must realize that negotiations have ended. Later, when Germany advances new proposals, the government could consider them, but now the matter should be brought back to the Knesset since its decision in favor of entering negotiations was based on assumptions that were proved wrong.

Moreover, the present international situation favors Germany, since both world camps are courting it, and thus its political need of a settlement with the Jewish people has dramatically decreased. There is now no chance that America would put pressure to bear on Germany in our favor. And the East has no interest in doing that. Consequently, the move you have taken has bogged down. It is now vital to put a stop to the negotiations process.

I think that all Knesset factions will now reconsider the whole matter, and I doubt whether the government will succeed in getting a majority this time. I hope not.

MK Zalman Aran (*Mapai*)**:** I am in favor of continuing negotiations and against bringing the matter before the Knesset. It is too early. Negotiations should be continued while our delegation retains its dignity and strives to reach its aim. I cannot deride accepting a sum of hundreds of millions of dollars which are needed by the State of Israel.

I reject the moral right of Mapam – a party identifying itself with the Soviet Union which pardons former Nazi officials – to argue against negotiations. I also reject the assumption that in view of the present international situation, our claim has no chance of a response. I still remember your claim in the late 40s that because of the international situation there was no chance for the establishment of a Jewish State.

When the government brought the matter of direct negotiations with Germany before the Knesset, it did not promise victory. It clearly said no one can be assured of positive results, but that making an attempt wuold be worthwhile. This attempt has not yet come to an end.

I understand the opposition is now celebrating the possible failure of these negotiations. I propose that we do not succumb to this mood. Let us continue, with dignity and courage, with these negotiations, and time will tell.

MK Yizhar Harari (*Progressives*)**:** My negative position regarding direct negotiations is well-known, but I am of the opinion that once the Knesset decided to enter negotiations, we all want them to succeed.

I think that we have reached a stage in which we should inform the Germans that if their debt to us is conditional upon payments to their Western creditors, there is no sense in continuing negotiations. If the Germans are really sincere in wanting to pay us, they would not give up that willingness because we discontinue negotiations. The chances are that they will accept our conditions.

MK Yohanan Bader (*Herut*)**:** The Germans' interest was, first and foremost, establishing direct contact with us. They were also interested in showing us good will. However, they were not interested in paying, certainly not out of their own pocket. Historic experience testifies to that. In line with this mood, Professor Böhm showed a maximum of good will for a cheap price. First they agreed on $750 million. Now, in London, a lesser sum will be discussed, and then they will ask that we be paid first, thus earning the good will of influential Jews abroad. I think we should believe Schacht,[1] who recently said that the "Germans have good intentions, but no ability." Had the government taken his words seriously, it would not have entered into negotiations.

I think the present situation is very serious indeed, but it is now possible to get out of this matter with a modicum of dignity by putting an end to negotiations and doing that with a thunderclap.

MK George Flesh (*General Zionists*)**:** I would like to ask the foreign minister what is, in his opinion, the minimal sum upon which we would be prepared to agree? We submitted a claim for $1.5 billion. We gave up $500 million on account of East Germany. Now we are told that we could conclude an agreement on $750 million. Where will the limit be drawn?

---

1   Hjalmar Schacht (1877-1970). German economist and banker. president of the Reichsbank under the Weimar Republic, federal minister of economics between 1934 and 1937. Was one of the primary architects of Germany's policy of redevelopment, reindustrialization and rearmament. Dismissed from the cabinet due to his differences with Hitler and other prominent Nazis in 1939. Arrested in 1944 by the Nazis, accused of taking part in the 20 July plot and ended World War II in a concentration camp.

I understand that the whole matter is soon to be deliberated and decided by the cabinet. I, too, propose that that the matter should be brought back to the Knesset after the cabinet's decision is made known. Therefore I propose that the Foreign Affairs and Security Committee reconvene before the matter is brought back to the Knesset.

Minister Moshe Sharett: This meeting is taking place before the cabinet has had time to convene and hear the delegation's report and reach a decision. Therefore, I cannot answer the various questions raised here. I can only bring the many opinions expressed here to the attention of the cabinet.

Nevertheless, I would like to say what the government's considerations could be. The government's intention in these negotiations, in submitting its claim, was to receive compensation of hundreds of million dollars from Germany. I cannot say exactly how much more. During negotiations, a new approach by the other side became apparent. The personal experience I have gained in past negotiations has taught me that there have never been serious political negotiations during which prior assumptions were not adjusted. Along the way from claim to implementation, facts unclear at the beginning become obvious, and in the meantime the general background of reality undergoes changes while new factors enter the scene. This is what happened during the reparations negotiations too.

However, the very fact that changes occurred should not deter us from our endeavor as long as chances of attaining our goal still exist. On the contrary, it is clear that had we not advanced our claim and then begun to carry it out, we could have remained indifferent to results, and said that our aim was to discontinue negotiations; indeed, this aim of achieving nothing would have been 100 percent successful. We took a different path. We said, let us make an effort aimed at achieving something positive, and hence we knowingly risked being faced with changes and surprises, for the road of action is forever fraught with changes and surprises.

One of the facts which has become decidedly obvious, although it was known beforehand, was that various forces are at work inside Germany, and that an internal struggle continues there between – in our traditional terminology – Zionist and non-Zionist forces: there are those Germans who deny any need to listen to us, and who therefore endeavor to pay the lowest sum possible; there are those Germans whose approach is based on a historic awareness and on an understanding of Germany's future interests and therefore admit Germany's obligation towards the Jewish people, and push for early payment on a large scale.

Now, if we aim at a concrete achievement, we should naturally try to strengthen one camp as much as possible and weaken the other. It may well be that by raising the slogan of discontinuing negotiations we will weaken the positive camp and strengthen the negative one. This slogan might also make it easier for the Western powers to stand aloof. At the same time, we cannot assume that the pro-reparations camp will defeat its rival all by itself; outside pressure must be brought to bear, along with action aimed at strengthening it.

We are facing a delicate moment. It stands to reason that we should announce our position; we could say that they, the Germans, are expected to reveal something by a certain date. Perhaps we do not have to commit ourselves to continue negotiating, but we also do not have to decide to discontinue. We could perhaps say that a certain stage of negotiations has ended, but we will not sever contact in order to evoke internal pressure in Germany so that they come out with a new proposal, and if that proposal is below a certain minimum we can always say "No." But first let us try all possible means of pressure with the purpose of influencing them to advance a final, acceptable proposal.

These considerations lead to drawing a certain line. Perhaps we will say nothing and wait till a certain date and then, when they advance a proposal, consider accepting it, or not. By saying this I am not expressing the government's position. I only outline a possible government position.

Chairman MK Meir Argov (*Mapai*): Since the foreign minister has to leave, I suggest that we discontinue the debate and start voting on the various proposals at hand.

MK Zalman Aran (*Mapai*): I doubt whether the committee can arrive at a decision today. I think the time is not yet ripe for decision. I propose that we convene again after the cabinet meeting.

MK Yaakov Riftin (*Mapam*): The foreign minister said here that he would like to know the Committee's opinion, and that can be ascertained only by taking a vote. Moreover, some Committee members have not yet spoken. I see no alternative but to vote on the various proposals.

MK Shalom Zysman (*General Zionists*): The committee is a sovereign body. Its sovereignty would be harmed if it does not sum up its opinion by taking a vote.

Chairman MK Meir Argov (*Mapai*): I put two proposals to the vote: one is for immediately voting on the various proposals. The other is to postpone voting until the next committee meeting.

The vote:
For the first proposal: 6
For the second proposal: 7
It was decided to postpone voting on the various proposals till the next Committee meeting.

[27] Waiting for a German Initiative

Mapai Political Committee Meeting, 5.5.1952

Moshe Sharett: I would like to open my report with a short remark about the current situation of the reparations negotiations. In my opinion, this meeting can make no decision. The government also cannot make one, and neither can the Knesset. Our decision will be made when Germany states clearly whether it will pay or it will not pay, how much it will pay and by what method. Only then should the decision be made whether to accept or reject it.

How did this matter of reparations unfold? First, there was our claim to the occupying powers. It had no effect and the matter stagnated. That was the first stage. In the second stage, we had various unofficial contacts with the Bonn government. As a result of these contacts, as well as of our request to the powers and of mind-searching and deliberations which took place inside Bonn government circles – the Social Democratic Party also had part in this process – as did reports on the Jewish and international public opinion response to Bonn, sent by Germany's representatives abroad – Chancellor Adenauer announced his willingness to pay reparations to the Jewish people. He immediately linked payment to the financial ability of the German people, and announced his readiness to negotiate with representatives of the Jewish people and the State of Israel.

His statement came also as a result of our request to the powers and as a result of mind-searching and deliberations in Bonn government circles. The Social Democratic Party also had a part in it, as well as various representatives of the Bonn government in Western capitals who report on Jewish and international public opinion responses.

There was an intermediate stage between these two in which the government of Israel, through the Jewish Agency, initiated a World Jewish Conference on this question. Its aim was to get the matter moving, to revive public interest and focus attention on it, and also to voice the interest of the Jewish people to the powers. Our aim was also to enlist American, British and French Jewry as well as to engage Germany so that it would become aware that this was not only the claim of a country in the Middle East that had to be dealt with but one with a universal constituency.

Adenauer's statement, made between the initiation and the convening of Conference of Jewish Organizations, established a new context. From a conference whose aim was solely to exert political pressure, it became a body representing concrete claimants of the Jewish people. Thus the matter became somewhat complicated, although not seriously, for now two bodies of claimants had formed. It was here that the third stage began. We said that Adenauer's statement in which he accepted our demand in principle was insufficient. It is nebulous and abstract and says nothing clearly, and we cannot enter negotiations on its basis. I would like to elucidate what I said to the cabinet: the entire question is whether Germany understands that it must pay hundreds of millions of dollars, or if it thinks it can acquit itself by paying only tens of millions of dollars. Consequently, we decided to clarify matters. There was the phase of unofficial contact with Adenauer himself as a result of which he sent a letter to Goldmann who had been elected chairman of the Jewish Conference and was accorded special status regarding this issue. His status was not just that of another Zionist leader, but that of an official, authorized figure enjoying the trust of the government of Israel. Adenauer's letter stated that Germany accepts the claim Israel presented to the powers as the basis for negotiations. The letter also alluded to Adenauer's statement to the Bundestag, and this had effective value in view of Germany's reservations about their capability of paying the sum they had acknowledged was due.

What was our response to this development? By no means did we accept the wording that they accept our claim as a basis for negotiations. We did not see it as undertaking to pay us $1 billion. Had Adenauer wanted to undertake payment he could have said, "I accept this claim," and not say, "I accept this claim as a basis for negotiation." Since he said "I accept it as a basis for negotiation," it meant it could be more, but it could also be less. Then we had the Knesset debate early in January. The government proposed what it proposed, the Knesset approved what it approved and we dispatched a delegation. Negotiations were conducted in the town of Wassenaar, near The Hague, during which several facts emerged.

Here I must make some preliminary remarks. Before the Wassenaar negotiations got under way, a conference convened in London, attended by Germany's creditors: banks and governmental institutions that had previous claims against Germany for monies they had lent Germany. This mainly touched upon Germany's debts from before the world war, but it also included several loans taken out by post-war Germany. As we were aware that this conference would soon take place, we tried to accelerate the Wassenaar negotiations, but our partnership with the Jewish organizations and our own unavoidable parliamentary processes in the Knesset and the Foreign Affairs and Defense Committee brought about a delay; this is always the price one has to pay for democracy's inefficiency.

Had it not been for the parliamentary process and the linkage with the Jewish conference, we could have started negotiating two months earlier, before the London conference convened.

From the outset, when we sat at the same table with the Germans in Wassenaar, they linked their undertaking to pay with two provisos: first, the German people's ability to pay, as mentioned in Adenauer's first statement; and second, the overall agreement they would reach with their creditors in London. I will not go into all the stories, the language spoken, did they smile or did not smile – we can skip over all that; it is a story that has no place in a political report.

On the issue of the ability to pay, a serious conflict arose in Wassenaar from which three positions emerged:

1. The Israeli delegation demanded an immediate and decisive commitment by Germany regarding the entire sum to be paid and how long it would take, and then moved on to the details of how much would be paid in currency, what amount would be in goods, and so forth.

2. The German delegation, or the majority of it, was represented by the head of their delegation, Professor Franz Böhm. He personally relied upon Adenauer, and perhaps upon a circle around him, particularly from the German Foreign Ministry. An intermediate position was formulated: it proposed the acceptance of payment of a certain sum regardless of the London Conference, and as far as possible to move the negotiations forward but not without a possible combination within the general framework of the German payments to the London creditor's conference.

3. The German delegation to the London conference, relying on the Bonn government's financial circles, argued that there was no possibility of binding the German government to something unrelated to the London settlement because there was no possibility of reaching a later settlement with the London Conference after an unrelated commitment had been given to us. In other words, the third position relies on simple logic. It says, "We admit we owe you a certain sum, but that does not mean we are able to pay it."

It is clear that we should have created an uproar over the reduction of the original sum to $750 million. In the interest of strengthening our position, it was not good that the Israeli press would take a positive view of the Germans' willingness to pay only $750 million. However, Israeli public opinion took the German position most seriously – it was shocked by Germany's readiness to pay $750 million only. How could it be? Germany owes us $1 billion and we are to loose $250 million?

Let me say frankly: had this matter been concluded with their agreement to $750 million, and then actually paying this entire sum, I would have viewed that result as a resounding success. Our agreement to 75 percent and not to 100 percent should not be viewed as revoking our word about our claim as a basis for negotiation.

For what is the crux of the matter? We adopted a certain basis for our claim. We said, "The 500,000 Jews we have absorbed into Israel cost us approximately that sum." The Germans could have argued, "You think that each person cost you whatever sum you say? But that is not exactly so." Or, they could have said: "Are you including the Jews of Romania and Bulgaria? We do not admit that they were all ruined by Hitler. We admit to three-quarters of them." They would have had a point here. Or they simply could have said, "You are claiming $1 billion? We are giving you $750 million. Isn't that fair?" The point is not the reduction in the sum, but the distinction between what they owe and what they could pay.

We have informed them that this is not in accordance with their commitment. We entered the negotiations on the basis of clear commitments. Otherwise, we would not have entered them. There is something deceitful here. Adenauer has put his name to it. This is simply not possible! On the face of it, we have suspended the negotiations, although in fact negotiations would have been suspended anyway due to the Passover recess. Anyway, there are no negotiations now, and we have gone back to unofficial contacts. One meeting between Goldmann and Adenauer has already taken place, and the second one was postponed until after the Zionist Executive Conference in mid-May.

The comings and goings within the German camp continue incessantly. Reshuffling occurs, and people move from camp to camp. There is a strong tendency in the German government to return to the basis of determining a specific sum unconnected to the London Conference, and to say, "We must undertake to pay such-and-such a sum to the Jewish people." It is clear that it will not be $750 million. On the other hand, some contend that this cannot be done without connecting it with the London Conference. This internal struggle in Bonn is still going on, and in my opinion nothing can be decided at the moment. The only decision that can be made is the complete cessation of negotiations and foregoing the entire matter. I am not even considering that solution. Nothing has happened that would justify it. I stand by my opinion: if we succeed in obtaining a sum of hundreds of millions, not tens of millions of dollars, then it is certainly worth our while. The process of Germany's reintroduction into the world is progressing; Germany is a member of equal standing in the West, and it is about to enter the Atlantic Alliance. The question is not whether we should delay this process or not, whether we should isolate Germany or not, but rather whether we will be isolating ourselves. The question is whether we can sell our acceptance of Germany's entrance into the world with full equal rights for a certain price to benefit Israel and the Jewish people. In my opinion we must obtain whatever we can from this.

I would like to add that we cannot rely on much assistance from the Western powers, especially America, for America is also part of the creditors' conference in London, and America although does not want the arrangement between Germany and Israel to be at its expense, in one form or another it must be at its expense. Germany knows this full well. It wants us to enlist American aid for Germany, and it wants America to free its frozen assets. All that is at America's expense. America is telling us, "You have our blessing, but on condition that Germany pays from within Germany, and not with our money that is in our hands."

I will not go into those details, which are extremely complex. I would like to state clearly that if America is paying lip service to the Germans and telling them "You have to arrange this," it is not exerting serious pressure on Germany to that end. It depends mainly on the feelings of the Bonn government about the importance of clearing this account with the Jewish people and the State of Israel. Moral factors are constantly at work here, as well as factors that are not moral but political and commercial alike. Undoubtedly, another consideration here is that if they pay us in goods it means that then perhaps they will be able to enter the Middle East market if there will ever be peace between Israel and the Arab states. There can be no doubt of this. At this point, considerations about the ability to pay are at work as well as arrangements with other creditors, about avoiding excessive reparations, about the status of the Bonn government within Germany, how these considerations can be used against the government, and so forth. It is a battle, it is a contentious political-financial matter, and we must strive to achieve the best possible results. The time of decision cannot be expedited. The stratagem must be to hold the Sword of Damocles – cessation of the negotiations – over their heads, in order to arrive at maximum results.

In any event, the pressure and contacts we have at our disposal include negotiations with the German Social Democrats. We should seek the assistance of this element, which is constantly growing inside West Germany. The Germans should be aware that we are awaiting the outcome of this internal struggle and looking forward to hearing their final word. From the parliamentary standpoint, we have no right to take the initiative. Should there be an initiative, it should come from Germany. Therefor we must undoubtedly remove from the agenda the demand to cease the negotiations.

[Following a discussion in which seven members of the political committee participated, Foreign Minister Moshe Sharett stated,]

I submit that we accept the proposal voiced by one of the speakers that the discussion of this matter, to take place tomorrow in the Knesset's Foreign Affairs and Defense Committee, should conclude with a decision that negotiations will not be renewed until Germany makes a clear statement. I think that would be an appropriate and beneficial solution, both internally and outwardly.

Chairman Meir Argov: There are two proposals:
  A.   The Foreign Affairs and Defense Committee concludes that at this stage, the negotiations should not be renewed until a new statement from Germany is received. This decision will be brought before the Knesset

in a statement on behalf of the Foreign Affairs and Defense Committee against the opposition's proposals. Furthermore, the foreign minister will respond not in a statement but as a participant in the debate.

B. In his reply to the Knesset after the debate of the proposals for the agenda, the foreign minister will announce that a statement on this matter will be forthcoming in the near future, and that then a debate will be possible.

The vote:

For proposal A: 13
For proposal B: 1
Proposal A was accepted.

*

The Knesset Foreign Affairs and Defense Committee convened again on May 6, and after discussing the current situation of the reparations negotiations, the following decision was accepted by a vote of 7 against 6:

The Committee recommends to the government non-renewal of the negotiations between the Israeli and West German delegations until the Bonn government submits a clear and binding proposal to meet Israel's claim for reparations, including dates of payment.

The Committee expresses its confidence that it will be given the opportunity of discussing such a proposal prior to a final government decision on whether to accept or reject the proposal.

[28] No Compromise on Reparations[1]

Knesset Session 77, 6.5.1952

Speaker Ze'ev Sheffer: Chairman of the Foreign Affairs and Defense Committee has the floor.

MK Meir Argov (*Chairman of the Foreign Affairs and Defense Committee, Mapai*)**:** Mr. Speaker, members of the Knesset, On 15.1.52 the Foreign Affairs and Defense Committee made the following decision: "Following the government's statement to the Knesset and the authority vested in the Foreign Affairs and Defense Committee by the Knesset, and after the committee heard the preliminary assumptions according to which the government seeks to act, the Foreign Affairs and Defense Committee decides to authorize the government to act on the question of reparations from Germany, including the possibility of direct negotiations, in accordance with present needs and circumstances. Once the government has determined its plan of action for the first stage, a report will be submitted to the Committee."

In accordance with that decision, the Foreign Affairs and Defense Committee heard two reports on the stages of negotiations on reparations with the Bonn government and was provided with comprehensive information by the government in this regard. In light of those reports, I should note that in these negotiations the Israeli delegation appeared with national dignity and responsibility and conducted itself in accordance with the instructions given to it by the government and within the limits set by the Knesset through the Foreign Affairs and Defense Committee. The full collaboration between the Israeli delegation and that of Jewish organizations from around the world should also be noted with great satisfaction. During the negotiations it transpired that the Bonn government set the overall sum of the reparations to Israel at less than the sum specified by our

---

1   Earlier on in this Knesset meeting, a no-confidence motion was forwarded by the Herut Party in protest against the government's policy regarding negotiations with West Germany on reparations. The motion was defeated by 57 votes against 3 (43 abstained).

government in its note to the occupying powers – the United States, the Soviet Union, Britain and France. In addition, the German delegation did not make a definite commitment that this sum would be paid but rather that it regards the sum determined – $715 million – as a nominal sum, in recognition of the debt only, without determining what sums will actually be paid.

The German delegation decided that payments and dates would be conditional upon the settlement of Germany's overall debt to various states that was deliberated at the London Conference. On this basis the Israeli delegation suspended the negotiations in order to receive fresh instructions from the government of Israel. After hearing the details of the negotiations, the committee proposed that the Knesset note the following decision: "The committee recommends to the government non-renewal of the negotiations between the Israeli and West German delegations until the Bonn government submits a clear and binding proposal to meet Israel's claim for reparations, including dates of payment. The committee expresses its confidence that it will be given the opportunity of discussing such a proposal prior to a final government decision on whether to accept or reject it."

When the Knesset reached its decision on the reparations claim from Germany, it viewed the claim as restitution of part of what was plundered from the Jewish people by the German people, since the value of the Jewish property lost to the Nazis is greatly in excess of the sum that the Bonn government is required to pay. However, we emphasized more than once that neither the government of Israel nor the Jewish people in the Diaspora view these reparations as atonement or conciliation for mass murder.

With this decision, the Knesset viewed it as a great privilege to determine a historical fact that there is a claimant for the plundered Jewish property and that the government of Israel together with world Jewish organizations would claim reparations. The State of Israel and its people do not imagine that this obligation can be avoided by unrealistic assurances, evading payment within a reasonable period and by delaying tactics. We think that we must again exert all possible pressure – including world opinion and the influence of the occupying powers – on the German government and people to meet this claim. This House would do well to unite behind this claim.

The Bonn government should know that it will not evade the issue and that we will continue to voice this claim everywhere and at every opportunity, for the plundered property, which is ours, will be channeled to building the Jewish homeland and the rehabilitation of the survivors of the Nazi sword, and that all the aforementioned is apart from the claim by Jewish communities throughout the world. From this podium we must announce to the entire world the renewal of our claim with all our moral, Jewish and political force. We must see to it that all available political factors are harnessed towards this purpose.

I recommend that the Knesset accept the committee's proposal. I will respond to the rest of the reservations after hearing their rationale.

MK Yaakov Riftin (*Mapam*): Members of the Knesset, the crisis in the negotiations between the Israeli and Germany delegations occurred at a very early stage. It seems that even the most pessimistic members in this House assumed that the Bonn government would make use of more complex and honorable means of camouflaging its intentions.

The Germans advanced an incredibly satanic proposal. They proposed a moral agreement between the Bonn government and the government of Israel regarding a certain sum which would be negotiated by both governments together at the London conference. This means that we are to award moral and political rehabilitation to the Bonn government without any concrete financial conclusions and that Bonn and the government of Israel would be fighting together against the occupying powers.

The State of Israel should not stop its struggle for obtaining reparations to the state and the Jewish people. But it should do so through the occupying powers. Direct negotiations should be terminated.

It should not be forgotten that while the concrete financial significance of these negotiations has declined, their negative political weight has soared. Dr. Adenauer and his government are desperately attempting to make West Germany the main basis for starting a new world war. Is there any justification for conducting negotiations through which the prestige of this government, which sees itself as a vital factor in the preparations for a third world war, is enhanced?

If only there had been at least some economic benefit from the continuation of negotiations! But it is already obvious today that any such benefit would be strictly limited, and thus the Knesset must ask itself whether such a benefit should be preferred to continuing the Jewish people's consistent struggle against the revival of Nazism, against making Germany an aggressive base, against the plan of igniting a new world war.

The Knesset must decide to stop the negotiations with the Bonn government.

MK Yochanan Bader (*Herut*): Mr. Speaker, members of the Knesset, what are Germans interested in most? They are interested in the negotiations themselves so that they can sit with the Jews, so that the world can see that the Jews do not hate them all that much, that the Jews relate to Germans as decent debtors who can be trusted, that they can be negotiated with, and everything will be fine. That is the most important thing for the Germans. The second, no less important factor, is the agreement itself. The third factor – as there is to be an agreement – is the step towards conciliation, and anything you say from this podium will not change it. When there is an agreement with Germans on $700 million, it will mean compromise, forgiveness, peacemaking, and at the very least the opening of a path towards compromise and forgiveness. The fourth factor, which they are not interested in at all, is real payment. And finally, what they most certainly do not want is quick payment.

Due to this order of priorities, and since the chronological order runs from the negotiations to the agreement and then to the payment, we – that is you, the government – must give the Germans everything they want in advance. You have already given them the contact and the togetherness, and you have not received a thing. You have already given the Germans the agreement – perhaps there will be an agreement – but an agreement is not payment. Once an agreement is reached, what will the Germans care about paying or not paying? If they do not pay they will be bad debtors, but what do the murderers, the Nazis care, the people who brought about a world war and murdered six million Jews and certainly many more millions of others. What do they care if the Jews say the German debtor cannot be trusted? The world has known this for a long time: they have never paid their debts, and they will not pay you this time, either. But they will have their negotiations, the Germans will have direct contact, the Germans will possibly have an agreement.

This is the road you are taking, you no longer think about honor or pride, and you are under pressure. Pressure of this kind, gentlemen, is a very bad counselor. You are taking a very bad road, and not only will you hurt tens of thousands of people like me in this country, not only will you sully national honor, not only will you aid the Germans, but you will obtain no money. If you have already heard the sums they are talking about, then why bother? Cease being so stubborn – desist!

Therefore, gentlemen, as one for whom six million is not a theoretical figure – and there are many like me in Israel – I implore you at the last minute: for God's sake, desist! You have had problems with the negotiations, you have internal troubles and you will have more, you are awakening tremendous forces and no one knows where it will all end. Desist! There are already Jews in Europe who have reacted extremely against your negotiations, like attempting to assassinate Adenauer,[2] and I would certainly not regret the demise of any German. Are you

---

2   *Davar* daily newspaper reported on 28.3.1952: "A package addressed to the West German chancellor exploded this evening at police headquarters in Munich. Karl Reichert, a Munich Fire Service explosives expert, and three policemen were seriously injured. Munich police chief Dr. Weissmann said that this afternoon two unnamed persons approached two young boys on a Munich street and gave them a package bearing the address: Chancellor Dr. Adenauer, Bonn. They asked the boys to post the package at the Munich central post office. The boys showed it to a tram driver who took them to a policeman, who handed the package in at a police station. The two unnamed persons were aged between 35 and 40. The explosion occurred as the package was being opened and the basement of the building was completely destroyed. Before going to press it was reported that the police explosives expert had died."
Additional information regarding this episode was uncovered in *Haaretz* daily newspaper 54 years later: "Eliezer Sudit, a former member of the Irgun, the man who sent an explosive parcel to Chancellor Adenauer, revealed that in doing so he acted on an order issued by

aware of what you are bringing about? Desist! You have aroused tremendous feelings of frustration, of bitterness, of despair, of resistance.[3] This country does not need shocks of this kind. The world does not need shocks of this kind. And you will not obtain any money, either.

You have made a mistake – admit you have made a mistake, and desist! Turn back from this road, for you will not obtain any money either!

MK Shalom Zysman (*General Zionists*)**:** Only a few years have passed since the Holocaust. Perhaps individual Jews or Jewish organizations can demand property from Germany, but the State of Israel, the sovereign representative of the Jewish people – what has happened to it? Why did it have to forgive the Germans in such a hurry? I would certainly receive as an answer: "We are not forgetting and not forgiving." But we know very well that these are empty declarations in view of our sitting together at the same table. The Germans' aim was only this: that the two delegations would be seated together.

Since the motion to hold direct negotiations was carried out by a small majority, the government should have ensured that the negotiations would not fail, that there would be a 100 percent chance of the reparations being paid, and paid in big sums. Now that the first stage of the negotiations is over, we all know their result: total failure.

We have lost our trump card, and for good. This card was our strong "No!" The Germans wanted to sit with us. They needed this for achieving their aims. Had we used that card and said "No!", we would have obtained loftier and far more beneficial moral stature than those millions of marks we hoped to receive. Now, won't the anti-Semites say: "Look at these kikes – six million of their sons and daughters were murdered and a few years later they agree to accept money!"

MK Menachem Begin. Sudit, in his first interview with the media, said he did not know why Begin and his comrades chose to 'keep their mouths shut' all these years. 'Today I think that in view of the failure of the operation, they had nothing to be proud of. I was a soldier who fulfilled orders, and all in all, I am satisfied that I did something against the Reparations Agreement.' Sudit added to the *Haaretz* correspondent who interviewed him that three meetings were held at Begin's home prior to the operation, in which several Herut leaders participated, including MKs Yohanan Bader and Haim Landau. Sudit prepared the explosive package in France. He also mailed two explosive envelopes to the Israeli delegation in Wassenaar in the name of 'The Jewish Partisans' Organization,' but they were both intercepted by the Dutch authorities and neutralized." (*Haaretz*, 14.6.2006).

3   On 5.10.1952, Dov Shilansky, a former Irgun member and one of its European operatives, was arrested at a basement door in the Foreign Office complex in Tel Aviv. He was carrying a bag containing a two-kilogram time bomb. In the *Herut* newspaper, MK Bader stated that Shilansky's arrest was nothing but a "Security Services provocation." In court on 28.11.1952, Shilansky admitted that he had decided to place the bomb in the building housing the department dealing with the reparations agreement in order to arouse a public reaction. He further claimed that he had warned the police about the explosion. He was sentenced to 21 months imprisonment, of which he served 11. In later years he was elected a member of the Knesset on the Herut ticket and served as its Speaker.

We will explain that it was not the money which we wanted; we wanted to build the State of Israel, but the anti-Semites will make a simple calculation: they received $60 or $100 million, so the cost of each victim was such and such, and they would conclude that it is possible to murder Jews and then sit together with them and calculate the cost involved. We have lost the opportunity for the big "No!"

The Arab states are awaiting our economic downfall. Had they known that we were not going to Germany in order to receive money, how much then would our position have been strengthened, for they would have realized that we are economically stable, that far more important spiritual assets enhance our nation.

History has taught us that the accursed German people have never paid compensation. To whom would we complain that the Germans did not keep their promise to us? Are you going to accuse a sadistic murderer when he ignores his promise to pay? Now that the first stage of negotiations is over, it is obvious that the Germans have won the whole front.

Members of the Knesset, what we are going to receive is not reparations, but alms. Germany will give us alms for the building of the country! Is this what you had in mind upon entering negotiations, when you spoke so eloquently from this podium on reparations? We have had our fill of damage and degradation. Enough! Stop it all now.

Foreign Minister Moshe Sharett: Mr. Speaker, Members of the Knesset, I have no intention of entering into polemics. As far as both the government and I are concerned, we are in the middle of this affair, not at its beginning or end, but in the middle. I therefore cannot allow myself the same freedom of expression as that enjoyed by some members. As far as it is possible, I would like to avoid a debate.

We are in the middle of this affair and the question is, what has been achieved so far, and what has not? We have heard a statement by the West German delegation – with its government's backing – that West Germany owes the State of Israel a sum of $715 million as reparations for the plunder of Jewish property during the Nazi regime. I know the account very well, and I know exactly what the discrepancy is between this sum and the sum stated in the claim. I also know that the discrepancy is between what we have not heard from East Germany and that part of the claim, which in our opinion depends upon it. That discrepancy, too, is very clear to me. This sum of $715 million is less than the $1 billion we sought to impose on West Germany. Nevertheless, I am not convinced that we can belittle the importance of the fact, both in principle and quantitatively, that in 1952 the West German government declared, or had it declared on its behalf, that it owes the State of Israel – the State of Israel that was established in 1948 – for Jewish property that was plundered in earlier years a sum of $715 million. In any event, as foreign minister, and not the finance minister, I cannot advise our government and the Knesset before which I appear to belittle this historic fact.

But a declaration is not sufficient for us. This statement still says nothing about the scope and timing of payments, which the Bonn government is prepared to "undertake immediately" – and I stress the words *to undertake immediately* – for the sum it will undertake immediately might not settle the whole account, and in our view it will not free West Germany from settling it in the future. There is, of course, great and perhaps decisive value in the commencement of payments, their size, frequency and character, and yet we have still not heard the binding, decisive statement.

When we embarked on this path it was so difficult – difficult on the international front and perhaps even more difficult on the home front – because from a psychological standpoint it is far easier to fight and argue with the United States and France and Britain on the one hand, and the USSR on the other. To enter into negotiations with Germany is easier than to debate this issue with, for instance, Rabbi Nurock. When we began, we started from zero. The claim sounded unrealistic, with no substantive background. The idea of a collective payment, the idea of the present Germany's responsibility for the crimes of Nazi Germany, the idea of their obligation to pay the State of Israel – all this was unprecedented. The very idea of the obligation of paying compensation not for war damage, but for the plunder of a people's property was unprecedented in international relations. From the international-political standpoint, the standpoint of international law, our claim was unprecedented. It was an attempt to create something *ex nihilo*. Still, we progressed stage by stage.

We submitted the claim to the four powers on March 13, 1951. It is not true to say that it did not help. It has not helped so far in East Germany, but it has in West Germany. The reverberations of this claim, which was addressed to the occupying powers, were reflected in Dr. Adenauer's statement – in September 1951, if I am not mistaken – in which he first admitted West Germany's responsibility for Nazi Germany's war crimes. Second, he accepted the principle of collective payment, not only of meeting individual claims. And third, he affirmed the status, authority and right of the government of Israel to claim and receive this compensation.

Then came Adenauer's famous letter in which our claim was accepted as a basis, and then came the admission of the debt. What failure is there here? What crisis was there here? This is a battle and we are in its midst. Today we are waiting to hear about the payment or payments that Germany is prepared to undertake immediately, in accordance with its acknowledged and standing obligation.

An attempt was made to link negotiations with us to the London conference. The London conference is a meeting of Germany's creditors, or of countries whose citizens or institutions are Germany's creditors. Our state, too, is registered there to ensure our rights and status.

There has been an attempt to link the final arrangement with us to the outcome of that global arrangement. We rejected it outright. We opposed any linkage whatsoever to the London arrangement. We stated that we would not accept it under any circumstances, and that Germany's firm stance on this linkage would be tantamount to its denial of our claim, for our claim was unlike all the other claims on the table in London: we had not lent money to the Germans; we did not offer financial aid to Germany at any time and now demand that Germany must repay this aid. We represent a wronged people, a robbed people, and we are claiming restitution of the plunder. We will not stand in line in London to receive our share, the share that we are convinced that Germany can and must restore to us.

We rejected this out of hand, and I have every reason to confirm that Germany fully understands our position on this matter. It also knows that there cannot be any compromise on it: either it can and will offer an absolute sum, not subject to the London arrangement in any formal way whatsoever, or it cannot – and then we will know. That is what we want to know today.

Our position on this matter is clear and the question facing the Bonn government today is also clear. The question is whether or not it is at present prepared to meet its commitment and announce a decisive undertaking to commence payments immediately.

Several draft resolutions demanding cessation of negotiations are now awaiting the Knesset's decision. All of them have been submitted by factions that demanded at the time that negotiations should not commence, and so there is nothing new in them. A month has elapsed and no such demand has been heard, since the Knesset was in recess. The Knesset has reconvened, and the same demand has been revived. It is a demand that could have been made yesterday, tomorrow or at any time. I will not discuss now the reasons behind this demand, for we have already had a comprehensive and trenchant debate on this issue, and a decision was made at that stage. We might possibly have a further incisive debate on this issue when a further stage for a decision is reached, but it has not arrived yet.

There is, perhaps, a certain innovation in Mapam's position as presented here by its spokesman, although in that historic Knesset debate of January 7-9 1952, if my memory serves me, the idea of demanding from the powers that they impose reparations payments on both parts of Germany had already been voiced.

Gentlemen, when was this advice given and to whom? It was given, then as now, to the very government that began the whole process by addressing the occupying powers so they would impose reparations on both parts of Germany. It was not made on Mapam's initiative, but to the governments! It was our appeal to the three powers that led to Adenauer's statement that enabled the start of the negotiations and put the entire issue on the road to implementation. Where we will reach on this road is still unclear, whether or not we will reach the end of the road is still unknown, but we are moving along at a promising pace.

I have every reason to believe that West Germany's authorities are fully aware of the significance of not forwarding a proposal, or of forwarding an unacceptable one. It may be assumed that they are putting their heads together and seriously considering this problem. It is no simple matter for them either, in view of their international situation, to trigger the failure of these negotiations by making a proposal that will be rejected by us. They know full well – they learned it at the negotiating table – what stuff we are made of. They certainly appreciate our abilities to negotiate and our resolve.

Our proposal to the three powers found an attentive ear in the Bonn government. This has not been the case with the East German government. It simply ignored us. How dare Knesset members now suggest that we renew our appeal?

There are parties for whom it is important to pay lip service in a Knesset vote that will later be inscribed on the tablets of Jewish history. The government's submission of the claim was not forwarded in order to pay lip service, though there are claims whose main significance lie in their presentation, not necessarily in their implementation. I do not belittle such claims, but from the outset the government's aim in this matter has been to achieve concrete results, and it still is. It is striving to achieve results not only by preserving the honor of the State of Israel but by enhancing it.

To all those members of this House who displayed such tension and anxiety lest the honor of Israel be sullied by these negotiations, I say, rest assured. The honor of Israel is safe in the hands of this government.

Chairman Ze'ev Sheffer: I put the following resolution to a vote: the Knesset notes the decision of the Foreign Affairs and Defense Committee, which recommends to the government non-renewal of the negotiations between the delegations of Israel and West Germany until the Bonn government submits a clear and binding proposal to meet Israel's claim for reparations, including dates of payment. The committee expresses confidence that it will be given the opportunity of discussing such a proposal prior to a final government decision on whether to accept or reject it.

The vote:
In favor of the Foreign Affairs and Defense Committee resolution: 50
Against: 34
The resolution was carried.

[29] Towards Renewal of Negotiations

Cabinet Meeting, 18.6.1952[1]

Prime Minister David Ben Gurion: The subject of this meeting is the reparations negotiations. We must give the Germans an answer, and I do not want to shoulder this decision by myself.

Minister Eliezer Kaplan: We have not yet received all the details, but some of them are at our disposal. The Germans have informed our delegation that they agree to pay Israel 3 billion marks, which are, at the present rate, about $715 million. They say that this agreement must be submitted to the Bundestag. They are prepared to agree on the timetable for payments and propose that the first two installments, which together will amount to 400 million marks, will be paid by the end of March 1954, and that 260 million marks will be paid annually in the next ten years.

The matter of the payment of 400-500 million marks – in addition to the sum of 3 billion marks – to the Jewish organizations has not yet been settled. This morning we received a cable from our delegation to the effect that in the meeting yesterday of the German cabinet, everything was approved except for the payment to the Jewish organizations. The delegation is asking for approval of the agreement, which in their opinion was fundamentally positive. They are still endeavoring to reach better conditions of payment, but there is not much hope there. They think that the ratification by the Bundestag will take place in September, and thus payments would start in October.

We must now decide whether to instruct the delegation to renew negotiations on this basis.

Minister David-Zvi Pinkas: The procedure is now clear. The government has been authorized by the Knesset to renew negotiations if a concrete German

---

1 Foreign Minister Moshe Sharett was absent from this meeting as he was away on a mission to the U.S.A.

proposal is presented, but it has promised to report developments to the Foreign Affairs and Defense Committee. An effort should be made to increase the first installment of the reparations.

Minister Behor Shitrit: We should make sure that in case of reunification of the two Germanies, the agreement will not relieve East Germany from its obligation.

Minister Eliezer Kaplan: Certainly.

It was decided:
To authorize the Israeli delegation to renew the reparations negotiations with the Bonn government on the basis of the proposals it submitted on June 16, 1952.

[30] Who Will Sign the Reparations Agreement?

Cabinet Meeting, 24.8.1952

Chairman, Foreign Minister Moshe Sharett:[1] I have something to report on reparations. This issue is nearing conclusion. Two days ago they had a seven-hour meeting in which they resolved two or three questions that were either still open or on which there was no agreement. The German draft is now ready. The English one is not, but the Bonn government must go over the German draft and approve it. If the German draft is approved, they will complete the English one and send it to us so that the government can study it before signing. Furthermore, we promised the Foreign Affairs and Defense Committee to bring the matter before it.

There is the question of whether approval of the draft by the West German government will take a long time or not. The Germans' opinions are divided: some say that the draft should be submitted to the government for its approval immediately, while others say it would be better to circulate it to all the ministries since otherwise the ministries might raise questions and create difficulties later. Therefore, perhaps it would be better to take the long road which would be shorter in the long run, and if so, the approval should take another week or two.

At a certain stage, we were informed by our delegation, Adenauer wishes to sign the Reparations Agreement himself as it is an historic event in which he is personally involved. Our delegation's impression was that he does not insist that a man equal to him in rank sign on our side; he would be satisfied if it is signed by the head of our delegation, but in view of his advanced age he would not want to travel, and thus the signing ceremony should take place in Bonn. Sometime later it transpired that this information was inaccurate. Adenauer said he is prepared to go to any agreed location; he does not insist that the signing take place on German soil, in Bonn, but it is desirable that it be as close to Germany as possible. But he does insist that the agreement be signed by a member of the other side's cabinet, not necessarily by the prime minister, but at least by a member of the cabinet.

---

1   Prime Minister Ben Gurion was absent as he was observing IDF maneuvers.

A few days ago I received a cable from the delegation and Dr. Nahum Goldmann imploring the government that I sign. I met Minister Moshe Shapira at the prime minister's office and the three of us together consulted on this matter. The outcome was that we cabled a question to the delegation: what would happen if we suggested that the minister of finance sign – we gave you credit, Levi Eshkol,[2] in your absence – in order to preserve the practical aspect of the agreement and not to accord it a political character.

In the meantime, Dr. Goldmann met with Adenauer on the substance of the agreement in order to push it forward. Among other things, Nahum reported what we already know: there has been constant and vigorous diplomatic activity by the Arabs in Beirut, Washington, London and Paris, and even directly in Bonn, all in vain. According to Goldmann, the Arabs offered the Germans huge and attractive orders, attractive from both the commercial and political standpoints. Again, all in vain. It was agreed that the signing would take place in Luxembourg on September 8, and he – Adenauer – expressed the hope that I would attend. There is also a cable in the same spirit from the delegation.

Earlier on, before this meeting, the prime minister advised me that I should sign the agreement facing Adenauer. Adenauer's signature on the agreement will endow it with a more binding character than that of the head of the German delegation, and if he does sign, it will mandate a certain degree of reciprocity. That is the question I bring before this meeting.

Minister Yosef Burg: Will the foreign minister's signature not undermine his stature with the Eastern bloc?

Chairman, Foreign Minister Moshe Sharett: On the contrary, once this matter is concluded we will shift to a serious attack on East Germany, a diplomatic attack, of course. I don't know if we will succeed, but we will make a concerted effort with the Soviet Union and say, you know what West Germany has done. What about you? In private conversations with our people, the Soviet diplomats are saying, "They are giving? Take it!"

It was decided:
The foreign minister will sign the reparations agreement on behalf of the government of Israel.

---

2   Following the death of Minister of Finance Eliezer Kaplan on July 13, 1952, Levi Eshkol
     was appointed in his place.

[31] It is an Honor to Shoulder the State of Israel's Obligations

An Exchange of Letters between the Legal Adviser of the Foreign Ministry
and the Foreign Minister

Confidential

To: Minister of Foreign Affairs, personal   1.9.1952
From: Shabtai Rosenne, Legal Advisor, Foreign Ministry

I am deeply concerned at the thought that it is you who will be sent to sign the
reparations agreement. I vi ew this as beneath the dignity of Israel's minister of
foreign affairs, and an act that might tarnish the name of Moshe Sharett in the
future.

I also do not consider that this agreement obliges Adenauer to sign on behalf of his
government. His signature cannot affect the implementation of the agreement.
It is therefore my duty to request that you reconsider this decision, as you may
have reached the conclusion that no intrinsic damage will be caused should the
heads of the delegations sign the agreement instead of the minister of foreign
affairs of Israel and the German chancellor.

Please bear with my candor,

Sincerely, Shabtai Rosenne

*

To: Legal Advisor   2.9.1952
From: Minister of Foreign Affairs

I herewith respond to the serious doubts you have raised regarding the wisdom of
the government's decision that the minister of foreign affairs sign the reparations
agreement with West Germany on behalf of the State of Israel when the cosignatory
is the head of the Bonn government.

I could dismiss your appeal by stating that the matter has already been decided, brought to the attention of the other party, and published in the press with no denials. In a situation such as this, no self-respecting government would recant and withdraw the matter for renewed discussion. And all the more so if this means forcing the other party to retract its decision, thus compelling it to reconsider the entire matter.

The fact of the matter is that I must unequivocally present to you all the binding circumstances and totally reject your assumption – which I can only view as extremely odd – that in the present situation we can allow ourselves to consider reversing our decision and that changing the procedure decided upon by mutual consent could be considered as "practical policy."

However, your arguments and considerations are of such weight that I cannot refute them either morally or politically. But the decisive fact remains that from the practical point of view, your appeal was made at least ten days too late. Nevertheless, your opinion merits a response.

You base your opposition first and foremost on moral reasoning: in your opinion it is beneath my dignity to sign the agreement with the Germans. I reject the morality of this reasoning with my utmost conviction. One or the other: if the entire matter of the reparations is moral, and if reaching an agreement requires negotiations and signing an agreement, it is obvious that conducting negotiations and signing the agreement are similarly moral. If the matter is immoral, then the claim should not have been made at all, and consequently we should not have entered negotiations and signed an agreement. If my basic assumption is correct, and it is the only one on which this issue can be based, then the claim is intrinsically moral. Therefore, all the conclusions and results deriving from it are moral, and then not only I am permitted to sign, but President Chaim Weizmann is also permitted to do so, and the question of the signatory's identity and status in the state hierarchy is purely a practical one.

In any event, I totally reject the logic of the assumption implicit in your letter: that I am permitted to send trusted colleagues whose dignity is dear to me no less than the dignity of any of us to the negotiations table, and at the same time evade the duty of standing at their head when political circumstances require it.

Your concern for my reputation is both touching and dear to me – just as dear as your awareness of and sensitivity to the moral quality of Israel's public appearances – but I must set your mind at rest. Should the verdict of history go against the whole reparations affair, then I have already tainted myself to such a degree that my absence at the signing ceremony would not mitigate my sentence. On the other hand, should history justify my actions, then not only would my signature not spoil the process, it would become a link in the chain and serve as an appropriate conclusion to a stable and enduring undertaking.

I can only conclude from your letter that either you do not wholeheartedly support the entire matter, or that your attitude towards it is overly fastidious which in my view does not reflect statesmanship and embodies a clear element of Diaspora sentimentality.

As to the seemingly practical reasoning to which you subscribe, that Adenauer's signature cannot affect the implementation of the agreement, I beg to differ. None of us can guess how much longer Adenauer will head the Bonn government. Even if due to his age he does not last much longer, either in government or in general, and even if he remains in his post for only another two or three years, those years are likely to prove critical to the agreement's implementation. And even if he departs and after his departure, the weight of his signature cannot be compared, as far as his colleagues, his party and the entire German public both inside and outside Germany are concerned, with the weight of the signature of Prof. Böhm or someone else.

But in view of the obligation it places on the other side, it is not only the importance of Adenauer's own signature which we should bear in mind. There is also the matter of justice with regard to Adenauer himself. He views the obligation that Germany is taking upon itself with the reparations agreement as an historic step, unprecedented in the history of civilized people in the same way that there was no precedent of such shame and disgrace for the massacre of the Jews and all the abhorrent acts of the Hitler regime. One cannot easily dispute the justness of this historic claim. But if it is just, then it is to Adenauer's personal credit that Germany is now taking this step, and thus Adenauer deserves the historical credit by signing personally. To deprive him of the act would be an ignoble, narrow-minded act, lacking a sense of history on our part; it would spoil things by lowering our own participation at the signing ceremony from that lofty level which he has achieved.

You may be surprised by my considerations of respect and reciprocity, and even my showing noble feelings towards a German chancellor. But in my opinion, this alone should be the approach of the independent State of Israel which from historical and moral standpoints was founded on the ruins of the Nazi regime but has now redeemed the honor of the Jewish people debased by that regime. The fear of taking such a step in our relations with Germany returns us to a status that belongs in the past: the status of a people lacking qualities of sovereignty and exempt from considerations of a state, a people secluded within its four walls, mourning the past, praying for the future and resolving the problem of its present relations with other nations by silently abhorring them. A sovereign nation must face the future, even though its current relations with others burden it with practical obligations that should be viewed as an honor to shoulder, as others, too, bear these same burdens towards it.

We must educate the nation towards this new perception of our honor, but first we need to educate ourselves.

Moshe Sharett

[32] Israel Labor Party Approves the Reparations Agreement

Mapai Political Committee Meeting, 5.9.1952

Moshe Sharett: This meeting was convened for two purposes. First, the Committee must be apprised of the situation before it is brought before the Foreign Affairs and Defense Committee. Second, our members of the Foreign and Defense Committee should be prepared, for its meeting is to convene today.

Let me refresh your memory and bring you back to the stage of the Knesset's last discussion of the reparations issue, the suspension of negotiations. At that stage the Germans said that they admit that the sum of $715 million is owed to the State of Israel and to the Jewish people and that they are prepared to declare this publicly, but they contended that the fact that this sum is due did not mean that they are able to pay it and to commit themselves to do so. They stated that they are willing to discuss the sum that they are able to pay and added that this would also depend on the results of the London Conference of Creditors.

We rejected both these contentions. First, we stressed that what is due is what should be paid. Second, we rejected any linkage of our negotiations to the negotiations taking place in London. The talks with the German delegations broke down over these two issues, and this led to a storm – Böhm and Küster[1] resigned from the German delegation, and Küster wrote and published a *J'accuse* letter in which he strongly protested against Adenauer and the German government. Adenauer then felt that his name was at stake. His party's colleagues rose to help him and the German Social Democrat Party with which we maintained close contact; we updated the party about the evolving situation, and, willingly and warmly, their leaders put pressure to bear in the Bundestag. We also mobilized the support of the American and British press, and succeeded in activating Adenauer's Washington and London colleagues – President Truman and Prime Minister Churchill - when they met in Paris to discuss the termination of the

---

1   Dr. Otto Küster, lawyer, dismissed from his post of judge in 1933 because of his anti-Nazi outlook. Headed the Reparations Department of the Ministry of Interior in the state of Baden-Württemberg.

occupation regime in Germany. Foreign Ministers Eden and Acheson also expressed themselves strongly on this subject in their separate meetings with Adenauer, and these steps enhanced his position vis-à-vis the cabinet members who opposed the whole subject of reparations.

In view of all the above, negotiations were renewed and advanced along a new path of complete separation from the London Conference. Second, the Germans decided that the agreed sum would be $715 million which we decided to demand instead of our former demand of $1 billion.

I would now like to describe the general background of the negotiations. Members of this committee should be aware that the issue of reparations does not concern the German public, and it is certainly not a topic high on its agenda. A small minority of Germans are in favor of the planned agreement, but the overall atmosphere there is of unwillingness, of seeing the whole proceeding as unnecessary and unjustly imposed, as something bound to burden German society and which it is not duty-bound to shoulder. Yes, indeed, there was a past regime in Germany that committed actions for which they are accused, but in fact there are ten thousand Germans in every German town whose living was destroyed because of the war, and are they receiving compensation? Why, then, should they finance compensation to the Jewish people? This whole matter is met with distaste, and moreover, there are cabinet ministers, headed by the minister of finance as well as business and banking circles surrounding him, who vehemently oppose the whole idea of reparations.

The commitment of paying an additional $450 million – not a small sum at all – to Jewish organizations gave rise to an acrimonious struggle. The minister of finance, for instance, contended that instead of payment to our country and to the organizations, he was prepared to earmark a certain sum to the German consuls so that they could allocate personal compensation to Holocaust survivors in the countries in which they live. He said that this policy of compensation, the dimensions of which are unheard of in history, would create much more good will towards Germany than global payments to the State of Israel and Jewish organizations.

However, for Adenauer and his group this is a moral issue. He is convinced that he is accomplishing a great historic deed that will guarantee him an honorable place in the history of humanity and that of the Jewish people, because Jewish history is a great treasure trove for preserving one's good name forever. Adenauer is also confident that the Jewish people wield enormous power and influence in the world, and thus by paying reparations, he is paving the way for gaining numerous benefits for Germany. These two considerations are his main driving motives. There are also Germans who think that the reparations agreement will open a profitable market for German goods in the Middle East.

In Germany I enumerated the factors which are conducive to the Reparations Agreement, but we should know that there are strong pressures there against it, and the struggle between these two camps is taking place against the background of a pre-election year. If this issue becomes a bone of contention in the election campaign, then certainly the general response to the agreement will be negative. First of all, this leads to the conclusion that finalizing the agreement is urgent. Our second conclusion is that there is no sense in stubbornly demanding corrections to the agreement which was reached following protracted and tiresome negotiations, corrections which, as has already been shown, are unattainable. Such stubbornness on our part will not pressure those willing to sign the agreement. On the contrary, it would relieve them from committing themselves to honoring the agreement because they will face their opponents' contention that it is impossible ever to satisfy us, in spite of our achievement which, according to all cold logic, is a unique one. They will say that these people – we Israelis – have got it into their heads that they are entitled to get just about everything from Germany, so in that case, is it not better to put an end to the whole affair?

During the revived negotiations the problem arose of the Templers'[2] property confiscated by us in several places around our country. It was agreed that this issue would be deliberated outside the Reparations Agreement four months after its signing. It was agreed that the payments for this property would be in German marks, and that they would be siphoned off from the annual reparations payments over 12 or 14 years.

I am aware that there are several comrades among us who see this issue of compensation payments to the Templers as a new and troubling burden on us. Can it be that these comrades assumed this property was ownerless? I am shocked that there are educated, sophisticated and ethical people among us who think in terms of the law of the jungle. Can it be that they assumed we had simply seized land and buildings with no need for accountability? Why did we seize this German property at all? When we did so, we said that it was morally justified since the German people had plundered Jewish property, to say nothing of the spilled blood. At the time, we saw no chance of receiving reparations, and supposing we could have, we could not know how much and when so that if property belonging to those people existed in our country, should we not take it, especially when victims of German atrocities were arriving here? However, it was quite clear at the time that if a day of judgment should arrive, the value of this property would be deducted from what is due to us; otherwise, how could proper negotiations be conducted while we remained in possession of seized German property? We rejected a claim

---

2   The German Protestant order of the Templers was founded in the midst of the 19th century with the aim of building urban and agricultural settlements in the Holy Land. Between 1869-1907, the Templers established seven settlements all over Palestine. When WW II broke out, the 1,200 members of these settlements were considered enemy citizens and deported to detention camps in Australia. After the war ended they were freed and became Australian citizens.

to pay the Templers, most of whom live in Australia, in Australian currency, but this does not mean that we will not pay at all.

Regarding my trip abroad for the signing of the agreement, I am convinced of its necessity in view of the need to grant maximum weight to the agreement. The signing of this agreement is not a matter of formality only. It is an act of international significance, for it is the first time in Jewish history that a demand for compensation follows plundering, and that such a demand is accepted.

Second, we want this agreement to be implemented, and we think that raising the signatories' stature would contribute to guaranteeing its implementation.

In addition, I think that signing of the agreement by Israel's foreign minister is important for an educational purpose: having succeeded in establishing a state of our own, we must educate our people to become a sovereign people instead of a Diaspora people. They should realize that we have a state of our own on the globe, and that on this globe there also exists a state called Germany. Our people cannot evade the existence of Germany unless it puts an end to its own state or transfers it to another planet. This truth must be harshly inculcated into the minds of this people until it becomes accustomed to it.

I would like inform you that during the signing ceremony, Adenauer and I will deliver short speeches. Possibly, the distance between the two speeches would be so great that it would be better if nothing were said. It might well be that there will be strong opposition to my speech, and if so there will be no speeches at all. I intend first of all to strongly condemn the Holocaust, the crime, and the impossibility of atonement. Incidentally, Ben Gurion is against my saying anything regarding the impossibility of atonement for the spilled blood; he thinks it is too cruel to touch upon that. If I say that we expect the evil spirit to be uprooted from the German people's mentality, it will mean that it has not yet been uprooted. I also intend to emphasize the importance of the Reparations Agreement being achieved out of a sense of moral responsibility and not under duress.

I am a Minister of the State of Israel, not just a slaughtered Jew. There will be somebody who will speak in the name of the six million slaughtered Jews. Dr. Goldmann will speak in the name of the Conference of Jewish Organizations, and my words regarding the spilt Jewish blood will be far more fiery than his.

Our people should be taught to fully absorb these truths and understand them. Instead of fearing how the Reparations Agreement will be received among Jews, they should be taught to think properly.

Chairman of the meeting Yona Kesse: I put to the vote the following proposal: "The political committee authorizes our Foreign Affairs and Defense Committee and the cabinet members to ratify the agreement's draft."

The proposal was accepted.

Eliezer Livne: I think the strength of the agreement would not be diminished were there no personal meeting. Is it still possible to propose that the foreign minister will not travel to meet with Adenauer?

The vote:
For: 2
Against: a majority
Abstained: 2
Eliezer Livne's proposal was rejected.

[33] The Foreign Affairs and Defense Committee Ratifies the Agreement

Knesset Foreign Affairs and Defense Committee Meeting, 5.9.1952

Chairman Mordechai Namir (*Mapai*)**:** As you know, the Knesset has decided that the government should bring its position on the reparations agreement with Germany to the Foreign Affairs and Defense Committee and has empowered the committee to decide on its behalf. We will now hear the foreign minister on this matter.

Foreign Minister Moshe Sharett: First of all I would like to apprise the Committee of the situation from the standpoints of procedure and order. We are gathered here today, September 5, and the situation is that negotiations between the two delegations have been concluded and a draft agreement has been submitted to the two governments. The German constitution mandates that such an agreement must be ratified by parliament after it has been signed by the government. The Israeli constitution does not mandate the agreement's ratification by parliament. The government does not only view itself as being authorized to sign the agreement – if it decides to sign it – but views its signing of the agreement as its absolute prerogative. Clearly, the Knesset can always discuss any matter and decide to annul the signing – its sovereignty is paramount – but then the question arises of the future of a government whose signature the Knesset has decided to annul. The government is bound by the Knesset's decision to submit the agreement to the Foreign Affairs and Defense Committee for its study and discussion. A decision on this matter cannot be taken today for two reasons. First, the issue has not yet been discussed by the Bonn parliament. Second, the Bonn government has not yet made a final decision on this draft; that decision will apparently be made on Monday morning. A bitter struggle is taking place over there regarding the draft, and one of the results of that struggle is the postponement of the cabinet meeting until Monday. It stands to reason that our government's decision will only be made once we know what the Bonn government has decided.

Negotiating the reparations agreement took five months. The draft which is now before you is the fruit of nine weeks of intensive negotiation over the formulation of all the agreement's details. I will not review the entire five-month period now, but let me remind you that at a certain stage a crisis occurred and the negotiations were suspended by us. A statement to that effect was made in the Knesset.

The crisis broke out due to our adamant opposition to two fundamental positions adopted by the other side. At a certain stage it emerged that the other side was drawing a distinction between two figures: the sum on which it is willing to agree that the West German government owes the State of Israel as reparations, and the sum it is able and undertakes to pay. Already at that stage the sum of $715 million, or 3,000 million marks, was invoked as the sum that West Germany admits is due to the State of Israel, but at the same time it was said: it is clear that West Germany does not see itself bound to pay this sum; the sum to be actually paid must be negotiated; and the sum it owes does not necessarily have to be linked with the sum due to the State of Israel but should be linked to Germany's ability to pay.

That was the first fundamental distinction. Second, on the basis of instructions it received from its government, the West German delegation informed us that the conclusion of the negotiations and a final binding agreement must be dependent upon the outcome of the London Conference of Germany's creditors. The reparations are one of Germany's debts that it acknowledges and is prepared to pay, and thus it could not be separated from all the others.

We vehemently rejected these two assumptions, and as a result negotiations were suspended. There were a number of developments during the break. First, there was the resignation of the German chief negotiator Prof. Böhm, and one of their delegation's principal members, the deputy head of the delegation, Dr. Küster. The reasons for both resignations were made public: both men accused the German government of breach of faith, of going back on the word given to the State of Israel.

The German chancellor, who apparently faced a difficult struggle with opponents of this whole issue, mulled it over and in the end decided against the opponents. He also forced Germany's chief negotiator at the London Conference, a man named Abs, to accept his decision not to make reparations to us conditional upon the London agreement.

We took steps to arouse world public opinion and to enlist direct pressure of world powers. These efforts bore fruit. A number of articles were published in influential American and British newspapers. Those published in the British press were most explicit and fervent. There were some similar ones in the American press. Following our foreign ministry's application to the American, British and French foreign ministers on the eve of their meeting with the West German chancellor in Paris, where the agreement on the termination of the occupation was signed,

Dean Acheson and Anthony Eden – each one separately, both before and after the signing – raised the question of reparations with Adenauer. They expressed their keen hope that the agreement would be fairly concluded in a way that would leave no room for Israel to justifiably blame him for breaking his promise. According to information received, the veracity of which is beyond doubt, Eden especially was most incisive. It seems that Adenauer himself did not need this pressure, but welcomed it as a card he could play against his opponents in the German cabinet and against German banking and financial circles.

In any event, as a result of all this, a fundamental turnabout occurred in the German position facilitating renewal of negotiations. In other words, it was agreed to separate negotiations with us from the London Conference. Second, the malignant distinction they attempted to introduce between the sum they admit as our due and the sum they undertake to pay was annulled and was replaced by a statement that Germany is willing to undertake payment of the entire sum of 3,000 million marks. We agreed to accept this as fair payment for the claims we submitted.

It is known that in his letter to Nahum Goldmann, Adenauer agreed to accept Israel's claim as the basis for negotiation. In other words, he accepted the claim of $1 billion, while $0.5 billion was left for our claim from the East German government; this will be dealt with once we sign the agreement with the Bonn government. This was accepted as the basis. We viewed the undertaking of a payment of $715 million as a sum with which we can be satisfied.

Germany's undertaking to pay has not ended there since it still faces the claim of the Jewish organizations. As you know – or perhaps you do not, so I will enlighten you now – the Claims Conference was established on the initiative of the State of Israel just as the entire issue of submitting a reparations claim was Israel's exclusive initiative. In view of West Germany's admission of its obligation to pay overall compensation, made before Adenauer made his first statement to the Bonn Bundestag on September 27, 1951 and which the Bundestag approved, we saw fit to increase pressure by Jewish public opinion, and therefore we proposed that the Jewish Agency convene a conference of Jewish organizations for the purpose of getting world-wide Jewish support for Israel's claim.

Meantime, between sending out invitations to the conference and the conference itself, a significant link was added to the chain: Adenauer's statement. In that statement the chancellor spoke not only about the State of Israel but also about the Jewish people outside the framework of Israel. His thinking was clear: if he takes upon himself an undertaking, he wants it to be final, so that no Jewish individual or body anywhere in the world could come along and say, "You haven't finished with us yet, Germany still owes us a great deal."

When this statement was brought before the Claims Conference, it felt itself bound, in addition to supporting Israel's monetary claim, to submit its own claim. At this table I admit, and for these minutes only, that at a certain stage we doubted whether the conference was right. We thought that the claim for a global payment should remain exclusively the State of Israel's and that it should not be weakened by submitting a second one. But ultimately, following deliberations with the Claims Conference, we struck a balance and decided that the Conference would also submit a global claim. It was particularly difficult to obtain the German government's agreement to this additional claim, and there was an even greater difficulty in Adenauer's struggle vis-à-vis his financial advisors on this issue. Ultimately, the German government agreed to pay the Claims Conference a sum of 450 million marks, or approximately $120 million.

That is the political background. I would like to add that in the meantime three factors have emerged making the agreement worthwhile for Germany. The first is the conviction that Germany is undertaking a great moral act that will go down in history. Second, that Germany is paving the way to closer understanding with and the possibility of aid from the great powers, especially America, where Jews are influential. Third, it is assumed that the agreement would benefit the German economy by opening a wide market in our area for German exports.

Just as Jewish influence in the world is exaggerated, so is the power of the State of Israel in the Middle East, but these are the current German assumptions. Still, we should bear in mind the main opposition to the reparations agreement is voiced by banking, economic and financial circles, which perceive this burden on Germany's economy as unjust and exaggerated, and claim that its dimensions are immense.

Now, after prolonged and exhausting negotiations during which every claim and position was a bone of contention, we are facing this draft. At this juncture I would like to praise our whole delegation and each of its members individually for the tremendous effort and great ability they have invested in the negotiations, and to express the government's conviction that in these negotiations we achieved everything we could expect. That does not mean that the government does not see serious weaknesses and flaws in what has been achieved, but taking the matter in its entirety, it cannot imagine that another delegation or different negotiations would have achieved more.

The agreement is now presented for your verdict.

In conclusion, I would like to bring to your attention a particular issue that arose in the course of the negotiations – that of the Templers' property.[1] There are two types of German property in our country, both held by the state: church property and property owned by civil bodies or individuals. With regard to church property, at the outset we adopted the principle of negotiating for its acquisition and our willingness to pay for it. Indeed, we are currently negotiating with church bodies and have made substantial progress. Regarding civil property, we have taken possession of it on the basis of the following consideration: we said to ourselves, the German people plundered and destroyed vast amounts of Jewish property. The German people owns property here in Israel? We shall appropriate it on

1   See document no. 32, note no. 2.

account of our claim . We reasoned that as long as the problem of the plunder of Jewish property were not settled, this German property, confiscated within our borders, would remain in our hands. Indeed, when the Australian government submitted a claim for payment for this property on account of its expenditure for the rehabilitation of the Germans Templers who have become Australian residents or citizens, we rejected that request in spite of the friendly relations between our two countries, and eventually the Australian government gave up pressing us in this regard. When the question of the Templers' property was raised by the Germans during the reparations negotiations, we objected to it being included in the wording of the agreement, but we did agree to negotiations on reparations no earlier than four months after ratification.

MK Yaakov Riftin (*Mapam*): The Committee should discuss the reparations agreement only after its approval by the German government.

MK Yitzhak Ben Aharon (*Mapam*): Study of the draft text has done nothing to change our attitude towards negotiations with the present Bonn regime which is unworthy of any other definition but that of a neo-Nazi regime. Accordingly, this agreement is an agreement with a neo-Nazi regime, and we shall oppose signing it.

I would, however, like to say a few words regarding the agreement itself. First, the period of payments. In light of world developments, in light of the development of Germany and its present status, in light of the experience accumulated about Germany's payment of debts in the past, under no circumstances can I believe that in this coalition government there are people who truly believe that this Germany will maintain payments over twelve years. (*Foreign Minister Moshe Sharett: You can make a note that I believe it possible.*) I do not believe that there are people who believe that Germany will pay such a global sum of three billion marks over twelve years. The Government of Israel can claim it has obtained reparations amounting to three billion marks, but what it has obtained is just a scrap of paper with the words "three billion marks" inscribed on it. There is no substance to it. You are misleading the public when you say that the government, together with the Jewish organizations, has obtained three billion marks from the Bonn government.

It is merely a scrap of paper from the standpoint of elementary political realism. I do not think there is one serious adult who believes in it. Perhaps the first payment and the second would be honored at the most, but this is just a mess of pottage. We are selling our honor, our forgiveness, our grant to them of a seal of approval from the civilized world, allowing them reintroduction into the community of nations, all that for a mess of pottage.

We therefore propose not to approve he agreement.

MK Yohanan Bader (*Herut*): First, I would like to state that the strong words I have uttered on this subject on various occasions still stand, and my whole opposition and its reasoning still exist and will continue to exist.

For this scrap of paper, which allows Germany to decide when and how it will pay us reparations, the Germans reap the benefits of which the foreign minister spoke, together with additional advantages. I deeply regret that I do not have words to appropriately express the gravity of this matter. In my opinion, serious damage will be caused by this agreement to the Jewish people and the State of Israel.

In conclusion, I have one further request: let the foreign minister of the State of Israel send somebody else to sign this agreement. Photographs will be taken there. There will be smiles and greetings. I think that going to that meeting will do no honor to the foreign minister of the State of Israel.

MK Zalman Aran (*Mapai*): I would like to commend the members of our delegation to the reparations negotiations for the part they played in an unprecedented undertaking in the history of our people. Jews were massacred and their property plundered time and time again, but never before has there been an attempt to redeem what was plundered. The delegation's members functioned to the best of their abilities, their personal talents being their only asset, and succeeded in bringing about the agreement. One should not idealize this achievement. It has its advantages as well as its defects, but it certainly is an historic event, opening up great possibilities for the State of Israel.

MK Yaakov Riftin (*Mapam*): I do not ignore the eventual partial benefits that this agreement can reap for the State of Israel, but I think that the damage is more serious. As I see it, the German government is at the forefront of the process of accelerating the world towards a new war, and the pace of West Germany's becoming involved in America's belligerent plans will also determine the fate of the Jewish people. It is my conviction that this agreement is part of those plans, and therefore I oppose it.

I come now to another issue – that of East Germany. I think that the Government of Israel is adopting a hostile line towards East Germany. It clearly pursues a policy of preferring West Germany to East Germany.

I also have grave doubts about the practicality of this agreement. I am not prepared to say that I believe that this agreement will not be upheld, but the long history of Germany's payments following the previous world war cannot be ignored. Judicial matters that arise here might be brought before the Hague International Court of Justice, but if the Jews appear as Shylock versus poor unfortunate Germany, I am not sure that international conscience will be on our side.

Foreign Minister Moshe Sharett: I would like to dwell on one point that I overlooked in my review, and that is the intensive Arab pressure exerted on Germany with the purpose of frustrating the agreement.

The Arabs raised a diplomatic campaign of the highest order. They appealed to West German representatives in various capitals and made *démarches* in Paris, London and Washington as well as in Bonn. Interestingly, it was Syria that orchestrated this campaign and was more active than any other Arab State. Quite recently Egypt has also entered the fray and attempted to tempt Germany with assurances of the large orders it would place if the reparations agreement is not signed. However, this attack was repulsed not only by the Bonn government but also, more vigorously perhaps, in the capitals of the Western powers. Why do I say "more vigorously"? Because it transpires that the Arabs have contacts within the Bonn government, and some troubling signs have come to light in this regard. I say this for your private and confidential knowledge since we cannot divulge our sources, and we might expose them if this information leaked out and the fact that it is at our disposal were made known. I hope that the committee members fully understand what I mean. We have been privy to documents forwarded by the Arabs, and have also become aware of internal German guidance which was given them. Certain arguments and claims used by the Arabs could not be put forward had they not been advised and guided by people who were well versed in the German cabinet's deliberations. We know that this activity did not cease till the last moment and is perhaps still continuing. There can be no doubt that if the agreement is finally signed, the Arabs will view it as a resounding defeat for themselves. It will certainly not demonstrate our weakness, as one Committee member contended previously.

As to the contention that East Germany did not reply to our request since we gave priority to the Bonn government, I reject it as pure nonsense. As you will recall, this entire campaign began with the note to the powers. That note was submitted simultaneously in the four capitals, including Moscow. It was the second note, for previously we had submitted one on the rights of individuals to compensation. We have received no response from Moscow to the first note, and indeed to this day East Germany has no legislation for meeting individual claims. The second note was submitted to the four great powers in March 1951. After a while we received responses from the Western powers, but a long time has elapsed, and we have not received a response from the Eastern power. We entered into negotiations with the Western powers but were unable to do so with the Eastern power. We have transmitted written and oral memoranda and demanded a response. At no point did we discriminate between the Bonn government and the Eastern government, for we approached neither the Bonn government nor the government of East Germany. At a certain stage Adenauer delivered a speech to the Bonn parliament (*MK Yitzhak Ben Aharon (Mapam): Without preliminary approaches?*) – without preliminary approaches from the State of Israel.

(MK Yohanan Bader (Herut): Was there not an approach by Dr. Goldmann?) Why did you, Mapam members, not try and do it? We obtained visas to East Germany for you. You had every right and the required permission, no less than from Dr. Nahum Goldmann, to approach the East Germans. For a long time Dr. Goldmann had no personal contact with Adenauer. The first time he saw Adenauer was a long time after that speech in parliament on September 27, 1951. Prior to that speech nobody had seen Adenauer while you saw the East Germans face-to-face.

At a certain stage we received a reply from the Soviet Union, which we did not make public because we did not want to weaken our position vis-à-vis West Germany. That reply was completely paltry, hardhearted and formalistic. It stated that a peace treaty had not yet been signed with East Germany, or with Germany in general, and therefore there could be no talk of payment of compensation. On the other hand, it said that we should approach East Germany. We replied to this and appended a copy of Stalin's speech that appeared in Pravda in which he spoke about the compensation being received constantly from East Germany. We thus based our reply on a very important source, the highest one of all. That is more or less the present situation, and that is the so-called preference we gave to the Bonn government.

My final remark: I would like to say that it certainly is a sacred Jewish duty not only not to forget, but also not to allow the Holocaust – the blood that was spilled and the victims – to be forgotten. But the Holocaust should not be the only or the most defining Jewish experience of our generation. I demand full rights for the experience of our new-born national independence because it is an integral, if not decisive part of Jewish consciousness today. It should not be forgotten even for a moment. I demand full rights for our new national experience. Our national cognition cannot be made up only of past experiences that have taken place innumerable times in Jewish life. Present Jewish consciousness is focused around the fact of our having a sovereign state. This new phenomenon demands its rightful place in that consciousness. The state has played a principal role in this matter of reparations, not as a beggar. True, it is indigent and that justifies many things, but it was not the state's indigence that decided the issue of reparations but rather its status as a claimant, and it is a claimant because it is a state, not only because it is poor. It is a claimant because it is a state. Even from a technical standpoint we based our claim on the 500,000 Jews the state has absorbed and rehabilitated.

Each of our people's historic catastrophes left it in a condition of need, but when did we receive compensation? Did we receive compensation for the Ukrainian pogroms? Did we receive compensation for the Khmelnitsky pogroms? Did we receive compensation for Hitler's destruction and plunder before the State of Israel was established? Was there any hope of the Claims Conference obtaining anything from this Germany had it not joined us?

This position incurs obligations. For if we derive benefits from having a state, if we voice claims as a state and if we receive reparations because we are a state, then we must also uphold the obligations imposed on a state in our relations with other countries. There is no escaping this. If you seek to receive something on account of being a state, you must also take on the obligations of a state. You don't want to receive? Then you would also not have any obligations: you do not receive and do not hope to receive, just go on living inwardly as if there were no state, as if there were nothing but a slaughtered Jewish people.

My position is totally different. While feeling that the Nazi slaughter will never be forgotten, neither in the consciousness of the Jewish people nor in that of the world, I am convinced we have the right to claim reparations. This is not giving up national honor. On the contrary, it is a demonstration of strength and honor emanating from the reality of Israeli statehood. Therefore the Israeli foreign minister will sign this agreement, and this act will embody the change that has taken place in the lives of the Jews with the establishment of the state.

I am not talking about the morality of sending our people to negotiate, of whether that is permitted? The members of the Israeli delegation to the negotiations may sit together with the Germans day and night – and a minister may not? Had Germany, from the outset, made entering the negotiations conditional upon participation of Israel's cabinet members – if you can imagine such a ridiculous conception! – would the government have cancelled the whole thing?

There are emotional factors that one should not ignore, but something has happened: we have concluded the negotiations and the Reparations Agreement is a solid fact. It is a fact. It is real. This document exists. And now we are faced with the question of its status. (*MK Eliezer Livne (Mapai): Is it possible that each party would sign the agreement in its own country?*) I reject such niceties. Do you think that I am not aware of such an alternative, that I shall sign in one room and he in another? It is unheard of! (*MK Eliezer Livne (Mapai): What was done to the Jews was unheard of, too.*) – I am cognizant of your views on this question, and I totally disagree with them. I claim the same right of being a proud Jew as you.

Chancellor Adenauer's signing of this document is in our interest. It was important for us that he came to this realization himself. He claimed this right for himself, for on the one hand he is not certain regarding the fate of the agreement in Germany, and he seeks to bind his successors to it as far as he is able. That is a noble gesture. On the other hand, he seeks to go down in history. It is not a vain pretension, for his name is linked with this endeavor. He could rightly think that had it not been for him, this agreement would not have come to be, and he wants, symbolically, to link his name with it. In his naiveté he seems to think that the memory of the Jewish people is an iron safe, and anyone depositing his name in it ensures his reputation forever. Would you utterly reject this consideration of his?

But once we sign this agreement as a state with another state, there is a universal signing protocol that can not be evaded. Moreover, it should have an interest in making the signing ceremony a significant event, not a negligible act. If it is made known that this agreement was signed by the German chancellor and the Israeli foreign minister, this would surely add weight to the event.

It is my conviction that while we must not do away with traditions evolved by our people's past generations, our present generation should be aware that it is essentially different, for it has created a new reality in Jewish history by bringing our people into the palace of independent nations. I therefore intend to invest all my energies and educational capabilities in inculcating our youth with this consciousness so that it behaves as a sovereign nation should.

Chairman Mordechai Namir: We shall now move on to voting.

MK Shalom Zysman (*General Zionists*)**:** I move that the Committee demand that the government not send a minister for the signing of the agreement.

MK Yohanan Bader (*Herut*)**:** The Committee decides that the government reject the agreement's draft.

MK Yitzhak Ben Aharon (*Mapam*)**:** The Committee rejects the agreement proposal.

MK Zalman Aran (*Mapai*)**:** I move that the Foreign Affairs and Defense Committee, having perused the reparations agreement's draft and deliberated its contents, assesses it as an important achievement and decides (a) to authorize the government to take into consideration the proposals for amending the draft agreement voiced in the Committee's meeting; (b) to authorize the government to reach a final decision regarding the approval and signing of the reparations agreement.

MK Yohanan Bader (*Herut*)**:** I take back my proposal and join that of MK Yitzhak Ben Aharon.

MK Eliezer Livne (*Mapai*)**:** I propose striking out the words "an important achievement" from the communiqué to the foreign press.

MK Zalman Aran (*Mapai*)**:** I do not oppose striking out the words "an important achievement."

Chairman Mordechai Namir: I put MKs Aran and Ben Aharon's proposals to a vote.

The vote:
In favor of MK Aran's proposal: 8
Against: 7
MK Aran's proposal was carried.

Chairman Mordechai Namir: I move now to MK Shalom Zysman's proposal against sending a cabinet minister to the agreement's signing.

MK Yona Kesse: The issue of who is to be sent for the signing was included in the decision to authorize the government to reach a final decision, so there is no place for taking a vote here.

The vote:
In favor of MK Zysman's proposal: 4
In favor of MK Kesse's proposal: 6.

[34] Israel Demonstrates its Strength

Telegram from Foreign Minister Moshe Sharett
to the Israeli Ambassador in Washington, 5.9.1952

The press, both Jewish and non-Jewish, must be briefed to welcome the reparations agreement after it is signed. It is important to prevent typical Diaspora-like expressions of regret and protest after the agreement has been signed by the foreign minister of Israel with Chancellor Adenauer. On the contrary, the historic importance of the agreement, the first of its kind in our annals, should be especially lauded because the signatories on the German side will be the chancellor and the foreign minister and on the Israeli side the foreign minister. It is important to emphasize the change that came about in the status of the entire Jewish people following the establishment of the state which demands accountability and compels its plunderers to pay a penalty. The participation of the Israeli foreign minister at this event should be perceived as a demonstration of strength honoring our country and the entire nation.

[35] On the Brink of Signing the Agreement

Cabinet Meeting, 7.9.1952

Foreign Minister Moshe Sharett: First I would like to brief the cabinet on developments in the internal debate. The Knesset Foreign Affairs and Defense Committee convened on September 5 and discussed the various aspects of the reparations agreement for about six hours. Members of the committee, who were able to peruse the agreement's draft the day before, pointed out its defects, such as an excessively drawn-out period of payments and the lack of assurance in the German currency's stability. We explained that what affected the length of the payments was the additional sum to be paid to the Claims Conference. If not for that, the period would have been shorter. Initially, the Germans did not take the Claims Conference undertakings seriously. They had in mind a shorter payment period for us alone. When they realized that in addition to our claim a global payment to the Claims Conference was unavoidable, they stated that the payment period would have to be extended.

In my reply I emphasized the fact that the Germans were insistent on this long period as they do not want to undertake payments beyond their capabilities. It may be assumed that they do not seek to shirk their obligations, although we cannot know what the future holds. Regarding the stability of currency, we explained that after American and Canadian dollars and the Swiss franc, the German mark is the most stable one.

The final decision of the Foreign Affairs and Defense Committee was carried by the usual majority on reparations votes: eight to seven. All members were present, and all took part in the vote.

Now, what is happening at the other end, in Bonn? The act of final approval of the agreement was postponed from last Wednesday [3.9.1952] until Monday [8.9.1952] to enable the German finance minister to meet a previous international engagement at the conference of the World Bank, and then to participate in the German cabinet meeting and argue his case against the agreement. Constitutionally, he has the right to veto the agreement at the first cabinet meeting, and that he will do. Apparently, it was agreed with the chancellor that the first meeting, at which the finance minister speaks and casts his veto, would be convened at 9 a.m. Then, at 11 a.m., the chancellor will convene the second meeting, at which the decision of approval will be passed by a simple majority.

Therefore, formally, the Bonn government has not yet approved the agreement, and the document before us is but a draft. Consequently I decided to leave the country only after Bonn's decision is made known to us; otherwise it might be thought that unless I rely on miracles, the two governments have conspired to sign the agreement, come what may. That would be undignified. In view of all this, the signing ceremony was postponed to Wednesday September 10, at 08:00, for Adenauer has another engagement at 09:00. I intend to fly to Brussels on Tuesday and travel by car to Luxembourg early on Wednesday.

Prime Minister David Ben Gurion: I would like to make four comments. The claim that by concluding this agreement we are helping Germany reenter the community of nations is totally unfounded. They have returned to the community of nations and they are being courted by the powers – Russia is courting its part of Germany, and Western Europe the other part. Each of the powers is pursuing its vital interests, and the reparations agreement with Israel carries no weight in this business. Second, not only was it permissible for us to conduct these negotiations, it was Israel's duty to obtain everything possible. A claim for payment of a debt is not suspended even if you are uncertain that it will be honored. Third, should this agreement be implemented, it will be one of the greatest accomplishments in the building of the State of Israel. It is of greater significance than any other accomplishment of ours since the end of the War of Independence. Its value is incalculable.

I would like to add a fourth comment, on the moral value of the agreement for all humanity. I say, humanity has been endowed with an unprecedented moral right, thanks to Israel. This is the first time in world history that the strong and mighty are paying compensation to the weak by force of a moral principle. In any event, I am not aware of anything like this ever happening before. It is obviously a precedent in human history, and we brought it about. Israel is to be commended for having wrought such a precedent in human history.

Foreign Minister Moshe Sharett: Only the question of my speech at the signing ceremony remains. I have read its text to the members of the cabinet. A few of them as well as some members of our delegation criticized it, saying it contained elements that could destroy the whole claim. I suggested some cuts and emendations. The members of the delegation view the signing ceremony not as an occasion for settling accounts with the Germans, but as the formal closure of the agreement while preserving our honor and moral standing. They know the other side very well: under no circumstances will the Germans be able to accept two things: (a) the implication that the entire German people was responsible for murder, and (b), the implication that there can be no atonement for their acts. The speech was acordingly shortened. (*Minister Pinhas Lavon: Can it not be signed without speeches?*) That was my first proposal, but neither Chancellor Adenauer nor Dr. Goldmann would agree to it.

The first part of the speech on the campaign of extermination remains in place. The part in which the idea that the agreement is a precedent for mankind has been cut out in its entirety. Opposition to it was heard on both sides. The part about how the agreement's implementation might ease the conscience of the German people to a certain degree has also been cut out.

I propose that the prime minister and I be authorized to make the final decision on the speech. Adenauer said he wished to sign and at the same time say what he has on his mind, how he perceives this agreement. We have seen the first draft of his speech, but changes to it will certainly be made. It is not the speech of a Jew, although there is nothing in it to which I would object. He is speaking to his audience. I speak to mine. There is not one hurtful word in what I have to say.

It was decided:

To continue the discussion at a special cabinet meeting to be convened on September 8.

[36] The Government of Israel Makes its Final Decision

Cabinet Meeting, 8.9.1952

Foreign Minister Moshe Sharett: I wish to inform the cabinet that at its meeting today, the Bonn government ratified the reparations agreement, as is, with no amendments. Accordingly, the signing will take place in Luxembourg on Wednesday September 10, 1952 at 8 a.m.

At the conclusion of the negotiating phase, which is the beginning of the implementation phase, I would like to mention two or three people who contributed to our reaching this historic agreement. First, I would like to make it clear that the previous Director General of the Finance Ministry, Mr. David Horowitz, played a pivotal role in initiating the reparations claim when it was submitted. The very idea of claiming reparations has been with us for a long time. A special clause was included in the note we submitted on January 16, 1951, but the dynamic, driving force behind the submission of the claim when we submitted it was Mr. David Horowitz. It was he who crystallized the framework of the argument on which the claim was based, and he who planned the first steps towards its implementation.

I would like to mention the author of the second note of March 12, 1951, Dr. Leo-Yehuda Pinhas Kohn. It was a document filled with dignity and profound Jewish feeling, and it made a strong impression throughout the world. It was a document that, from the viewpoint of the Jewish people, brought honor upon the State of Israel as well as upon Jews everywhere. It detailed the basic reasoning of the claim – the cost of immigrant absorption – which later played a crucial role in the negotiations. This reasoning was not much to our liking. The claim could have been based differently, but it was an argument that in fact played a decisive role, indeed an irresistible one.

Third, I would like to commend our ambassadors and their staff in Washington, London and Paris. In Washington and London their efforts bore fruit. The French, however, did not lift a finger to help us.

Last but not least, I would like to mention the historic endeavor of Dr. Nahum Goldmann. As someone who was at the heart of the entire matter, I hereby state that had it not been for him, I doubt whether we could have reached the signing of this agreement. He accomplished this by exerting moral pressure on Chancellor Adenauer, whose role was so significant, and by obtaining his agreement to accept the sum in our claim as the basis of the negotiations.

According to recent information, the Bonn government is now in dire straits; it has not prepared public opinion to accept the agreement, and it fears its negative response. It is also concerned lest the agreement lead to complications with the London Conference of Creditors.

I now propose that the cabinet makes a decision to ratify the agreement and authorize me to sign it.

Prime Minister David Ben Gurion: Another name must be added to that list of people who played a decisive part in attaining the reparations agreement – that of Moshe Sharett – although this custom of giving praise is not one we usually follow among our selves.

We will ratify the agreement and authorize the foreign minister to sign it.

It was decided:

(a) To ratify the reparations agreement between the Government of Israel and the Government of West Germany, and to authorize the foreign minister to sign the agreement on behalf of the Government of Israel.

(b) To authorize the journey of the foreign minister to Luxembourg for the signing of the agreement.

[37] An Historic Achievement for the State of Israel

Foreign Minister Moshe Sharett's Telegram to Israel Legations Abroad, 8.9.1952

The following is the minister's assessment of the reparations agreement. Explain it to the Jewish and non-Jewish press immediately after ratification of the agreement by the Bonn government on Monday in order to direct the press response to the signing of the agreement on Wednesday. The contents of this brief may be used freely, but it should not be ascribed to the foreign minister or to any other state source.

1. The reparations agreement is an historic achievement for the State of Israel. Not only was the entire campaign initiated by Israel, but the appearance of the state as a claimant compelled the other side to accede, and for the first time in our people's history part of its plundered property has been restored to it. From that standpoint the agreement constitutes a most valuable innovation in international relations, a precedent for rectifying wrongdoing by the strong to the weak, a warning to any future oppressor that it will pay the penalty; all of this depends on the implementation of the agreement. Whether or not the agreement is honored is impossible to foresee. However, it is imperative to claim one's due, even if the successful conclusion of the claim is not assured.

2. The Claims Conference was also formed on the initiative of the state whose proposal it was that the Jewish Agency convene it. Once it began functioning, it demonstrated the unity of the Jewish people in its claims from Germany and its support of Israel's claim. Bonn's commitment to the conference about further legislation in the sphere of compensation ensures that individual claims will be met, including those of tens of thousands of Israeli citizens, in far greater numbers than we have so far seen. The conference will also receive reparations for rehabilitating victims of Nazism in the Diaspora. With these payments and by ensuring the conference's rights through arbitration, the State of Israel has become the protector of the Diaspora for the first time as a party to an international agreement. The Claims Conference's total identification with Israel's claim, its close ties with the Israeli delegation throughout the negotiating process, and Israel's vigorous support of the conference goals should be highlighted and commended.

3. The agreed total sum of reparations amounts to a high percentage of the sum of our original claim, which Bonn had agreed to accept in advance only as the basis for negotiation. The attempt made by Bonn further on during negotiations to differentiate between the sum due to us and the sum to be paid – resulting in suspension of the negotiations – was rejected, and now Bonn is obliged to pay all that is due to us. The attempt to make their payment conditional upon the outcome of the London conference negotiations also came to naught. The sum to be paid to Israel was presented on a separate and independent basis and not as an integral part of Germany's other payment commitments. The payment periods of the other creditors, spread over 40 years, are far longer than ours. Moreover, payment to us will commence immediately while others will start receiving payments only in five years time.

4. Israel will receive much-needed goods financed by almost the full sum of its reparations and those due to the Claims Conference. Tens of thousands of Israeli citizens and the Israeli economy alike will benefit from the further large sums due to individuals from now on. This arrangement will facilitate full cover of our expenditure on purchasing British fuel which until now has been an unbearable financial burden. Apart from that, the agreement ensures a huge flow of basic materials into Israel and will benefit production, while the small percentage of consumer goods coming into the country is also vital.

5. The following is for internal information only: the sum total of the reparations constitutes one-third of our balance of payments. This will greatly enhance our economic situation as well as our credit rating and expedite our progress towards complete economic stability. Of all the state's external income, this is the smoothest and least expensive part of it.

6. The payment period is much longer then we had envisaged. It was drawn-out in part because of the addition of payments to the Claims Conference.

7. The following two paragraphs, too, are for internal information only: from Germany's point of view, it should be noted that the reparations agreement is due mainly to the personal endeavor of Chancellor Adenauer, who views this matter as a moral duty and who believes it will place him in Jewish and world history and will pave the road towards peace with Israel and world Jewry; he considers that this will exert a favorable influence on decision makers in the United States and other countries. The forces in Germany supporting the reparations agreement are, first, the Social Democrats; second, Chancellor Adenauer's supporters; third, a number of senior officials seeking to enhance their status abroad; fourth, the minister of economy and others who think that in time this matter will be economically advantageous to Germany by opening additional markets and forging new commercial ties; and fifth, a number of figures – like Prof. Böhm – who in good faith seek forgiveness for their people's crimes. German public interest in the agreement is on the wane and many openly oppose it. The out-and-out opponents are the minister of finance and banking circles who contend that the entire claim

is groundless and the sum of the reparations is highly inflated. In view of all this, it is clear that our rejection of the draft, while attempting to enlarge the total sum, would only have reinforced the opponents, weakened the proponents and caused missing-out on a unique historic opportunity.

8. David Horowitz, Leo Kohn and Dr. Nahum Goldmann each made a most valuable contribution toward reaching an agreement. The main burden of the negotiations fell on the shoulders of our delegation, whose members, one and all, worked wisely, boldly and relentlessly, in complete unison and mutual coordination. They deserve our deep appreciation.

9. In all communications to news services, the decisive personal role of Bonn's Chancellor Adenauer should be emphasized both in the Jewish and the non-Jewish press.

Chancellor Konrad Adenauer signing the Reparations Agreement [source unknown]

Foreign Minister Moshe Sharett signing the Reparations Agreement.
To his left: Dr. Nahum Goldmann; to his right: Dr. Giora Yoseftal [source unknown]

372

[38] Moshe Sharett: A Speech Not Made

Signing Ceremony Speech Draft[1], 10.9.1952

Your Excellency, Ladies and Gentlemen,

The agreement signed between us is unique in the field of international relations.

The campaign of extermination conducted by Nazi Germany against the Jewish people was unprecedented in the history of the world. This horrifying wound in the memory of our people has not healed. It is difficult to conceive forgiveness for the killing of millions of innocent people. Israel and the Jewish people expect to see racial hatred completely uprooted from the heart of the German nation.

The step taken by the government of the Federal Republic of Germany – led by Your Excellency and on your initiative – of undertaking to pay to the State of Israel and the Conference on Jewish Material Claims Against Germany an overall sum in compensation for part of the material damage suffered by the Jewish people, in addition to the compensation due to individuals who suffered such damage, is an act of historic importance particularly as it has been done out of free will and recognition of moral responsibility.

Implementation of the obligation that has been signed will aid in the building of the economy of the State of Israel, the country that has absorbed numerous war refugees and whose gates are open to every persecuted Jew lest another helpless victim fall pray to blind hatred and sinister instincts.

By paying this debt to Israel and to the Jewish people, Germany will demonstrate its decision to somewhat rectify the wrong done and make a contribution to law and justice in human society.

---

1   Before leaving for Luxembourg to sign the reparations agreement, Foreign Minister Moshe Sharett drafted his speech for the ceremony. On reaching his destination, the draft was handed over to the other side and Chancellor Adenauer's speech was given to the Israelis, as is customary on such occasions. Chancellor Adenauer refused to approve the foreign minister's speech due to a number of expressions it contained, saying "I am prepared to hear this – Germany is not." As the foreign minister was not prepared to shorten or change parts of his speech, the parties agreed that no speeches would be made at the ceremony.

ARTICLE 17

(a) The present Agreement shall be ratified with the least possible delay in accordance with the constitutional procedures of the Contracting Parties.

(b) The instruments of ratification shall be exchanged as soon as possible by accredited representatives of the Contracting Parties, at the Secretariat of the United Nations in New York.

A procès-verbal shall be drawn up by the Secretary-General of the United Nations, who is hereby requested to furnish each Contracting Party with certified copies thereof.

(c) The present Agreement shall come into force upon the exchange of the instruments of ratification.

IN FAITH WHEREOF the undersigned representatives duly authorized thereto have signed the present Agreement.

DONE at *Luxembourg* this *tenth* day of September, 1952, in two originals in the English language, one copy of which shall be furnished to each one of the Governments of the Contracting Parti...

For the Federal Republic of Germany

For the State of Israel

M. Sharett

The last page of the German-Israeli Reparation Agreement (September 10, 1952)

[39] The Political and Moral Value of the Reparations Agreement by far Outweighs its Economic Significance

The Day After: Foreign Minister Moshe Sharett at a Press Conference, Paris 10.9.1952

The agreement signed yesterday in Luxembourg between the State of Israel and the Federal Republic of Germany is unique in the annals of international relations.

Our memory is still haunted by the catastrophe inflicted on the Jewish people by the German Nazi regime in which two out of every three European Jews and one out of every three Jews in the world at large were put to death.

This horrific wound has not healed in our people's memory. No atonement is possible for the slaughter and torture of these innocent millions. Together with all civilized humanity we expect the German nation to eradicate the evil spirit which brought about these horrendous deeds.

Today we are confronting a new, highly significant fact: the Federal Republic of Germany has committed itself to the payment of general reparations for a part of the damage caused to the Jewish people. These reparations are fraught with historic importance. The commitment to implement this agreement was resolved of its own will and in response to the demand for the assumption of moral responsibility. These reparations will play an educational role in the life of the German people and serve as a precedent in the history of humanity.

The implementation of the agreed upon commitment will contribute to the building and the strengthening of Israel which has absorbed so many of the Holocaust survivors and whose gates are wide open to any persecuted Jew so that Jews will no longer fall prey to blind hatred and ignorant prejudice.

By carrying out its commitments to the State of Israel and to the Jewish people, Germany will provide concrete proof that it has indeed, to a certain extent, taken upon itself the correction of the crimes perpetrated, and at the same time it will make a valuable contribution to establishing law and justice in human society.

It is my opinion that the agreement's importance is both material and moral, but that its political and moral value by far outweighs its concrete economic significance.

I shall not argue with the agreement's opponents. Much has already been said regarding this subject. However, I find it necessary to disagree with some of the agreement's supporters: those who see it as an unavoidable negative step, taken only because there is no other choice and those who view it as a material achievement but one stained by immorality.

I totally reject this attitude. The fact is that we have succeeded in bringing Germany to admit its responsibility for the Holocaust. By committing themselves to pay reparations to the State of Israel and to the Jewish people in view of the property plundered and destroyed, we have gained a most valuable political achievement not only for our people but for humanity at large. Let it be stressed that this feat was a direct result of the existence of the State of Israel, of its role as the Jewish people's spokesman. The very fact that the state has successfully fulfilled its mission must give us deep moral satisfaction.

By meeting with Chancellor Adenauer of the Federal Republic of Germany and signing the Reparations Agreement together with him, I felt only satisfaction and pride in view of this agreement's demonstration of Israel's moral power and the consequent growth of its prestige in the international arena. I also felt highly honored personally by my mission of representing our country at that solemn and historic event.

May I add that I personally felt sincere appreciation towards Dr. Adenauer for the step he took in the name of his government, a step for which the responsibility lies first and foremost on his shoulders. He here has indeed demonstrated, more than any other, civil courage and moral strength.

In my conversation with Dr. Adenauer, we discussed the chasm separating our two people in view of what has happened. The conversation was conducted in German, not in Hitler's German but in the language of Goethe, a language we had both learned before Hitler's rise to power.

[40] Political Wisdom and Moral Pragmatism
Moshe Sharett and the Beginning of Relations with Germany

A Retrospective by Benyamin Neuberger[1]

In the early 1950s a dramatic episode occurred in the realm of Israel's foreign relations. The Jewish State – in spite of the Holocaust, which was still most strongly imbedded in the collective memory of all Israelis – decided to enter into direct negotiations with the government of the Federal Republic of Germany's government over the European Jews' property plundered by the Nazis. This led to the signing of a historic reparation agreement with her and eventually, step by step, the establishment of mutual economic, political, military and cultural relations. This course of action was led in Israel by David Ben Gurion (Prime Minister in the years 1948-1953 and 1955-1963) who referred to West Germany in those days as "the other Germany," and Moshe Sharett (Foreign Minister 1948-1956 and Prime Minister 1954-1955). On the subject of Israel's relations with postwar Germany, these two bitter political rivals saw eye-to-eye and successfully cooperated with each other.

While Israeli historian Yehoshua Jelinek, who has extensively researched Israeli-German relations, sees Ben Gurion and Sharett – alongside German Chancellor Konrad Adenauer, Jewish leaders Nahum Goldmann and Jacob Blaustein and the American high commissioner in Germany, John McCloy – as architects of the reparations agreement[2], Niels Hansen, a former German ambassador to Israel, who wrote the most comprehensive account of the beginning of relations between the two countries, sees Sharett, not Ben Gurion, in the dominant Israeli role who formulated policy vis-à-vis West Germany in the early 1950s[3]. Gabriel Sheffer, Sharett's biographer, sees it this way also, considering

---

1 Dr. Neuberger is a political scientist at the Open University, Israel.
2 Y. Jelinek, *Deutschland und Israel 1945-1965 – ein neurotisches Verhältnis*, 2004, p.215.
3 N. Hansen, *Aus dem Schatten der Katastrophe: Die deutsch-israelischen Beziehungen in der Ära Konrad Adenauer und David Ben Gurion*, 2002, p.215.

him to be the "motive force" and "main proponent" acting "backstage" towards abandoning the policy of boycotting Germany.[4]

Hansen and Sheffer both claim that Sharett's policy towards Germany was a "well-planned", "active" "long-term view" characterized by its "sustainable capability" in spite of the fact that in regard to this issue, Sharett remained in Ben Gurion's "shadow." Thus, for instance, Hansen and Sheffer say that the critical meeting between Nahum Goldmann and Konrad Adenauer in London, December 1951, was prepared by Sharett, and that "the positive results that were an outcome of his far-seeing view and his decisive policy" rather than that of the Prime Minister.[5]

Whatever the differences of opinion regarding the political roles of Ben Gurion and Sharett, all agree that Sharett was the leading figure in Israeli-German negotiations in the years 1951-1952 and from the outset of the establishment of contact between the two countries until his removal from the post of foreign minister in June 1956 by Ben Gurion who, at the same time, continued to lead the selfsame policy towards Germany in the following years. There is also a consensus that in the early 1950s, the Foreign Ministry led by Sharett was the decisive factor in navigating the policy of Israel, and that its superb diplomatic staff headed by Sharett – Walter Eytan, Abba Eban, Gershon Avner, Shabtai Rosenne, Maurice Fisher, Haim Yahil, Eliezer Shinar – played a critical role in the bringing about of the reparations agreement.

Sharett – a liberal and moderate statesman, the "moral conscience" of the Israeli government regarding its policy toward the Arabs – emphasized raison d'état necessitating a constructive attitude towards the establishing of direct contact with post-war Germany. He pointed to the need for the state "to take stock of every shift in the balance of power around it and in the world at large" since "a dispersed, powerless people can, and perhaps should, live only on past memories and a ssianic hope for eventual salvation," but "a state cannot."[6]

Undoubtedly, considerations of the political balance of power are the realist's classic rationale. Indeed, Sharett recognized the need for establishing relations with West Germany in view the inevitability of its becoming an important power in the international arena and a weighty member of NATO. He saw no purpose in boycotting Germany while no country in either the Western and Eastern blocs did so. Indeed he even saw the danger of Israeli hostility to Germany pushing her into closer relations with the Arab countries. He maintained that as a sovereign state Israel must care for its existence and security as well as its economic interests. Thus, Israel's political isolation, its lack of intensive backing by a world power, and its catastrophic economic situation during the early 1950s due to the absorption

---

4   Sheffer, Moshe Sharett: *Biography of a Political Moderate*, 1996, p. 1002.
5   Sheffer, ibid., p. 608; Hansen, ibid., p.35
6   Sharett's speech in the Knesset, 9.1.1952, doc. 18, pp. 269-270.

of waves of mass immigration convinced him that Israeli-German relations must be promoted.

However, in the same way that his moderate policy towards Israel's Arab neighbors was not contrary to the state's interests, Sharett's Realpolitik as regards the German issue was not contradicted by moral percepts. He regarded an independent Israel as a haven for the Holocaust survivors and considered it his moral duty to strengthen it in order to safeguard their future. He also saw nothing immoral in regaining the Jewish property plundered by Nazi Germany before and during the Holocaust years and in preventing a recurrence of "Hast thou killed, and also taken possession?"[7]

The importance of the Jewish state's representing the Jewish people's case and the fact that for the first time in the history the Jewish people it was able to demand reparations from its tormentors, were not lost on Sharett. Perhaps this is not a purely moral lesson, but neither is it Realpolitik in its negative sense. Sharett was vehement in rejecting the notion of the German people's collective guilt. He maintained that blaming every German for the Holocaust even if he was not an accomplice to the crime, even if he was an anti-Nazi, to say nothing of the young generation which could not have been Nazi was a racist attitude. He took the line of the Prophet, who said: "The fathers shall not be put to death for the children, neither shall the children be put to death for the fathers: every man shall be put to death for his own sin."[8]

Sharett also saw the reparations agreement as a historic precedent of universal importance, as a contribution to the human community's law and justice, and as a lesson that enmity between peoples, could be overcome. Indeed, ridden as our world is with ingrained enmities, it is possible time and again to point to what ensued in Israeli-German relations and learn from it that no such thing as "eternal enmity" is acceptable. In spite of a history of terrible shedding of blood, reconciliation is always possible.

The distinction maintained by many in Israel about the early 1950s between the proponents of "realism," acting according to calculations of power and profit, and the "moralists" acting in the name of values, conscience and moral purity is simplistic. It does not reflect the true debate and is unjust toward Israel's leaders in those years.

It is not true that the position of the "moralists" who opposed establishing contact with Germany was free of political and Realpolitik considerations. The leaders of leftist Mapam and the Israeli Communist Party supported establishing relations with communist East Germany while vehemently condemning any contact whatsoever with what they called "neo-Nazi" West Germany. What determined their position were considerations relating to the cold war and sympathy toward the Soviet Bloc – not pure moral principles or deep emotional

---

7   1 Kings, 21:19
8   Deuteronomy, 24:16

attitudes. Similarly, their assertion that relations between Bonn and Jerusalem should be resisted since they were part of a Western scheme to "legitimize" Germany in order to pave the road to attacking the Soviet Union, was not based on morals and emotions. Even Menahem Begin, whose passionate emotions regarding Germans and Germany cannot be doubted, did not flinch from using Realpolitik arguments in order to buttress his position. In his opinion, the increasing contact between Israel and West Germany endangered Israel's relations with the Soviet Union ("we are worsening without justification the national-political relations between Israel and that hugely influential factor"). In the name of "the state's benefit," not emotions and morals, he called for a change in policy towards Germany, in order to "lessen the hostility" of the Soviet Union towards Israel.[9]

A fitting definition of the policy adopted by Israel's leaders in the 1950s towards Germany might be "moral pragmatism." This policy, pragmatic in form but moral in substance, was rooted in deep moral soul-searching.

Indeed, the relations between Israel and Germany clearly demonstrate that a dichotomy between realism and morals in foreign policy could be erroneous. As we have seen, the "realists" who advocated establishing relations with Germany acted not alone from considerations of benefits and power, whereas the "moralists" did not ignore interests and political tendencies. In this case, the distinction between "national egoists," whose position towards other nations is defined by national interests, and the "idealists," whose position is characterized by ideals above and beyond the national interest, is surely invalid. Lo and behold, no concrete change in Israel's policy towards Germany occurred after the torch bearers of morality came to power.

It is of course permissible to disagree with Sharett's German policy, but the fact is that almost all his opponents – Golda Meir in Mapai, the leadership of leftist Mapam (and Ahdut Ha'avoda which seceded from it in 1954), the liberal General Zionists and even the Herut right-wingers over the years accepted the path outlined by him. This is a rare example of a courageous and unpopular stand against a popular view which eventually succeeded in overcoming it.

Golda Meir, who in the early 1950s objected to any contact with Germany and saw every German as a Nazi ("I would like to state that I hold a racist view; as far as I am concerned, all Germans are a priori Nazis"[10]) pursued a totally different policy during her tenure as foreign minister (1956-1965). Nevertheless, in this period intimate military relations developed between Israel and Germany and formal diplomatic relations were established. She considered it the Israeli leaders' moral duty to overcome personal feelings and to do everything possible for the state's security. The leadership at that time rightly believed that economic relations would enhance Israel's security. Thus the "dry" statistics of Israel's deficit trade

---

9   "Ha'uma" (Hebrew) no. 58, p. 263.
10   Meir's speech in Mapai's Central Committee, doc. 13, p. 130.

balance and its lack of foreign currency took on, in Ben Gurion's and Sharett's eyes, a moral dimension which usually does not play a part in the formulation of economic policy.

When diplomatic relations between Israel and Germany were established in May 1965, the emotional resistance, which was still fierce, was already much weaker than in 1952. Herut and Mapam still demonstrated against this rapprochement, but their objection lacked the intensity of the 1950s; as for the General Zionists and Ahdut Ha'avoda, they no longer completely objected to maintaining relations with Germany. Begin still proclaimed that there will never be proper relations between Israel and the murderers, but the public was no longer eager to respond. This time, wide sectors thought that the decisive consideration should be the buttressing of the state's political and military interests, not over-heated emotions.

In May 1977, the right-wing "moralists", who had vehemently opposed any relations with Germany, came to power. All eyes turned towards Prime Minister Menahem Begin, who in 1952 had called for the storming of the Knesset in order to abort the reparations negotiations. As Prime Minister, however, Begin acted differently from his past position as head of the opposition. In June 1977, when asked what he would do when he would have to shake a German statesman's hand, he replied, "I will conduct myself as a Prime Minister."[11]

Consequently, Begin did not sever the relations with Germany and his government maintained the pragmatic policy of its predecessor. Political scientist Dr. Lily Gardner-Feldman defined Begin's approach during 1977-1983 as very sensitive to the past but always pragmatic.[12] Begin held talks with German politicians and diplomats – an action that as leader of the opposition he used to denounce as treasonable. Herut members in the government no longer boycotted Germany; Herut's foreign ministers Yitzhak Shamir, Moshe Arens, David Levy and Silvan Shalom visited Bonn. Herut activist Eliyahu Ben-Elissar, a Holocaust survivor who still tried to put restraints on Israeli-German relations, said that "the national camp cannot ignore international reality, Germany's status in it and Israel's need to maintain relations with the Federal Republic."[13]

In 1987, all Herut ministers supported President Chaim Herzog's visit to West Germany, and regarding the unification of Germany in 1990, the prime minister, foreign minister and minister of defense – all of them Herut members – raised no real objection. Later Prime Ministers Binyamin Netanyahu, Ariel Sharon and Ehud Olmert, all of them past or present Likud members, continued to maintain proper relations with Germany.

Similarly, members of Mapam and Ahdut Ha'avoda totally changed their attitude when serving in senior government positions. Yigal Alon, who in the

---

11   "Ha'uma", ibid., p. 263.
12   Lily Gardner-Feldman, *The Special Relationship Between West Germany and Israel*, 1984.
13   "Ha'uma", ibid., p. 263.

1950s was one of the main opponents of establishing relations with Germany, maintained close contact with its leaders as foreign minister ("I feel among friends," he said upon arriving in Bonn on 26th February 1975.[14])

The extent of the relations with Germany nowadays proves how much Sharett was right in all he said in the 1950s. Germany today is a major power. It maintains "special relations" with Israel – all German governments have committed themselves to regarding these relations as a "primary factor" or "cornerstone" of German foreign policy. This commitment crosses all political party boundaries and has been maintained both for Social Democrat governments and those led by Christian-Democrats (and their major coalitions). Thus, in 2005, the Bundestag, with the assent of all parties (Christian Democrats, Christian Socialists, Social Democrats, the "Greens," and the Democratic Socialists) committed itself to Israel's existence "within secure borders and free of threats, fear and terror".[15]

Time and again, Germany has supplied Israel with weapons vital to its defense. In the early 1960s Germany delivered tanks, helicopters, artillery and hundreds of other military items. Later, gas masks were flown from Germany following the eruption of the Gulf War. Again, following threatening speeches by Iran's president, the German government decided to supply Israel with modern submarines that are apparently capable of carrying nuclear missiles, giving Israel a second strike capability. Indeed, Chancellor Gerhard Schroeder (1997-2005) promised that Israel would receive all that it needs for safeguarding its security and would get it at the time it needs it.

Economic relations between Germany and Israel are of a major significance as well. The extent of trade, which amounted to $93 million in 1960, grew to $4.6 billion in 2004. After the United States, Germany is second in importance for Israeli exports. Israel is Germany's most important trading partner in the Middle East, ahead of rich, important, or populace countries such as Egypt, Saudi Arabia and Iran. German investments in Israel as well as Israeli hi-tech companies' investment in Germany amount to billions of dollars. German tourism is also significant.

The extent of relations with Germany in matters of science, education and culture, youth exchanges, twinning of cities, contacts between political parties, trade unions, universities and research institutes, museums and professional associations is unprecedented. German investments in Israeli science are significantly larger than those of any other country except for the United States. Relative to the size of its population, no country – including the United States – approaches the extent of German investment in Israeli science.

Moshe Sharett supervised operations of the Israeli delegation during the historical negotiations over the reparations, and was the primary and constant

---

14   Yohanan Meroz, *Was it All in Vain? – An Israeli Ambassador in Germany's Summing Up* (Hebrew), 1988, pp. 52-53
15   "Das Parlament", 17.5.2005

bearer of the brunt of the conflict with the opponents to the direct reparations negotiations in the Knesset, its Foreign Affairs and Security Committee, the government, and the high echelons of the ruling Mapai Party. He played a most critical role in all these developments. It is true that many of these achievements came to being after Sharett's removal from the Israeli political arena, but they all sprouted from the fertile ground of the reparations agreement, symbolically signed by him and no other Israeli, together with the West German Chancellor Konrad Adenauer. This is how Herbert Blankenhorn, one of the negotiators over the reparations on the German side and a confidant of Konrad Adenauer, characterized Sharett: "his is a restrained and strong personality radiating authority, a dedication to purpose, and a strong attachment to the problems of the present and to the historical background which are both full of suffering. His talk is quiet and is the outcome of organized thinking, free of any empty slogans."[16]

Moshe Sharett, who is almost forgotten in Israel, was an exalted statesman. He was right on the issue of Germany; he was right about Israel's western orientation, and was apparently right in his approach towards the Arab-Israeli conflict. In all these, his was the voice of reason and foresight.

16   Hansen, ibid., p. 261.

Appendices

Appendix A

200 Hurt As Police Defend Knesset From Herut Riot

The Jerusalem Post, 8.1.1952

In the face of an organized attempt by the Herut Party of former Irgun Zvai Leumi terrorists to prevent a parliamentary discussion, the Knesset yesterday began a ten-hour debate on the subject of Israel's claim for reparations from Germany. Police riot squads, wearing steel helmets and gas masks, battled with more than 1,000 demonstrators who used tear gas to break through cordons and barbed-wire barriers and then stoned the Knesset building,[1] smashing windows and filling the chamber with clouds of tear-gas. The rioters were dispersed after a two-hour battle by police using tear-gas and batons. Platoons of troops in full battle gear were called out but stood by without going into action. 92 policemen were injured, of whom ten were hospitalized, and 70 rioters were arrested. Over 30 civilians were treated for injuries by the Israeli anbulance service Magen David Adom first aid organization and five were taken to hospital. But it is believed that about 100 more were treated privately to evade the police. The debate in the Knesset was opened by the prime minister at 4.30, but about an hour later it became stormy and hectic when Herut and communist members called out from the floor that police were behaving savagely outside. Eyewitnesses of the riots, however, praised the police's restraint in the face of violent provocation.

Police in Two-hour Battle

Violence surged in the streets of Jerusalem for two hours yesterday in the wake of a Herut demonstration opposing the Knesset debate with Germany. Police barbed-wire barricades were broken through, parked cars overturned and rocks thrown into the Knesset chamber and at police protecting the building. Injuries were inflicted on 92 policemen and 36 civilians when at 7 P.M, an army

---

1   The Knesset building at the time was on King George Boulevard, in the city center, not far from the Zion Square where the demonstrators gathered before marching towards the Knesset.

detachment arrived on the scene and drew up in formation alongside the Knesset. By 7.30 P.M. order has been restored, and the littered streets before the Knesset were virtually abandoned.

Several hundred people stood in a thin drizzle at the mass meeting in Zion Square to hear Herut leader Menachem Begin voice sharp opposition to any negotiations with Germany for reparations payment to Israel. Mr. Begin spoke with emotion, frequently shouting, interspersing his words with biblical quotations. He referred to the Government statement in support of Germany reparations discussing as the culmination of the policies of "that maniac who is now prime minister."

Midway through his harangue, Mr. Begin drew a note from his pocket, held it aloft dramatically and said,

"I have not come here to enflame you; but this note which has just been handed to me states that the police have grenades which contain gas made in Germany, the same gas which was used to kill your fathers and mothers. We are prepared to suffer anything – torture chambers, concentrations camps and subterranean prisons – so that any decision to deal with Germany will not come to pass."

No policemen were to be seen in Zion Square during the meeting which closed with the singing of the national anthem. Then groups of youth led the march up Ben Yehuda Street in the direction of the Knesset building. A number carried haversacks loaded with stones. Many bragged openly that they had come from Tel Aviv and Haifa and had brought "our arms with us."

Earlier in the day police had cordoned off a large section of the city's center, running from Jaffa Road to Terra Sancta College. Barbed wire concertinas blocked the roads, and bus routes were temporarily changed. Pedestrians with business in the area were permitted to pass the barrier, although they were kept away from the immediate Knesset environs. Heavy detachments of police, estimated to number 600, patrolled the cordoned off area. Most were armed with shields, batons, steel helmets and gas mask kits.

The lower barrier on Ben Yehuda Street at the corner of Ha'poalim Street was broken through in short order, with little apparent police resistance. As the crowds of demonstrators swelled, however, and violence became evident, groups of police went to the roofs of nearby buildings and lobbed down gas-bombs in an attempt to disperse the mob.

District Police Superintendent Levi Avrahami reported, however, that the tear-gas was first employed by the demonstrators who, by this means, were able to break past the first barrier. The light wind wafted the gas into the faces of the police, away from Ben Yehuda Street and in the direction of the Knesset.

The shrieking sirens of Magen David Adom ambulances, the billowing clouds of tear-gas and the ring of pistol shots fired by the police above the heads of the mob soon made the area resemble of a street battle.

As road blocks were removed forcibly by the marchers, the police, who had been ordered to observe extreme self-restraint in dealing with the demonstrators, fell back to positions around the Knesset. The crowd showered the police with stones and even Magen David Adom ambulances rushing first aid to the injured were stoned and halted. Attempts were made to drag out the injured.

During the first hours of the demonstrations, 12 policemen were injured, among them Deputy Superintendent Moshe Ayalon who sustained a serious injury from a flying rock.

A car parked outside the Knesset was overturned by the demonstrators. As the gasoline poured out of the tank, a tear-gas bomb apparently ignited it. The blaze was put out by the Jerusalem Fire Brigade. A number of cars parked along the King George Boulevard and the Jewish Agency compound were also damaged.

At this point no one was permitted to enter or leave the Knesset building which was in fact in a state of siege.

Ten of the 92 injured policemen were hospitalized, Magen David Adom gave first aid to 69 policemen and 31 civilians, many of these firemen. Because of shortage of space, many injured policemen were transferred from the Magen David Adom building to police headquarters where a temporary infirmary was set up.

Debate in Atmosphere of Violence

The question of an approach to Bonn for reparations was debated yesterday in the Knesset in an atmosphere of violence unprecedented in Israeli parliamentary life. The shouting of the mob not far off, the intermittent wail of police and ambulance sirens, sporadic explosions of gas grenades and the glow of flames from a burning car appeared through the windows of the Knesset building, and later the widow panes were splintered by rocks and the fumes of tear-gas bombs from the battle-scarred street outside permeated the chamber. One member was hit in the head by a stone.

Through all this disturbance, the meeting went on. The section of the hall where stones and glass splinters fell, the Mapam, General Zionists and Hapoel Hamizrahi benches, was vacated and members stood around elsewhere. But later the proceedings were interrupted by obstruction within the Knesset itself when Mr. Menachem Begin called the prime minister "a hooligan" and refused to recant. He also declined to leave the platform when ordered to do so by the Deputy Speaker, saying, "If I don't speak, no one will speak." The meeting was closed by the Deputy Speaker amidst an uproar.

After the recess, Mr. Begin returned to the platform and apologized. He added that he was waiving his Knesset immunity, that it would be his last appearance in the second Knesset which most listeners thought was a threat to go underground if an attempt were made to negotiate with Germany.

During Mr. Yaakov Chazan's (*Mapam*) speech, Dr. Yohanan Bader (*Herut*) burst into the chamber crying, "Gas against the Jews! With that you will win!" He had just returned from the demonstration outside. Other Herut members joined in the denunciation, and with some difficulty the Speaker, Mr. Yosef Sprinzak (*Mapai*), restored order.

During a speech by Mr. Itshak Raphael, Mr. Meir Vilner, followed by Mrs. Esther Vilenska, both communists, entered the chamber excitedly shouting, "We sit here and argue while people are being murdered outside. They are shooting!"

Shortly afterwards the first stones came through the windows, over the heads of Mapam members who took shelter from the splinters. More stones came crashing through and the fumes of tear gas moved slowly across the hall. At the cabinet table and in the U-shaped tiers occupied by members, men and women rubbed swollen eyes with a handkerchief.

Some members made a bold effort to remain in their places. Dr. Hanan Rubin (*Mapam*) was hit in the head and left, holding a handkerchief over his head. The stoning continued when Mr. Begin took the platform. He took issue with the prime minister's statement that the wrath had been "staged." He read a list of rabbis, scholars and poets who had signed a petition opposing negotiations with Germany. Mr. Ben Gurion, who had been remarkably quiet throughout, rose from his place and pointed to the windows. "They are not identified with your hooligans in the street," he said.

It was here that Mr. Begin said to the prime minister: "You are a hooligan." This had not been the worst epithet hurled across the floor. In the frequent exchanges, Mr. Begin had called the prime minister a "murderer," and Mr. Pinhas Lavon (*Mapai*) had called Mr. Begin a "madman." But this was the first such statement from the platform, and Dr. Serlin (*General Zionists*), who in the meantime had taken over the chairmanship of the session, called for an apology. Mr. Begin insisted that Mr. Ben Gurion should first apologize. This caused the meeting to break down.

Appendix B

Biographical Index

Aram, Moshe (1896-1978). Born in Russia. Emigrated to Palestine in 1924. One of the leaders of Poalei Zion Smol, a small Zionist-leftist party. Member of the Histadrut Executive. His party joined Mapam and after its split he joined the Ahdut Ha'avoda splinter.

Aran Zalman (1899-1970). Born in Russia. Emigrated to Palestine 1926. Member of Mapai since its establishment in 1930. Member of the Zionist Executive Committee in 1946 and of its Presidium in 1948. Member of the First through Sixth Knessets. Chairman of the Foreign Affairs & Defense Committee. In 1953 served as minister without portfolio and in 1954 was minister of transportation. From 1955 to 1960 and again from 1963 to 1969, he was minister of education and culture.

Argov, Meir (1905-1963). Born in Russia. Emigrated to Palestine 1927. Member of Mapai since its establishment in 1930. Member of the Jewish National Council 1930-1948. Volunteered in 1940 to the British Army and fought in the Jewish Brigade in Italy. Elected to the First Knesset in 1949; retained his seat in elections in 1951, 1955, 1959 and 1961, serving as Chairman of the Foreign Affairs & Defense Committee from 1951 onwards.

Bader, Yohanan (1901-1994). Born in Poland. A lawyer and economist. In 1939 escaped the Nazis by fleeing to Russia. Arrested by the Soviets in 1940. Was released in 1941 under the terms of the Soviet-Polish Agreement and left the Soviet Union. Joined the Free Polish Army in August 1942 and arrived with it in Palestine in 1943 where as a member of the Revisionist Party he joined the Irgun. In 1945 was arrested by the British and imprisoned until May 1948. One of the founders and ideologists of the Herut Party in 1948 and editor of its newspaper

"Herut". Member of the Knesset from 1949 to 1977, a regular member of the Finance Committee, and the economic spokesman of his party.

Bar-Yehuda, Israel (1895-1965). Born in Russia. Arrested in 1922 by the Soviets for Zionist activity and exiled to Siberia. In 1924, his banishment was converted to deportation. Emigrated to Palestine in 1926. Joined Kibbutz Yagur in 1930. Member of Mapai since its establishment in 1930. Was one of the leaders of a leftist faction which seceded from Mapai and established the Ahdut Ha'avoda Party in 1944 (which later joined Mapam and then seceded from it). Member of the First and Second Knessets for Mapam and for Ahdut Ha'avoda to the Third through Fifth. Was minister of interior from 1955 to 1962 and then minister of transportation.

Begin, Menachem (1913-1992). Born in Poland. Key disciple of Ze'ev Jabotinsky, founder of the militant, nationalist Revisionist Party which seceded from the World Zionist Organization in 1935. In September 1939, after Nazi Germany invaded Poland, he escaped to Lithuania, shortly to be occupied by the Soviets. Was arrested in 1940 and sent to a Gulag camp where he stayed until May 1942 when he joined the Free Polish Army. Arrived in Palestine with his unit and joined the underground military organization – the Irgun (Etzel) – which had split from the Yishuv's Jewish military organization – the Haganah – in 1931, becoming its commander in 1944. Soon after he assumed command, a formal "Declaration of Revolt" against the British Mandate authorities was publicized by the Irgun, and armed attacks against British forces were initiated. The Irgun was forcefully disbanded in 1948 after the establishment of the State of Israel when it attempted to independently land a ship (*Altalena*) carrying arms and volunteers. Begin was elected to the First Knesset as head of the Herut Party founded by Irgun veterans and supporters of the Revisionist Party. He remained in opposition in the eight consecutive elections (except for a national unity government around the 1967 War). His 1977 electoral victory and premiership ended three decades of political dominance by Mapai and its inheritor, the Israel Labor Party. Begin's most significant achievement as prime minister was signing a peace treaty with Egypt in 1979 for which he and Anwar Sadat shared the Nobel Prize for Peace. Later, Begin's government promoted the construction of Israeli settlements in the West Bank and the Gaza Strip. Begin authorized the IDF invasion into Lebanon (the 1982 Lebanon War). As IDF forces remained mired in Lebanon and public pressure mounted, Begin gradually withdrew from public life until his resignation in October 1983. His last years were spent in complete isolation.

Ben Aharon, Yitzhak (1906-2005). Born in Rumania. Emigrated to Palestine in 1928. Member of Mapai since its establishment in 1930. Joined Kibbutz Givat Haim in 1933. In the summer of 1935 he served as the envoy for a Zionist youth organization in Nazi Germany until he was expelled by the Gestapo. From 1938-1939, he was Secretary of Mapai. Enlisted in the British army in 1940 to fight against Nazi Germany. In 1941 he was captured in Greece by the German army along with more than 1,000 soldiers from the Yishuv. They were released in 1945. After the war he joined Mapam and became one of its leaders. In 1954, when Mapam split, he joined the Ahdut Ha'avoda faction. Was a member of 7 Knessets and was minister of transportation 1958-1962.

Ben Eliezer, Aryeh (1913-1970). Born in Lithuania. Emigrated to Palestine in 1920. As a member of the Revisionist Party he joined the Irgun and in 1943 became one of its commanders. In 1944 was imprisoned by the British and exiled to a detention camp in Eritrea. Escaped in 1947 and reached France where he was one of the organizers of the *Altalena* mission. Returned to Israel in 1948 and was one of Herut's founders. Member of the first 7 Knessets.

Ben Gurion, David (1886-1973). Born in Poland. Emigrated to Palestine in 1906. In 1909 he joined the Hashomer, an organization of watchmen who defended isolated Jewish settlements. Studied Ottoman law at Istanbul University in 1912. When WW I broke out he returned to Palestine. Was expelled by the Ottoman authorities in 1915 for Zionist activity. Moved to the USA and in 1918 volunteered in the British Army, joining the Jewish Legion which operated in Palestine. In 1920 he was one of the founders of the Histadrut and became its general secretary. Was a founding member of Mapai in 1930. Was elected chairman of the Executive Committee of the Jewish Agency in 1935, a role he kept until the establishment of the State of Israel in 1948. Played an instrumental role in the founding of the State of Israel. It was under his leadership that the People's Council decided to declare the state's establishment on May 14th, 1948. As prime minister and defense minister during the War of Independence, Ben Gurion oversaw the nascent state's military operations. Remained prime minister and defense minister until 1963, except for a period of nearly two years between 1954 and 1955 (during which Moshe Sharett was prime minister). Ben Gurion had a major role in the IDF retaliatory operations in the first half of the 50's and in the waging of the 1956 Sinai War – Israel's first "war of choice". Ben Gurion stepped down as prime minister for what he described as personal reasons in 1963 and was replaced by Levi Eshkol. In 1965 a serious rift occurred between him and Eshkol and as a result he broke away from Mapai and formed a new party, Rafi, which won 10 Knesset seats. In 1968, when Rafi merged with Mapai, Ben Gurion refused to reconcile with his old party. He formed another new party, the National List, which won 4 seats in the 1969 general elections. A year later Ben Gurion retired from politics and spent his last years living in a modest home in Kibbutz Sde Boker in the Negev. He is buried there.

Ben Zvi, Yitzhak (1884-1963). Israel's second president (1952-1963). Born in Russia. Emigrated to Palestine in 1907. Studied Ottoman law in Istanbul University in 1912-1914 together with David Ben Gurion. Returned to Palestine in August 1914 but was expelled by the Ottoman authorities in 1915 for his Zionist activity and went to New York. Returned to Palestine in 1918. Member of Mapai since its establishment in 1930. Since 1931 chairman and later president of the Jewish National Council. Member of the first two Knessets.

Bentov, Mordechai (1900-1985). Born in Poland. Emigrated to Palestine in 1920. A leading member of Hashomer Hatzair, a Zionist, Marxist and pro-Soviet movement which established the Mapam Party. Member of Kibbutz Mishmar Ha'emek. In 1949 was elected to the First Knesset as a member of Mapam. Was re-elected in 1951 and 1955, after which he was appointed minister of development, a post he held until 1961.

Berger, Herzl (1904-1962). Born in Russia. Emigrated to Palestine in 1934. Joined Mapai. Member of the editorial board of *Davar*, the Histadrut daily. Knesset member from 1951 through 1961.

Bernstein, Peretz (1890-1971). Born in Germany. Emigrated to Palestine in 1936. Became editor of the *Haboker* daily, mouthpiece of the General Zionists Party. Director of the Jewish Agency's Economic Department between 1946 and 1948. Was elected to the First Knesset in 1949 as a member of the General Zionists, was re-elected in 1951 and became minister of trade and industry. Returned to the Knesset in 1955 and 1959 but did not regain his cabinet position. When in 1961 the General Zionists merged with the Progressive Party to form the Liberal Party, Bernstein was elected one of its two presidents. Was re-elected to the Knesset later that year. Lost his seat in the 1965 elections.

Berman, Abraham (1906-1978). Born in Poland. During the Nazi occupation of Poland he was one of the leaders of the Warsaw Ghetto's anti-Nazi underground. After the war was elected to the Polish parliament and in 1947 became chairman of the Jewish Committee in Poland. Emigrated to Israel in 1950 and joined Mapam. Was a Knesset member from 1951 through 1955, but in 1954 left Mapam and joined the Israeli Communist Party. Was a member of the presidium of the World Organization of Jewish Partisans.

Boger, Haim (1876-1963). Born in Russia. Emigrated to Palestine in 1906. One of the founders of the Herzlia Hebrew Gymnasium where he was one of the first teachers and later principal, working at the school from 1919 until 1951. Joined the General Zionists Party. Was elected to the Knesset on the General Zionists list in 1951, but lost his seat in the 1955 elections.

Chazan, Yaakov (1899-1992). Born in Russia. Emigrated to Palestine in 1923 where he became a member of Kibbutz Mishmar Ha'emek and a central figure in the Hashomer Hatzair Party. Was one of the founders of Mapam in 1948. A staunch Marxist and pro-Soviet politician, he became a vehement critic of communism following the Prague Trials of 1953. Member of the First through Seventh Knessets, 1949 to 1973.

Harari, Yizhar (1908-1978). Born in Palestine. A lawyer. Member of the Supreme Command of the *Haganah* and later a Lieutenant-Colonel in the IDF. He was elected to the First through Fourth Knessets for the Progressive Party, which later merged into the Liberal Party, from which he was elected to the Fifth Knesset. Joined the Labor Party in 1968 and was elected to the Seventh Knesset.

Horowitz, David (1899-1979). Born in Poland. Emigrated to Palestine in 1920. Founder of Kibbutz Beit Alfa and its member till 1925. Director of the Jewish Agency's Economic Department from 1935 to1948. Director-General of the Ministry of Finance from 1948 to 1952. Founder of the Bank of Israel and its first governor.

Kaplan, Eliezer (1891-1952). Born in Russia. A construction engineer. Emigrated to Palestine in 1920. Director of the Technical Department of Tel Aviv Municipality between 1923 and 1925. Elected to Tel Aviv city council in 1925, remaining on the council until 1933. A member of Mapai Party since its establishment in 1930. In 1933 joined the Jewish Agency Executive and served as its treasurer until 1948. Upon the establishment of the State of Israel was appointed minister of finance. Elected to the First Knesset and retained his seat and portfolio following the 1951 elections. In June 1952 he became the country's first deputy prime minister.

Kesse, Yona (1907-1985). Born in Russia. Arrested by the Soviets for Zionist activity. His imprisonment was converted to deportation, and he emigrated to Palestine in 1926. Member of Mapai Party since its establishment in 1930, and its general secretary in the 40's. Knesset member for Mapai till his death.

Lavon, Pinhas (1904-1976). Born in Russia. Founder of the "Godinia" Zionist youth movement in Poland. Emigrated to Palestine in 1929. Member of Mapai Party since its establishment in 1930. Member of the first 4 Knessets for Mapai. In 1952 was appointed minister without portfolio. Following Ben Gurion's resignation, was appointed minister of defense in 1954 and became a pronounced "hawk". Following the "Egyptian Mishap" in 1953, in which several Egyptian Jews were caught while carrying out sabotage operations in Cairo and Alexandria, directed by the IDF Intelligence Branch, he resigned from the Cabinet. Was general secretary of the Histadrut 1954-1955 and remained a Knesset Member following elections in 1955 and 1959.

Levin, Yitzhak-Meir (1893-1971). Born in Poland. A founder of the non-zionist, religious party of Agudat Israel in Poland, he was elected to the World Agudat

Israel presidium in 1929. In 1937 was elected as one of the two co-chairmen of the organisation's executive committee, and in 1940 became the sole chairman. Between 1937 and 1939 was a member of the Sejm, the Polish parliament, representing Agudat Israel. Emigrated to Palestine in 1940. Elected to the First Knesset in 1949 as a member of the United Religious Front, an alliance of the four major religious parties. Was appointed minister of welfare in the first and second governments. After retaining his seat in the 1951 elections, he rejoined Ben Gurion's government as minister of welfare but resigned in 1952 in protest at the National Service Law for Women. Remained a member of the Knesset until 1971.

Livne, Eliezer (1902-1975). Born in Poland. Emigrated to Palestine in 1920. Member of Kibbutz Ein Harod for many years. Member of Mapai since its establishment in 1930. From 1933 to 1935 was a Jewish Agency emissary to Germany, seeking to encourage emigration of German Jews and transfer of their assets to Palestine. At the outbreak of WW II became an unofficial spokesman for the Haganah and was co-founder and editor of its monthly *Ma'arachot*, dealing with military matters. In 1940 became an editor of *Eshnav*, a weekly of the "activist" faction of Mapai. From 1942 to 1960 edited *Beterem*, a literary-political monthly. After the establishment of the State of Israel, was elected on Mapai's ticket to the First and Second Knessets. Left Mapai in 1959. Was co-founder in 1960 of the Committee for Denuclearization of the Middle East. After the 1967 war, was one of the founders of the Movement for Greater Israel.

Mikunis, Shmuel (1903-1982). Born in Russia. Emigrated to Palestine in 1921. Joined the Palestine Communist Party and became secretary of its central committee in 1939. When the Israeli Communist Party was formed in 1948, he became its secretary until 1974. A member of the first 5 Knessets on ICP's list.

Naftali, Peretz (1888-1961). Born in Germany. Joined the Social Democratic Party in 1911. Served in the German army between 1911 and 1912 after which he started to work as a journalist on economic affairs, returning to the army for a spell in 1917-1918 to fight in WW I. In 1921 became editor of the economic department of the *Frankfurter Zeitung*, a post he held until 1926, when he became head of a trade union's economic research department. In 1921 published a book, *How to Read the Economic Section of the Newspaper*, which was a bestseller. In 1925 joined the Zionist Organization. Emigrated to Palestine in 1933 and became director-general of Bank Hapoalim in 1938, a post he held until 1949. Elected to the Knesset in 1949 on Mapai's list. After being re-elected in 1951, was appointed minister without porfolio and later minister of agriculture, a role he held until the 1955 elections, after which he reverted to being a minister without portfolio. In January 1959 became minister of welfare, but lost his Knesset seat and place in the cabinet in the 1959 elections.

Namir, Mordechai (1897-1975). Born in Russia. In 1924 was arrested by the Soviet authorities for his Zionist activity, and upon his release in that year he emigrated to Palestine. Member of Mapai since its establishment in 1930. In 1935 was a member of Tel Aviv's city council and from 1936, secretary of the workers' union in the city. Between 1949 and 1950 was Israel's minister in Moscow. From 1950 to 1956, Namir served as the General Secretary of the Histadrut. Was Knesset member on behalf of Mapai from 1951 until 1969. From 1956 until 1959 was minister of labor and was mayor of Tel Aviv between 1960 and 1969.

Pinkas, David-Zvi (1895-1952). Born in Hungary. Emigrated to Palestine in 1925. Joined the Hamizrahi Party and became director of Bank Hamizrahi in 1932, the same year he was elected to Tel Aviv city council. Three years later was appointed head of the city's Education Department. Between 1947 and 1948 served as a member of the Jewish National Council's directorate. In Israel's first elections in 1949 he was elected to the Knesset as a member of the United Religious Front, an alliance of the 4 religious parties represented in the Knesset. In 1950 was also elected deputy mayor of Tel Aviv. After the 1951 elections was appointed minister of transportation.

Riftin, Yaakov (1907-1978). Born in Poland. Emigrated to Palestine in 1929. One of the leaders of the Hashomer Hatzair movement in Poland and the Hashomer Hatzair Party in Palestine, and later of the Mapam Party. Joined Kibbutz Ein Shemer in 1931. Was a member of the Jewish National Council, and in that capacity was a member of the Yishuv's Security Committee. Riftin was a member of the first 5 Knessets.

Rimalt, Elimelech (1907-1987). Born in Poland. Emigrated to Palestine in 1939. Was a school headmaster in Ramat Gan. In 1951 was elected to the Knesset on the General Zionists list. Following the formation of a national unity government after the 1969 elections, was appointed minister of postal services. Left the cabinet in 1970. The following year he became chairman of the Liberal Party (into which the General Zionists had merged), a role he held until 1975 having been an MK for just under 26 years.

Rokach, Israel (1886-1959). Born in Palestine. In 1922 was elected to the city council of Tel Aviv. In 1929 was appointed deputy mayor. In the 1936 municipal elections he represented the right-wing parties and lost to the candidate of the workers' parties. Nevertheless, the British high commissioner forced Rokach's appointment to the mayoral post despite public uproar. Served as mayor of Tel Aviv until 1953. A member of the first 3 Knessets as member of the General Zionists Party, of which he was the main leader. In the fourth and fifth governments, between 1952 and 1955, Rokach served as minister of the interior.

Rosen, Pinhas (1887-1978). Born in Germany. Studied law in universities in Freiburg and Berlin, graduating in 1908, and later served in the German army in WW I. Was an active Zionist and served as Chairman of the Zionist Federation in Germany from 1920-1923. Emigrated to Palestine in 1926 where he practiced as a lawyer and helped create the Central European Immigrants Association. In 1942 Rosen founded the New Aliya Party, which later evolved into the Progressive Party. In 1948 helped to draft Israel's Declaration of Independence. Elected to the Knesset in 1949. Israel's first minister of justice. Retained his seat and ministerial position in the 1951, 1955 and 1959 elections. After the 1959 election the Progressive Party merged with the General Zionists to form the Liberal Party. This new party won the third largest number of seats in the 1961 elections but was not invited into the coalition, and Rosen lost his ministerial position. When the Liberal Party merged with Herut, Rosen and seven of his colleagues founded the Independent Liberal Party, and he was elected to the Sixth Knesset. Towards the end of 1968 he resigned from the Knesset and retired from politics.

Sapir, Yosef (1902-1972). Born in Palestine. From 1928, a member of the Farmers Organization's Executive and a pronounced leader of the right-wing political camp. From 1940 until 1951 he was mayor of the town of Petah Tikva. In 1951 was elected to the first Knesset on the General Zionists Party ticket and served as Knesset member till his death. Between 1952 and 1955 was minister of transportation, and between 1967 and 1970 as minister without portfolio.

Shapira, Moshe (1902-1970). Born in Russia. In 1924-1925 studied in the Hildesheimer Rabbinical Seminary, Berlin. Joined Hamizrahi Party. Emigrated to Palestine in 1926 and became leader of the Labor Mizrahi Party. In 1935 was elected to the Jewish Agency's Executive as deputy member and appointed director of its Immigration Department. Following Austria's occupation by Nazi Germany he went to Vienna, met there with Adolf Eichmann and succeeded in rescuing many Austrian Jews. In 1946 became a full member of the Jewish Agency's Executive. Was a Knesset member from the First Knesset until his death. He was instrumetal in the establishing of the United Religious Front, served as minister of the interior in the first government and later as minister of religious affairs and welfare.

Sharett, Moshe (1894-1965). Born in Russia. Emigrated to Palestine in 1906. His family settled in the Arab village of Ein Sinya, north of Ramallah, where he became fluent in Arabic. In 1908 his family moved to Tel Aviv where he graduated from the first class of the Herzliya Gymnasium. In 1913 began to study law at the University of Istanbul, but time there was cut short due to the outbreak of World War I. He returned to Palestine and in 1916 was conscripted into the Ottoman Army and served as 1st Lieutenant until the end of the war. In 1922 went to London and studied political science at the London School of Economics. Returning to

Palestine in 1925, became deputy editor of *Davar* daily until 1931. Was a member of Mapai since its establishment in 1930. In 1931 became the Secretary of the Jewish Agency's Political Department, headed by Dr. Haim Arlozoroff. In 1933, following Arlozoroff's assassination, became the head of the Agency's Political Department, holding that position until the formation of Israel when he became Israel's first foreign minister. As head of the Agency's Political Department, Sharett was instrumental in the volunteering of 30,000 Palestinian Jews into the British Army and in subsequent convincing of Churchill's cabinet to establish the Jewish Fighting Brigade which fought in Italy and after the end of the war helped to organize displaced Jewish refugees – Holocaust survivors – to illegal emigration to Palestine. In June 1946 was arrested by the British authorities and detained for 4 months in the Latrun camp for his share in authorizing the Haganah to execute armed attacks against British installations in view of Britain's anti-Zionist policy. In 1946-1947 orchestrated the Zionist political pressure which subsequently brought about the UN decision of Nov. 29, 1947 to partition Palestine into a Jewish and an Arab state. In 1953, when Prime Minister and Defense Minister Ben Gurion retired and went to Kibbutz Sde Boker in the Negev, Sharett became prime minister while retaining his post as foreign minister. He now constantly struggled against the hawkish tendencies of the defense establishment, headed by Defense Minister Lavon and Chief of Staff Moshe Dayan, backed from afar by Ben Gurion, which continuously pressed for carrying out military retaliations against Israel's neighboring countries. This rivalry intensified upon Ben Gurion's return to the post of defense minister, and even more so when Ben Gurion assumed premiership after the 1955 general elections. Eventually, Ben Gurion, eager to wage war on Egypt, ousted Foreign Minister Sharett from the government in the summer of 1956, thus ridding himself of an obstacle which could frustrate his military plans. Sharett then stepped out of the political arena. In 1961 he assumed the post of chairman of the World Zionist Organization and the Jewish Agency and held it until his death.

Shazar, Zalman (1889-1974). Born in Russia. Emigrated to Palestine in 1924. A member of Mapai since its establishment in 1930. From 1944 to 1949 was the editor-in-chief of *Davar* daily. Was elected to the first Knesset in 1949 as a member of Mapai and was appointed minister of education in Ben Gurion's first government. He was not a member of Ben Gurion's second government, but retained his Knesset seat in 1951 and 1955. In 1952 became a member of the Jewish Agency Executive. Resigned from the Knesset in 1956, and from 1956 to 1960 was acting chairman of the Jewish Agency's Jerusalem Executive. In 1963 was elected president of Israel and served two terms until 1973.

Shprinzak, Yosef (1885-1959). Born in Russia. Emigrated to Palestine in 1910. A member of Mapai since its establishment in 1930. Served as the Histadrut general secretary from 1946 to1949. Knesset member and its Speaker from 1949 till his death.

Sneh, Moshe (1909-1972). Born in Poland. In 1941 became the editor of the *Warsaw Nova Slova* newspaper in 1931, and the political editor of the Yiddish daily *Heintt* in 1933. In 1932 was elected to the central committee of the Zionist Federation of Poland and was a leader of the radical faction of the General Zionists. In 1935 also became a member of the Zionist Executive Committee. Worked as a doctor until 1939, including in the Polish Army following the outbreak of WW II. Emigrated to Palestine in 1940. Upon arriving in Palestine, he joined the Haganah and was head of its national staff between 1941 and 1946. From1945 to 1947 was a member of the Jewish Agency's Executive. In June 1946, when the British arrested several members of the Executive, succeeded in hiding and fleeing to Paris. In 1947 left the Jewish Agency's Executive upon changing his political outlook, becoming a Marxist and a pro-Soviet politician. Joined Mapam in 1948 and was appointed deputy editor of the party's newspaper, a position he held until 1953. In 1949 he was elected to the first Knesset and was re-elected in 1951. He joined the Israeli Communist Party in 1954, and became a Knesset member on the IPC list until 1965 and again from 1969 until his death.

Vilenska, Esther (1918-1975). Born in Lithuania. Emigrated to Palestine in 1938. Joined the Communist Party in 1940 and became the editor of its daily newspaper. She was a member of the Histadrut's Executive and a member of several Knessets from 1949.

Vilner, Meir (1918- 2003). Born in Lithuania. Emigrated to Palestine in 1938. Member of the Communist Party's central committee since 1944. Member of Knesset since 1949 until his death.

Yosef, Dov (1899-1980). Born in Canada. Volunteered to the Jewish Legion in WW I and came with it to Palestine in 1918. Studied law in Canada and England. Joined Mapai in 1933. From 1936 served as the legal advisor to the Jewish Agency's Executive and in 1945 was appointed a member of the executive. In June 1946 was detained for four months by the British in the Latrun Camp. Member of the first three Knessets. Minister of supply and rationing in 1949, and later minister of agriculture, transportation, justice, industry and commerce, and health.

Zysman, Shalom (1914-1967). Born in Poland. Studied law at the University of Warsaw. Emigrated to Palestine where he joined the Haganah. During World War II served in the Jewish Brigade. In the War of Independence he was a major, and deputy head of the IDF's publicity department. In 1951 was elected to the Knesset on the General Zionists ticket, but lost his seat in the 1955 elections.

Index

Ablasszette 205
Abs, Hermann Joseph 352
Achison, Dean 79 134 294 347 353
Adenauer, Konrad 89 90 98 106 11 115
    116 118 122 123 127 134-137 143 144
    146 147 149 153 155 158 170 173 179
    180 190-195 201-205 209 216 217 225
    231 232 236 240 249 251 279 294 295
    300 303 305 306 308-312 314 317-319
    324-327 332 333 337 341-343 345-347
    349 353 354 357-359 362 364 365 367
    369 370; Statement in the Bundestag
    27.9.1951 336
Afrika Corps 216
Agudat Yisrael 93 164 182 261 262 266 291
Akiva, Rabbi 229n
Al Hamishmar 138 213
Algeria 177
Altalena 185 248 273 390 391
Amalekites 1 12 37 45 102 104 109 115
    116 124 126 129 148 149 182 183 193
    229 230 233
American Export Import Bank 46 295
American Jewish Committee 90-92 95 242
    261 266 292
American Jewish Conference 261
American Jewish Congress 90 242 266
American Jewish Labor Committee 90 91
American People 181 209
American Press 346 352
American Zionist Council U.S.A. 90
Anglo-Jewish Association 242
Anti-Semitism 28 71 104 116 184 197 203
    207 210 232 334
Antiochus 149
Arab refugees and compensations to 46 47
    108 118
Arab Revolt 213

Arabs 121 122 125 150 174 216 223 229
    328 335 342 357; in Israel 244; in
    Palestine 288
Aram, Moshe 233
Aran, Zalman 144 210 218 301 320 323
    356 360 361
Argov, Meir 49 60 86 112 119 133 155 160
    227 238 301 302 316 323 328 330
Arlosoroff, Haim 120
Armenians 122
Auschwitz 28 63 64 68 111 182 189 203 243
    266; Survivors' Committee 269
Australia 85 348n 355
Avner, Gershon 313 316 320

Babah, Simcha 237
Bader, Yohanan 174 175 221 322 334n 356
    358 360 376
Balfour Declaration 106
Bar Kochba 29n
Bar Yehuda, Israel 215 219 224 265
Basel plan 106
Bavaria 71
Begin, Menahem 53 56 60 79 86-88 152 153
    178 183 184 188 190 192 194 195 211
    215 219 221 226 239 247 248 273 275
    334n 375-377
Beit Dagan 266
Belgium 53 65n 82 83 87
Belorussia 74
Ben Aharon, Yitshak 70 76 154 217 319 355
    357 360
Ben Ami, Oved 263
Ben Eliezer, Aryeh 53 82 101 102
Ben Gurion, David 39-43 48 93 94-96 98 11
    115 123 128 134 138 161 179-181 183

185 201-204 230 231 233 254n 294 304
309 310 339 341n 349 364 367 377
Ben Zvi, Yitzhak 109
Bergen Belsen 238
Berger, Gotlob 69 75
Berger, Herzl 127 243
Berlin 133 179 225 230 239 246 249 262
270 275; East 104 213 262
Berman, Avraham 241 249 266
Bernadot, Folke 228n
Bernstein, Peretz 49 152 153 154 319
Bevin, Ernest 240n
Bialik, Haim Nachman 181
Birobidjzan 169
Blaustein, Jacob 306-310
Blood libels 286
Bnei Brith 90
Board of Deputies of British Jews 261
Boger, Chaim 227 270
Böhm, Franz 3 312 313 317 321 326 345
346 352 369
Bonn 179 230 245 305
Boycott (ostracizing) of Germany 2 6 10 11
14 20 24 27 30 32 39 40 58 59 80 84 106
107 127 133 139 154 207 221 268 269
278 286 290
Brauer, Max 133
Brentano, Heinruch von 205
Brisk 186
Britain 27 32 36 39 40 51 61 71 80 84 113
120 136 139 143 154 164 206 231 239
289 290 294 336 352 366; Army 215
238 256 287 288; in Palestine 29 30 64
71 185 257 287n 288 289; King of 279
294 295
British Labor Party 130
British press 346 352
Buckstein, Morris 92
Bulgaria 64 127
Bundestag 16 17 89n 94 100 136n 149 152
164 205 306 312 325 339 346 351 353
357 358
Burg, Yosef 304 342
Bürgenstock 9
Byelorussia 74
Byzantion 168

Canadian Jewish Congress 266
Catholic Church 105 205
Casablanca 177
Chazan, Yaakov 172 195 213 244 265 273
376
China 58

Christian Democratic Union 232
Churchill, Winston 154 181 201 203 247
294 346
Claims Conference 4 18 47 89 90 92-94 101
104 107 114 136 144-147 153 164 165
212 242 245 247 260 266 277 303 306
and n 307-309 312 316 317 319 324 325
330 331 339 349 353-355 358 363 368
369 372
Cohen, Herman 230
Cominform 192 232
COMISCO 11
Communism/communists 86 104 119 124
125 127 173 179 191 207 246 249 265
282 284 284n
Concentration Camps 24 63 68 74 117 133
179 187 203 232 238 263 290 321
Conference: Berlin (World Federation of
Trade Unions) 104 213n.; Brussels
(four powers) 84 254 255; Geneva 63n;
London (Germany's creditors) 303 304
312 313 317 319 326 327 331-333 336
337 346 347 352 367 369; New York
Conference of Jewish organizations see
Claims Conference; Paris (Four Foreign
Ministers) 44 50 51 53 56 57 66 85
164; Potsdam 15 84 159 202 203 255;
Yalta 15 84 159 255; Zurich (Socialist
International) 130 224
Consuls of Germany: London 45; New York
29 30 58; Zurich 95
Consul of Israel: Los Angeles 9; Munich
46 119; New York 29 30 59 93; Zurich
9 59 95
Crimea 169
Crusaders 124
Czarist Russia 235
Czechoslovakia 122 127 238239

D.I.A.A. 266
Dachau 63 148
Damaskus blood libel 286
Davar 85 333n
Day of Atonement 169
Dayan, Shmuel 66
De-Nazification 28 30 84 85 202 203 216
232
Death Camps 62 69 163; Squads 68
Death march 148
Deutsch, Abraham 108
Deir Yassin 129
Democracy 284 296 301 325

Democratric Republic of Germany (G.D.R.)
33 35 38 61 62 75-77 85 94 104 110 144
146 147 149 161-163 165 170 176 177
179 192 203 204 207 211 213 216 220
224 228 232 235 239 240 244-246 248
249 262-264 270 318 335 336 338 342
356-358
Diaspora see Jewish Diaspora
Die Letzte Vertreibung der Juden aus Wien
197
Dinur, Benzion 97 125 139 304
Dobkin, Eliahu 119
Dvorzhetsky, Meir 114 116 119 120 122 123
125 126 128

East Germany see Democratric Republic of
Germany
Eastern bloc see Soviet bloc
Eban, Obery-Abba 92 101
ECOSOC 58
Eden, Antony 294 306 347 353
Egypt 206 255
Eichman, Adolf 63 64
Einsatzgruppen 63 64
Eisenhaur, Dwight 306
Eitan, Walter 40 41
El Al 278
England see Britain
Erinpura 256n
Eshkol, Levi 97 314
Essen 119
European army see NATO; Council 234
Expulsion of Jews 197 198 278; from Spain
30 74 79 105 74 105 127 148 193 197
Extermination of Jews see Holocaust

Falkenhausen, Alexander von 53
Fascism 84 85 109 195 213 232-236 241
242 246 276 282 284
Federal Republic of Germany (West
Germany/ Bonn) passim; Army 174
213 234; Chancellor 93 100 108 134
150 164 165 170 228 251 273 313 352
353 360; Chancellor's statement, 27.9.51
100 103 106 108 113; Länder 260 261
264 307 308; Ministry of economy 310
369; Ministry of foreign affairs 69 326;
Ministry of finance 310 311 347 363
369; Police 46
Ferenc, Benjamin 307
Final Solution 63 63n 64
Fischer, Morris 307

Flash, George 298 321
Food and Agriculture Organization 58
France 27 32 40 42 51 58 61 71 80 82 83 87
113 120 129 127 136 164 239 294 336
366; National Assembley 234; Socialist
Party 130
Frank, Karl Hermann 64
Frankfurt 230
Freedom Fighters of Israel (Stern gang) 228

General Zionists 110 112 140 191 214 218
259 263 267 272 273 280 282 283 360
Genocide 68 70
German Palestine Committee 310
German people, Germans 16 66 72 78 103
109 110 115 116 124 128 130 132 143
149 150 157 170 180 193 199 212 221
224 235 239 243 245 247-251 270 271
276 293 374; Language 375
Gestapo 63 179
Ghetto 62 63 123-125 130; Vilnius 114n
121 123; Warsaw 68 79 106 173 197 203
215 216 241 242 243 249
Ginzburg, Asher 148
Goethe, Wolfgang 375
Goldman, Frank 308
Goldmann, Nahum 47 90-93 101-103 124
136 206 303 304 307-310 312 314 325
342 349 353 358 365 367 376
Goldstein, Israel 92
Govrin, Akiva 271
Great powers (Britain, France, U.S.A & the
Soviet Union) 17 33 47 48 50-53 59 87
105 161 206 213 216 233; Britain France
& U.SA see Western powers
Gromiko, Andrei 85
Grotewohl , Otto 104 191 203
Guderian, Heinz 233

Haaretz 333n 334n
Haboker 214
Hadrian 148
Haganh 65n 190n 215 287n
Haifa 256 287 289
Halpern, Leivik 106 121 243
Haman 208
Hamburg 133
Hamizrachi 182 261 272
Hapoel Hamizrach 182 273
Harari, Yizhar 108 221 254 258 321
Hasmonean War 207
Heidegger, Martin 115

Heidrich, Reinhard 63
Heine, Heinrich 205 206
Held, Adolph 310
Herzl, Theodore 169 189 206 285 286
Herzliya gymnasium 270n
Heuss, Theodore 310
Herut 1 59 111 124 125 175n 177 and n
     185 187n 211 214 219 244 254n 272-274
     282 283 334n 360 374 377
Himmler, Heinrich 69 104
Histadrut 140n 245 391
Hitler, Adolf / Hitlerism 64 84 96 104 111
     115 116 127 132 133 141 154 156 162
     169 179 190 191 194 197n 199-204
     207 208 209 210 212 213 215 291 220
     224-226 232 233 240-246 249 251 256
     259 275 277 286 288 290 294 321n 327
     345 358 375
Hoess, Rudolf 63
Holland 4 65n 82
Holocaust (Nazi atrocities, crimes) 2 6 14 24
     51 53 59 62 63 71 81 86 94 100 116-118
     121 123 129-131 142 147 149 151 157
     161-164 166 167 171 172 193 202 204
     207 216 217 225 245 246 252 253 269
     313 314 349 358 359 375; Victims/
     Survivors 1 14 6 24 35 52 54 64-66 81
     87 91 94 96 114n 115 142 145 162-164
     166 168 171 172 178 221 243 266 269
     277 289 313 314 316 331 347 368 374
Horowitz, David 3 16 17 47 98 144 366 370
Horst Wessel 203
Hungary 122 238 239
Husseini, Amin el- 213

Idelson, Beba 128
Immigration to Palestine/Israel 5 6n 13 16 21
     46 47 52 64-66 81 87 115 116 141 163
     191 218 243 253 262 287 314 316 318
International Compensation Commission 206
International court of Justice, Hague 105 356
International Labor Organization 124
International Refugee Organization 164
International Students Organization 45 58
International Wheat Council 10 11 27 29-31
     45 58
Inquisition, Spain 74 123 148
Iraq 124
Irgun (Etzel) 129n 185 186 190n 274 333n
     374
Iron Curtain 247
Isfahan 177
Italy 65n

Israel: Establishment of 64-66 70 75 90 92
     97 131 140 158 172 197 198 200 238 267
     278 280 320 331 293 320 368; Foreign
     Minister 53 54 69 70 72 75 79 87 88 94
     98 101 102 104 108-110 112 136 139
     152 153 155 178 203 221 222 228 247
     250 295 297-299 301-303 313n 319 321
     323 329 334n 335 342 343 349 352 356
     359 360; Government 11 13 23 41 89 91
     136 137 139 150 165 203 303 322 325
     341 363 366; Ministry of Finance 3 23
     26 119 150 303 342; Ministry of Foreign
     Affairs 4 17 26 27 32 34 36 37 42 46 48
     70 72 97 343; Mission in Germany 31
     36 38 40 41 43; Notes to the occupation
     powers: 16.1.1951 13 19 54 55 61 73
     161 366; 12.3.1951 13 18 19 44 47
     50-53 54-57 60 61 73 80-83 86 88 91
     94 100 113 136 and n 139 142-145 147
     153 158 161-166 178 180 244 254 257
     265 295 300 324 325 331 336 337 357
     366; Note to the Soviet Union 241; Police
     46; Prime minister 26 36 41 121 137 145
     183 186 194 196 203 238 254 273 300
     341 365 374 376 377
Israel Defense Forces 174 185n 240 250
Israel-Germany: Diplomatic relations with
     Federal Republic of Germany (Recognition
     of FRG) 7 12 13 25 34 35 37 38 56 79 83
     88 98 105 107 111 120 126 147 149 150
     152 174 175 202 204 205 231-233 271
     301 379 380; State of War with Germany
     7 10 11 27 29-32 37-41 209 275 280
Israel-Poland Friendship Association 122
Israeli Arabs 182
Israeli Bonds 46 223
Israeli Communist Party (ICP) 1 104 111
     112 124 125 130 176 191 204 213 239
     243 248 272 283 374
Istanbul 287n
Italy 289

Jabotinsky, Ze'ev 6n 120n 157n 190 390
Jeremiah 124
Jerusalem 130 246
Jesus 229 230
Jewish Agency 3 6n 7 9 26 33 36 47 48 51
     55 56 70 78 90-92 99 101 105 107 119
     120 132 134 164 165 206 212 240 242
     243 261 267 277 289 291 300 308 310
     313 324 353
Jewish Brigade 65 129 162 215 229 238 239
Jewish Chronicle 146

Jewish Diaspora 2 8 30 33 38 62 85 87 90
91 95 99 116 123 124 141 150 153 165
178 181n 186 197-199 208 210 211 228
229 233 238 247 248 250 252 253 266
268 278 279 280 282 286 288 289 292
307 331 345 349 362 368 369
Jewish National Fund 214
Jewish Organizations 51 57 105 138 261
279; see Claims Conference
Jewish People passim; Argentina 85 101
186; Austria 62 64 85; Baltic States 63;
Belgium 62 82 83 87; Britain 101 164
324; Bulgaria 62 64 157 327; Canada
101; Czechoslovakia 62 64 82 122 238;
Denmark 62; Egypt 13 46; Estonia 63;
Europe 62 64 81 100 217 237; France
62 69 87 101 164 324; Germany 6n 8
41 55 62 64 120 142 162 191 207 262
276 286 287; Greece 62; Holland 62 82;
Hungary 62 64 85 122 238; Iraq 13 46
73 125 144; Italy 62; Lithuania 79 118;
Moslem countries 177; North Africa 13
46 101; Norway 62; Palestine see Yishuv;
Poland 62 123 149 238 243; Romania 13
46 47 62 125 243 287n 327; South Africa
101 165; Soviet Union 62; Ukraine 156
157n 192 238; United States 23 55 101
131 141 181 186 199 203 237 292 324
354; Yemen 124; Yugoslavia 62 82
Jewish property plundered by Nazi Germany
7 54 61 81 100 103 107 113 129 141
142 161-163 165 166 173 216 221
241 250 256 264 271 276 281 289-291
331 368; Individual Claims 5-8 13 23
24 33 38 43 44 46 48 50 55 57 61 87
101 105 110 113 120 121 125 128 130
139-141 143-146 157 161 163 165 166
194 212 244 245 256 259 260 262 266
276 277 291 307 308 317 334 336 353
367 368 374
Jewish refugees see Holocaust survivors
Jewish Restitution Successor Organization
(JRSO) 5 55-57 212 261 263 307n.
Jewish War Veterans 90
Joint Distribution Committee 48 55 91 114
120 261 289 291 307n 308
JRSO see Jewish Restitution Successor
Organization
Judah Ish Kariot 119 229
Judaism 207 208
Judenvermögensabgabe 307
Judenrat 103 204 242

Kant, Immanuel 229
Kaplan, Eliezer 42 96 305 309 314 315 339
340
Kaufman, David 197
Kempner, Robert 42
Kesse, Yona 72 103 116 152 247 349 361
Khmelnitzky, Bogdan 124 148 149 156 193
358
Kishinev 189 198 207
Kohn, Leo Yehuda 366 370
Kol Nidrei 169
Knesset passim
Krupp 216
Küster, Otto 317 346 352

Landau, Haim 298 334n
Latvia 127
Lavon, Pinhas 182 187 194 195 206 209
234 235 365
Levin, Yitshak Meir 94 95 98 137 138 315
Lidovsky, Eliezer 116
Lipov, Dov 128
Lithuenia 79 118 127 186
Livitt, Moses, 307-310
Livne, Eliezer 74 107 147 152 153 156 274
303 359 360
Lübe, Paul 205
Luchinsky 184
Lurie, Arthur 93
Luxemburg 342 364 366 367 372n 374

Maariv 20
Maidanek 111 171 189 203 243
Maimom, Yehuda Leib 42 43
Mandel, Meir 125
Mapai 1 2 14 15 138 140n 157 214 231
232 233 243 245 247 249 253 261 263
267 271 280 281n 283 284 288 323 360
377; Central Committee 11 113; political
committee 324 346 349
Mapam 1 104 111 112 138 140 141 157 176
191 192 195 212 213 and n 224 239 248
249 261-263 267 272 273 279 283 291
294-296 320 337 358 360 376 377
Marrakesh 177
Marshal Plan 8
Marx, Karl 214 245
Mauritious 287n.
McCloy, John 47 49 89 97 116 272
McGhee, George 310
Meir, Golda 39 42 91 95 97 130 133 224 304
Mendelsohn, Kurt 205

Menuhin, Yehudi 115
Middle East 85 111 231 235 256 287 301
    328 347 354; Command 219n 231 246
    248 265
Mikunis, Shmuel 102 103 111 200 215 240
    272
Mintz, Benjamin 109 227
Moch, Jules 234
Molotov, Vyacheslav 284
Morgentau, Henry 184
Morrison, Herbert 79
Moscow see Soviet Union
Moyne, Walter 228n

Naftali, Peretz 96 132 305
Naftali committee 5 6
Namir, Mordecahi 156 351 360 361
NATO 192 203 213 231 233 244 246 327
Nazis/Nazism (Nazi Germany) 28 30 34
    70-72 74 78 85 88 104 105 109 111
    117 121 124-126 130 131 150 163 165
    173-175 178-181 192 195 196 199 200
    201 203 204 216 222 231 233-236 246
    247 256 283 290 332 333
Nazi Atrocities/Crimes/persecution see
    Holocaust
Nazi Germany (the Third Reich) 8 9 52-54
    64 65 69 77 79 84 91 108 128 129 136
    145 148 157 162 173 225 249 264 268
    269 287 289 307 318 320 331 336 372
Nazi War Criminals 49 53 59 60 67-70 73-75
    82-86 88 149 206 232; Extradition of 53
    54 60 83
Neo-Nazis, Neo-Nazism 102 111 174 207
    215 216 232 233 245 256 270 355
Netanya 253 262 263
Netherlands 4
New York Conference of Jewish organizations:
    see Claims Conference
New York Times 201
New Zionist organization 190n
Nir Refalkes, Nahum 61 66 67
Norway 12 35 40
Noy, Melech 117
Nüremberg Trials 34 42 49 52 62 64 67 69
    70 128
Nurok, Mordechai 77 80 81 104 105 168
    191 204 211 215 217 220 232 254 255
    257 261 272 336

Occupation powers (American, British,
    French, Soviet) 12 13 16 19 20 25 33
    38 43 45 47 48 52 71-73 78 84 86-88 91
    136 139 142 147 254 256 260 289 300
    306 332 337 364; American 23 25 32 49
    57 69 260 261; British 25 32 260 261;
    French 25 32 260 261; Soviet 25 88 203;
    Western occupation powers see Western
    bloc; Western occupation powers' note to
    Israeli gov. (15.7.1951) 16 257 357
Operation "Stubble" 69

Pakistan 206 255
Palestine 64 106 120 124 191 199 207 286
    348n.; Partition of 3 22 210 288 310
Paris 16 17
Partisans, Jewish 249 334n.
Patent convention 31
Patria 287
Paulus, Friedrich von 75
Peel, William 210n
Peel commission 22
PEN Club 115
Petliura, Semion 156 190 198
Pick, Wilhelm 203 245
Pinkas, David Zvi 96 97 218 305 339
Pinsk 184 195 196 198
Plehve, Vyacheslav 189 207 285 286
Pogroms 124 126 189n 194 198 207 238n
    358
Poland 69 71 77 79 82 118 122 127 149 157
    184 238 239 249
Polizeiamt 46
Ponari 182
Potsdam see Conference

Raphael, Yitzhak 101 103 175 183 273 377
Raubritter 78 205
Raziel Naor, Ester 272
Referendum 155 158 182 218 219 237 266
    298 301
Reich, third 9, 264 see Nazis
Reichsbank 64
Reichsfluchsteuer 264
Reichstag 205 207; Burning of 188
Remez, David 42
Remmer, Otto 170
Reparations agreement: German delegation
    315-318 326 335; Israeli delegation 9
    31-34 38 29 41 42 43 88 228 305 316
    317 325 326 334n 339 340 342 356
    364; Signing of 341-345 356 359 360
    362-367 372
Revenge see Vengeance

Revisionist Party 185
Reuter, Ernest 133
Ribbentrop, Joachim von 179 191
Riftin, Yaakov 153 158 219n 245 265 298 323 332 355 356
Riga 63
Rimalt, Elimelech 166 188b 189 191 194 214 220 237 243 264 273
Robber Barons 105
Robinson, Yaakov 41 307
Rokach, Iisrael 101 110 241 252 259 262
Romania 46 127
Romans, Rome 148 149 168 187 229
Rommel, Erwin 216
Rosen, Pinhas 41 42 194
Rossene, Shabtai 343
Rubin, Hanan 191 249 272 377
Russia see Soviet Union
Russian people 250

S.A. 179
S.S. 68 179 192 242
Saar 77
Sapir, Yosef 110 208 211 272
Saxony 76
Scandinavia 36
Schacht, Hjalmar 321
Schumacher, Kurt 130 133
Schuman Plan 240
Schuman, Robert 234 294
Schwartz, Kalman 126
Seidlitz, Walter von 75
Serlin, Yosef 183 194 273 377
Shabbos Goy 99 114 119 122
Shapira, Haim Moshe 39 96 134 314 311 342
Shapiro, Herman Zvi 230
Sharett, Moshe 44 49 55 65n 67 79-81 89 93 94n 96-98 100 102 105 134-137 139 142 145 157 158 178 180 206 217 219n 229 242 246 252 253 273 275 281 297 298 303 305 306 312 314-316 318 322 324 328 335 336 339n 341-343 345 346 351 355 357 362-364 366-368 372n 374
Shazar, Zalman 196
Shefer, Ze'ev 194 2771 272 330 338
Sheftel, Arieh 118-123 125 128
Sheetrit, Bechor 340
Shilansky, Dov 334n
Shimoni, David 98
Shinar, Pinhas 307
Shprinzak, Yosef 100 102 103 110 112 114 127 161 166 175 377
Shtern, Avraham 228n

Shylock 119
Slavinsky, Maxim 190
Sneh, Moshe 84 88 111 280
Social Democratic Party, Germany 11 16 130 131 144 207 284n 324 328 346 369
Socialism 131 133 207
Socialist International 130 243; Youth Congress 117
Sokolovsky, Vasili 88
Soviet (Eastern) bloc 1 206 244 270
Soviet-Nazi pact 157 191 284n.
Soviet Union 51 63 71-73 75 76 78 80 84 85 87 88 104 111 113 118 120 122 137 138 142 150 163 177 191 192 203 204 213 220 221 226-228 232 234 235 238 239-241 247-249 257 258 265 279 283 294 320 336 342 357 358 364
Spanish Expulsion see Expulsion
Stalin, Yosif 104 240n 358
Stalingrad 75
Struma 287
Stuttgart 263 277
Sudetland 77
Sudit, Eliezer 333n 334n
Sviridov 85
Syria 357
Sweden 40

Talmud 207
Tehran 177
Tel Aviv 252 253 256 262 263 287 289
Templers 348 349 354 355
Temple: First 172n.; Second 148 168 187 211
The People's Voice 248
Third Reich see Nazi Germany
Third World War see World War III
Tissen 216
Titus 198
Torah 102 182 264
Transfer (of German Jews' property to Palestine) 6 24 76 79 106 120 190 191 214 237 268 286 287
Treaty of Versailles 198
Treblinka 63 118 203 243 266
Truman, Harry 154 201-204 231 247 294 309 346
Tunisia 177
Turkey 246

Uganda 169
Ukraine 74 124 127 156 157n 192 358
Uman 126

UNESCO 58
United Israel Appeal 214
United Nations 9 10 11 30 40 47 58 73 88
    105-107 118 122 124 141 150 165 275
    206 275 287 293; General Assembly 3
    58 88 94 111 135 165 250 269-271 276
    280 288 293
United Religious Front 12
United States: Government 17 27 32 34
    36 39 40 42 44 46 49 51 57 58 61 67
    69-72 75 80 113 120 136 143 163 164
    195 201-203 206 215 219n 223 231 34
    5 265 279 280 294 309 320 327 328 336
    354 366; Grant to Israel 44 94 100 214
    295; High Commissioner in Germany 12
    33 34 67-69 73 84 86; President 352;
    State Department 92 102 158 233 240
    245 246 265 318; White House 318
Uruguay 26
USSR see Soviet Union

Vengeance (Revenge) 75 121 122 127 129
    193 195 211 229 230 239 250 275
Vespaianus 148
Vilenska, Ester 231
Vilner, Meir 104 191 377
Vilnius 79 118 121; Ghetto see Ghetto
Vishinsky, Andrei 79

War of Independence 39 172 237 246 255
    287 295 364
Warhaftig, Zerach 255
Warsaw Ghetto see Ghetto
Wassenaar 4 312 317 318 320 325 326 334n
Weissmann (Munich police) 333n
Weizmann, Chaim 240n 344
Wehrmacht 201 204 242
West, Binyamin 121
West Germany see Federal Republic of
    Germany
Western Bloc/powers 1 4 7 8 10 11 13 15 27
    29 34 38-42 45 56 59 71-73 76-78 85 91

111 113 137 144 150 174 215 216 218
    221 236 240 241 244 248 250 254 257
    261 270 275-277 279 280 289 290 295
    300 301 306 320 321 324 327 338 352
    354 357 364
Wiedergutmachung 137 180
World Federation of Trade Unions 104 213
World Jewish Congress 3 48 52 55 78 79
    91 105 106 164 206 207 212 242 261
    262 266 318
World Jewry see Jewish Diaspora
World War I 35 57 108 118 119 129 174
    216 236 319
World War II 29 37 52 53 62 64 97 102 116
    119 122 128 142 143 159 165 174 181
    189 192 206 208 220 225 232 238 244
    251 255 256 262 268 276 278 287 288
    325 333 348n 356
World War III 84 111 154 174 202 215-217
    231 232 240 246 268 276 279 280 295
    332

Yahil, Haim 120
Yalta see conference
Yellow Patch 63
Yishuv (Jewish community of Palestine) 3 52
    64 65 79 117 120 131 162 190 190n 191
    210 216 229 230 247 249 251 287
Yosef, Dov 39 40 42
Yoseftal, Giora 307 312 313 316
Yugoslavia 58 82 150

Zionism 21 22 131 141 166 168 169 169n
    181 189n 194 196 199 215 250 251 262
    267 280-282 284-288 296 316 322
Zionist Executive 70 78 190 206 262 280
    327; Congress 21 22 78 93 169n 219 206
    262; Organization 3 181n 189-191 206
    207 210 261 262 266
Zysman, Shalom 298 323 334